D1548188

COASTAL AND OCEAN MANAGEMENT LAW

IN A NUTSHELL®

FOURTH EDITION

by

DONNA R. CHRISTIE
Elizabeth C. & Clyde W. Atkinson
Professor of Law
Florida State University
College of Law

RICHARD G. HILDRETH
Frank E. Nash Professor of Law
University of Oregon School of Law

Mat #41649779

Nutshell Series, In a Nutshell and the Nutshell Logo are trademarks registered in the U.S. Patent and Trademark Office.

*To the memories of our dear friends, mentors
and colleagues,*

*Bill Burke
and
Jon Jacobson*

Professor Christie dedicates this edition to Aidan.

*Professor Hildreth dedicates this edition
to Caroline, Ian, and Emily,
with appreciation for the research assistance
of Lindsay Gaesser.*

OUTLINE

TABLE OF CASES

References are to Pages

XIII

COASTAL AND OCEAN MANAGEMENT LAW

IN A NUTSHELL®

FOURTH EDITION

INTRODUCTION

Coastal and ocean management law is perhaps unique, because it focuses on a *place* rather than on a generally recognized field of law. Coastal and ocean law comprises aspects of property, land use regulation, water law, natural resources law, constitutional law, federal and state statutory law, and international law in the special context of the coastal and ocean environment. Natural interrelations of land, water, and natural resources are complex and have equally intricate legal consequences that have resulted in ongoing conflicts over public and private rights, boundaries, jurisdictions, and management priorities.

The term "coastal zone" was coined by the Commission on Marine Science, Engineering, and Resources, also known as the Stratton Commission, in its 1969 report, *The Nation and the Sea*. The Commission observed that:

> The coast of the United States is, in many respects, the Nation's most valuable geographic feature. It is at this juncture of the land and sea that the great part of this Nation's trade and industry takes place. The waters off the shore are among the most biologically productive regions of the Nation.

The Commission found, however, that the value of the coastal zone as a vital natural system and as a focal point for trade and recreation was threatened by increasing population concentration and

commercial,   recreational,   and   residential
development.

The recognition that the coasts are a national
resource in need of more effective management led to
enactment of the Coastal Zone Management Act of
1972 (CZMA). The CZMA provided federal funding
for states to develop and administer coastal programs
according to guidelines set out in the Act. Although
state participation was voluntary, the incentives
provided by the CZMA—federal funding and the
promise that federal actions would be consistent with
state plans—led to the participation of all U.S.
coastal states and territories in the program. The
CZMA allowed for a great deal of flexibility and a
wide range of approaches for coastal management
programs. These programs range from networks of
existing state laws to special regulatory regimes
created to manage development in the coastal zone.
Most of the effort during the first decades, however,
was focused on the land side of the coastal zone.

More than thirty years later, domestic and
international developments have brought more
attention to the coastal zone's "wet side." Ocean
fisheries have collapsed; dead zones have proliferated
around the world; and global warming is leading to
dangerous ocean acidification. Global warming has
also led to melting of the Arctic icecap, exposing the
potential for exploitation of Arctic's continental shelf
and leading to controversies over sovereignty over
Arctic resources. The *Deepwater Horizon* oil spill led
to new questions about our management of ocean
resources. The oceans are also seen as the sites and

sources of renewable energy production, but as these uses intensify, more user conflicts and additional impacts on the ocean environment will develop.

The United States Commission on Ocean Policy (USCOP), created by the Oceans Act of 2000 to comprehensively review national ocean policy, found that "[o]ur failure to properly manage the human activities that affect the nation's oceans, coasts, and Great Lakes is compromising their ecological integrity, diminishing our ability to fully realize their potential, costing us jobs and revenue, threatening human health, and putting our future at risk." USCOP, Executive Summary, *An Ocean Blueprint for the 21st Century: Final Report of the U.S. Commission on Ocean Policy* (2004). In 2010, President Obama established the United States' first national ocean policy, creating an ethic of stewardship of the oceans and intended:

> . . . to ensure the protection, maintenance, and restoration of the health of ocean, coastal, and Great Lakes ecosystems and resources, enhance the sustainability of ocean and coastal economies, preserve our maritime heritage, support sustainable uses and access, provide for adaptive management to enhance our understanding of and capacity to respond to climate change and ocean acidification, and coordinate with our national security and foreign policy interests.

The implementation of this policy without a legislative mandate or dedicated funding will be a challenge in the next decades.

Ocean and coastal law are now at a point where major changes are needed to assure that marine and coastal ecosystems will remain viable and sustainable in this new century. This book focuses on the special environmental and institutional concerns of the area where land and water meet. The user conflicts, the jurisdictional gaps and overlaps, and the clash of public and private, state and national, and national and international interests all contribute to a legal regime that continues to evolve to attempt to address the challenges of sustainability.

CHAPTER I

PUBLIC AND PRIVATE RIGHTS
IN THE COASTAL ZONE

A. OWNERSHIP OF LAND UNDER
NAVIGABLE WATERS

An analysis of public and private rights in the coastal zone must begin with a discussion of basic property interests and boundaries between public and private ownership. This discussion necessarily involves a look at the historical evolution of these property interests in the United States.

Under English common law, the King exercised both ownership and dominion over lands subject to the ebb and flow of the tides, often referred to as lands under navigable waters. In *Shively v. Bowlby*, 152 U.S. 1, 14 S.Ct. 548, 38 L.Ed. 331 (1894), the United States Supreme Court explained that ownership by the sovereign was based on the fact that such lands were incapable of cultivation and private occupation. Because the natural uses of these lands—navigation, commerce, and fishing—were public in nature, title to these lands vested in the King, as sovereign and representative of the nation.

Upon settlement of the colonies, these rights of the King passed to the grantees in the royal charters. When the American Revolution took place, title and dominion over lands under tidal waters vested in the original states subject to the rights surrendered by the Constitution to the federal government. *Martin v. Waddell's Lessee*, 41 U.S. 367, 10 L.Ed. 997 (1842). As the United States acquired territory by treaty, cession from states, or discovery and settlement, the United States government held title to the lands under tidal or navigable waters for the benefit of the states that would be created from the territory. Under the "equal footing doctrine," as explained in *Pollard v. Hagan*, 44 U.S. 212, 3 How. 212, 11 L.Ed. 565 (1845), states admitted into the Union after adoption of the Constitution are entitled to the same rights as the original states in the tidal waters and in the submerged lands. In *Pollard,* the Supreme Court held that Alabama, a state created from lands ceded to the United States by Georgia, succeeded to all the sovereign rights and jurisdiction formerly possessed by Georgia. In *Shively v. Bowlby*, 152 U.S. 1, 14 S.Ct. 548, 38 L.Ed. 331 (1894), the Supreme Court confirmed that the admission of Alabama on an equal footing with respect to lands under navigable waters was not based merely on the terms of the cession of the territory to the United States by Georgia, but that such rights in navigable waters were "inherent in her character as a sovereign independent State, or indispensable to her equality with her sister States."

Lands under navigable waters acquired by the United States could be conveyed prior to statehood. In *Shively v. Bowlby*, 152 U.S. 1, 14 S.Ct. 548, 38 L.Ed. 331 (1894), the United States had conveyed lands bounded by the Columbia River to private owners while Oregon was a territory. The state of Oregon later sold the adjacent land below the high water mark. A dispute arose over the effect of the previous federal grant on the lands below the high water line. The U.S. Supreme Court indicated that grants of land under navigable waters would be narrowly construed because of the special governmental and trust capacity in which these lands were held. In contrast to the usual rule of construction that provides that ambiguities in a grant or deed are construed strictly against the grantor, the Court held that land under navigable waters could only be conveyed by express grant. The Court explained as follows:

> The rule of construction in the case of such a grant from the sovereign is quite different from that which governs private grants. The familiar rule and its chief foundation were felicitously expressed by Sir William Scott: "All grants of the Crown are to be strictly construed against the grantee, contrary to the usual policy of the law in the consideration of grants; and upon this just ground, that the prerogatives and rights and emoluments of the Crown being conferred upon it for great purposes, and for the public use, it shall not be intended that such prerogatives, rights and emoluments are diminished by any grant, beyond what such grant by necessary and unavoidable construction shall take away." *The Rebeckah*, 1 C. Rob. 227, 230.

Id. at 10. Because there was no explicit language, the federal grant, the Court held, conveyed no title or right in the land below the high water mark.

When territories were acquired by the United States by cession or treaty, property rights acquired by the landowners under the former sovereign depended on the terms of cession or treaty. In general, the United States was obligated to recognize earlier French, Spanish, and Mexican land grants, and courts apply the law of the grantor nation in interpreting a grant. The result is that the determination of choice of law in interpreting grants of coastal property may be extremely complex. *See, e.g., Miller v. Letzerich*, 49 S.W.2d 404, 408 (Tex. 1932) (explaining that "the validity and legal effect of contracts and of grants of land made before the adoption of the common law must be determined according to the civil law in effect at the time of the grants"). French and Spanish civil law of the period, however, also recognized that the sovereign owned the lands under navigable waters.

B.   THE BOUNDARY BETWEEN PUBLIC AND PRIVATE LANDS

The simplicity of the principle that the state owns lands beneath navigable waters while the upland is subject to private ownership begins to break down immediately when one considers that the line between the water and coastal uplands is in constant flux. With some exceptions, there are two high tides and two low tides daily. The daily high and low tides do not have the same reach. The reach of the tides also varies with the time of the month and the time of the year. The major force affecting tides is the moon, and during the monthly phases of full moon and new moon, higher tides, called spring tides, occur. During the first and third quarter phases of the moon, lower tides, or neap tides, occur. The moon goes through other long-term periodic changes, such

as variation in its cycle, declination, and distance
from earth. The moon completes a cycle of all its
variations in approximately 18.6 years. Tides are also
affected by weather with many areas experiencing
higher tides in winter when the winds affect the
reach of the water. On most beaches, the line of
vegetation is an indicator of the highest reach of the
ocean water. See Frank E. Maloney & Richard C.
Ausness, *The Use and Legal Significance of the Mean
High Water Line in Coastal Boundary Mapping*, 53
N.C.L. Rev. 185, 195–198 (1974).

In *Borax Consolidated, Ltd. v. City of Los Angeles*,
296 U.S. 10, 56 S.Ct. 23, 80 L.Ed. 9 (1935), the U.S.
Supreme Court was required to determine the
boundary between an 1881 federal grant of land on
Merman Island and the "tidelands and submerged
lands" adjacent to the island in Los Angeles Harbor
conveyed by the state of California to the city in 1911.
Applying federal law to interpret the extent of the
federal grant, the Court held that tidelands
controlled by the state extend to the high water
mark. The Court reviewed the meaning of ordinary
high water in civil and common law and rejected both
the civil law's definition of the highest reach of the
waves in winter and the English common law rule of
the average of the medium tides between the spring
and neap tides. In order to include all lands that are
normally covered by tides, the Supreme Court
concluded that the boundary must be the mean of *all*
the high tides. The definition was borrowed from the
United States Coast and Geodetic Survey that had
noted that the average should be taken over a

"considerable period of time" and that the periodic variation in tides had a period of 18.6 years.

Although *Borax* sets out the federal rule, most states have also adopted the mean high tide line and the *Borax* definition of the mean high tide as the boundary between public and private property as the rule of state law. There are variations, however. For example, Texas law defines the boundary as the mean of the higher of the two daily high tides. Hawaii's Supreme Court defines the boundary as the "highest reach of the highest wash of the waves." *In re Sanborn*, 57 Haw. 585, 589 (1977). In Louisiana, public ownership extends to the reach of the highest tide in winter. Maine, Massachusetts, Delaware, Pennsylvania, and Virginia recognize the mean low tide as the public/private boundary. Until relatively recently, New Hampshire had also been widely considered a "low tide state." In 1994, however, the New Hampshire Supreme Court issued an advisory opinion indicating that the state, as early as 1889, had rejected the 1647 Massachusetts colonial ordinance establishing a low tide line boundary. *Opinion of the Justices*, 139 N.H. 82, 649 A.2d 604 (1994). Subsequent legislation attempting to assert public rights to "the furthest landward limit reached by the highest tidal flow" was found, however, to be an unconstitutional taking of private property. *Purdie v. Attorney General*, 143 N.H. 661, 732 A.2d 442 (1999).

Even when the definition of the boundary is certain, physically determining the mean high water line may be difficult. The tidal range is the vertical height the water moves, not the distance on the ground between the low and high tide lines. It is not a physical mark made on the ground by the waters. The tide line is the intersection of the tidal plane with the land. *See Borax Consolidated v. Los Angeles,* 296 U.S. 10, 22 (1935). The amount of land covered by the high tide, therefore, varies depending on the coastal topography. In some areas, particularly along the coast of the Gulf of Mexico, the slope of the land is so slight that minor discrepancies in tidal calculations can affect hundreds of acres of land. Dynamic sandy beaches also create a problem in fixing a high tide boundary line, because the profile of the beach is in such constant flux that the intersection of the beach with the tidal plane can change radically from day to day.

C. AMBULATORY BOUNDARIES

Shorelines are rarely stable and are subject to constant, gradual change from natural processes and human activities. Storms and flooding may drastically change the character of the coast in a very short time. Most states consider the legal boundary, as well as the physical water boundary, ambulatory. A littoral owner may gain or lose land affected by the processes of accretion, erosion, avulsion, or reliction.

Accretion is the process by which upland is created by the gradual depositing of sand or sediment along the shore by the waters. The material that is deposited is known as alluvion. The accumulation of alluvion must be gradual and imperceptible. In general, when the water boundary moves seaward by the process of accretion, the property boundary also moves. In *St. Clair County v. Lovingston*, 90 U.S. 46, 23 L.Ed. 59 (1874), the Supreme Court identified three reasons for the rule of accretion: First, the Court noted the maxim *de minimis non curat lex.* (The law does not care for small things.) The point here is not that the total accretions over a period of time must be small, but that the amount of land accreted at any moment is so small as to be imperceptible. Second, the rule preserves the landowner's right of access to the water. In *Hughes v. Washington*, 389 U.S. 290, 88 S.Ct. 438, 19 L.Ed.2d 530 (1967), the U.S. Supreme Court noted that "[a]ny other rule would leave riparian owners continually in danger of losing the access to water which is often the most valuable feature of their property." The final reason for the accretion rule is that the owner bearing the burden of potential losses of property in contiguity to water should also receive any benefits from accretion.

The cause of the accretion may be relevant in determining whether the boundary changes. A well-established exception to the accretion rule is that a riparian or littoral owner does not gain title to accreted property that is the result of acts of that owner. Courts have found that to permit acquisition of such accreted land would be tantamount to allowing the owner to take state property. Whether the accretion is natural or caused by human activities, often called "artificial" accretion, may be relevant even in circumstances where the upland owner is not directly involved. The U.S. Supreme Court, in *St. Clair County v. Lovingston,* id., established the federal rule that whether accreted land is the result of natural or artificial causes is irrelevant to the boundary determination. Some states, most notably California, have taken the position that artificial accretion, whether caused by the littoral owner or unrelated parties, cannot result in extension of the upland boundary, reasoning that the accretions are merely manmade deposits on state public trust lands. The California Supreme Court later mitigated the harshness of this rule by holding that accretions are deemed artificial only if directly caused by human activities in the immediate vicinity of the accreted land. *California v. Superior Court of Sacramento County*, 44 Cal.Rptr.2d 399, 900 P.2d 648 (1995).

Erosion is the gradual wearing away of land by water. Erosion also results in movement of the property boundary.

Avulsion is any sudden and perceptible change in the shoreline by action of the water. Because the change occurs quickly and the original boundary is still considered identifiable, the boundary does not change. The state of Texas does not, however, recognize the doctrine of avulsion in regard to coastal shorelines. Noting that the result of applying the general rule of avulsion to fluctuating coastlines "would be unworkable, leaving ownership boundaries to mere guesswork," the Texas Supreme Court reaffimed that "[t]he division between public and private ownership remains at the mean high tide line in the wake of naturally occurring changes, even when boundaries seem to change suddenly."

Severance v. Patterson, 345 S.W.3d 18, 32–34 (Tex. 2009).

Stresses on today's environment have also produced two other phenomena that can affect boundary changes. First, withdrawal of large amounts of petroleum and water from coastal areas, particularly in Texas and Louisiana, has caused the land to sink or subside allowing encroachment of water. Second, global warming is leading to sea level rise that is already detectable in many areas. Although such gradual changes would seem to be of the type that justifies boundary relocation, Texas courts have recognized a limited right of reclamation of subsided land. In *Coastal Industrial Water Authority v. York*, 532 S.W.2d 949 (Tex. 1976), the Texas Supreme Court distinguished subsidence from erosion. Unlike erosion, subsidence does not involve the removal of land from its location and is not an ordinary hazard of riparian ownership. Unless the public is already using the site for navigation, the owner has a right to protect or reclaim the land, "rather than to watch helplessly as his boundary retreats."

Professor Joseph Sax has noted that sea level rise also differs from the circumstances giving rise to the traditional common law rules:

The rate and magnitude of the rising sea levels are physically quite different from the historical experience out of which the common law rules grew. The rising sea level is neither gradual like traditional accretion, erosion, or reliction; nor is it sudden and violent like

traditional avulsion. We are facing a historically
distinct situation that is not a good factual fit
with the "background" rules.

See Joseph L. Sax, *Some Unorthodox Thoughts About
Rising Sea Levels, Beach Erosion, and Property
Rights*, 11 Vt. J. Envtl. L. 641, 645 (2010). He has
proposed that resolution requires "a balance between
the littoral owner's claimed property rights and the
state's property rights as the owner of the land
seaward of the MHTL." *Id* at 646. He proposed
application of a balancing approach to accommodate
"the fact that both owners have a legitimate interest
and are innocent victims of a phenomenon beyond
their control." Id.

The uncertainties caused by ambulatory
boundaries have led some states to attempt to fix
water boundaries at a certain date. Because federal
common law recognizes ambulatory boundaries, the
law chosen to interpret a grant may be critical to
determination of the boundary.

Hawaii's law had recognized the right to accretions
and, consequently, an ambulatory boundary, but
required upland owners to register such claims and
prove by a preponderance of the evidence that the
accretion is natural and permanent (in existence at
least twenty years). In 2003, the Hawai'i State
Legislature passed Act 73 providing that owners of
oceanfront lands could no longer register or quiet
title to accreted lands unless the accretion restored
previously eroded land. Act 73 also provided that
lands accreted after the date of the Act would be
"[p]ublic lands" or "state land." The Intermediate

Court of Appeals of Hawai'i held that Act 73's permanent fixing of the boundary divested a littoral owner's rights to any existing accretions to oceanfront property that were unregistered or unrecorded as of the effective date of Act 73. The court did find, however, that property owners "have no vested right to future accretions that may never materialize and, therefore, Act 73 did not effectuate a taking of future accretions without just compensation." See *Maunalua Bay Beach Ohana 28 v. State*, 122 Haw. 34, 222 P.2d 441 (2009).

The supreme court of the State of Washington interpreted the 1889 state constitution as fixing coastal boundaries as of the date of statehood. In *Hughes v. Washington*, 389 U.S. 290, 88 S.Ct. 438, 19 L.Ed.2d 530 (1967), the Hughes' oceanfront land had been transferred to a private owner by the federal government prior to statehood. Hughes' ownership of accretions to the land depended upon whether state or federal law governed. The U.S. Supreme Court held that federal law must govern a federal grant of lands bordering tidelands. The Court reasoned that coastal boundaries are too closely related to the vital interest of the United States in its international boundaries to be governed by state law.

Hughes was followed in *Bonelli Cattle Co. v. Arizona*, 414 U.S. 313, 94 S.Ct. 517, 38 L.Ed.2d 526 (1973), in applying federal law to determine an ambulatory boundary issue involving the navigable Colorado River. However, in *Oregon ex rel. State Land Board v. Corvallis Sand & Gravel Co.*, 429 U.S. 363, 97 S.Ct. 582, 50 L.Ed.2d 550 (1977), the Court overruled *Bonelli,* holding that state law applies to the question of whether state title to a riverbed follows the course of a navigable river as it moves. The Court explained that although the equal footing doctrine dictates that federal law applies for purposes of determining the boundaries of a navigable riverbed upon a state's admission to the Union, state property law thereafter controls boundaries.

In *California ex rel. State Lands Commission v. United States*, 457 U.S. 273, 102 S.Ct. 2432, 73 L.Ed.2d 1 (1982), the Supreme Court considered whether *Corvallis Sand & Gravel* overruled *Hughes* as well as *Bonelli.* The United States owned property on the north side of the entrance to Humboldt Bay continuously since California's statehood. Because of jetties built at the mouth of the bay by the United States, 184 acres of land accreted on the north shore. California argued that the reasoning in *Corvallis* also required that state law be applied to tidelands boundaries. The Supreme Court disagreed, noting that *Bonelli* had not expressly relied on *Hughes* and that the *Corvallis* opinion recognized that federal law would continue to apply if "there were present some other principle of federal law requiring state law to be displaced." The Court reiterated the finding in *Hughes* that oceanfront property is "sufficiently different . . . so as to justify a 'federal common law' rule of riparian proprietorship." The Court also distinguished the case from both *Corvallis* and *Hughes* by observing that the case involved land in which the United States had never terminated its interest, and not merely the interpretation of a

federal grant to a private landowner. An alternative
statutory holding was based on section 5(a) of the
Submerged Lands Act of 1953, 43 U.S.C.A. § 1313(a),
which expressly withheld from the grant to the states
all accretions to lands reserved by the United States.
The concurring justices found that the Submerged
Lands Act was controlling and that the discussion of
Hughes was consequently dicta. The "continuing
vitality" of *Hughes* may, therefore, still be in
question.

Fixing the boundary between private and public
ownership is also a normal part of the procedure for
beach restoration projects. In general, the
government will survey and establish the mean high
water line boundary prior to filling the state lands
seaward of boundary. Most state laws addressing
beach restoration provide for that boundary to
remain fixed after the project. In *City of Long Branch
v. Jui Yung Liu*, 4 A.3d 542 (N.J. 2010), the New
Jersey Supreme Court applied both the public trust
doctrine and the principle of avulsion in finding no
taking of the Liu's property.

> [T]he doctrine of avulsion itself is founded on
> principles of equity. The beach replenishment
> program—which the Court determines
> constituted an avulsion—erected a buffer
> protecting the Lius' property, and therefore the
> Lius were a direct beneficiary of the
> replenishment program. In the end, however,
> under the public trust doctrine, the people of
> New Jersey are the beneficiaries. Because the
> old mean high water mark remains the

boundary line between private and public property, there was no true loss of land to the Lius or gain to the State.

Id. at 485. In *Stop the Beach Renourishment, Inc. v. Fla. Dep't of Envtl. Prot.*, 560 U.S. 702 (2010), the U.S. Supreme Court unanimously held that the state supreme court's upholding of a beach restoration statute fixing the boundary did not constitute a judicial taking of the upland property owner's vested right to accretions. In *New Jersey v. New York*, 523 U.S. 767, 784 (1998), the U.S. Supreme Court recognized analogous activity, artificial land-filling increasing the area of Ellis Island, as an avulsive event under federal law, leaving the boundary in place.

D. THE SIGNIFICANCE OF PUBLIC OWNERSHIP

1. THE PUBLIC TRUST DOCTRINE

Tidelands and lands below navigable waters are owned by the state in a special capacity—in the public trust. The public trust doctrine can be traced to Roman law. The Institutes of Justinian provided that "[b]y the law of nature these things are common to mankind—the air, running water, the sea, and consequently the shores of the sea." The air, sea, shore, and water, as *res communes,* were not subject to private ownership. The doctrine seemed to disappear during the Middle Ages, but reemerged in Tudor England, apparently as a basis for the Crown to control tidelands and navigable waterways. Under

English common law, public trust or sovereignty lands were not *res communes.* Title, *jus privatum,* was held by the King as sovereign, while dominion over the lands, *jus publicum,* was vested in the Crown as a trust for the benefit of the public. The public trust doctrine was adopted in the United States as part of the English common law.

The classic rationale for the public trust doctrine was elaborated by the Supreme Court in *Shively v. Bowlby,* 152 U.S. 1, 14 S.Ct. 548, 38 L.Ed. 331 (1894):

> Lands under tide waters are incapable of cultivation or improvement in the manner of lands above high water mark. They are of great value to the public for the purposes of commerce, navigation and fishery. Their improvement by individuals, when permitted, is incidental or subordinate to the public use and right. Therefore the title and the control of them are vested in the sovereign for the benefit of the whole people.

Id. at 57. Modern jurisprudence has not limited the purposes of the trust to the traditional public uses of commerce, navigation, and fishing. The doctrine has evolved to reflect the public's contemporary interests in navigable waters and tidelands. See generally, Joseph L. Sax, *The Public Trust Doctrine in Natural Resources Law: Effective Judicial Intervention,* 68 Mich. L. Rev. 471 (1970). Most states recognize recreational use as part of the public trust. State courts have also identified environmental and ecological protection and preservation of scenic beauty as within the trust. See, e.g., *Marks v.*

Whitney, 98 Cal.Rptr. 790, 491 P.2d 374 (1971) (One of the most important public uses of tidelands is preservation of land in its natural state for open space, habitat, scientific study, and its favorable effect on scenery and climate.); *Kootenai Envtl. Alliance, Inc. v. Panhandle Yacht Club, Inc.*, 105 Idaho 622, 671 P.2d 1085 (1983) (The public trust doctrine protects "navigation, fish and wildlife habitat, aquatic life, recreation, [and] aesthetic beauty."); *State v. Trudeau*, 139 Wis.2d 91, 408 N.W.2d 337 (1987) ("The rights Wisconsin's citizens enjoy with respect to bodies of water held in trust by the state include the enjoyment of natural scenic beauty. . . ."). The California Coastal Act of 1976 (Pub. Resources Code, § 30000 et seq.) provides that: "The scenic and visual qualities of coastal areas shall be considered and protected as a resource of public importance. Permitted development shall be sited and designed to protect views to and along the ocean and scenic coastal areas, to minimize the alteration of natural land forms, to be visually compatible with the character of surrounding areas, and where feasible, to restore and enhance visual quality in visually degraded areas. . . ." Cf. *Schneider v. California Coastal Comm'n*, 140 Cal. App. 4th 1339 (2006) (holding that the Commission had no authority to impose development conditions to protect views of the coastline from offshore, ocean-based vantage points).

The public trust doctrine has also been proposed as an important common law tool for governments in development of strategies to respond to climate change and sea level rise. See, e.g., Tim Eichenberg, et al., *Climate Change and the Public Trust Doctrine: Using an Ancient Doctrine to Adapt to Rising Sea Levels in San Francisco Bay*, 3 Golden Gate U. Envtl. L.J. 243 (2010); Margaret E. Peloso & Margaret R. Caldwell), *Dynamic Property Rights: The Public Trust Doctrine and Takings in a Changing Climate*, 30 Stan. Envtl. L.J. 51 (2011).

By broadening the substantive scope of the doctrine, states have created more opportunities for public trust values, e.g., navigation and environmental protection, to come into conflict with each other. In *Weden v. San Juan County*, 135 Wash.2d 678, 958 P.2d 273 (1998), the Washington Supreme Court was required to address the controversial issue of regulating personal water craft (PWC). In determining that a county ordinance prohibiting navigation and recreational use by PWCs is consistent with the state's public trust doctrine, the court found that "it would be an odd use of the public trust doctrine to sanction an activity that actually harms and damages the waters and wildlife of this state." See also *Renard v. San Diego Unified Port Dist.*, 328 Fed. Appx. 575 (2009) (holding that boaters do not have a constitutional right to unregulated long-term anchorage in public navigable waters); *Samson v. City of Bainbridge Island,* 149 Wn. App. 33, 202 P.3d 334 (Wash. Ct. App. 2009), *cert. denied*, 166 Wash. 2d 1036, 218 P.3d 921 (2009) (holding that a local government ban on private recreational docks to protect scenic vistas did not violate the public trust doctrine by restricting access to the water by waterfront owners).

The public trust doctrine itself establishes no priorities among protected uses. Legislatures and agencies generally must balance or prioritize competing interests based on the appropriateness of the use to the particular area of the coast or ocean. See generally, Donna R. Christie, *Marine Reserves, the Public Trust Doctrine and Intergenerational Equity*, 19 J. Land Use & Envtl L. 427 (2004).

A violation of the public trust doctrine by a private individual would generally be considered a public nuisance and, therefore, not subject to abatement by members of the public. Some states have, however, specifically recognized citizens' rights to sue a private party to prevent or abate a violation of the public trust doctrine. See, e.g., *Gillen v. City of Neenah*, 219 Wis.2d 806, 580 N.W.2d 628 (1998); *Marks v. Whitney*, 98 Cal.Rptr. 790, 491 P.2d 374 (1971); *Paepcke v. Public Bldg. Comm'n*, 46 Ill. 2d 330, 340–41, 263 N.E.2d 11, 18 (1970). See also, Richard J. Lazarus, *Changing Conceptions of Property and Sovereignty in Natural Resources: Questioning the Public Trust Doctrine*, 71 Iowa L. Rev. 631, 646 (1986).

2. THE GEOGRAPHIC SCOPE OF THE PUBLIC TRUST DOCTRINE

Public trust lands are lands beneath navigable waters. However, the term "navigable" has no plain meaning in law and can only be defined in its statutory or common law context. In England, navigable waters were apparently those affected by the ebb and flow of the tide. See *Phillips Petroleum*

Co. v. Miss., 484 U.S. 469, 477–478 (1988). In an early case, *The Propeller Genesee Chief*, 53 U.S. 443, 12 How. 443, 13 L.Ed. 1058 (1851), the U.S. Supreme Court extended admiralty jurisdiction beyond tide waters to all waters of "navigable character." In *The Daniel Ball*, 77 U.S. 557, 19 L.Ed. 999 (1870), the Supreme Court explained that virtually all waters in England that are in fact navigable are tidally influenced. The Court distinguished the circumstances of the United States which contains mighty inland rivers and large lakes which bear commerce. In determining that a "different test" must be applied to determine the navigability of rivers in the United States, the Court held that:

> [t]hose rivers must be regarded as public navigable rivers in law which are navigable in fact. And they are navigable in fact when they are used or are susceptible of being used, in their ordinary condition, as highways for commerce, over which trade and travel are or may be conducted in the customary modes of trade and travel on water.

Although *The Daniel Ball* involved a question of the scope of the federal Commerce Clause, this definition of navigability has come to be known as the federal title test and has been adopted by many states as the definition of navigability for purposes of the state title to submerged lands.

Navigability in fact, as defined in *The Daniel Ball,* is not directly determined by merely establishing the depth or width of a water body, nor does it require proof of actual use. See *Utah v. United States,* 283

U.S. 64, 82 (1931) ("[W]here conditions of exploration and settlement explain the infrequency or limited nature of such use, the susceptibility to use as a highway of commerce may still be satisfactorily proved."). The definition has an element of local custom. Even narrow streams may have been plied by fur traders in canoes, and shallow streams may have been susceptible to commerce by barges with a shallow draft. At the time of statehood, the relevant point of time for establishing navigability for state title purposes, these types of vessels represented in many instances the "customary modes of trade and travel on water." See *The Montello*, 87 U.S. 430, 440–441 (20 Wall.) (1874).

Modern recreational use of waters has occasionally been viewed as evidence of navigability. For example, New York's legislature has found the common law standard for navigability based on commercial use to be anachronistic and inconsistent with state policy to develop state waters for beneficial uses, including recreation. New York courts have found use by canoeists relevant to the issue of commercial navigability. E.g., *Adirondack League Club v. Sierra Club*, 92 N.Y.2d 591, 706 N.E.2d 1192 (N.Y. 1998). The Mississippi Supreme Court specifically recognized that navigability in fact and customary modes of travel are terms with a "dynamic quality." Therefore, waters of modest size and capacity that are currently capable of use by fishermen and recreational boaters are navigable in fact. The court noted that reliance on *The Daniel Ball's* commercial navigability test is misplaced and confusing when the scope of federal Commerce Clause jurisdiction is not the issue. *Ryals v. Pigott*, 580 So.2d 1140 (Miss. 1990). The North Carolina Supreme Court has also found that if a water is navigable for purposes of pleasure boating, it is navigable at law even if the water has never been used for trade or commerce. *Gwathmey v. North Carolina*, 342 N.C. 287, 464 S.E.2d 674 (1995).

Navigability in fact for title purposes must be established for the water body at the time of statehood on a case-by-case basis. The U.S. Supreme Court recently clarified in *PPL Montana, LLC v. Montana*, 132 S.Ct. 1215 (2012), that reliance on present day recreational use has limited application in determination of state title. The Court held that the "Montana Supreme Court . . . erred as a matter of law in its reliance upon the evidence of present-day, primarily recreational use of the Madison River." While the court could consider such evidence, it was limited to "that which shows the river could sustain the kinds of commercial use that, as a realistic matter, might have occurred at the time of statehood. Navigability must be assessed as of the time of statehood, and it concerns the river's usefulness for 'trade and travel,' rather than for other purposes. . . ." Evidence of present day recreational use is relevant only to the extent that it "may bear upon susceptibility of commercial use at the time of statehood" and "informs the historical determination [of] whether the river segment was susceptible of use for commercial navigation at the time of statehood." The Montana Supreme Court's reliance upon present-day, recreational use, "at least without further inquiry," was held to be "wrong as a matter of law." Id. at 1233–1234. This case calls cases such as *Ryals* and *Gwathmey* into question.

For over a century it was a matter of debate as to whether such cases as *The Propeller Genesee Chief* and *The Daniel Ball* rejected or merely supplemented, the English ebb and flow of the tide test for defining the scope of navigable waters for state title purposes. ("The doctrine of the common law as to the navigability of waters has no application in this country. Here the ebb and flow of the tide do not constitute the usual test, as in England, or any test at all of the navigability of waters." *The Daniel Ball* at 563). The U.S. Supreme Court addressed this issue directly in *Phillips Petroleum Co. v. Mississippi*, 484 U.S. 469, 108 S.Ct. 791, 98 L.Ed.2d 877 (1988). The case involved the ownership of submerged land several miles north of the Mississippi Gulf coast. The waters over these lands were not navigable in fact, but were influenced by the tides. The Mississippi Supreme Court had found that all lands subject to the tides up to the present day high tide line are navigable *in law* and are owned by the state. The U.S. Supreme Court agreed that cases extending the definition of navigability to all waters that are navigable in fact did not withdraw application of admiralty jurisdiction and the public trust doctrine from waters subject to the ebb and flow of the tide. As a matter of *federal* law, title to lands under all waters that are navigable in law passed to the state upon entry to the Union. The Court noted that once title passed to the state, state law controlled the subsequent disposition of public trust lands. The Supreme Court found that Mississippi law had consistently held that public trust lands include tidally affected lands and upheld Mississippi's claim to submerged lands under tidewaters although the waters were not navigable in fact.

Because federal law had played its role once title had transferred to the states, the law concerning public trust lands has not developed uniformly among the states. As noted earlier, the substantive scope of public trust uses may differ among states, and several states have acknowledged ownership by the riparian owner to the low tide line. A number of states also limit the test for navigability to either the navigability in fact test or the ebb and flow of the tide test. See Frank E. Maloney & Richard C. Ausness, *The Use and Legal Significance of the Mean High Water Line in Coastal Boundary Mapping,* 53 N.C.L. Rev. 185 (1974).

3.   DIVESTMENT OF PUBLIC TRUST LANDS

Public trust lands, held by states in this special governmental capacity, can be alienated, but the trust imposes certain limitations. The leading case explaining these limitations, *Illinois Central Railroad Co. v. Illinois*, 146 U.S. 387, 13 S.Ct. 110, 36 L.Ed. 1018 (1892), involved the validity of an 1869 grant by the Illinois legislature of virtually all the submerged lands in the harbor of Chicago to Illinois Central Railroad. Four years later the statute was repealed, and Illinois filed suit to establish ownership of the harbor. The U.S. Supreme Court described the nature of the state's obligation in the following excerpt:

The trust devolving upon the State for the public, and which can only be discharged by the management and control of property in which the public has an interest, cannot be relinquished by a transfer of the property. The control of the State for the purposes of the trust can never be lost, except as to such parcels as are used in promoting the interests of the public therein, nor can be disposed of without any substantial impairment of the public interest in the lands and waters remaining. . . . A grant of all the lands under the navigable waters of a State has never been adjudged to be within the legislative power; and any attempted grant of the kind would be held, if not absolutely void on its face, as subject to revocation. . . .

. . . The ownership of the navigable waters of the harbor and of the lands under them is a subject of public concern to the whole people of the State. The trust with which they are held, therefore, is governmental and cannot be alienated, except in those instances mentioned of parcels used in the improvement of the interest thus held, or when parcels can be disposed of without detriment to the public interest in the lands and waters remaining.

The Court found that the attempted transfer of the submerged lands of Chicago Harbor was an abdication of the public trust and was voidable or void.

The Eleventh Circuit used a similar rationale more recently in *Marine One, Inc. v. Manatee County*, 898

F.2d 1490 (11th Cir. 1990), to find that a permit
holder had no protectable property interest in a
permit to build a marina. The court found that a
permit to build on state-owned submerged lands is a
mere license which may be revoked without
compensation if the use interferes with the interests
of the public under the public trust doctrine.

The Supreme Court seemed to retreat somewhat
from the *Illinois Central* holding in *Appleby v. City of
New York*, 271 U.S. 364, 46 S.Ct. 569, 70 L.Ed. 992
(1926). Where the City of New York had transferred
several blocks of land under the navigable waters of
the Hudson River for purposes of filling for
waterfront improvements, the Court held that the
city did not have unrestricted power to control
navigation and wharfage in the waters over the lots.
Although Appleby had not subsequently filled the
entire area, the city had expressly conveyed the *jus
publicum* as well as the *jus privatum* in the lands and
had not required that the lands actually be filled. The
Court distinguished the right of the public to
continue to ply the waters over the lots from the city's
power to dredge the lots or appropriate for profit the
use of the waters for moorings for adjoining piers—
uses which largely excluded the owners' use of the
land and waters.

Clearly, states have alienated and continue to
alienate submerged trust lands. In general, the
courts will not construe conveyances to incorporate
public trust lands unless *expressly* included. See
Shively v. Bowlby, 152 U.S. 1, 14 S.Ct. 548, 38 L.Ed.
331 (1894). In addition, even in the case of express

conveyances by the state, some courts will find that the waters are still impressed with the *jus publicum,* unless the transfer expressly conveys the title free of public trust rights. See, e.g., *Gwathmey v. North Carolina*, 342 N.C. 287, 464 S.E.2d 674 (1995).

Many transfers of public trust lands have related to the improvement of commerce and navigation by building docks, wharves, navigation channels, or other harbor improvements and are generally characterized as within trust purposes. Courts have also upheld transfers of trust lands for uses less directly related to the public's trust interests in navigable waters. In *City of Madison v. State*, 1 Wis.2d 252, 83 N.W.2d 674 (1957), the Wisconsin Supreme Court found that the transfer by the state of a portion of the submerged lands of Lake Monona for filling to build a public auditorium was consistent with the public's use of the land for recreation and did not impair the former uses of the lake. The California Supreme Court found in *Boone v. Kingsbury*, 206 Cal. 148, 273 P. 797 (1928), that leasing ocean tidelands and submerged lands to oil prospectors furthered the public trust by promoting commerce. *Morse v. Oregon Division of State Lands,* 285 Or. 197, 590 P.2d 709 (1979), found that extension of an airport runway into state-owned estuary tidelands could be justified under the public trust doctrine. The Illinois Supreme Court held in *People v. Chicago Park District*, 66 Ill.2d 65, 360 N.E.2d 773 (1976), however, that "to preserve meaning and vitality in the public trust doctrine," the public interest served by the grant of state submerged land must not be "only incidental and remote."

The Third Circuit Court of Appeals in *West Indian Co. v. Government of the Virgin Islands*, 844 F.2d 1007 (3d Cir. 1988), analyzed and succinctly summarized the standard reviewing courts have applied to transfers of trust lands as follows:

> The courts carefully scrutinize any conveyance of submerged lands to determine if it is in complete congruence with the fiduciary obligations owed to the public by the sovereign. If the conveyance represents a deliberate and reasonable decision of the sovereign that the transaction of which the conveyance is a part affirmatively promotes the public interest in submerged lands, the courts have deferred to the sovereign's decision.

Id. at 1019. See also, e.g., *Caminiti v. Boyle*, 107 Wash.2d 662, 732 P.2d 989 (1987).

Most states have allowed individuals to acquire state lands through adverse possession. Although many state statutes on adverse possession do not specifically exclude public trust lands, courts have generally been unwilling to apply the adverse possession doctrine to such lands. See, e.g., *State ex rel. Rohrer v. Credle*, 322 N.C. 522, 369 S.E.2d 825 (1988); *O'Neill v. State Highway Dep't*, 50 N.J. 307, 235 A.2d 1 (1967); *Coastal States Gas Producing Co. v. State Mineral Bd.*, 199 So.2d 554 (La.App. 1967). Some courts have, however, applied the doctrine of equitable estoppel to validate claims to public trust lands. Courts have often found the application of equitable or legal estoppel to be justified when the parties have relied upon an invalid state conveyance of public trust lands, developed the land, and paid taxes for an extended period. Because such lands have usually been filled and used privately for many years, quieting title in private parties has been found not to interfere with public uses of navigable waters or the exercise of governmental powers. See, e.g., *Trustees of the Internal Improvement Fund v. Lobean,* 127 So.2d 98 (Fla. 1961).

Marketable title acts, passed to simplify land transactions, may also affect state title to public trust lands. These acts extinguish claims that are not part of the recorded chain of title for a requisite number of years, giving the owner a marketable title subject only to interests specifically exempted in the statute. Public trust lands have not always been specifically exempted in the statutes, but it is not clear that application of marketable title acts to these lands would meet the trust obligations of state governments. The Florida Supreme Court, in *Coastal Petroleum Co. v. American Cyanamid Co.*, 492 So.2d 339 (Fla. 1986), did not address the issue of whether the government had the power to make such a disposition of public trust lands, finding instead no legislative intent to apply the law to trust lands without "some indication that [the legislature] recognized the epochal nature of such revocation [of the public trust doctrine]." The court held that the legislature would not be found to have overturned "well-established law" and to have "casually dispose[d] of irreplaceable public assets" without specific reference to public trust lands.

If a marketable title act is found to be applicable to public trust lands in a particular state, an additional issue will arise: Can the record title owner exclude public use of navigable waters? In other words, does the act vest only bare title, *jus privatum*, or does the act also extinguish the *jus publicum?*

The statute of limitations of the federal Quiet Title Act of 1972 (QTA), 28 U.S.C.A. § 2409a, has been interpreted to foreclose state claims to public trust lands that are also claimed by the federal government. In *Block v. North Dakota ex rel. Board of University & School Lands*, 461 U.S. 273, 103 S.Ct. 1811, 75 L.Ed.2d 840 (1983), North Dakota attempted to use the act's waiver of the federal government's sovereign immunity to make a claim to an allegedly navigable river in which the United States had been issuing riverbed oil and gas leases to private entities. Although the U.S. Supreme Court held that the case was barred by the QTA's statute of limitations, the Court also found that the act did not effectuate a transfer of title if the state actually had title to the land. Obviously sympathetic to the state's claims, the Supreme Court intimated that the state should continue to press the claim until the United States was induced to file a quiet title action and settle the issue on the merits. Upon Congress' amendment of the QTA in 1986 to exempt states from the statute of limitations, North Dakota again brought suit, but failed to establish that the waters of the Little Missouri River were navigable at the time of statehood. *North Dakota ex rel. Bd. of Univ. & School Lands v. United States*, 972 F.2d 235 (8th Cir. 1992).

E. RIGHTS OF RIPARIAN OR LITTORAL OWNERS

1. THE SCOPE OF RIPARIAN OR LITTORAL RIGHTS

Riparian land borders running waters; littoral land borders a lake or ocean. The term "riparian" is often used in both circumstances, however, and the rights associated with ownership of both types of land seem to be mostly the same.

As members of the public, riparian owners have all the rights of the public in navigable waters. In addition, riparian owners have common law rights attributable to their ownership of lands contiguous to navigable waters. In general, common law riparian rights include a right of access to reach the water, the right to accretions, a qualified right to wharf out, the right to make commercial use of water access, the right to make reasonable use of the water, and the right of navigation in common with the public. Riparian rights are considered vested property interests.

The right of access includes a number of different aspects and forms the theoretical basis for most of the other riparian rights. Beachfront owners have an exclusive right of access over their property to reach the water. (The public has no right to cross private land to reach navigable waters.) The right to an unobstructed view, recognized in some states, can be considered a recognition of the riparian's right of visual access to the water—a right to a viewscape not generally recognized as a property interest. See, e.g., *DBL, Inc. v. Carson*, 262 Ga. App. 252, 255, 585 S.E. 2d 87, 91 (2003) (docks obstructing view). Recent litigation on this issue has involved beach restoration projects where dunes were constructed to protect the upland property and extend the project life of the restored beach. In condemnation proceedings related to the easement acquired for the dune, property owners claimed that they were entitled to severance damages to compensate for the remaining property's loss of value due to loss of the view. In *Borough of Harvey Cedars v. Karan*, 214 N.J. 384 (2013), the New Jersey Supreme Court overturned a $375,000 jury award and held that in such a "partial taking," just compensation must take into account not only the reduction in fair market value attributable to the loss of view, but also the "quantifiable benefits arising from the storm-protection project." Florida's legislature addressed the issue by amending its beach restoration legislation to provide:

> In any action alleging a taking of all or part of a property or property right as a result of a beach restoration project, in determining whether such taking has occurred or the value of any damage alleged with respect to the owner's remaining upland property adjoining the beach restoration project, the enhancement, if any, in value of the owner's remaining adjoining property of the upland property owner by reason of the beach restoration project shall be considered. If a

taking is judicially determined to have occurred as a result of a beach restoration project, the enhancement in value to the owner's remaining adjoining property by reason of the beach restoration project shall be offset against the value of the property or property right alleged to have been taken. If the enhancement in value shall exceed the value of the damage, if any, to the remaining adjoining property, there shall be no recovery over against the property owner for such excess.

Fla. Stat. § 161.141. Florida has, however, specifically found a compensable taking of the right of view when a bridge obstructed the view of a homeowner to the navigable waterbody. *Lee County, Florida v. Kiesel*, 705 So.2d 1013 (Ct. of Appeals, 1st Dis. 1998).

The right to exploit the riparian's access commercially is also clearly derivative of the exclusive right of access. The right to accretions may also be considered an aspect of access. If accreted lands did not inure to the upland owner, the land would no longer border the water, i.e., would not be riparian lands. The right of access, along with other exclusive riparian rights, could be lost. But cf., *Stop the Beach Renourishment* (2010); *Maunalua Bay Beach Ohana 28* (2009).

The riparian's right to accretions and alluvion, the material deposited, may also arise in a different context. Longshore currents, or littoral drift, constantly carry sand from beaches, but they also deposit new sand on beaches. Depending on whether more sand is carried away or deposited, the beach erodes or expands. Groins, jetties, or other structures intended to stabilize shorelines and navigation channels interrupt the longshore currents, causing deposition of suspended sand and resulting in "starvation," i.e., erosion, of downdrift beaches. In cases where the downdrift beaches are some distance away from the structures and multiple factors may contribute to the erosion, verifying causation presents a problem in establishing liability for the downdrift property damage. See, e.g., *Applegate v. United States*, 1996 WL 208458 (Fed. Cl. 1996). Where causation can be established, finding a theory upon which to base liability has been the major obstacle.

Most courts have rejected the "common enemy rule," which shields an owner from liability for diversions of surface water that cause accumulation of water on neighboring lands, as a defense in such cases. In *Lummis v. Lilly*, 385 Mass. 41, 429 N.E.2d 1146 (1982), a contiguous landowner constructed a groin that caused the beach to narrow on Lummis' downdrift property. The Massachusetts Supreme Court declined to invoke the common enemy rule and applied instead riparian law that allows each riparian reasonable use of the common waters. Reasonable use may result in diminution, obstruction, or change in natural water and sediment flow, but must consider the common rights of other riparian owners. The court found that the same rule should be applicable to littoral owners. The standard of reasonableness will also be applicable to cases that use a nuisance theory of liability.

The right to alluvion more directly provides the basis for liability for downdrift erosion in an emerging concept called "sand rights." The argument is that the littoral owner has a vested property interest in the sand that would be naturally transported to the shore. In California, where the sand rights doctrine was conceived, the protection of the sand transport system is viewed as an extension of the public trust doctrine. See Michael A. Corfield, Comment, *Sand Rights: Using California's Public Trust Doctrine to Protect Against Coastal Erosion,* 24 San Diego L. Rev. 727 (1987).

If coastal erosion is caused by a government project, affected property owners may claim that the government has unconstitutionally "taken" property without compensation. In *Applegate v. United States*, 1996 WL 208458 (Fed. Cl. 1996), more than 300 property owners south of the Canaveral Harbor Project sought compensation for loss of their property above the mean high-water mark due to erosion and flooding caused by the building and maintenance of the port and navigation channels. The court did not recognize a right to the continued flow of sand, but instead analogized the situation to dam flooding cases. The Federal Claims Court found that it is well "settled that flooding and attendant erosion of private property by the Government amount to a taking." Although the court recognized the basis for the plaintiffs' takings claims, issues involving proof of loss and causation may preclude any recovery or compensation by property owners in the case. See also *Banks v. United States*, 78 Fed. Cl. 603 (2007) (where the Army Corps of Engineers conceded liability for erosion caused by jetties and was liable for the part of the erosion above the high water mark that it caused to plaintiffs' properties and failed to mitigate).

The littoral owner's right of access is generally recognized to include the ability to reach the navigable part of the adjacent waters. The riparian does not have, however, a right of free navigation superior to the rights of the public in general. An often-litigated scenario involves the limitation of a riparian owner's navigation of adjacent waters by the construction of a low bridge or causeway or by the plugging of canal because of pollution problems. The overwhelming majority of cases have found that once the riparian has been afforded the ability to access navigable waters, the riparian's special rights go no further. Interference with the public's general right of navigation is not an actionable injury to a riparian. See, e.g., *Miller v. Mayor of New York*, 109 U.S. 385, 3 S.Ct. 228, 27 L.Ed. 971 (1883); *Gilman v. City of Philadelphia*, 70 U.S. 713, 18 L.Ed. 96 (1865); *Becker v. Litty*, 318 Md. 76, 566 A.2d 1101 (1989); *Colberg, Inc. v. State*, 67 Cal.2d 408, 62 Cal.Rptr. 401, 432 P.2d 3 (1967); *Thiesen v. Gulf, F. & A. Ry. Co.*, 75 Fla. 28, 78 So. 491 (1917); *Carmazi v. Board of County Comm'rs*, 108 So.2d 318 (Fla. App. 1959). The few cases finding a cause of action in the riparian involved a statutory right or application of the principle that a riparian may suffer special injury, different from the public, when navigation is obstructed. See *Ritter v. Standal*, 98 Idaho 446, 566 P.2d 769 (1977) (Idaho statute made obstruction of a navigable estuary a public nuisance); *Webb v.*

Giddens, 82 So.2d 743 (Fla. 1955) (boat rental business cut off from navigable portion of lake by causeway); *Game & Fresh Water Fish Comm'n v. Lake Islands, Ltd.*, 407 So.2d 189 (Fla. 1981) (prohibition on airboats denied island property owners access to island).

The qualified right to wharf out is related to the right to reach the navigable part of the water. This right has also been interpreted to include the right to fill in or dredge shallow areas to provide access to deeper waters. Historically, states encouraged erection of wharves, piers, and docking facilities to stimulate commerce and navigation through so-called "riparian acts." Some states have even granted private ownership of submerged lands when the riparian made such improvements. See *Jackson v. Revere Sugar Refinery*, 247 Mass. 483, 142 N.E. 909 (1924). However, several states that originally granted private ownership of submerged lands when the riparian made such improvements have since amended their laws or overruled these decisions. See *City of W. Palm Beach v. Board of Trustees of the Internal Improvement Trust Fund*, 714 So.2d 1060 (Fla. Dist. Ct. App. 4th Dist. 1998); *Clement v. Burns*, 43 N.H. 609 (1862). Today, the right to wharf out is strictly limited, if it can be said to exist at all. Virtually all states regulate the construction of wharfs, docks, and piers through pollution control or dredge and fill legislation and through zoning and other police power regulation at the local level. See e.g., *Dep't of Ecology v. City of Spokane Valley*, 167 Wn. App. 952 (2012) (holding that the "owner-noncommercial use" exemption of the Shoreline

Management Act was inapplicable to a real estate developer because the planned docks would not be built for the applicant's private use); *Samson v. City of Bainbridge Island*, 218 P.3d 921 (Wash.2009) (upholding a local government ban on private recreational docks by waterfront property owners to protect scenic vistas).

States may also require permission to use or occupy state lands below the high water line. In navigable waters, such structures require a permit from the U.S. Army Corps of Engineers. At this point, the right to wharf out may be better described in most states as merely creating a priority for a riparian owner to construct an adjacent dock.

The right of the riparian to wharf out inherently conflicts with public use of the foreshore and the obstructed navigable waters. In the absence of an exclusive lease or specific legislation, the riparian cannot exclude the public from waters around or under a pier. See *Capune v. Robbins*, 273 N.C. 581, 160 S.E.2d 881 (1968) (swimmer attempting a trip from Coney Island to Florida on a paddleboard could not be prohibited from passing under defendant's pier). Most jurisdictions require piers and other coastal structures to be built in a manner that does not obstruct passage by the public along the foreshore. See, e.g., *Barnes v. Midland R.R. Terminal Co.*, 218 N.Y. 91, 112 N.E. 926 (1916); *Caminiti,* 107 Wash.2d 662, 732 P.2d 989 (1987); cf. *Va. Marine Res. Comm'n v. Chincoteague Inn*, 61 Va. App. 371 (2013) (holding that although a portion of the floating platform to accommodate overflow seating from the

Inn's restaurant was temporarily moored over state-owned bottomlands, it was not encroaching over the bottomlands such that it violated the rights of the people of the Commonwealth to use the bottomlands).

Wharves or docks that unreasonably interfere with navigation may be a public nuisance. A private nuisance may arise where docks or piers cut off the access to navigable waters of other riparians. There is no single formula for equitably apportioning a "line of navigability" between or among riparians in all situations. Courts have tried extension of the land boundary lines, lines perpendicular to the shore, and in the case of lands abutting a cove, drawing a line across the mouth of the cove and extending boundaries to that line in a way to create areas roughly in ratio to the riparians' water frontage. Each case is a fact specific, equitable determination that, as much as possible, preserves the owners' access to a navigable channel and unobstructed view. See, e.g., *Langley v. Meredith*, 237 Va. 55, 376 S.E.2d 519 (1989) (apportioning areas for wharfs for adjacent owners by applying a ratio of the water frontages to the line of navigability); *Hayes v. Bowman*, 91 So.2d 795 (Fla. 1957); *Dorrah v. McCarthy*, 265 Ga. 750, 462 S.E.2d 708 (1995).

2. LIMITS ON RIPARIAN RIGHTS—THE NAVIGATION SERVITUDE

The navigation servitude, because of its link to navigable waters and the protection of navigation, is often confused with the public trust doctrine. The navigation servitude, however, is a paramount federal servitude on navigable waters based on the commerce power rather than on ownership or trust responsibilities. One commentator asserts a link, however, arguing that the American navigation servitude results from a mistaken interpretation of the English public trust doctrine by U.S. courts. See William B. Stoebuck, *Condemnation of Riparian Rights: A Species of Taking Without Touching,* 30 La. L. Rev. 394, 436–37 (1970).

The navigation servitude allows removal of any impediment to navigation without compensation to an owner and in some cases severely limits traditional riparian uses. See, e.g., *Palm Beach Isles Assocs. v. United States,* 58 Fed. Cl. 657 (2003); *United States v. 30.54 Acres of Land,* 90 F.3d 790 (3d Cir. 1996); *Donnell v. United States,* 834 F.Supp. 19 (D.Me. 1993); *Lewis Blue Point Oyster Cultivation Co. v. Briggs,* 229 U.S. 82, 33 S.Ct. 679, 57 L.Ed. 1083 (1913). In addition, many of the values associated with riparian ownership are not compensable if riparian property is condemned in conjunction with an exercise of Congress' power over navigation, even if the benefit to navigation is incidental. See *Oklahoma v. Guy F. Atkinson Co.,* 313 U.S. 508, 61 S.Ct. 1050, 85 L.Ed. 1487 (D.C. Okl. 1941); *United States v. Twin City Power Co.,* 350 U.S. 222, 76 S.Ct. 259, 100 L.Ed. 240 (1956). The navigation servitude has often been criticized as being at odds with the Fifth Amendment. See generally, Eva H. Morreale, *Federal Power in Western Waters: The Navigation Power and the Rule of No Compensation,* 3 Nat. Res. J. 1 (1963); Eugene J. Morris, *The Federal Navigation*

Servitude: Impediment to the Development of the Waterfront, 45 St. John's L. Rev. 189 (1970).

In *United States v. Chandler-Dunbar Water Power Co.,* 229 U.S. 53, 33 S.Ct. 667, 57 L.Ed. 1063 (1913), the U.S. Supreme Court found that no compensation was due Chandler-Dunbar for the removal of works in the river or the loss of the water power of the stream when the federal government condemned a portion of the upland riparian property for a navigation project which required the entire flow of the St. Marys River for improvement of navigation. The Court found that no private property rights could arise in the "running water in a great navigable stream." The Supreme Court followed this holding in *United States v. Twin City Power Co.,* 350 U.S. 222, 76 S.Ct. 259, 100 L.Ed. 240 (1956), in which the power company argued that the value of condemned upland property must include its value as a hydroelectric site. The Court found that no value derived from the flow of the stream itself was compensable.

Subsequently, the U.S. Supreme Court in *United States v. Rands,* 389 U.S. 121, 88 S.Ct. 265, 19 L.Ed.2d 329 (1967) refused to require the federal government to compensate an owner for the value of condemned property on the Columbia River as a port site. Congress responded by enacting section 111 of the Rivers and Harbors Act of 1970, 33 U.S.C.A. § 595(a). The section provides that in condemnation proceedings to acquire riparian property for river, harbor, and waterway improvement, "the compensation to be paid . . . shall be the fair market value of such real property based upon all uses to which such real property may reasonably be put, . . . any of which uses may be dependent upon access to or utilization of such navigable waters." Clearly overruling *Rands,* Congress has demonstrated that the navigation servitude does not constitutionally compel it to follow the no compensation rule.

The geographic scope of the navigation servitude is not coextensive with the reach of the Commerce Clause. In *Kaiser Aetna v. United States*, 444 U.S. 164, 100 S.Ct. 383, 62 L.Ed.2d 332 (1979), developers had dredged channels in a privately owned, nonnavigable waterbody (Kuapa Pond; now Hawaii Kai Marina), increased the clearance of a bridge, and connected the pond by an eight-foot deep channel to a navigable bay. The U.S. Army Corps of Engineers (Corps) later asserted that permits had to be obtained for further excavation or development in the pond and that public access to the pond was required. The U.S. Supreme Court held that Kuapa Pond clearly lies within the definition of navigable waters delimiting the reach of the Corps' regulatory authority under the Commerce Clause, but the Court also explained that the Corps' attempt to turn the privately owned pond into a "public aquatic park" amounted to a taking of private property without compensation. The navigation servitude was described as "the important public interest in the flow of interstate waters that in their natural condition are in fact capable of supporting public navigation." The Court also emphasized that the pond was private property under Hawaiian law and not a "great navigable stream [incapable] of private ownership," quoting *United States v. Chandler-Dunbar Water Power Co.*, 229 U.S. 53, 33 S.Ct. 667, 57 L.Ed. 1063 (1913). See also *Dardar v. Lafourche Realty Co., Inc.*, 985 F.2d 824 (5th Cir. 1993).

Many states also assert a navigation servitude, based on the state police power or the public trust doctrine, which is subordinate to the federal servitude. In *Wernberg v. State*, 516 P.2d 1191 (Alaska 1973), the Alaska Supreme Court reviewed three general approaches to state navigation servitudes. The general rule requires compensation to the riparian for interference with property rights unless the harm is caused in aid of navigation. The public purpose rule requires no compensation for harm if the project is for any public purpose. See, e.g., *Colberg, Inc. v. State ex rel. Dep't of Pub. Works*, 67 Cal.2d 408, 62 Cal.Rptr. 401, 432 P.2d 3 (1967). The Louisiana exception extends the servitude to projects in aid of navigation even if located a great distance from the water body. Although the Alaska Supreme Court found that the state applies the public purpose rule, it refused to apply the navigation servitude to the particular case. In the factual situation where a bridge project cut off a right of access that had been exercised for twenty years, the court held that the Alaska constitution required compensation for taking such littoral property rights. See generally Daniel J. Morgan & David G. Lewis, Comment, *The State Navigation Servitude,* 4 Land & Water L. Rev. 521 (1969).

CHAPTER II

PUBLIC ACCESS TO BEACHES AND SHORES

As commercial, industrial, residential, and recreational uses of the coasts create a wall of development along the ocean's edge, the public not only loses the view of the beach and ocean, but also often loses the ability to access navigable waters and the publicly owned beach seaward of the mean high tide line. Developers seek to maximize the value of coastal properties by creating "private" beaches, but this happens at the expense of the public, who may have rights in the dry sand as well as the wet sand area of certain beaches. The access problem is exacerbated by loss of beaches due to erosion and sea level rise. Preserving the rights of the public as coastal populations continue to grow and beaches disappear is one on the most formidable problems faced by coastal managers.

A. COMMON LAW THEORIES FOR BEACH ACCESS

The beaches below the high tide line, the wet sand, is part of the public trust—open to the public for swimming, recreation, and fishing. As a general proposition, lateral or horizontal access along the wet sand area is a public right. (Even in most of the states that recognize the low tide line as the boundary of private property, public access to the wet sand area is allowed for fishing and navigation). Enjoyment of the waters and the wet sand area is often dependent upon being able to reach the beach from the upland, perpendicular access, or upon being able to use the adjacent dry sand area. Although the area above the high tide line is subject to private ownership, the public may acquire the right to use perpendicular access routes or to use the dry sand area. These rights may arise under the common law doctrines of prescription, dedication, customary use, or the public trust.

1. PUBLIC EASEMENTS BY PRESCRIPTION

A prescriptive easement is acquired by continuous, uninterrupted, exclusive use that is open and notorious and adverse under claim of right. Most states recognize that easements by prescription may arise when the public makes continual use of beach property for the prescriptive period, which may range from as little as five years to as much as thirty years depending on state's law. In *Gion v. City of Santa Cruz*, 84 Cal.Rptr. 162, 465 P.2d 50 (1970), the California Supreme Court explained: "Litigants . . . must also show that various groups of persons have used the land. If only a limited and definable number of persons have used the land, those persons may be able to claim a personal easement but not [an easement in] the public."

The notion of establishing a prescriptive easement by public use is conceptually problematic. It can be argued that seasonal use by diverse members of the public can never meet the requirements of continuous or exclusive use. See, e.g., *Ivons-Nispel, Inc. v. Lowe*, 347 Mass. 760, 200 N.E.2d 282 (1964) (the general public is too broad a group to acquire a prescriptive easement to use a private beach for recreation); *State ex rel. Haman v. Fox*, 100 Idaho 140, 594 P.2d 1093 (1979). Beachfront owners have also maintained that because it is impossible to bring an ejectment or trespass action against the general public, the public should not be able to gain rights through prescription. See, e.g., *State ex rel. Thornton v. Hay*, 254 Or. 584, 462 P.2d 671 (1969). In spite of these conceptual hurdles, most states have recognized that an easement can be established by the public.

Establishing adverse use can be the greatest obstacle to overcome in acquiring a public prescriptive easement. Permissive use can never ripen into an easement. In recreational resort areas, a court may find, for example, that use of the beach by the public actually promotes the interests of the ocean front owner. See *City of Daytona Beach v. Tona-Rama, Inc.*, 294 So.2d 73 (Fla. 1974) (public use of beach around the owner's recreational pier was not adverse, but was in furtherance of the owner's interest). The so-called "open fields doctrine," which creates a presumption that unenclosed and undeveloped areas are used by the public by license of the owner, is applied in many jurisdictions. In *Gion v. City of Santa Cruz*, 84 Cal.Rptr. 162, 465 P.2d 50 (1970), the California Supreme Court rejected the presumption of permissive use of open beaches. The "preferable view" the court found was to treat the question of adverse use as "ordinarily one of fact, giving consideration to all the circumstances and inferences that can be drawn therefrom."

Some courts have rejected the principle that public use must be adverse in the same sense as in adverse possession cases, finding that a claim of right adverse to the owner is established when "whoever wanted to use [the beach] did so . . . when they wished to do so without asking permission and without protest from the landowners." *Seaway Co. v. Attorney Gen. of Texas*, 375 S.W.2d 923 (Tex. Civ. App. 1964); see also *Gion v. City of Santa Cruz*, 84 Cal.Rptr. 162, 465 P.2d 50 (1970).

Landowners attempting to interrupt the continuous use of the public and prevent the ripening of an easement by prescription have occasionally faced significant hurdles. In *Concerned Citizens v. Holden Beach Enterprises*, 329 N.C. 37, 404 S.E.2d 677 (1991), signs, fences, gates and guardhouses failed to stop the public from using the property, and the owner's futile attempts established the adverseness of the public's use. At trial, the frustrated agent of the owner asked: "[W]hat does it take to keep somebody out of the place [?] . . . [H]ave you got to set a tank up, a machine gun or what [?]" Id. at 51, 404 S.E.2d at 686.

2.   IMPLIED DEDICATION

Unlike prescriptive easements, dedication of property to public use does not necessarily require a specific time period, but does depend on intent. In *Gion v. City of Santa Cruz*, 2 Cal.3d 29, 84 Cal.Rptr. 162, 465 P.2d 50 (1970), the California Supreme Court held that "dedication of property to the public can be proved either by showing acquiescence of the owner in use of the land under circumstances that negate the idea that the use is under a license or by establishing open and continuous use by the public for the prescriptive period." In the case of dedication by acquiescence, the owner's intent is the determinant factor, and the length of public use is not relevant. Maintenance or patrolling of a beach by municipal authorities and the expenditure of public funds is relevant to the owner's knowledge and intent to acquiesce to public use. In the case of implied dedication by adverse use for the prescriptive period, the intent of the public—the intent to use without asking or receiving permission—becomes the controlling factor. See also *Seaway Co. v. Attorney Gen. of Texas*, 375 S.W.2d 923 (Tex. Civ. App. 1964).

In *Gion,* the public had used the shoreline land involved since at least 1900. The city had paved a parking lot, installed landslide alarms, maintained the land against constant erosion, and had collected trash on the beach. Occasionally, an owner had posted private property signs that had quickly disappeared. In *Dietz v. King,* 2 Cal.3d 29, 84 Cal.Rptr. 162, 465 P.2d 50 (Cal. 1970), a case considered concurrently with *Gion,* the public had used a beach and a beach access road for at least a hundred years. Although no previous owners of the land had excluded the public, the Kings attempted to block the road with timber and had put up "no trespassing" signs. Neither action was effective in deterring the public from using the land. In both cases, the California Supreme Court found that a dedication to the public had taken place.

The California court's approach in *Gion* and *Dietz* created a landowner's dilemma: As a matter of law, ineffective attempts to exclude public use would not negate intent to dedicate; and even when intent to dedicate could not be found because the landowner attempted to exclude the public, the same evidence could provide the basis for a prescriptive claim by establishing adverse use for the prescriptive period. Moreover, the same evidence that establishes that the public's use is permissive, which negates a finding of prescription or dedication by adverse use, may also support a finding of dedication by acquiescence. The California legislature reacted by allowing landowners to record an instrument declaring that public use of the described land is permissive and by providing that such a recording is conclusive evidence of consent that cannot ripen into dedication or a prescriptive public right.

The Hawaii Supreme Court has specifically rejected *Gion's* theory of implied dedication. In *In re Banning*, 73 Haw. 297, 832 P.2d 724 (1992), the Hawaii court held that while continuous adverse public use may raise a rebuttable presumption of implied dedication, if public use is the only evidence of dedication, it must continue for much longer than the prescriptive period. Application of *Gion* was also found to be inconsistent with state policy that not only encourages property owners to open their lands and waters to the public for recreational purposes, but also specifically prohibits the public from acquiring any rights by prescription in the property as a result of such use.

3.   CUSTOM

In *State ex rel. Thornton v. Hay*, 254 Or. 584, 462 P.2d 671 (1969), the Oregon Supreme Court found that evidence supported a finding of a public prescriptive easement to use the beach property that the owners had fenced, but declined to decide the case on that basis. In order to avoid tract-by-tract litigation, the court resurrected the English doctrine of custom to apply uniformly to "ocean-front lands from the northern to the southern border of the state." The Oregon court ignored an early Connecticut case rejecting application of the custom doctrine on the basis that it is unadapted to United States' society. *Graham v. Walker*, 78 Conn. 130, 61 A. 98 (1905). Referring to Blackstone's Commentaries, the court defined the requirements of custom to be public use that is ancient, exercised without interruption, reasonable, peaceable, obligatory, and not repugnant to other custom or law. The use of the dry-sand area of the Pacific shore by the public was found to be "an unbroken custom running back in time as long as the land has been inhabited." This decision has been criticized for adjudicating the rights of coastal property owners in Oregon who were not parties to the litigation. See also *Stevens v. City of Cannon Beach*, 317 Or. 131, 854 P.2d 449 (1993). The Oregon court later refused to extend the doctrine to areas not actually adjacent to the high tide line and not customarily used by the public. See *McDonald v. Halvorson*, 308 Or. 340, 780 P.2d 714 (1989).

A number of other states have adopted the doctrine of custom to protect public access to beaches. In Hawaii, the state's supreme court has held that long-standing public use of the state's beaches to a recognizable boundary, the seaweed or debris line, has ripened into a customary right. *In re Ashford*, 50 Haw. 314, 50 Haw. 452, 440 P.2d 76 (1968). The Florida Supreme Court has found that the public has customary rights to use the dry sand area of certain beaches in the state. *City of Daytona Beach v. Tona-Rama, Inc.*, 294 So.2d 73 (Fla. 1974). A Washington Attorney General's Opinion, 1970 AGO No. 27, has also concluded that the public is entitled to free use of the wet and dry sand beaches of the state based on the doctrine of custom. In denying an oceanfront owner the right to fence off a beach, the federal court for the District of the Virgin Islands held that "custom" is part of federal common law. *United States v. St. Thomas Beach Resorts, Inc.*, 386 F.Supp. 769 (D.V.I. 1974). In North Carolina, however, a suit by beachfront owners challenging the state's claim that the public has a customary right to use all natural dry sand beaches was dismissed on procedural grounds. *Fabrikant v. Currituck County*, 174 N.C.App. 30, 621 S.E.2d 19 (2005).

4.   THE PUBLIC TRUST DOCTRINE

Because the public's right to enjoy public trust uses of the area below the high water line may depend on access to and across the foreshore, New Jersey courts have allowed the public trust doctrine to creep landward. In *Borough of Neptune City v. Borough of Avon-by-the-Sea*, 61 N.J. 296, 294 A.2d 47 (1972) and

Van Ness v. Borough of Deal, 78 N.J. 174, 393 A.2d 571 (1978), the New Jersey Supreme Court held that the public trust doctrine requires that municipal beaches must be open to all members of the public on equal terms. In *Avon-by-the-Sea,* the court struck down a requirement for nonresidents to pay a much higher fee than residents to use a municipal beach. The court held in *Deal* that the public could not be excluded by a town's dedication of a beach for use by its residents only. Subsequently, in *Matthews v. Bay Head Improvement Ass'n*, 95 N.J. 306, 471 A.2d 355 (1984), the New Jersey court extended the public trust doctrine to include: (1) a right of feasible access to the beach dependent on the particular circumstances of an area; and (2) the public's use of the sandy beach "where use of the dry sand is essential or reasonably necessary for enjoyment of the ocean."

The Bay Head Improvement Association owned, or leased from private owners, a substantial part of the beach in the Borough of Bay Head, New Jersey, and limited daytime access to members of the Association. There was no public beach in the borough. The Association carried out the same activities as a municipality and received significant funding from the borough. To assure that such a strategy was not adopted broadly to foreclose the public from local beaches, the New Jersey Supreme Court held that the public trust doctrine required that membership in the Association must be open to the public at large. The court did not hold that all privately owned beachfront property must be open to the public, but the court's rationale—"that the public must be given both access to and use of privately owned dry sand areas as reasonably necessary"—supports that conclusion. The New Jersey Supreme Court recently reaffirmed this principle in *Raleigh Avenue Beach Association v. Atlantis Beach Club, Inc.*, 185 N.J. 40, 879 A.2d 112 (2005), (holding that the public had the right to use a privately owned, dry sand beach).

The state of Maine attempted to statutorily broaden the scope of the public trust doctrine in the intertidal zone to include recreational use. Maine had originally been part of the Massachusetts Bay Colony, and intertidal ownership was governed by a colonial ordinance providing that a shoreline owner's title extends to the low water line subject only to the public's right to fish, fowl, and navigate. In a four-three opinion, the Maine Supreme Court found that by declaring the intertidal zone to be impressed with a public trust which included recreational use, the 1986 Public Trust in Intertidal Land Act constituted an unconstitutional taking of private property. See *Bell v. Town of Wells*, 557 A.2d 168 (Me. 1989). See also, *Opinion of the Justices*, 365 Mass. 681, 313 N.E.2d 561 (1974) (an advisory opinion of the Massachusetts Supreme Court finding that a legislative expansion of the public trust doctrine in that state would be unconstitutional). More recently, however, the Maine court held that the public's rights in the intertidal area were not strictly limited to fishing, fowling and navigation. In extending public trust rights in Maine to include the public's right to walk across intertidal lands for purposes of scuba diving, the court recognized a necessity to "strike a reasonable balance between private ownership of the intertidal lands and the public's use of those lands." *McGarvey v. Whittredge*, 28 A.3d 620 (2011).

The Michigan Supreme Court held recently that the scope of shoreline ownership and the scope of the public trust doctrine are not necessarily the same. In *Glass v. Goeckel*, 473 Mich. 667, 703 N.W.2d 58 (2005), the Michigan court found that even where statutory provisions may have affected the boundary between privately owned, littoral land and state-owned, submerged lake-bottom, the private title of littoral landowners remains subject to the public trust beneath the historic ordinary high water mark. The court held that the land up to the historic ordinary high water remained subject to the *jus publicum*—*the* public rights preserved under the public trust doctrine—even if the title to the land had passed into private ownership. The court also reaffirmed that "walking along the lakeshore is inherent in the exercise of traditionally protected public rights." See *Glass v. Goeckel*, 473 Mich. 667, 703 N.W.2d 58 (2005).

B. STATUTORY AND REGULATORY ACCESS REQUIREMENTS

Legislation or regulations creating new rights of public access to or across private lands to facilitate exercise of public trust use of beaches and waters is subject to challenge as a taking of private property by authorizing a permanent physical invasion. See, e.g., *Nollan v. California Coastal Comm'n*, 483 U.S. 825, 107 S.Ct. 3141, 97 L.Ed.2d 677 (U.S. 1987); *Bell v.*

Town of Wells, 557 A.2d 168 (Me. 1989); *Opinion of the Justices (Public Use of Coastal Beaches)*, 139 N.H. 82, 649 A.2d 604 (1994). However, many states have statutes designed to protect existing public access and to mitigate the impacts of shoreline activities on existing access ways.

Florida, for example, has a provision prohibiting development or construction that interferes with accessways created through public use, dedication, or other means unless a comparable alternative accessway is provided. See Fla. Stat. § 161.55(6). Coastal development regulatory programs, such as in California, and more general land use statutes regulating subdivision or planned unit development of land have routinely required, as a condition for development or subdivision approval, that the impacts of development on established public rights to the shoreline be mitigated. These types of regulations can be inherently ineffective for protecting public accessways established by common law principles: If the regulation is enforced at the state level, regulators may not be fully aware of local, customary uses that create public rights and easements; if regulation is at the local level, municipalities may lack the incentive or resources to identify and enforce common law easements.

The Texas Open Beaches Act, Tex. Nat. Res. Code Ann. ch. 61, deals directly with the protection of existing beach access rights. The statute imposes penalties for obstructing access where the public has acquired a right to reach or use the sandy beach. It is also illegal to post signs indicating that the public has no right to use a public beach. Perhaps most importantly, the Texas legislature has found that the nature of the use of sandy beaches in the state justifies a rebuttable presumption that the beaches are public from the mean low tide line to the line of vegetation. In 2009, voters in Texas added access to public beaches to the state constitution's Bill of Rights. Art. I, sec. 33(b) provides: "The public, individually and collectively, has an unrestricted right to use and a right of ingress to and egress from a public beach. The right granted by this subsection is dedicated as a permanent easement in favor of the public."

C.   THE NATURE OF A PUBLIC EASEMENT

If the public establishes an easement to use a beach above the high tide line, what happens to the easement when natural forces move the beach? Does an easement follow the beach or dunes as they move due to erosion or avulsion? Generally, an easement is considered a "static real property concept." But the North Carolina Supreme Court did not reject a finding of a public easement over shifting, windswept sand dunes because the traveled way varied as the topography of the dunes changed. The court found that the requirement of "substantial identity" for a prescriptive easement must take into account the dynamic nature of the landscape. *Concerned Citizens v. State ex rel. Rhodes*, 329 N.C. 37, 404 S.E.2d 677 (1991).

Similarly, Texas appellate courts had posited that "[a]n easement fixed in place while the beach moves

would result in the easement being either under
water or left high and dry inland, detached from the
shore. . . . The law cannot freeze such an easement at
one place any more than the law can freeze the beach
itself." *Matcha v. Mattox ex rel. People*, 711 S.W.2d 95
(Tex.Civ.App.1986). This concept, called a "rolling
easement," has been applied in Texas to prevent
rebuilding and to require removal of structures that
obstruct beach access, even when the beach had move
substantially due to an avulsive event, such as a
hurricane. The Texas Supreme Court did not,
however, address the rolling easement as a matter of
Texas law until 2012.

In *Severance v. Patterson*, 370 S.W.3d 705 (2012),
the Texas Supreme Court held in an advisory opinion
that Texas does not recognize a "rolling" public
beachfront access easement. Texas recognizes that
the MHW boundary between state submerged lands
and private upland moves with the changing
shoreline; it is irrelevant whether the change is
caused by erosion or avulsion. The court held that
easement boundaries, however, may only shift when
gradual changes alter the location of the beach. Id. at
723 ("It would be impractical and an unnecessary
waste of public resources to require the State to
obtain a new judgment for each gradual and nearly
imperceptible movement of coastal boundaries
exposing a new portion of dry beach"). If an avulsive
event, such as a hurricane, moves the MHW line and
vegetation line suddenly and perceptibly, causing the
former dry beach to become part of state-owned wet
beach or become completely submerged, the adjacent
private property owner is not automatically deprived

of her right to exclude the public from the new dry beach. The land encumbered by the easement is lost to the public trust, along with the easement attached to that land. Id. at 723–24. See also *Trepanier v. County of Volusia*, 965 So.2d 276 (Fla. Dist. Ct. App. 2007) (finding that the migration of the public's customary use with the movement of the beach is a matter of proof).

The Hawaii Supreme Court impliedly rejected the concept of a "rolling" or shifting public easement in *In re Banning*, 73 Haw. 297, 832 P.2d 724 (1992). The court refused to extend a public easement to adjacent accreted lands in spite of state arguments that because the beach is subject to constant change, specifically bounded descriptions of public access easements are insufficient. The court maintained that an easement by prescription or dedication must be confined to a "definite and specific line," and that "vague description of the easement literally allows members of the public to redefine its location each time they use the land."

D.   PUBLIC BEACH ACCESS AND TAKINGS JURISPRUDENCE

Beach access statutes and public access conditions on development have been subject to continual challenges alleging that such access requirements are a taking of property, particularly the owner's right to exclude. In some instances, the public's right of access may even preclude any development of a parcel of property, reducing its value to the point that the owner may also base a takings claim on the severe or total reduction in the value of the property.

1.   PROTECTION OF EXISTING PUBLIC BEACH ACCESS

Clearly, laws that do no more than protect existing public beach easements do not effect a taking of private property. In *Lucas v. South Carolina Coastal Council*, 505 U.S. 1003, 112 S.Ct. 2886, 120 L.Ed.2d 798 (1992), discussed fully infra at Chapter III. D.1, the U.S. Supreme Court found that even in cases where regulation left the property with no economically viable use, government enforcement of a limitation on property rights based on background principles of law does not constitute a compensable taking of property, because the right to such use was never part of the owner's rights. Justice Scalia noted specifically that the Court "assuredly would permit the government to assert a permanent easement that was a pre-existing limitation on the landowner's title."

In spite of this specific language in *Lucas,* Justice Scalia wrote a strong dissent to the Court's denial of certiorari for *Stevens v. City of Cannon Beach*, 317 Or. 131, 854 P.2d 449 (1993). Stevens sought review of an Oregon Supreme Court decision finding that Stevens did not suffer a compensable taking when he was denied permits to build a seawall on the dry sand beach that was necessary to further develop his land. The Oregon court found that the doctrine of custom was a background principle of state property law, and that Stevens never had the right to obstruct the dry sand beach that was subject to public use based on custom. Justice Scalia found the reliance on *Thornton v. Hay*, 254 Or. 584, 462 P.2d 671 (1969), problematic both substantively and procedurally:

I believe that petitioners have sufficiently preserved their due process claim, and believe further that the claim is a serious one. Petitioners, who owned this property at the time Thornton was decided, were not parties to that litigation. Particularly in light of the utter absence of record support for the crucial factual determinations in that case, whether the Oregon Supreme Court chooses to treat it as having established a "custom" applicable to Cannon Beach alone, or one applicable to all "dry-sand" beach in the State, petitioners must be afforded an opportunity to make out their constitutional claim by demonstrating that the asserted custom is pretextual. If we were to find for petitioners on this point, we would not only set right a procedural injustice, but would hasten the clarification of Oregon substantive law that casts a shifting shadow upon federal constitutional rights the length of the State.

Stevens v. City of Cannon Beach, 510 U.S. 1207 (1994) (Scalia, J. dissenting).

Justice Scalia's strong objection to the application of the doctrine of custom to Oregon's beaches suggests that novel use of common law theories, such as custom or the public trust doctrine, may meet resistance in some courts. While these common law doctrines may be within the realm of "background principles of law," courts may find that newly devised applications of the doctrines to further public access to beaches do not meet the requirements of the Fifth Amendment.

2.   BEACH ACCESS CONDITIONS ON DEVELOPMENT PERMITS

To protect public access to beaches in furtherance of California's constitutional provisions and the state's coastal management program, the California Coastal Commission routinely includes public access as a condition for approval of coastal development permits. For example, on a segment of Faria Beach, forty-three of fifty-seven permits for development on beachfront properties included easements for lateral public access across the properties above the mean high water mark, facilitating the public's use of the public beaches at each end of Faria Beach. In *Nollan v. California Coastal Commission*, 483 U.S. 825, 107 S.Ct. 3141, 97 L.Ed.2d 677 (1987), the owners of a lot on Faria Beach objected to the Coastal Commission's imposition of a similar easement on their lot as a condition for receiving a permit to demolish a small bungalow and replace it with a larger house. Analogizing the factual situation to *Kaiser Aetna v. United States*, 444 U.S. 164, 100 S.Ct. 383, 62 L.Ed.2d 332 (1979), see *supra* Chapter I.E.2, Justice Scalia stated that the requirement of a public easement across the beachfront would undoubtedly constitute a permanent physical occupation, and therefore a *per se* taking of the Nollan's property, unless the condition furthered a land use regulation that "substantially advance[s] legitimate state interests." The Commission argued that it could have exercised its police power to deny the permit based on the interference with visual access and the "psychological barrier" to public use of the beach presented by the wall of development along the beach. This being the case, the Commission maintained that a permit condition serving the same legitimate purposes should not be found to be a taking. The Court agreed, but could not understand how lateral access to the beachfront related to visual access from the street and found that "the condition substituted for the prohibition utterly fails to further the end advanced as the justification for the prohibition." Conditions not related to the legitimate purposes underlying the authority to restrict development were depicted by the Court as "an out-and-out plan of extortion."

Although *Nollan* found that there must be an "essential nexus" between the exaction and the effects of the development, the Court did not explain how close the fit must be. In *Dolan v. City of Tigard*, 512 U.S. 374, 114 S.Ct. 2309, 129 L.Ed.2d 304 (1994), the Court reaffirmed *Nollan's* standard and further explained that the "essential nexus" required is a "rough proportionality" between the dedication of property rights and the "nature and extent" of the impact of the proposed development. This scrutiny of whether the regulation substantially advances a legitimate state interest goes well beyond the traditional consideration by the courts of land uses measures, i.e., consideration of whether the conclusions of the government are "fairly debatable." *Euclid v. Ambler Realty*, 272 U.S. 365, 47 S.Ct. 114,

71 L.Ed. 303 (1926). In *Lingle v. Chevron*, 544 U.S. 528, 125 S.Ct. 2074, 161 L.Ed.2d 876 (2005), the Supreme Court clarified *in dicta* that *Nollan's* heightened scrutiny and more rigorous analysis of the fit between the burden and the exaction applies only in adjudicative decisions where the government imposes conditions requiring dedication of land or access—requirements that would be found to be per se takings outside the permitting context. Although *Lingle* limits the scope of the *Nollan/Dolan* analysis to cases involving an application of the doctrine of "unconstitutional conditions," the application of the standard to beach access easements is clear. The Court noted in *Nollan* that where property rights, such as the right to exclude, are abridged, the police power must "substantially advance" a legitimate state interest and that this requirement is not just a matter of semantics. The Court will "be particularly careful about the adjective where the actual conveyance of property is made a condition to the lifting of a land-use restriction." See also *Koontz v. St. Johns River Water Management District*, 133 S.Ct. 2586 (2013) (holding that the government's demand for property from a land-use permit applicant must satisfy the requirements of *Nollan* and *Dolan even when the government denies the permit and even when its demand is for money*).

CHAPTER III

MANAGEMENT OF COASTAL RESOURCES

A. COASTAL ZONE MANAGEMENT

1. THE COASTAL ZONE MANAGEMENT ACT AND RELATED LEGISLATION

The federal Coastal Zone Management Act of 1972 (CZMA), 16 U.S.C.A. §§ 1451–1464, was passed "to preserve, protect, develop, and where possible, to restore or enhance, the resources of the Nation's coastal zone for this and succeeding generations." Enacted during the same period as other major federal environmental legislation, the CZMA differed substantially from legislation like the Clean Air Act or the Clean Water Act. First, state participation in coastal zone management planning was completely voluntary. Federal standards or management would not be imposed if the state did not develop a plan. Second, although there was a recognized national interest in effective coastal management, Congress also recognized that the type of land use planning and management required was traditionally within the domain of state and local governments. See generally, Alison Rieser, Donna Christie, Richard Hildreth & Joseph Kalo, Ocean and Coastal Law 249–311 (2013).

The CZMA provides federal funding for states to develop and administer coastal programs according to guideline set out in the Act. Funding for program development and administration is a traditional incentive for encouraging state cooperation. The CZMA provides, however, an additional incentive for state participation—the so-called federal consistency requirement. This provision creates a kind of reverse preemption that assures a state that, with certain exceptions, federal agency activities and activities that are sponsored or permitted by the federal government will be consistent with the state created and federally approved coastal management plan.

The states are given great flexibility in their approaches to coastal management and even in determining the area to be covered by the program. The CZMA only generally defines the coastal zone to include the territorial sea and adjacent lands "to the extent necessary to control shorelands, the uses of which have a direct and significant impact on the coastal waters." 16 U.S.C.A. § 1453(1). Each state defines the limits of its coastal zone for purposes of its management program.

The Washington coastal program was the first to receive federal approval in 1976. With approval of the Illinois program in 2012, all thirty-five eligible states and territories (including the Northern Marianas, Puerto Rico, the Virgin Islands, Guam, and American Samoa) had successfully developed federally approved programs. In 2011, however, the legislature of Alaska failed to extend the state program and officially withdrew from the federal program on July 1st of that year. An initiative added to 2012 ballot to reinstate the program in Alaska failed.

The CZMA has been amended a number of times. The 1973 Arab oil embargo and energy crisis of the mid-1970s led to major amendments to the CZMA in 1976 to facilitate energy facility siting and other energy development. The 1980 amendments continued to focus attention on coastal states incorporating national interests in coastal planning. With the original development period ending, funding for the CZMA was substantially reduced and new program goals and policies were introduced to enhance coastal management. The Coastal Management Reauthorization Act of 1985 included new procedures for the review and amendment of state coastal programs. The Coastal Zone Act Reauthorization Amendments of 1990 made major changes in the federal consistency provision to clarify its scope and application. A new Coastal Zone Enhancement Grant Program was created to encourage states to improve their plans in one or more of eight areas of coastal concern, including: (1) coastal wetlands protection, (2) management of development in high hazard areas, (3) public access, (4) control of marine debris, (5) studying cumulative and secondary impacts of coastal development, (6) special area management planning, (7) ocean resources planning, and (8) siting of coastal energy and government facilities. 16 U.S.C.A. § 1456b(a). The amendments also created a major new requirement for state coastal programs, a Coastal Nonpoint Pollution Control Program, for protecting coastal waters from pollution from shoreline land uses. See id. at § 1455b(a). The 1996 CZMA amendments did not make major substantive changes.

The latest reauthorization expired in 1999; although several new provisions have been introduced, Congress has repeatedly been unable to pass reauthorization language. A 2010 report outlines why this has been the case and why reauthorization has become controversial:

    1.   Numerous stakeholders (participants, use and development interests, and environmentalists); and

    2.   Changing context, including events (like Hurricane Katrina and the BP oil spill), new scientific information (like knowledge concerning marine dead zones), economic trends (like rising energy prices), and climate change.

See generally Harold F. Upton, Coastal Zone Management Background and Reauthorization Issues (Congressional Research Service Report 10–16, Sept. 29, 2010).

The National Estuarine Sanctuaries Program, which was created in 1972 as a part of the Coastal Zone Management Act, has evolved into the current National Estuarine Research Reserve System. 16 U.S.C.A. § 1461. The purpose of the reserve system is to provide natural field laboratories of representative estuarine types for research and to enhance public understanding of estuaries and their functions by creating opportunities for education and interpretation. NOAA is responsible for developing estuarine research guidelines to establish common research principles and objectives for the national reserve research system. Financial assistance may be available to the states to acquire lands for management, educational, and interpretive purposes.

Twenty-eight estuarine research reserves have been designated nationally that are characteristic of different coastal regions and estuarine types. State governors nominate areas for inclusion in the program. NOAA designates an estuarine area upon finding that it is a representative estuarine ecosystem suitable for long-term research and that state laws provide sufficient protection to "ensure a stable environment for research."

Area-based coastal management is also carried out under the National Estuary Programs (NEP) established under § 320 of the Clean Water Act administered by the federal Environmental Protection Agency (EPA). State governors nominate estuaries of national significance for preparation of non-binding management plans by private and public stakeholders. Congress specified 16 estuaries to which EPA was to give priority in administering the program. One expert has summarized the NEP this way:

The NEP is a watershed-based management approach to protecting our nation's estuaries. Acceptance into the NEP leads to a comprehensive evaluation of all the problems in a given estuary and the development of strategies to address the most serious problems threatening the long-term health of the estuary.

Public participation in this effort is one of the conceptual cornerstones of the NEP, although meaningful participation by the public may not be fully realized in all cases. Management plans created under the NEP do not have the force of law, but they can and do motivate federal, state and local regulators into action.

Matthew W. Bowden, *An Overview of the National Estuary Program*, 11 Natural Resources & Environment 35 (1996).

The Chesapeake Bay Program authorized by Clean Water Act § 117 served as a model for the NEP. That program proceeded one significant step further to a multi-party agreement in which the member states have agreed to watershed level regulation of land use and water quality to meet agreed ecosystem performance goals such as a 40% reduction in controllable nitrogen and phosphorus loadings to the bay toward which there has been significant progress. Maryland, Virginia, Pennsylvania, the District of Columbia; over 50 federal agencies, and more than 2,000 local governments have implemented the program without laws that mandate such cooperation. See Harry R. Hughes and Thomas W. Burke, Jr., *The Cleanup of the Nation's Largest Estuary: A Test of Political Will*, 11 Natural Resources & Environment 30 (1996).

On the west coast, the state-federal CALFED Bay-Delta Program (now the Delta Stewardship Council) focused on San Francisco Bay and its tributaries with goals of improving statewide water supply reliability, and protecting and restoring the Delta ecosystem.

The process has led to adoption of a Delta Plan in 2013 and state legislation, the Delta Reform Act, which requires state and local agencies to be consistent with the Delta Plan.

Also, under the Estuary Restoration Act of 2000, 33 U.S.C.A. § 2901, EPA, NOAA, Fish and Wildlife Service, Army Corps of Engineers, and Department of Agriculture, work in concert to restore estuaries. The purpose of the Act is to promote the restoration of estuary habitat; to develop a national Estuary Habitat Restoration Strategy for creating and maintaining effective partnerships within the federal government and with the private sector; to provide federal assistance for and promote efficient financing of estuary habitat restoration projects, and to develop and enhance monitoring, data sharing, and research capabilities. The final Estuary Habitat Restoration Strategy was approved in 2012 and attempts to focus program efforts and limited resources on areas not addressed by other federal programs.

2.   DEVELOPMENT AND APPROVAL OF STATE CZM PROGRAMS

The development stage for state coastal management programs turned out to be a long, arduous process in most states. In general, states lacked statutory bases to implement coastal management programs, and local governments often balked at what was perceived as state usurpation of local planning and zoning functions.

The CZMA currently sets out the requirements for a state management program to receive federal approval at 16 U.S.C.A. §§ 1455–1456. The requirements can be broadly categorized as informational and definitional, institutional and organizational, procedural, and planning. Informational and definitional requirements include identifying boundaries of the coastal zone, defining permissible land and water uses, inventorying areas of particular concern, and defining "beach." Institutionally, the program must identify the means and legal authorities by which the state can carry out the program and the organizational structure to implement the program. The program must include procedures for intergovernmental coordination and public participation. Planning processes must be developed for prioritizing uses in the coastal zone, identifying and preserving areas of special "conservation, recreational, ecological, historical, and esthetic values," and for dealing with shoreline erosion and sea level rise. See id. at § 1452(2)(B) and (3). Finally, the program must include a planning process for energy facilities that "provides for adequate consideration of the national interest."

The Secretary of Commerce, through the National Oceanic and Atmospheric Administration's (NOAA) Office of Ocean and Coastal Resources Management (OCRM), has the responsibility for determining whether a program meets the requirements of section 1455 and the purposes and policies of the CZMA. Programs are generally submitted in the form of an environmental impact statement meeting the requirements of the National Environmental Policy Act (NEPA), 42 U.S.C.A. § 4332. Program approval must include a determination that the views of federal agencies affected by the program have been "adequately considered."

In *American Petroleum Institute v. Knecht*, 456 F.Supp. 889 (C.D.Cal. 1978), the American Petroleum Institute (API) challenged the approval of the California Coastal Zone Management Program (CZMP). API's primary arguments were that the CZMP lacked the specificity necessary to meet the CZMA's requirements and that the program did not adequately consider the national interest. API contended that the program should "include detailed criteria establishing a sufficiently high degree of predictability to enable a private user of the coastal zone to say with certainty that a given project [met the standards of the CZMP]." The federal district court first considered Congress' definition of a "management program," which emphasized that the program set "forth objectives, policies and standards to guide public and private uses of . . . the coastal zone." The court determined that there was no intent to require a "zoning map" or a predictive device for private users to rely upon. Instead, the program is intended to create a framework within which the state can make rational decisions balancing competing interests. The court also rejected the argument that adequate consideration of the national interest entailed "affirmative accommodation of energy facilities [as] a quid pro quo for [program] approval."

Approved coastal programs are subject to continuing review by NOAA to determine the extent to which the state is implementing and enforcing the program. Program approval may be withdrawn or financial assistance may be suspended under certain circumstances.

In the 1987 review of California's coastal program, NOAA required that the Coastal Commission prepare and submit for approval guidelines that would provide greater predictability for parties seeking consistency determinations for proposed activities affecting the Outer Continental Shelf. The Commission refused, and NOAA withheld most of the program's administrative funding. Congress enacted legislation restoring the funds, but the NOAA grant continued to be conditioned on the state adopting consistency guidelines that would be submitted to NOAA "for review and approval as a program change." In *California v. Mack*, 693 F.Supp. 821 (N.D.Cal. 1988), the state challenged NOAA's authority to coerce modification of a previously approved program by conditioning further federal funding. The federal district court held that NOAA does not have the authority to revisit the provisions of an approved plan or to coerce, through its power over funding, an alteration of the approved program itself. The court viewed NOAA's action as a reversal of its position in *American Petroleum Institute v. Knecht* concerning the specificity of state programs and an attempt "to manipulate the coastal policy of the states . . . by forcing a state to choose between modifying the program and losing federal financial assistance under the CZMA." Id. at 826. The court enjoined NOAA from withdrawing program approval or withholding funds based on the unlawfully imposed condition.

The 1990 amendments to the CZMA clarify the procedures necessary for NOAA to withdraw funds or approval of a state coastal program. If a state fails to adhere to its approved program or the terms of a grant, financial assistance may not be suspended until NOAA provides the state's governor with specifications and a schedule for compliance. Program approval may not be withdrawn unless the state fails to take the actions required for compliance. See 16 U.S.C.A. § 1458(c)–(d).

States may amend or modify an approved coastal program by submitting the amendment to the Secretary for review. In general, the Secretary must approve or disapprove the amendment within a maximum of 120 days unless additional time is necessary to meet NEPA requirements. If the amendment is not disapproved within that period, it is conclusively presumed to be approved. Id. § 1455(e)(1)–(2). Until the amendment is approved, it cannot be considered an enforceable policy for purposes of consistency determinations. Id. § 1455(e)(3)(B). NOAA regulations distinguish between a program amendment and routine program implementation. See 15 C.F.R. § 923.80–923.84. An "amendment" involves "substantial changes in, or substantial changes to, enforceable policies or authorities related to" certain aspects of a coastal management plan, 15 C.F.R. § 923.80(c), and requires approval under section 1455(c). "Routine program implementation," however, is a "[f]urther detailing of a State's program that is the result of implementing" the approved program and is not subject to the amendment approval process. 15 C.F.R. § 923.84(a).

In *AES Sparrows Point LNG, LLC v. Smith*, 527 F.3d 120 (4th Cir. 2008), Baltimore County had attempted to stop development of an LNG terminal by passing a categorical ban on LNG terminals in the Chesapeake Bay Critical Area that the CMP did not previously contain. The legislation was, however, never presented to NOAA for approval as part of the CMP. The court found that "[t]his, in our view, constitutes a 'substantial change' in the 'uses subject to management' by the CMP. It also implicates the 'national interest' in the 'the siting of facilities such as energy facilities which are of greater than local significance.' " 16 U.S.C. § 1455(d)(8). Without the approval of the change by NOAA, the ban could not become part of the CMP.

3.   OPERATION OF THE CZMA

a.   Program Approaches

Some states, such as North Carolina, South Carolina, Washington, and California, have passed comprehensive legislation to create their coastal management programs; other states, such as Oregon and Florida, have "networked" existing legislation and regulations under the umbrella of an executive order or policy statement. See Gilbert L. Finnell, Jr., Coastal Land Management in Florida, 1980 Am. B. Found. Res. J. 307. The CZMA gives states a great deal of flexibility in programmatic approaches. The

Act recognizes three general approaches a state may adopt:

(A) State establishment of criteria and standards for local implementation, subject to administrative review and enforcement.

(B) Direct State land and water use planning and regulation.

(C) State administrative review for consistency with the management program of all development plans, projects, or land and water use regulations, including exceptions and variances thereto, proposed by any State or local authority or private developer, with power to approve or disapprove after public notice and an opportunity for hearings.

16 U.S.C.A. § 1455(d)(11).

b. Coastal Zone Boundaries

The definition of "coastal zone" in the CZMA at 16 U.S.C.A. § 1453(1) reads as follows:

(1) The term "coastal zone" means the coastal waters (including the lands therein and thereunder) and the adjacent shorelands (including the waters therein and thereunder), strongly influenced by each other and in proximity to the shorelines of the several coastal states, and includes islands, transitional and intertidal areas, salt marshes, wetlands, and beaches. The zone extends . . . seaward to the outer limit of State title and ownership under

the Submerged Lands Act. . . . The zone extends inland from the shorelines only to the extent necessary to control shorelands, the uses of which have a direct and significant impact on the coastal waters, and to control those geographical areas which are likely to be affected by or vulnerable to sea level rise. Excluded from the coastal zone are lands the use of which is by law subject solely to the discretion of or which is held in trust by the Federal Government, its officers, or agents.

The 1990 CZMA amendments changed the seaward boundary provisions to include all state ocean waters to correct the anomaly in Florida's coastal zone program. Although Florida's state waters in the Gulf of Mexico extend nine nautical miles, the CZMA had formerly limited its "coastal zone" to three miles. The definition of the landward boundary of the coastal zone allows major variation from one state to another. For example, North Carolina's Coastal Area Management Act defines the inland portion of the coastal zone as the area encompassed by all the counties bounded by coastal waters; Hawaii's coastal zone includes the entire state; California, on the other hand, defines the land portion of its coastal zone as a 1,000-yard strip extending inland from its coastal waters; Massachusetts' coastal zone extends landward 100 feet beyond the first major land transportation route encountered (e.g., a road, highway, or rail line), and also includes all of Cape Cod, Martha's Vineyard, Nantucket, and Gosnold.

Federal lands are excluded from the definition of "coastal zone." This does not mean, however, that activities on federal enclaves within a state's coastal zone are not subject to any state regulation. In *California Coastal Commission v. Granite Rock Co.*, 480 U.S. 572, 107 S.Ct. 1419, 94 L.Ed.2d 577 (1987), a mining company asserted that the California Coastal Commission had no authority to impose environmental permit conditions upon its mining activities on unpatented mining claims located in a national forest. Granite Rock argued that the Commission's permit requirements were preempted by several federal statutes including the CZMA's exclusion of federal lands from the definition of "coastal zone." The U.S. Supreme Court did not decide whether the federal lands involved were in fact excluded from the definition of "coastal zone," but concluded "that even if all federal lands are excluded from the CZMA definition of coastal zone, the CZMA does not automatically preempt all state regulation of activities on federal lands." In *Secretary of the Interior v. California*, 464 U.S. 312, 104 S.Ct. 656, 78 L.Ed.2d 496 (1984), the Supreme Court pointed out that the CZMA's consistency provisions were intended "to reach at least some activities conducted in those federal enclaves excluded from the . . . definition of the coastal zone."

c. The CZMA and the Commerce Clause

State coastal management plans can significantly obstruct industrial and energy development. For example, Delaware prohibits all new heavy industry within two miles of the coast, and a number of states

ban oil drilling in all or part of the coastal zone. In
Norfolk Southern Corp. v. Oberly, 822 F.2d 388 (3d
Cir. 1987), Norfolk Southern's plan to initiate a coal-
lightering service in Delaware Bay ran afoul of the
Delaware Coastal Zone Act (CZA) provisions banning
bulk product transfers in the coastal zone. In
response to Norfolk Southern's claim that the CZA
violates the dormant Commerce Clause, Delaware
argued that approval of its coastal program under the
federal CZMA constitutes Congressional consent for
the ban or, alternatively, that the ban does not offend
the Commerce Clause.

The Third Circuit Court of Appeals found that
although Congressional consent may be a defense to
a Commerce Clause challenge, neither the language
of the CZMA, the legislative history, nor case law
indicates an intent in the CZMA to expand or to alter
state authority in relation to the Commerce Clause.
However, in applying a deferential standard of
review to balance the incidental burdens on
interstate commerce with the "putative local
benefits," the court found that the nondiscriminatory
burden does not violate the Commerce Clause.

In *Ray v. ARCO*, 435 U.S. 151, 98 S.Ct. 988, 55
L.Ed.2d 179 (U.S. 1978), however, the U.S. Supreme
Court had summarily rejected the state of
Washington's arguments that approval of its coastal
management plan, which incorporated the
Washington Tanker Safety Law, precluded the law's
preemption by the federal Ports and Waterways
Safety Act.

4. INTERGOVERNMENTAL COOPERATION AND THE CZMA—THE FEDERAL CONSISTENCY REQUIREMENT

Federal grants to assist states in developing and administering coastal management programs provided an initial impetus for states to participate in coastal zone planning. But the so-called federal consistency requirement provides the major incentive for states to continue and maintain their programs. Prior to the 1990 amendments, CZMA section 307(c)(1), 16 U.S.C.A. § 1456(c)(1), provided that federal actions and activities "directly affecting the coastal zone" must be conducted "in a manner which is, to the maximum extent practicable, consistent with approved state management programs." In addition, federally-permitted activities "affecting land or water uses in the coastal zone" had to be "conducted in a manner consistent with the program." Specific provisions required outer continental shelf (OCS) exploration and development plans to be consistent with state programs. Id.

In *Secretary of the Interior v. California*, 464 U.S. 312, 104 S.Ct. 656, 78 L.Ed.2d 496 (1984), the state of California and others sued the Secretary of Interior on the ground that a proposed sale of oil and gas leases on outer continental shelf (OCS) tracts off the California coast could not be conducted without the Department of Interior making a consistency determination as required by CZMA section 307(c)(1). The Secretary argued that because the proposed lease sale was not an "activity directly affecting" the California coastal zone, no consistency determination was required.

The Outer Continental Shelf Lands Act (OCSLA), 43 U.S.C.A. §§ 1331–1356, divides the process for development of oil and gas OCS resources into four stages. A fifth stage, decommissioning, has been created by Interior Department regulations. 30 C.F.R. Parts 250, 256. The first is the five-year leasing plan prepared by the Department of Interior. Id. at § 1344. The second stage is the lease sale itself. Id. at § 1337. A lease purchaser acquires only the right to conduct limited preliminary activities on the OCS, such as geophysical and other surveys. The issue in *Secretary of the Interior v. California* was whether these preliminary activities "directly affect" the coastal zone. The third stage, exploration, and the fourth stage, production, cannot take place until after plans have been submitted for review and approved by the Secretary of the Interior. At these stages, the Outer Continental Shelf Lands Act, 43 U.S.C.A. § 1340(c)(2), itself, as well as section 307(c)(3)(B) of the CZMA, refer to the CZMA consistency requirement, and a consistency determination is specifically required.

In a five-four decision of the Supreme Court, Justice O'Connor delivered a majority opinion that left the consistency doctrine in a state of confusion. The Court rejected the state's argument that "leasing sets in motion a chain of events that culminates in oil and gas development, and that leasing therefore 'directly affects' the coastal zone within the meaning of Section 307(c)(1)." The Court noted that the lease sale authorized only preliminary exploration "that has no significant effect on the coastal zone" and is only one "in a series of decisions that may culminate in activities directly affecting that zone." The Court went on to suggest that only federal activities conducted "in" the coastal zone could have direct effects. "Section 307(c)(1)s 'directly affecting' language was aimed at activities conducted or supported by federal agencies on federal lands physically situated in the coastal zone but excluded from the zone as formally defined by the Act." Ultimately, however, the Court was persuaded by the fact that although consistency of OCS activities during the exploration and development stages is addressed in both the OCSLA and CZMA, neither act specifically requires consistency review at the lease sale stage. The Court stated:

> As we have noted, the logical paragraph to examine in connection with a lease sale is not Sec. 307(c)(1), but Sec. 307(c)(3). . . . [L]ease sales can no longer aptly be characterized as "directly affecting" the coastal zone. Since 1978 the sale of a lease grants the lessee the right to conduct only very limited, "preliminary activities" on the OCS. . . .

> It is argued, nonetheless, that a lease sale is ɐ crucial step. Large sums of money change hanᵈ and the sale may therefore generate momenᵗ that makes eventual exploration, develop· and production inevitable. On the other is argued that consistency review at ' sale stage is at best inefficient, anʳ

impossible: Leases are sold before it is certain if, where, or how exploration will actually occur.

The choice between these two policy arguments is not ours to make; it has already been made by Congress. In the 1978 OCSLA amendments Congress decided that the better course is to postpone consistency review until the two later stages of OCS planning, and to rely on less formal input from State Governors and local governments in the two earlier ones. It is not for us to negate the lengthy, detailed, and coordinated provisions of CZMA Sec. 307(c)(3)(B), and OCSLA Secs. 1344–1346 and 1351, by a superficially plausible but ultimately unsupportable construction of two words in CZMA Sec. 307(c)(1).

Id.

The Court held that section 307(c)(1) did not mandate consistency review for OCS lease sales, but some agencies read the case more broadly. The U.S. Army Corps of Engineers, for example, adopted the interpretation that federal activities must be conducted "in" the coastal zone to have direct effects. See, e.g., Corps Ocean Dumping Regulations, 53 Fed. Reg. 14,902 (1988).

After several years and a number of proposed amendments to CZMA section 307 to reverse *Secretary of Interior v. California,* the 1990 Coastal Management Act Reauthorization Amendments readdressed the federal consistency requirement. The federal consistency provision of CZMA section

307(c)(1)(A), 16 U.S.C.A. § 1456(c)(1)(A), currently provides:

(1)(A) Each Federal agency activity *within or outside* the coastal zone that *affects* any land or water use or natural resource of the coastal zone shall be carried out in a manner that is consistent to the maximum extent practicable with the enforceable policies of approved State management programs. A Federal agency activity shall be subject to this paragraph unless it is subject to paragraph (2) [federal development projects] or (3) [federally licensed or permitted activities and OCS exploration and development plans]. (Emphasis added.)

Note that the amendments do not specifically address OCS lease sales. The section does, however, specifically negate the interpretation that only activities conducted within the coastal zone are subject to consistency review. See *California v. Norton*, 311 F.3d 1162 (9th Cir. 2002) (Interior's suspension of leases held to "affect" the coastal zone). It remains possible for the Secretary of Interior to find that a particular lease sale does not "affect" a particular state's coastal zone.

The CZMA imposes certain limitations on state exercise of a "veto power" over federal agencies by use of the federal consistency requirement. First, a state must demonstrate that the activity is inconsistent with "enforceable policies" of its coastal management plan. Enforceable policies are "[s]tate policies which are legally binding through constitutional provisions, laws, regulations, land use plans, ordinances, or

judicial or administrative decisions, by which a
[s]tate exerts control over private and public land and
water uses and natural resources in the coastal
zone." 15 U.S.C.A. § 1453(6a). Through the phrase "to
the maximum extent practicable," the federal laws
applicable to the agencies' operations limit federal
agency compliance with state programs. The CZMA
also provides a mechanism to exempt inconsistent
elements of a federal agency's activity from
compliance "if the President determines that the
activity is in the paramount interest of the United
States." 16 U.S.C.A. § 1456(c)(1)(B). A finding by a
state that OCS plans or a federal permittee's
activities are not consistent with the state coastal
plan may also be overridden by the Secretary of
Commerce if the activity is "consistent with the
objectives of [the CZMA] or is otherwise necessary in
the interest of national security." Id. at
§ 1456(c)(3)(A)–(B).

a. Effects Triggering Consistency Review

Courts have disagreed as to what kinds of effects
will trigger consistency review by a federal agency.
The primary controversy has arisen in considering
the effects of offshore oil and gas exploration and
development. In *Kean v. Watt*, 1982 WL 170985
(D.N.J. 1982), the only significant effect of potential
OCS development in the coastal zone was the
financial burden on commercial fishermen that
destruction or obstruction of an OCS fishery would
have. There was no evidence that the development
would have any environmental effects on resources in
the coastal zone. The federal district court held that

federal activities outside the coastal zone that affect only commercial activities in the coastal zone, and not the natural environment, do not directly affect the coastal zone and trigger the federal consistency requirement.

The federal district court in *Conservation Law Foundation v. Watt*, 560 F.Supp. 561 (D.Mass. 1983), specifically rejected the *Kean* court's conclusion. In a challenge to an OCS lease sale by the state of Massachusetts, the Conservation Law Foundation, and ten other environmental groups, the court found that the CZMA, by its own terms, recognized economic development within the Act's purposes and that the legislative history supported the consideration of both the social and economic effects in the coastal zone.

The 1990 amendments changed the language of section 307(c)(1) from "directly affecting the coastal zone" to "affects any land or water use or natural resource of the coastal zone." This change was not particularly illuminating and can be read to support either court's position. The only legislative history concerning the provision seems to support the broader reading of the statute. The chairman of the House Merchant Marine and Fisheries Committee explained:

> The question of whether a specific federal agency activity may affect any natural resource, land use, or water use in the coastal zone is determined by the federal agency. The Committee intends this determination to include effects in the coastal zone which the

federal agency may reasonably anticipate as a result of its action, including cumulative and secondary effects. Therefore, the term "affecting" is to be construed broadly, including direct effects which are caused by the activity and occur at the same time and place, and indirect effects which may be caused by the activity and are later in time or farther removed in distance, but are still reasonably foreseeable.

136 Cong. Rec. H8068, 8075–76 (daily ed. Sept. 26, 1990).

Current regulations provide that:

[t]he term "effect on any coastal use or resource" means any reasonably foreseeable effect on any coastal use or resource resulting from a Federal agency activity or federal license or permit activity (including all types of activities subject to the federal consistency requirement under subparts C, D, E, F and I of this part.) Effects are not just environmental effects, but include effects on coastal uses. Effects include both direct effects which result from the activity and occur at the same time and place as the activity, and indirect (cumulative and secondary) effects which result from the activity and are later in time or farther removed in distance, but are still reasonably foreseeable. Indirect effects are effects resulting from the incremental impact of the federal action when added to other past, present, and reasonably foreseeable actions, regardless of what person(s) undertake(s) such actions.

15 C.F.R. § 930.11(g) (2006).

b. Interstate Consistency

The consistency provisions can also lead to interstate conflicts when an activity that requires a federal permit or approval is not consistent with the coastal program policies of another state that may be affected by the activity. See 15 C.F.R. § 930.150(a); *In the Consistency Appeal of Islander East Pipeline Company, L.L.C. From an Objection by the State of Connecticut* (2004). The CZMA does not specifically address whether consistency applies in such situations. In *In the Consistency Appeal of the Virginia Electric and Power Company from an Objection by the North Carolina Department of Environment, Health and Natural Resources* (1994), the state of North Carolina objected to water being drawn from Lake Gaston, on the boundary of the two states, to provide water to Virginia Beach. On the appeal of North Carolina's determination that the activity is inconsistent with its coastal program, the Secretary of Commerce found that the plain language of the statute required that the federal government apply the consistency provision to such activities. Specifically addressing the sensitive issue of allowing one state an effective "veto" over another state's activities, the Secretary stated:

> While the CZMA does not give one state direct authority to control activities in another state, the CZMA does grant to states with federally approved coastal management programs the right to seek conditions on or prohibit the

issuance of federal permits and licenses that would "affect" their state. Thus, Congress has, in effect, granted to states with a federally approved coastal management program, in exchange for their protecting the nation's coasts, the right to ensure that federal permittees and licensees will not further degrade those coasts. The ability to prevent the granting of federal permits and licenses is a federal authority which has been granted to coastal states, not a state authority which has been usurped from the states. However, as a safeguard to a state's unrestrained use of this authority, an applicant can, as the City has, appeal for an override by the Secretary of Commerce.

Id.

Regulations adopted in December 2000 also recognize the requirement of consistency for "interstate coastal effects." 15 C.F.R. § 930.150(a) provides:

A federal activity may affect coastal uses or resources of a State other than the State in which the activity will occur. Effective coastal management is fostered by ensuring that activities having such reasonably foreseeable interstate coastal effects are conducted consistent with the enforceable policies of the management program of each affected State.

The regulations also impose limitations on application of the consistency requirement in the interstate context. 15 C.F.R. § 930.154 requires states to list the kind and geographic location of activities for which they intend to conduct interstate consistency review. States must also demonstrate the effects of such activities, as well as "include evidence of consultation with States in which the activity will occur, evidence of consultation with relevant Federal agencies, and any agreements with other States and Federal agencies regarding coordination of activities." The listing must be approved by NOAA as a routine program change in order for a state to subject a federal action to interstate review.

c. Federal License or Permit

The consistency requirement applies to applicants for federal licenses or permits. See *Mountain Rhythm Resources v. FERC*, 302 F.3d 958 (9th Cir. 2002); *United States v. San Juan Bay Marina*, 239 F.3d 400 (1st Cir. 2001). But different statutes also refer to a wide range of other types of federal "approvals" that may be required for particular activities. The term "license or permit" has been defined broadly in NOAA's regulations to include:

> any authorization that an applicant is required by law to obtain in order to conduct activities affecting any land or water use or natural resource of the coastal zone and that any Federal agency is empowered to issue to an applicant. The term . . . does not include OCS plans, and federal license or permit activities described in detail in OCS plans . . . or leases issued pursuant to lease sales conducted by a Federal agency (e.g., outer continental shelf (OCS) oil and gas

lease sales conducted by the Minerals Management Service or oil and gas lease sales conducted by the Bureau of Land Management). Lease sales conducted by a Federal agency are Federal agency activities under subpart C of [the CZMA].

15 C.F.R. § 930.51(a).

The definition of "license or permit" was modified in new consistency regulations issued in 2006 to assure the term is not "overly-inclusive." Discussion of the regulation states that the definition creates a four-part test "to capture *any form* of federal license or permit that is: (1) Required by Federal law, (2) authorizes an activity, (3) the activity authorized has reasonably foreseeable coastal effects, and (4) the authorization is not incidental to a federal license or permit previously reviewed by the State." 71 Fed. Reg. 787 (2006).

d. Maximum Extent Practicable

While federal permittees and OCS developers must carry out their activities in a manner consistent with an affected state's coastal plan, federal agencies are only charged with consistency "to the maximum extent practicable." 16 U.S.C.A. § 1456(c)(1). This is not an escape clause for federal agencies to invoke when consistency with state programs is inconvenient, but is an affirmative obligation. NOAA regulations explain the phrase as follows:

The term "consistent to the maximum extent practicable" means fully consistent with the enforceable policies of management programs unless full consistency is prohibited by existing law applicable to the Federal agency.

15 C.F.R. § 903.32(a)(I).

In many cases it is not clear whether other federal statutory provisions preempt the CZMA's consistency requirement. For example, the eighth circuit Court of Appeals held in *Minnesota v. Hoffman*, 543 F.2d 1198 (8th Cir. 1976), that section 404 of the Clean Water Act exempts the Corps of Engineers from any state requirements relating to the discharge of dredged spoil. The Corps has also maintained that the Ocean Dumping Act, 33 U.S.C.A. §§ 1401–1445, may preempt the CZMA. See 33 C.F.R. § 336.2(C). The Ninth Circuit Court of Appeals held, however, that the Navy was required to obtain a state permit under Washington's Shoreline Management Act, part of the state coastal program, before continuing with dredging for a homeport project. *Friends of the Earth v. United States Navy*, 841 F.2d 927 (9th Cir. 1988); accord, *California Coastal Commission v. United States*, 5 F.Supp.2d 1106 (S.D.Cal. 1998).

e.   Positive Consistency

In *Cape May Greene, Inc. v. Warren*, 698 F.2d 179 (3d Cir. 1983), the Third Circuit Court of Appeals addressed the issue of whether the federal government can deny, limit, or condition assistance to an activity that is consistent with a state's coastal management program. The federal Environmental Protection Agency (EPA) had conditioned funding for

an indispensable sewage treatment plant on the
denial of new hookups to development in the
contiguous floodplain and other sensitive lands,
areas that had been designated as development areas
in both the local comprehensive plan and the state
coastal management plan. The New Jersey
Department of Environmental Protection had
previously approved a 244-unit residential
development within the floodplain and found it in
compliance with the state's coastal management
program. Because the EPA had also indicated that
the area was unsuitable for septic tanks, the funding
conditions would have effectively prohibited new
development. The court held that the EPA had acted
arbitrarily and capriciously, particularly in failing to
act consistently with the state's coastal program to
the maximum extent practicable as required by the
CZMA. The court reasoned that "[w]hen federal
assistance is provided for what is essentially a state
or local activity, the congressional preference for
having policies initiated at the state level must be
respected."

In a case remarkably similar to *Cape May Greene,*
the Fourth Circuit Court of Appeals upheld a
condition on a federal grant for a municipal sewage
collection plant that limited access by new
development to the federally funded project. The
court in *Shanty Town Associates Ltd. Partnership v.
Environmental Protection Agency*, 843 F.2d 782 (4th
Cir. 1988), distinguished *Cape May Greene* by
recognizing that the "grant conditions do not actually
forbid development . . . ; they simply forbid the use of
federal funds to encourage such development." The

court also noted that the CZMA specifically provides that nothing in the federal consistency provisions diminishes or modifies existing federal laws or "shall in any way affect any requirement" imposed by the Clean Water Act. See 16 U.S.C.A. § 1456(e)–(f). The EPA was not interfering in local land use decisions, but acting on specific findings that limitations were necessary to prevent a decline in water quality.

NOAA regulations attempt to preclude an interpretation that the CZMA imposes a "positive consistency" requirement by providing that federal agencies may continue to impose stricter standards notwithstanding more permissive criteria in a state coastal program. See 5 C.F.R. § 930.39(d). However, *Cape May Greene* can certainly be read as requiring "positive" federal consistency in relation to local land use decisions. See Michael C. Blumm, *Wetlands Protection and Coastal Planning: Avoiding the Perils of Positive Consistency,* 5 Colum. J. Envtl. L. 69 (1978).

In *Loveladies Harbor v. Baldwin*, 751 F.2d 376 (D.N.J. 1984), the federal district court addressed "positive consistency" in the context of Army Corps of Engineers wetland permitting. The property owners in *Loveladies Harbor* had received a state permit and water quality certification, but were refused a federal permit to fill in wetlands. The court found *Cape May Greene* inapplicable, primarily because the state permits involved were issued as exceptions to the state wetlands policy and did not comply with state law. The Corps was, therefore, "not arbitrary in deciding that it was not practicable under the CZMA to be consistent with a state permit issued in defiance of state standards."

f.   Appealing Consistency Determinations

The CZMA provides two procedures for dealing with disagreements concerning consistency determinations: 1) a mediation process for disagreements between federal agencies and coastal states, 16 U.S.C.A. § 1456(h); and 2) a Secretarial appeal process for federal permits and OCS exploration and development plans that are found by a state to be inconsistent with the state program. 16 U.S.C.A. §§ 1456(c)(3)(A)–(B). Technically, the term "appeal" is a misnomer. The Secretary examines the state's objection for compliance with the CZMA and conducts a *de novo* inquiry of whether the activity is consistent with the objectives of the CZMA or necessary in the interest of national security. The Secretary does not review whether the state was correct in its determination that the proposed activity was inconsistent with its coastal management program.

The fact that states that are dissatisfied with the mediation process can appeal consistency determinations in the courts and seek to enjoin agency actions that do not meet the requirements of CZMA section 307 has led to some concern that the federal consistency requirement may not serve the national interest. The 1990 amendments to the CZMA dealt with that contingency by providing a Presidential exemption in certain circumstances. After a court judgment finding a federal agency has not complied with the consistency provisions and a certification by the Secretary of Commerce that mediation is unlikely to resolve the compliance problem, the Secretary may request presidential intervention. Certain elements of the agency's action may be exempted from compliance if the President finds the activity is "in the paramount interest of the United States." 16 U.S.C.A. § 1456(1)(B).

Federal permit applicants or OCS developers who are denied permits or plan approval because of a state's negative determination on consistency can appeal the decision to the Secretary of Commerce. The Secretary can override the state decision and allow the permit to be issued if she or he finds that the activity is "consistent with the objectives of the [CZMA] or is otherwise necessary in the interest of national security." In order for the Secretary to override a state's consistency determination on the former grounds, the applicant must meet all three criteria set out at 15 C.F.R. § 930.121:

(a) The activity furthers the national interest as articulated in § 302 or § 303 of the Act, in a significant or substantial manner.

(b) The national interest furthered by the activity outweighs the activity's adverse coastal effects, when those effects are considered separately or cumulatively.

(c) There is no reasonable alternative available which would permit the activity to be conducted in a manner consistent with the enforceable policies of the management program. The Secretary may consider but is not limited to considering previous appeal decisions, alternatives described in state objection letters and alternatives and other information submitted during the appeal. The Secretary shall not consider an alternative unless the State agency submits a statement, in a brief or other supporting material, to the Secretary that the alternative would permit the activity to be conducted in a manner consistent with the enforceable policies of the management program.

The Secretary will not override a state determination if the applicant fails to establish all the above criteria, unless necessary on national security grounds. The national security exception requires that "a national defense or other national security interest would be significantly impaired if the activity were not permitted to go forward as proposed." 15 C.F.R. § 930.122.

Section 930.121(a) was revised in 2000 to add the requirement that the activity "further the national interest . . . *in a significant or substantial manner.*" This change was intended to exclude from the appeal process projects with only minimal connection to the national goals of the CZMA, and to focus the process on assuring that national interests are fully considered in the state certification process. NOAA's discussion of the 2000 regulations notes that "a project can be of national import without being quantifiably large in scale or impact on the national economy. . . . To determine whether a project

significantly or substantially furthers the national
interest, NOAA encourages appellants and States to
consider three factors: (1) The degree to which the
activity furthers the national interest; (2) the nature
or importance of the national interest furthered as
articulated in the CZMA; and (3) the extent to which
the proposed activity is coastal dependent." 65 Fed.
Reg. 77150 (2000). Consistency determinations that
are fundamentally local land use decisions will no
longer be matters for appeal to the Secretary.

Related to the appeal process is the question of who
has authority to appeal or even enforce consistency
decisions. The Secretarial appeal process, for
example, is not available to disgruntled individuals
or to local governments who would like to challenge
a state's positive determination of consistency of an
activity with the coastal program. And courts
disagree as to whether the CZMA creates a right for
private citizens or local governments to challenge
developments that are inconsistent with an approved
state coastal management plan. Compare *City of
Sausalito v. O'Neill*, 386 F.3d 1186 (9th Cir. 2004)
(city had standing to challenge consistency) with
Town of North Hempstead v. Village of North Hills,
482 F.Supp. 900 (E.D.N.Y. 1979) (finding the CZMA
"is neither a jurisdictional grant, nor a basis for
stating a claim upon which relief can be granted," the
court dismissed a CZMA claim against village by
neighboring town). See also *Save Our Dunes v.
Alabama Dep't of Envtl. Management*, 834 F.2d 984
(11th Cir. 1987) (holding plaintiffs had no standing
to appeal a coastal permit decision); *Serrano-Lopez v.
Cooper*, 193 F.Supp.2d 424 (D.P.R. 2002) ("The zone

of interests regulated by the CZMA includes a state's protection of their coastal zones and not an individual's attempt to seek further protection once the CZMA requirements have been complied with.").

Perhaps more frustrating to the purposes of the CZMA is a decision holding that the CZMA creates no implied right of action for a state to enjoin a federal permittee's activities that are inconsistent with the state coastal plan. In February 1986, John DeLyser applied to the Corps of Engineers for a permit to build a dock and boathouse on pilings. The permit was issued, but DeLyser instead began construction of a two-story residence with sanitary facilities. The Corps issued a cease and desist order and required DeLyser to submit an after-the-fact permit application. Because the state of New York found the project inconsistent with its coastal management program, the Corps denied the permit. DeLyser's appeal to the Secretary of Commerce was also unsuccessful. Despite the adverse rulings, DeLyser completed the building and took up residence. The Corps declined to enforce its order citing consideration of funding allocations and the failure of any party other than the state to object to the structure. The court held that the state had no authority under the CZMA to require DeLyser to remove the structure. See *New York v. DeLyser*, 759 F.Supp. 982 (W.D.N.Y. 1991).

B.   REGULATION OF
COASTAL DEVELOPMENT

The most sensitive and dynamic areas of the coastline—beaches, dunes, and barrier islands—are also the most attractive areas for recreation and development. Climate change and sea level rise have added an additional dimension to coastal development regulation as communities attempt to adapt to the sea's encroachment and more intense storms.

Development on beaches and dunes has already caused serious erosion of these areas, resulting in loss of recreation areas, habitat, public facilities, and the storm protection the beaches and dunes had provided. Federal, state, and local governments have, perhaps inadvertently, encouraged growth in these sensitive areas by providing infrastructure, flood insurance, and disaster relief. See Dana Beach, Coastal Sprawl: The Effects of Urban Design on Aquatic Ecosystems in the United States (Pew Oceans Commission 2002).

There are two primary approaches that have been taken to regulate development on beaches, dunes, and barrier islands. First, because federal, state and local government subsidies have stimulated coastal growth, withholding governmental support for development on barriers and beaches may provide an indirect means of controlling development. In addition, growth can be regulated directly through land use planning and by restricting or prohibiting structures that will contribute to destruction of

habitat or erosion of the shore or that will be located
in unsafe or unstable areas.

1.   LIMITING INFRASTRUCTURE FUNDING AND OTHER SUBSIDIZATION OF COASTAL DEVELOPMENT

Much of the exploding development on the nation's
coasts could not take place without federal and state
assistance and subsidies. Federal and state
programs, including flood insurance, highway
programs, sewage treatment facility funding and
disaster relief, have tended to subsidize and
encourage growth on barrier islands and other
coastal areas. Such development involves
tremendous public costs beyond the original
expenditures: Average annual storm damage to
coastal property, for example, amounts to billions of
dollars.

One of the best examples of government
subsidization of coastal development is the National
Flood Insurance Program (NFIP), which was created
by Congress in 1968. The NFIP was intended to
reduce federal flood disaster relief by providing
guaranteed flood insurance coverage for communities
that adopt building standards and land use controls
that minimize flood damages and property losses. See
also Part III.B.2. The exponential growth in coastal
areas subsequent to the passage of the program is
often attributed to the availability of inexpensive
flood insurance.

Recent litigation has highlighted the
environmental impacts of development facilitated by

the NFIP and FEMA's obligations to take these factors into account. In *Fla. Key Deer v. Paulison,* 522 F.3d 1133 (2008), the Eleventh Circuit Court of Appeals upheld an injunction prohibiting FEMA from issuing flood insurance for new developments in the habitats suitable for the endangered Key deer species in Monroe County, the county encompassing the low-lying Florida Keys, on the basis that FEMA failed to fulfill its consultation obligations under section 7 of the Endangered Species Act (ESA). But see, *Nat'l Wildlife Fed'n v. FEMA*, 345 F. Supp. 2d 1151, 1155 (W.D. Wash. 2004) (holding that the issuance of flood insurance is a nondiscretionary act and not subject to section 7 of the ESA). In *Coalition for a Sustainable Delta v. FEMA*, 812 F.Supp.2d 1089 (U.S. Eastern District of California 2011), the court denied FEMA's motion for summary judgment in regard to its practice of allowing persons to artificially fill the floodplain to actually remove it from its floodplain status, and thus from regulations and requirements associated with the NFIP. The court found that such action could trigger the ESA duty to consult because it allowed land to be removed from the floodplain and could jeopardize certain endangered species.

Hurricanes and coastal storms since 2005 have strained the NFIP with unprecedented numbers of insurance claims. In July 2012, the U.S. Congress passed the Biggert-Waters Flood Insurance Reform Act of 2012 (BW–12) in an attempt to reduce the debt of the NFIP after claims outpaced revenue following Hurricane Katrina, Hurricane Ike, Tropical Storm Debby, and super-storm Sandy. BW–12 affects all the

major components of the NFIP, including insurance
rates, flood maps, grant programs, and flood plain
management plans. Key provisions of the legislation
require the NFIP to raise rates to reflect true flood
risk, making the program more financially stable and
changing how Flood Insurance Rate Map (FIRM)
updates impact policyholders. Other provisions
eliminate subsidies for vacation homes and non-
primary residences. The changes have been
controversial, however, and the future of the program
remains the subject of debate and legislative
proposals and even litigation by states seeking to
delay flood insurance rate hikes. See e.g., Rawle O.
King, *The National Flood Insurance Program: Status
and Remaining Issues for Congress,* Congressional
Research Service Report No. 7–5700 (February 6,
2013); Arthur D. Postal, *Mississippi Sues to Stop
NFIP Rate Hikes*, Credit Union Times (Sept. 30,
2013). Ultimately, however, the goal of NFIP reform
is not to limit subsidization that encourages coastal
growth, but to limit the impact of that growth on the
federal budget. Earlier legislation more directly
addressed the issue of the effects of the program on
rampant coastal development.

To stem the impact of the NFIP and other federal
subsidies on the still undeveloped areas of the
nation's coast, Congress enacted the 1982 Coastal
Barrier Resources Act (CBRA), 16 U.S.C.A. §§ 3501–
3510 (reauthorized by P.L. 109–226 in May 2006), the
second generation of a program that coordinates
environmental protection with federal fiscal policy.
CBRA's purposes include preserving the natural
resources of coastal barrier islands, minimizing loss

of human life from hazardous coastal development, and restricting federal support for such development. Within Congressionally designated, undeveloped coastal barrier areas called the Coastal Barrier Resources System (CBRS), the Act restricts federal assistance or expenditures for new development. This includes NFIP coverage, government loans, non-emergency disaster relief, new bridges, roads and other infrastructure, and other forms of federal assistance and subsidies. The intent is that the expense and the risks of new development must be borne by the developer of coastal barrier island property. It is not clear at this time whether the approach has actually inhibited growth in the affected areas. See Elise Jones, *The Coastal Barrier Resources Act: A Common Cents Approach to Coastal Protection,* 21 Envtl. L. 1015 (1991). As developable coastal land becomes more and more scarce, developers are more likely to be willing to bear the increased private coast of development.

In *Bostic v. United States,* 753 F.2d 1292 (4th Cir. 1985), developers and landowners of property on Topsail Island, North Carolina, asserted that CBRA had wrongly designated their land as part of an undeveloped coastal barrier, making them ineligible for federal flood insurance. The *Bostic* court held, however, that since the map adopted by Congress specifically designated the island as an undeveloped coastal barrier, Congress unquestionably intended to include it in the CBRS, and the designation was not a reviewable agency action. The court also found that inclusion of the property in the CBRS was substantially related to the purposes of CBRA.

Some states have followed the lead of the federal government in discouraging subsidization of development in sensitive coastal areas. For example, the coastal infrastructure policy of Florida's Coastal Zone Protection Act of 1985 reinforced the expenditure limitation approach originally imposed by an executive order. Section 380.27(1), Florida Statutes, mandates that no state funds be used for constructing bridges or causeways to coastal barrier islands that are not currently accessible by bridge or causeway. The coastal infrastructure policy also emphasizes state-local cooperation by allowing state allocation of funds to expand infrastructure only if the construction is consistent with the approved coastal management element of local government comprehensive plans. The states' local government planning legislation provides that it is the intent of the legislature that local governments also cooperate in developing funding policies. Local governments are instructed to design their comprehensive plans to "limit public expenditures in areas that are subject to destruction in natural disaster." Fla. Stat. § 163.3178(1).

Government infrastructure to protect vulnerable areas from storm impacts and floods, such as New Orleans' system of levees, also leads to development in sensitive or dangerous areas of the coast. Litigation surrounding the failure of the U.S. Army Corps of Engineers (the Corps) to armor susceptible areas in a timely manner and the breaching of existing levees during Hurricane Katrina may lead to less reliance by property owners on these government protections when building in coastal areas. In the protracted litigation against the Corps for damages, the Fifth Circuit Court of Appeals applied the immunity provisions of the Flood Control Act of 1928 ("FCA"), 33 U.S.C. § 702, to deny claims of the residents of New Orleans' Lower Ninth Ward for levee breaches and held that "discretionary function" immunity further protected the Corps from liability. *Robinson v. United States* (*In Re Katrina Canal Breaches Litig.*), 696 F.3d 436 (2012). The court read the FCA's immunity provisions broadly, recognizing "immunity for any flood-control activity engaged in by the government, even in the context of a project that was not primarily or substantially related to flood control." Id. In the case of damages not subject to FCA immunity, i.e., damage due to the Corps' failure to armor certain areas, the court found the discretionary function exception (DFE) "completely insulates the government from liability." Id. The DFE bars suit on any claim that is "based upon the exercise or performance or the failure to exercise or perform a discretionary function or duty on the part of a federal agency or an employee of the Government, whether or not the discretion involved be abused." 28 U.S.C. § 2680(a). Id., quoting the Federal Tort Claims Act.

2.   COASTAL CONSTRUCTION REGULATION

Indiscriminate development on the coastline has created a multitude of problems. Development located on or seaward of protective dunes is much more vulnerable to storms and encroachment by an eroding coastline. Such development even exacerbates these problems by damaging the beach

and dune system, causing increased erosion and
potentially damaging adjacent lands as well.
Structures that are not designed or built to withstand
coastal hazards not only subject the owners to the
threat of loss of life and property, but also create a
hazard to others when parts of the structure are
driven by wind or water. In addition, coastal
structures can interfere with visual access and public
use of the shoreline. In some areas, development has
also displaced or disrupted vital nesting areas for
endangered sea turtles. Finally, poorly designed and
poorly located coastal construction has led to major
expenditures of public funds for flood and disaster
relief. It is clear that the needs and public purposes
served by strict coastal construction regulation go far
beyond the normal purposes and advantages created
by orderly land use planning and regulation in inland
areas.

Coastal setbacks have historically been a primary
tool in coastal construction regulation.
Approximately half of the coastal states have
implemented a retreat policy of some degree by
creating zones at the ocean's edge where
development is prohibited or strictly regulated. See
John M. Houlahan, *Comparison of State
Construction Setbacks to Manage Development in
Coastal Hazard Areas,* 17 Coastal Mgmt. 219 (1989).
Early setback lines generally prohibited or limited
construction in areas within a prescribed distance
from a baseline, usually the mean high water line,
the vegetation line, or a line associated with the
primary dune. See *Buechel v. State Dept. of Ecology,*
123 Wash.2d 1019, 875 P.2d 635 (1994). The

distances were relatively arbitrary and generally ranged from 40 feet to 100 feet. As understanding of beach and dune processes increased and as coastal engineering became more sophisticated, delineation of setback lines also became more sophisticated and highly technical. Many states now have a second type of regulatory setback lines based on complicated calculations of seasonal shoreline fluctuations, vulnerability to storms and storm surges, and the rate of shoreline erosion. See, e.g., *Island Harbor Beach Club, Ltd. v. Department of Natural Resources*, 495 So.2d 209 (Fla. App. 1986) (finding that because of the complexity of the technical and scientific issues and the high degree of scientific uncertainty involved, agency determinations of coastal construction control lines should be given great deference). Although this second type of setback line has more scientific validity, the complexity is confusing to landowners who can more readily understand the impact of a fixed setback distance in conceiving their expectations of uses of the land. The prior determination and public recording of these kinds of setback lines provides clearer notice to landowner's than ad hoc or case-by-case calculations.

Hawaii uses the first type of setback line for controlling coastal development. Construction must be located landward of "[s]etbacks along shorelines [that] are established of not less than twenty feet and not more than forty feet inland from the shoreline." The "shoreline" is defined as the highest wash of the waves during high season, typically a debris or vegetation line. See Haw. Rev. Stat. § 205A–43. See also, *Diamond v. Dobbin*, 319 P.3d 1017, 132 Haw. 9

(2014), demonstrating that determination of the shoreline from which the setback is measured, however, can be a complicated process. The use of this method is more useful for Hawaii's beaches, which have not been subjected to the high rate of erosion that the Atlantic coast beaches, for example, have experienced.

South Carolina's 1988 Beachfront Management Act (BMA), S.C. Code Ann. §§ 48–39–270 to 48–39–360, was one of the country's most comprehensive coastal construction laws. Under the state's coastal management program, the South Carolina Coastal Council has jurisdiction to regulate beachfront construction. The BMA required the Coastal Council to establish a baseline on the Atlantic coast at the "crest of an ideal primary oceanfront sand dune." From this baseline, a setback line was calculated at a distance of forty times the average annual erosion rate, but at a minimum distance of twenty feet landward of the baseline. The area within twenty feet landward of the baseline was a "dead zone" in which major structures were not permitted. In the remaining area between the baseline and the setback line, construction is limited to habitable structures not larger than 5000 square feet, located as far landward on a lot as possible, and meeting other demanding conditions. In the wake of Hurricane Hugo and a host of legal challenges, the BMA was amended in 1990 to eliminate the twenty-foot dead zone, making all construction between the baseline and setback line subject to the same standards. See Newman Jackson Smith, *Analysis of the Regulation of Beachfront Development in South Carolina,* 42

S.C.L. Rev. 717 (1991). See also *Esposito v. South Carolina Coastal Council*, 939 F.2d 165 (4th Cir. 1991); *Beard v. South Carolina Coastal Council*, 304 S.C. 205, 403 S.E.2d 620 (1991); *South Carolina Coastal Conservation League v. South Carolina Dept. of Health*, 345 S.C. 525, 548 S.E.2d 887 (2001).

Florida has similar legislation with two beachfront regulatory lines. See the Coastal Zone Protection Act of 1985, Fla. Stat. §§ 161.52–.58. The coastal construction control line (CCCL), based generally on the 100-year storm surge and publicly recorded, creates a zone in which construction is subject to state permitting and strictly regulated. The second zone of jurisdiction is created on a case-by-case basis by projecting the seasonal high water line as it will exist thirty years after the construction permit application. In this zone, all major construction is prohibited, except for certain single-family dwellings that can be constructed landward of the frontal dune structure. See generally Donna R. Christie, *Growth Management in Florida: Focus on the Coast*, 3 J. Land Use & Envtl. L. 33 (1987). Note that Florida's "retreat" policy is not as rigorous as South Carolina's original policy; it allows some habitable development in areas that are projected to be in the water in thirty years and provides for no future buffer zone.

Retreat strategies generally apply only to undeveloped beachfront property. Existing development is usually "grandfathered in" to lessen the impact of the regulation. There is also some underlying rationale that these existing structures are temporary, i.e., until the next big storm. Existing structures may become subject to new regulation if they are expanded, improved, or destroyed. Two major problems have arisen in relation to grandfathering of existing structures. First, in areas that were almost fully developed prior to the new regulation, new prohibitions on development that apply only to the remaining undeveloped lots may appear to be unreasonable (leading to takings challenges). See *Lucas v. South Carolina Coastal Council*, 505 U.S. 1003, 112 S.Ct. 2886, 120 L.Ed.2d 798 (1992); but see, Fla. Stat. § 161.053(5)(b) (creating a variance from some CCCL permitting requirements where existing adjacent structures form a "reasonably continuous and uniform construction line" seaward of the CCCL and the existing structures have not been "unduly affected by erosion").

The second problem concerning existing structures relates to the determination of when they may become subject to the new regulatory scheme. South Carolina's Beachfront Management Act places new limitations on rebuilding structures that are "destroyed beyond repair" and originally banned their reconstruction within the dead zone or seaward of the baseline. Destroyed beyond repair means "more that sixty-six and two-third percent of the replacement value of the habitable structure . . . has been destroyed." See S.C. Code Ann. § 48–39–270(11). Such standards can undoubtedly trigger a "battle of the experts."

Reacting to the widespread impact of the Act on beachfront homeowners in the wake of Hurricane

Hugo, the South Carolina legislature amended the BMA in 1990 to give the Coastal Council the authority to issue special permits to allow reconstruction of habitable structures under certain conditions, even if they were located seaward of the baseline. The Florida Coastal Zone Protection Act provides that CCCL and thirty-year erosion zone requirements will apply to all new construction except "modification, maintenance, or repair to any existing structure within the limits of the existing foundation which does not require . . . any additions to, or repair or modification of, the existing foundation." See Fla. Stat. § 161.053(12).

Storms like Sandy, Katrina, Ike, and Hugo also highlight the need for strict building codes for coastal construction. Substandard housing is not only subject to greater damage in a storm, but also creates a hazard for other nearby properties. The creation of the National Flood Insurance Program (NFIP) by the National Flood Insurance Act of 1968, 42 U.S.C.A. §§ 4001–4128, has led to widespread adoption of minimum federal building standards for flood-prone areas, including beaches. The NFIP is intended to reduce federal flood disaster relief by supplying guaranteed flood insurance coverage to communities that adopt building standards and land use controls that minimize flood damages and property losses. State and local regulation may be stricter than federally imposed safety and building standards, and governments are encouraged to adopt land use regulations that guide development away from flood hazard areas.

In addition to guaranteeing flood insurance for communities participating in the program, the NFIP also imposes penalties for nonparticipation. If a community with areas susceptible to flooding does not join the program, federal agencies, like the Small Business Administration and the Veterans Administration, are prohibited from providing federal assistance for development in flood-prone areas. See 42 U.S.C.A. § 4106(a). The NFIP has been held neither to be an unconstitutional coercion or imposition of strict federal building standards on the states, nor to be a taking of private property as a result of diminished property values in nonparticipating communities. See *Adolph v. Federal Emergency Management Agency*, 854 F.2d 732 (5th Cir. 1988); *Texas Landowners Rights Ass'n v. Harris*, 453 F.Supp. 1025 (D.D.C. 1978).

Unregulated coastal construction can also interfere with the habitat values of a beach. For example, beaches from North Carolina to Texas are nesting sites for sea turtles, most of which are threatened or endangered species. Many states strictly regulate the construction of vertical walls and the placement of riprap on the beaches of turtle nesting areas and limit other coastal construction during the nesting season. In addition, because hatchling turtles gravitate toward light, public safety needs must be balanced against protection of the young turtles in regulating light for coastal buildings and highways.

C. BEACH EROSION, SEA LEVEL RISE, AND SHORELINE PROTECTION

According to a 2000 report by the Heinz Center for FEMA, "80 to 90 percent of the sandy beaches in the United States are eroding." The Atlantic coast has an average annual erosion rate of about 2 to 3 feet/year, while the Gulf coast states average 6 feet/year. Major storms events can produce erosion as much as 100 feet. On the Pacific coast, cliff erosion, although "site specific and episodic," can remove "tens of feet at one time." The report estimates that without additional beach restoration or structural protections, as many as 1,500 homes per year (and the land they stand on) could be lost to coastal erosion. Sea level rise exacerbates shoreline erosion: "a sustained rise of 10 cm in sea level could result in 15 meters of shoreline retreat. This amount of erosion is more than an order of magnitude greater than would be expected from a simple response to sea level rise through inundation of the shore." See H. John Heinz III Center for Science, Economics and the Environment, *Evaluation of Erosion Hazards* (2000).

The response to the retreat of the shoreline due to erosion and adaption to sea level rise are two of the most important issues for coastal managers today. Coastal states and counties often have a major economic dependence on the recreation and tourism opportunities created by beaches, but beaches also protect lives and upland property and serve as essential habitat for species that range from shorebirds to sea turtles. Government responses can be generally categorized as restoration, structural armoring, and retreat.

1.   RESTORATION

The economic importance of beaches to many coastal economies has led governments to conclude that restoration is an economic necessity. The process is not only expensive, however, but also perpetual. New beach engineering technologies may mean that a restored beach may last 5–10 years without renourishment—or it may be washed away the next week by a storm. The high cost of this management technique is argued to be justified by the revenues generated by the beaches and the protection afforded to upland properties. In a comprehensive study, the National Research Council (NRC) supports beach renourishment as a viable method for protecting the shoreline from erosion and for restoring lost beaches. The report also contains important warnings:

> Although proven engineered shore protection measures exist, there are no quick, simple, or inexpensive ways to protect the shore from natural forces, to mitigate the effects of beach erosion, or to restore beaches, regardless of the technology or approach selected. Available shore protection measures do not treat some of the underlying causes of erosion, such as relative rise in sea level and interruption of sand transport in the littoral systems, because they necessarily address locale-specific erosion problems rather than their underlying systemic causes.

National Research Council, *Beach Nourishment and Protection* (1995).

Beach restoration projects now go on routinely, and most states, by common law or statute, provide for ownership of the created beach by the state and protection of the littoral owners' access rights. In spite of the protection and enhancement of upland property values afforded by government restoration projects, some beachfront owners have brought legal challenges charging that projects have devalued or "taken" their property by obstructing their ocean view, *City of Ocean City v. Maffucci*, 326 N.J.Super. 1, 740 A.2d 630 (Superior Court of New Jersey, Appellate Division 1999) (holding that severance damages must include the loss in the value due to the obstruction of view by dunes associated with a beach restoration project); but see *Borough of Harvey Cedars v. Karan*, 70 A.3d 524 (July 8, 2013) (holding that calculation of severance damages must also include the value added to retained property attributable to the protective dune system); by restricting beach access routes to protect sea turtle habitat after a restoration project, *Slavin v. Town of Oak Island*, 160 N.C.App. 57, 584 S.E.2d 100 (North Carolina Court of Appeals 2003) (holding that a littoral property owner's right of access to the ocean is a qualified one, subject to reasonable regulation that does not require compensation); by "taking" the riparian right to accretion, *Walton County v. Stop the Beach Renourishment*, 998 So.2d 1102 (Fl. S.Ct. 2008) (holding that the right to accretions is a contingent right and not implicated in beach restoration); and by claiming state ownership of land created by the restoration project, *Michaelson v. Silver Beach Improv. Asso.*, 342 Mass. 251, 173 N.E.2d 273 (1961) (holding that shoreline land created by the commonwealth belonged to the littoral owners) and *City of Long Branch v. Liu*, 363 N.J. Super. 411, 833 A.2d 106 (Law Div. 2003) (holding that the sand beach created by a government restoration project belongs to the state). Older cases dealing with ownership of the created beach tended to focus on whether the activity was accretion or avulsion. A better approach for courts to analyze modern beach restoration statutes is to consider beach restoration as *sui generis* and evaluate whether the statute reasonably balances the important public and private interests involved.

2.   STRUCTURAL ARMORING

Armoring or coastline "hardening" are terms that encompass seawalls, bulkheads, revetments, rip-rap, groins, and other fixed structures intended to stabilize the shoreline. Although armoring can provide short-term protection to endangered land and structures, it is not a preferred management tool. Evidence indicates that armoring increases the rate of erosion of adjacent beaches and causes damage to adjacent properties, loss of habitat, and loss of beach access. When a seawall is used, for example, the beach seaward of the wall often completely disappears, eliminating the public's access and use of the beach as well as habitat the beach and intertidal area provided. Because the seawall causes land at each end of the wall to erode at a greater rate, the seawall can also be considered a private nuisance.

One can argue that all armoring should be prohibited because shoreline property owners have assumed this risk of erosion, and armoring is an unreasonable approach for long-term management. In fact, a number of states have developed policies to prohibit "hard armoring" or to allow only temporary armoring in emergency situations. States imposing bans on permanent coastal erosion control structures include Maine, North Carolina, Rhode Island, and South Carolina. Property owners, on the other hand, argue that they have a right to protect their property.

In *Shell Island Homeowners Ass'n v. Tomlinson,* 134 N.C. App. 217, 517 S.E.2d 406 (1999), condominium owners challenged North Carolina's "hardened structure rule" which prohibited use of permanent erosion control structures, including bulkheads; seawalls; revetments; jetties, groins and breakwaters. The owners had been denied permits to attempt to stop the erosion of their property which was threatening the destruction of the nine-story condominium building. The court dismissed the owners' non-constitutional claims for failure to address administrative remedies, but addressed whether the rule effected a Fifth Amendment taking of their property. The plaintiff's primary argument was that "the protection of property from erosion is an essential right of property owners. . . ." The court refused to recognize this proposition as a "legally cognizable property interest" and stated that it has "no support in the law." The court attributed any losses on naturally occurring migration of the beach—a "consequence of being a riparian or littoral landowner." The takings claim was dismissed. (As an aside, a suit by the Shell Island Resort Homeowner's Association against state agencies and the Coastal Resources Commission for negligence in granting a permit to the developers of the Shell Island Resort was also dismissed.)

The "common enemy doctrine" is sometimes cited as a basis of a property owner's right to protect land from the encroaching sea. Although the doctrine primarily applied to diffuse surface waters, in his 19th century treatise, John M. Gould, noted:

> The owners of lands exposed to the inroads of the sea . . . may erect walls and embankments to prevent the wearing away of the land or to protect it from overflow. *It is lawful to embank against the sea*, even when the effect may be to cause the water to beat with increased violence against the adjoining land. . . .

Gould, A Treatise on the Law of Waters 320–21 (Chicago, Callaghan & Co. 2d ed. 1891) (Emphasis added). Recently, the state of Washington, which had apparently applied the common enemy rule to seawalls, rejected the language of an 1896 case, *Cass v. Dicks*, 44 P. 113, 114 (Wash. 1896), as *dicta* and held that the common enemy rule does not apply to sea water. *Grundy v. Thurston County*, 155 Wn.2d 1, 117 P.3d 1089 (Wash. 2005). Because the issue in the *Grundy* case was whether the doctrine provided a defense for damage to a neighbor's property, however, it is not clear whether the case addresses other language in *Cass v. Dicks* recognizing a landowner's right to erect a seawall as a matter of self-defense, "having a right to protect his land and his crops from inundation." Id.

In *United States v. Milner*, 583 F.3d 1174 (9th Cir. Wash. 2009), coastal erosion had caused the tideland property boundary to intersect with shore defense structures erected by Washington homeowners. The United States, who holds the tidelands in trust for the Lummi nation, brought suit for removal of structures that were seaward of where the MHW boundary *would be* if the shore defenses had not been erected. The Ninth Circuit Court of Appeals adopted a novel approach advocated by Professor Joseph L. Sax in *Some Unorthodox Thoughts about Rising Sea Levels, Beach Erosion, and Property Rights*, 11 Vt. J. Envtl. L. 641 (2009). The dispute was characterized as one between two adjacent landowners. This view made the common enemy doctrine "inapposite because the water is not acting as a 'common enemy' of the parties involved." One party's loss was the other's gain. The common enemy doctrine could, therefore, not provide a basis for one party to permanently fix the boundary. The court found that both parties have a vested right to an ambulatory boundary and seemed to adopt a reasonable use doctrine. Although the homeowners were recognized as having a right to build structures to prevent erosion and storm damage, they "cannot use their land in a way that would harm the Lummi's interest in the neighboring tidelands." The court found that even though the shore protection structures were legal when erected, this was not a defense to the trespass action and could not justify unilaterally fixing the ambulatory boundary. *Milner* at 1188–1191.

3.   RETREAT

The third management option is one that is necessary where beach and dune systems are so dynamic that neither restoration nor armoring is feasible, when the economic costs of restoration cannot be justified, and when environmental concerns, e.g., preservation of coastal wetlands, outweigh justifications for armoring or restoration. It is also a strategy for planning for sea level rise. Retreat may involve strict construction regulations within the sensitive beach/dune system or complete construction prohibitions within particularly sensitive or hazardous areas. The use of setback lines is discussed in Chapter III.B.2.

A version of the retreat strategy, called the rolling easement, has been advocated by many commentators, but the current version of the concept is attributed to James G. Titus, the project manager for sea level rise in the Climate Change Division of the U.S. EPA. Titus's strategy allows areas that could eventually become submerged to be developed or continue to be used until the use must be abandoned. No efforts would be allowed to protect the shore or hold back the sea. A rolling easement would further require removal of structures as they became seaward of a specifically designated migrating boundary, such as the dune vegetation line, mean high water, or the upper reaches of tidal wetlands.

Ecosystems would be allowed to migrate inland, protecting access and habitat in the long term.

The idea is that there must be clear, definitive planning about what lands will be subject to the rolling easement so markets and investors have the certainty necessary to incorporate and manage the risk of sea level rise. "If some lands must give way to the rising sea, the economic, environmental, and human consequences could be much less if the abandonment occurs according to a plan rather than unexpectedly." See James G. Titus, *Rolling Easements* 4–10 (U.S. Environmental Protection Agency 2011), available at http://water.epa.gov/type/oceb/cre/upload/rollingeasementsprimer.pdf.

Titus's rolling easement is not an "easement" at all, but a range of strategies, including both regulatory and property rights approaches, to accomplish the goals of the rolling easement described above. His 2011 report provides a comprehensive "primer on more than a dozen approaches for ensuring that wetlands and beaches can migrate inland, as people remove buildings, roads, and other structures from land as it becomes submerged" as a guide for governments in planning for sea level rise. Titus, *Rolling Easements*, id.

D. PROTECTING COASTAL WETLANDS

Coastal wetlands are among the world's most productive ecosystems. In addition to providing nursery and habitat for numerous birds and marine species; wetlands are also vital for food chain production, water quality, aquifer protection and recharge, storm protection and flood control. See 33 CFR 320.4(b)(2). Section 404 of the Clean Water Act (CWA), 33 U.S.C. § 1344, provides a nationwide scheme controlling alteration of wetlands by discharges. Section 404 permitting authority is in the U.S. Army Corps of Engineers (Corps), with ultimate administrative authority in the Environmental Protection Agency.

A threshold issue in wetlands permitting is what constitutes a wetland, i.e., what is the scope of the Corps' jurisdiction? Interestingly, CWA § 404 does not mention the term "wetland." Instead, the Act creates a permitting system for discharges of dredged and fill material into navigable waters. "Navigable waters" are defined as "the waters of the United States, including the territorial seas." 33 U.S.C.A. § 1362(7). This lack of preciseness in the statute has led to continuing controversy over § 404 jurisdiction. See, e.g., *United States v. Riverside Bayview Homes, Inc.*, 474 U.S. 121, 106 S.Ct. 455, 88 L.Ed.2d 419 (1985) (holding the Corps' permitting jurisdiction over wetlands that were adjacent to, but not directly connected to or flooded by, a navigable water body); *Solid Waste Agency of Northern Cook County (SWANCC) v. U.S. Army Corps of Engineers*, 531 U.S. 159, 121 S.Ct. 675, 148 L.Ed.2d 576 (2001) (holding that isolated wetlands are not subject to Corps jurisdiction); and *Rapanos v. United States*, 547 U.S. 715, 126 S.Ct. 2208, 165 L.Ed.2d 159 (2006) (the four-justice plurality opinion finding that wetlands may not be considered "adjacent to" remote "waters of the United States" based on a mere hydrologic connection; but Justice Kennedy, concurring, stating that wetlands are subject to Corps § 404 jurisdiction if they, alone or in combination with similarly situated wetlands in the region, significantly affect the chemical, physical, and biological integrity of traditional navigable waters). In April 2014, the EPA and Corps published a jointly proposed rule to clarify what waters are protected by CWA § 404. See 79 Fed. Reg. 22188 (April 21, 2014). The proposed rule adopts Justice Kennedy's approach in *Rapanos*, commonly referred to as the "significant nexus" test.

In the case of coastal wetlands, however, it is clear that tidally-affected water bodies are subject to § 404 at least as far inland as the mean high tide line and the head of tide on coastal rivers, see, e.g., *Leslie Salt Co. v. Froehlke*, 578 F.2d 742 (9th Cir. 1978). The principle coastal impact of *SWANCC* and *Rapanos* will be to exclude isolated, non-tidal wetlands that have no significant nexus to tidal coastal wetlands from CWA § 404.

Once an area is determined to be within the definition of a wetland constituting waters of the United States, the issue becomes whether the activity involved requires a permit. The section 404 permit system regulates only the "discharge of dredged and fill material." Before 1993 the Corps had not required a permit for dredging that did not involve disposing of the material in a wetland. Likewise, draining of a wetland without a discharge (by pumps or channels, for example) had not been regulated. See *Save Our Community v. United States EPA*, 971 F.2d 1155 (5th Cir. 1992). Land clearing is another activity that does not clearly fit within the plain meaning of "discharging." See *Avoyelles Sportmen's League v. Marsh*, 715 F.2d 897 (5th Cir. 1983). As part of a settlement in a suit involving draining and filling wetlands, the Corps amended its regulations in 1993 to prohibit wetlands destruction by removing wetlands vegetation and to assert jurisdiction based on even *de minimis* discharges that result in significant changes to the character of a water body. 33 C.F.R. § 323.2(d) (1995); see also *North Carolina Wildlife Federation v. Tulloch*, Civ. No. C90–713–CIV–5–BO (E.D.N.C. 1992). Two cases, however, required the Corps to rethink significantly its position on these issues. In *United States v. Wilson*, 133 F.3d 251 (4th Cir. 1997), the court held that "[s]ide-casting from ditch-digging . . . effects no addition of a pollutant, and if the ditching successfully dries out the wetland prior to the addition of other materials, no violation of the Clean Water Act results because adding fill to dry land cannot be construed to be polluting the waters of the United States." In *National Mining Association v. U.S. Army Corps of Engineers*, 145 F.3d 1399, 330 U.S.App.D.C. 329 (D.C.Cir. 1998), the Court of Appeals found that the Corps had exceeded its jurisdiction by defining incidental fallback as an "addition" to waters of the United States and upheld a nationwide injunction on application of the regulation. See 64 Fed. Reg. 25150.

Some activities in wetlands are specifically exempted from section 404. Most significantly, section 404(f)(1) exempts "normal farming, silviculture, and ranching activities." 33 U.S.C.A. § 1344(f)(1)(A). Courts have generally applied this exemption narrowly to ongoing activities and not to activities that bring wetlands into a new use. See, e.g., *United States v. Brace*, 41 F.3d 117 (3d Cir. 1994).

If a regulated activity occurs in waters of the United States, what criteria are applied to determine whether and under what conditions a permit will be issued? Section 404(b)(1) of the CWA requires the Corps to apply guidelines developed by the EPA, as well as its own regulatory review standards. 40 C.F.R. §§ 230.1–230.71 (1996). The EPA's 404(b)(1) Guidelines create a presumption against filling waters for non-water-dependent purposes by prohibiting a permit if there is "a practicable alternative to the proposed discharge which would have less adverse impact on the aquatic ecosystem, so long as the alternative does not have other significant adverse environmental consequences" and presuming practicable alternatives exist unless an applicant clearly demonstrated otherwise. See 40 C.F.R. § 230.10; see also *Bersani v. United States EPA*, 850 F.2d 36 (2d Cir. 1988); *Sylvester v. United States Army Corps of Eng'rs*, 882 F.2d 407 (9th Cir. 1989); *Sierra Club v. Van Antwerp*, 41 ELR 20346 (D.C. Cir. 2011); Jon Schutz, *The Steepest Hurdle in Obtaining A Clean Water Act Section 404 Permit: Complying with EPA's 404(b)(1) Guidelines' Least Environmentally Damaging Practicable Alternative Requirement*, 24 UCLA J. Envtl. L. & Pol'y 235 (2006).

The public interest test is the focus of the Corps' regulatory review. The broad standards for determining whether a project should be permitted are set out in the following regulation:

33 C.F.R. § 320.4(a) *Public Interest Review.*

(1) The decision whether to issue a permit will be based on an evaluation of the probable impacts, including cumulative impacts, of the proposed activity and its intended use on the public interest. Evaluation of the probable impact which the proposed activity may have on the public interest requires a careful weighing of all those factors which become relevant in each particular case. The benefits which reasonably may be expected to accrue from the proposal must be balanced against its reasonably foreseeable detriments. The decision whether to authorize a proposal, and if so, the conditions under which it will be allowed to occur, are therefore determined by the outcome of this general balancing process. That decision should reflect the national concern for both protection and utilization of important resources. All factors which may be relevant to the proposal must be considered including the cumulative effects thereof: among those are conservation, economics, aesthetics, general environmental concerns, wetlands, historic properties, fish and wildlife values, flood hazards, floodplain values, land use, navigation, shore erosion and accretion, recreation, water supply and conservation, water quality, energy needs, safety, food and fiber production, mineral needs, considerations of property ownership and, in

general, the needs and welfare of the people. . . . Subject to the . . . applicable criteria and guidelines, a permit will be granted unless the district engineer determines that it would be contrary to public interest.

See also 33 CFR 320.4(b)–(l).

The EPA, which implements all other sections of the CWA, has joint responsibility to administer section 404 and ultimate authority to interpret the statute. EPA also has authority to veto a permit issued by the Corps. 33 U.S.C.A. § 1344(c). See *James City County v. Environmental Protection Agency*, 12 F.3d 1330 (4th Cir. 1993).

Corps permits issued under either the Rivers and Harbors Act or the Clean Water Act are also subject to state veto under the state water quality standard compliance certification requirements of CWA section 401, 33 U.S.C.A. § 1341, see *Friends of the Earth v. Hall*, 693 F.Supp. 904 (W.D.Wash. 1988); and the state coastal program consistency certification requirements of CZMA section 307(c)(3)(A), 16 U.S.C.A. § 1456(c)(3)(A). See *Anton v. South Carolina Coastal Council*, 321 S.C. 481, 469 S.E.2d 604 (1996); *Ogburn-Matthews v. Loblolly Partners*, 332 S.C. 551, 505 S.E.2d 598 (1998).

In addition, many states regulate coastal wetlands alterations either through their CZM programs, see *Kirkorowicz v. California Coastal Commission*, 100 Cal.Rptr.2d 124 (Cal. App. 2000); *1000 Friends of Oregon v. LCDC*, 85 Or.App. 18, 735 P.2d 645 (Or. App. 1987); or specific dredge and fill legislation that requires permits for wetland alteration. See, e.g., Conn. Gen. Stat. §§ 22a–28 to 22a–35; Fla. Stat. §§ 373.403–373.443; Me. Rev. Star. Ann. tit. 12, §§ 4751–4758; N.J. Star. Ann. §§ 13:9A–1 to 13:9A–10; Or. Rev. Stat. §§ 196.800–196.990.

Section 404 of the CWA provides for delegation of some, but not all, wetland permitting authority to states that meet statutory requirements. 33 U.S.C.A. § 1344(g)–(1). However, only Michigan (1984) and New Jersey (1994) have been delegated § 404 permitting authority. 40 C.F.R. §§ 233.70, 71. State permits issued under delegated § 404 authority are also subject to EPA veto.

Finally, Corps administration of the Rivers and Harbors Act and CWA § 404 is subject to the environmental impact assessment requirements of the National Environmental Policy Act (NEPA) (see, e.g., *Ocean Advocates v. U.S. Army Corps of Engineers*, 402 F.3d 846 (9th Cir. 2004); *Shoreacres v. Waterworth*, 420 F.3d 440 (5th Cir. 2005)), the permit coordination and consistency requirements of the CZMA discussed above, the Endangered Species Act and Marine Mammal Protection Act discussed infra. See, e.g., *Florida Marine Contractors v. Williams*, 378 F.Supp.2d 1353 (M.D.Fla. 2005).

E.   COASTAL MANAGEMENT AND THE TAKINGS ISSUE

The Fifth Amendment of the United States Constitution provides that private property "shall [not] be taken for public use without just compensation." When there has been a permanent

physical invasion or appropriation of land by the
government, it is generally incontrovertible that
there has been a taking of property requiring
compensation. *Loretto v. Teleprompter Manhattan
CATV Corp.*, 458 U.S. 419, 102 S.Ct. 3164, 73 L.Ed.2d
868 (1982) (holding that even a slight, permanent
physical invasion under government authority is a
compensable *per se* taking). However, the question of
when a regulation that severely affects the value or
utility of land constitutes a "taking" has become one
of the most complicated and pervasive questions in
land use and environmental law.

The genesis of modern regulatory takings analysis
is *Pennsylvania Coal Co. v. Mahon*, 260 U.S. 393, 43
S.Ct. 158, 67 L.Ed. 322 (1922), in which Justice
Holmes stated: "The general rule at least is, that
while property may be regulated to a certain extent,
if regulation goes too far, it will be recognized as a
taking." The U.S. Supreme Court described the
conundrum of regulatory taking as follows:

Government hardly could go on if to some
extent values incident to property could not be
diminished without paying for every such
change in the general law. As long recognized,
some values are enjoyed under an implied
limitation and must yield to the police power.
But obviously the implied limitation must have
its limits. . . . One fact for consideration in
determining such limits is the extent of the
diminution [of value]. When it reaches a certain
magnitude, in most if not all cases there must be

an exercise of eminent domain and compensation to sustain the act.

In *Pennsylvania Coal,* the Court found that a Pennsylvania statute that made it unlawful for mining operations to cause subsidence of public buildings, public streets, and private residences had "gone too far." The support estate, an interest in land that is separate from the surface and mineral estates, is recognized in Pennsylvania. The statute effectively barred the coal company's exercising rights to the mineral and support estates, interests owned by the coal company that had not been transferred by the deed to the Mahons, the private owners of the surface estate. The Court found that the law had "very nearly the same effect for constitutional purposes as appropriating or destroying" the property.

In *Penn Central Transportation Co. v. City of New York,* 438 U.S. 104, 98 S.Ct. 2646, 57 L.Ed.2d 631 (1978), the Court acknowledged its inability to develop a set formula to evaluate regulatory taking claims, but set out "several factors that have particular significance": The economic impact of the regulation and the extent to which it interfered with distinct or reasonable investment-backed expectations must be balanced against the "character of the government regulation." In *Andrus v. Allard,* 444 U.S. 51, 65, 62 L. Ed. 2d 210, 100 S. Ct. 318 (1979), the Court noted that "government regulation—by definition—involves the adjustment of rights for the public good." Government action that "merely affects property interests through 'some public program adjusting the benefits and burdens of economic life to promote the common good,' " is less likely to be found a regulatory taking. See also *Lingle v. Chevron*, 544 U.S. 528, 125 S.Ct. 2074, 161 L.Ed.2d 876 (2005). The Supreme Court considered Penn Central's expectations and concluded that, at least where the regulation does not interfere with existing use of the property, such long use constitutes the "primary expectation concerning the use of the parcel." Even though New York's landmark legislation prohibited the development of the air space above Grand Central Terminal, the terminal could continue to be used profitably as it had been for 65 years.

Most recent takings cases have placed emphasis on the economic impact of the regulation on the property owner. See *Lucas v. South Carolina Coastal Council*, 304 S.C. 376, 404 S.E.2d 895 (1991) (creating a second category of *per se* taking in cases where a regulation destroys all economic use or value of the property). The outcome of a case often turns, however, on the methodology used to determine the economic impact or the extent of diminution in value caused by the regulation. When the property retains some economically viable use, courts will usually find that there has been no taking. In *Penn Central,* the Supreme Court made it clear that diminution of value would be determined on the basis of the value of the property as a whole as affected by the regulation.

> " 'Taking' jurisprudence does not divide a single parcel into discrete segments and attempt to determine whether rights in a particular

segment have been entirely abrogated. In deciding whether a particular governmental action has effected a taking, this Court focuses rather both on the character of the action and on the nature and extent of the interference with rights in the *parcel as a whole. . . .*" (Emphasis added.)

The Court refused to consider whether all the value of the air space above the terminal had been taken by the regulation, focusing instead on the total value of the property, including the transferable development rights provided by the regulation.

State courts have applied a variety of tests in the absence of a single rationale for determining a taking in the context of the federal or most state constitutions. In *State v. Johnson*, 265 A.2d 711 (Me. 1970), the Maine Supreme Court applied a diminution of value test to find that a permit denial under the Wetlands Act constituted a taking. In a zoning case, however, the same court affirmed the police power to set standards for development where "the use is actually and substantially an injury or impairment of the public interest." *In re Spring Valley Dev.*, 300 A.2d 736 (Me. 1973). In *Turnpike Realty Co. v. Town of Dedham*, 362 Mass. 221, 284 N.E.2d 891 (1972), the Massachusetts Supreme Judicial Court based the taking test on the distinction between creating public benefit and prevention of public harm. The denial of a permit to fill a New Hampshire salt marsh was held to be a valid regulation because it would prevent future harm to the public. *Sibson v. State*, 115 N.H. 124, 336

A.2d 239 (1975). In *Graham v. Estuary Properties, Inc.*, 399 So.2d 1374 (Fla. 1981), the Florida Supreme Court found that the denial of a dredge and fill permit to destroy 1,800 acres of coastal mangrove wetlands was not a taking because the owner could not have had reasonable expectations to develop the property in a manner that would seriously affect the environment.

In *Palazzolo v. Rhode Island*, 533 U.S. 606, 121 S.Ct. 2448, 150 L.Ed.2d 592 (2001), the U.S. Supreme Court confronted the takings issues raised by permit denials for proposed filling of Rhode Island coastal wetlands protected under Rhode Island's coastal zone management program. The case was remanded for reconsideration by the state supreme court based on the *Penn Central* analysis because the property still retained value and economic use. Upon remand, the trial court ruled that there had been no taking. *Palazzolo v. State*, 2005 WL 1645974 (R.I.Super.Ct. 2005). See also *Gove v. Zoning Board of Appeals of Chatham*, 444 Mass. 754, 831 N.E.2d 865 (Sup.Ct. 2005) (building prohibition on coastal lot subject to flooding held not a taking based on *Penn Central*).

Because so many major takings cases have focused on use of coastal lands and wetlands, these areas will be considered individually.

1.   COASTAL CONSTRUCTION REGULATION

Beachfront property is often wedged between a coastal highway and the mean high water mark, leaving little flexibility for locating structures on the land. Setback lines and other restrictive zones may incorporate an entire shoreline lot. Coastal land has always been in jeopardy from storms and erosion, and is now the target of sea level rise. In addition, new coastal construction regulations may disproportionately affect unimproved lots in developed coastal areas. All of these factors make regulation of coastal construction particularly susceptible to claims that the regulation "goes too far" in impairing the use and value of the land when regulation affects development or protection of the property.

South Carolina's Beachfront Management Act (BMA), as passed in 1988, created a "dead zone" landward of a baseline at the crest of the primary dune within which no development would be permitted. The statute precluded the development of two lots on an extensively developed beach on the Isle of Palms that had been purchased in 1986 by David Lucas. Lucas filed suit in state court contending that the BMA had taken his property without compensation. The trial court found that the BMA deprived Lucas of all economically viable use of the land, rendering it "valueless." The South Carolina Supreme Court reversed, holding that the BMA was intended to prevent a serious public harm and required no compensation regardless of the effect on property value. *Lucas v. South Carolina Coastal Council*, 304 S.C. 376, 404 S.E.2d 895 (1991).

Although the BMA was amended in 1990 to provide for special permits for development in the former "dead zone," the U.S. Supreme Court granted certiorari to determine whether the BMA had effected a "temporary taking" of the Lucas property. See *First English Evangelical Lutheran Church of Glendale v. Los Angeles*, 482 U.S. 304, 107 S.Ct. 2378, 96 L.Ed.2d 250 (1987) (holding that compensation is due for the period during which a regulation that effects a taking is in place, even if the regulation is subsequently withdrawn). Justice Scalia, writing for the majority, identified two categories of regulatory actions that required compensation without any balancing of the public interests served. The first category comprises regulations that authorize a permanent physical invasion. The situation in *Lucas v. South Carolina Coastal Council*, 505 U.S. 1003, 112 S.Ct. 2886, 120 L.Ed.2d 798 (1992), fell within the second category—"where regulation denies all economically beneficial or productive use of land." The Court rejected the notion that no compensation is required in situations that can be characterized as preventing a harmful or "noxious" use. Justice Scalia asserted that the distinction between preventing a public harm and creating a public benefit is meaningless, dependent primarily upon a subjective determination of the values of competing uses of property. In addition, the Court stated, the recitation in early cases that "a regulation prevents a public harm" was merely a statement "of the police power justification necessary to sustain (without compensation) any diminution in value." Noting that although situations where a regulation confiscates all value of land would be rare, such regulations should be treated as "similar" to a physical occupation, i.e., as a *per se* taking of property without compensation.

The only exception to the compensation requirement in the case of a regulation that deprives land of all beneficial use, the Court said, is when the "proscribed use interests were not part of [the] title to begin with." The Court further stated:

> Any limitation so severe cannot be newly legislated or decreed (without compensation), but must inhere in the title itself, in the restrictions that background principles of the State's law of property and nuisance already place upon land ownership. A law or decree with such an effect must, in other words, do no more than duplicate the result that could have been achieved in the courts—by adjacent landowners (or other uniquely affected persons) under the State's law of private nuisance, or by the State under its complementary power to abate nuisances that affect the public generally, or otherwise.

The Court described a "total taking inquiry" into state nuisance law as normally including:

> an analysis of, among other things, the degree of harm to public lands and resources, or adjacent private property, posed by the claimant's proposed activities, the social value of the claimant's activities and their suitability to the locality in question, and the relative ease with which the alleged harm can be avoided through measures taken by the claimant and the government (or adjacent landowner) alike.

(Citations omitted). The history of nuisance law suggests that this balancing test is similar to, but perhaps even more complicated than, the balancing of public interests served and private burdens imposed as applied in previous takings cases. This analysis adds very little certainty to the process of determining when a regulation denying all use effects a taking. The Court exacerbated the uncertainty by also recognizing that "changed circumstances or new knowledge may make what was previously permissible no longer so." It seems that the major differences in the two balancing tests (the *Penn Central* test and the "total takings" test) is that in the total takings analysis the burden of proof is shifted to the government and the court's judgment is substituted for the legislature's.

In *Lucas,* the Court found it probative that similarly situated owners had made the same use of land and are permitted to continue to make residential use of the land. In remanding the case to the South Carolina Supreme Court to determine the relevant background principles of state law, the U.S. Supreme Court observed:

   It seems unlikely that common law principles would have prevented the erection of any habitable structure or productive improvements on petitioner's land; they rarely support prohibition of the "essential use" of land.

In the remand of the *Lucas* case, the South Carolina Supreme Court found no common law basis for prohibiting Lucas' proposed use of the land and remanded the case to the trial court for a determination of the actual damages Lucas sustained for the temporary taking of his property. Interestingly, the state supreme court determined that the temporary taking began with the 1988 enactment of the BMA and continued through the date of that court's order, rather than finding that the taking continued only to the time of the Amendment of the BMA in 1990. *Lucas v. South Carolina Coastal Council*, 309 S.C. 424, 424 S.E.2d 484 (1992).

Although the U.S. Supreme Court specifically discussed nuisance law in *Lucas,* the Court did not explain what is incorporated in the concept of "other background principles" of state property law, leaving state courts to decide the parameters of this exception in total takings analysis. The Oregon Supreme Court has held that the doctrine of custom in the context of public beach access is such a background principle. See *Stevens v. Cannon Beach*, 317 Or. 131, 854 P.2d 449 (1993). And the public trust doctrine and federal navigation servitude have been identified as background principles justifying the denial of compensation to land owners denied permits to develop lands periodically overflowed by tidewaters. See *Esplanade Properties, LLC v. City of Seattle*, 307 F.3d 978 (9th Cir. 2002); *McQueen v. South Carolina Coastal Council*, 354 S.C. 142, 580 S.E.2d 116 (2003); *Palm Beach Isles Associates v. United States,* 58 Fed.Cl. 657 (2003).

The Virginia Supreme Court held that landowners could not base a total takings claim on the loss of value of land acquired subject to preexisting regulatory restrictions. The court reasoned that because the land was acquired with knowledge of the restrictions on development, the "risk of economic loss" was assumed by the landowners as part of their title. The court found it unnecessary to analyze the Coastal Primary Sand Dune Protection Act to determine whether the Act prevented a nuisance. "Such an inquiry is irrelevant" since the owner never acquired, as part of his title, the right to freely develop the property. See *Virginia Beach v. Bell*, 255 Va. 395, 498 S.E.2d 414 (1998). In *Palazzolo*, 533 U.S. 606, 121 S.Ct. 2448, 150 L.Ed.2d 592 (2001), however, the U.S. Supreme Court declined to interpret the Fifth Amendment as including such a limitation. "A regulation or common-law rule cannot be a background principle for some owners but not for others. . . . A law does not become a background principle for subsequent owners by enactment itself." Id.

The Supreme Court has, however, applied a different kind of "temporal" element to its takings analysis in a case involving a land use moratorium halting development in particularly sensitive waterfront areas pending the preparation of comprehensive plans controlling future development. The Court refused to combine the rationales of *First English* and *Lucas* to characterize a prohibition on development during a 3-year moratorium as a *per se* "temporary, total taking" requiring compensation. In *Tahoe-Sierra Preservation Council, Inc. v. Tahoe Regional Planning Agency*, 535 U.S. 302, 122 S.Ct. 1465, 152 L.Ed.2d 517 (2002), the Court found "total taking" analysis inapplicable. In considering the impact of a regulation on the property "as a whole," a temporary restriction on use of the property is not a permanent deprivation because the property will recover, and perhaps even increase, its value after the moratorium is lifted.

Within days of the *Lucas* decision, the U.S. Supreme Court denied certiorari in another takings challenge to South Carolina's Beach Management Act (BMA). In *Esposito v. South Carolina Coastal Council*, 939 F.2d 165 (4th Cir. 1991), owners of residences located at least partially within the "dead zone" argued that the restrictions on rebuilding if the structures were destroyed diminished the present value of the property and constituted a taking. The federal court of appeals found that the BMA allowed the owners to continue the existing use of their land and dwellings, consistent with their expectations. Diminution of market value alone was not enough to establish that a taking had occurred.

2.   WETLANDS REGULATION

If the U.S. Army Corps of Engineers denies a Clean Water Act § 404 permit, the validity of that denial may be challenged in federal district court. Because the Corps' jurisdiction and broad scope of review are well established, many permit denials are now taken directly to the U.S. Claims Court under the Tucker Act. The Tucker Act, 28 U.S.C.A. § 1491, gives the Claims Court jurisdiction to hear any constitutional claims against the United States for damages. By choosing the forum of the Claims Court, the permit applicant accepts the validity of the permit denial, but alleges that the denial constitutes an uncompensated taking of private property.

The first such takings challenges to denials of section 404 permits were brought in 1981. In cases like *Deltona Corp. v. United States,* 228 Ct.Cl. 476, 657 F.2d 1184 (1981), and *Jentgen v. United States*, 228 Ct.Cl. 527, 657 F.2d 1210 (1981), the Claims Court followed traditional Supreme Court analysis in considering the public purpose and legitimacy of the regulation, whether the property retained economic use, and the degree to which investment-backed expectations had been frustrated. The court held that the permit denials did not amount to takings. *Loveladies Harbor, Inc. v. United States*, 28 F.3d 1171 (Fed.Cir. 1994), however, reached a different conclusion on the takings issue in similar circumstances. The major difference in the case appears to be in the court's method of determination of diminution of value or degree of deprivation of use.

In footnote 7 of *Lucas v. South Carolina Coastal Council*, 505 U.S. 1003, 112 S.Ct. 2886, 120 L.Ed.2d 798 (1992), the Supreme Court noted the imprecision of determining when all economically viable use of property is taken. The result is dependent upon "the 'property interest' against which the loss of value is to be measured." In *Penn Central Transportation Co. v. City of New York*, 438 U.S. 104, 98 S.Ct. 2646, 57 L.Ed.2d 631 (1978), the Court identified the "denominator in [the] deprivation fraction" as the value of the property as a whole as affected by the regulation. Applying this approach in *Deltona* and *Jentgen,* the court considered the value of applicants' entire development as the relevant denominator. In *Loveladies Harbor,* however, the Claims Court refused to consider the areas for which the permits were denied in the context of the applicants' larger holdings, resulting in determinations that over 95 percent of the value had been deprived. *Loveladies Harbor v. United States*, 21 Cl.Ct. 153 (1990). On appeal, the Federal Circuit upheld the trial court conclusion that only land developed or sold after the wetlands became subject to regulation could be included in the denominator. *Loveladies Harbor v. United States*, 28 F.3d 1171 (Fed.Cir. 1994). In *Good v. United States*, 189 F.3d 1355 (Fed. Cir. 1999), the Federal Circuit found no taking had occurred through a Corps coastal wetland fill permit denial because the claimants could not have had reasonable expectations of receiving a permit when they acquired the property in 1973. Accord, *Norman v. United States*, 429 F.3d 1081 (Fed.Cir. 2005).

Mitigation is a common requirement of wetlands permits to offset impacts of the wetland loss. When such requirements involve dedication of land, *Nollan* and *Dolan* clearly require a "nexus" and "rough proportionality" between the exaction and the effects of the landowner's proposed action. See Part II.D.2. In *Koontz v. St. Johns River Water Management District*, 133 S.Ct. 2586 (2013), the Water Management District (WMD) denied a state wetlands permit when the applicant refused to provide any of the mitigation options proposed by the WMD. In the 5–4 decision, the U.S. Supreme Court stated that *Nollan* and *Dolan*'s principles apply whether "the government *approves* a permit on the condition that the applicant turn over property or *denies* a permit because the applicant refuses to do so." The Court also found that monetary exactions or "in lieu" fees are "functionally equivalent to other types of land use exactions" and must also satisfy the *Nollan/Dolan* requirements. In holding that "the government's demand for property from a land-use permit applicant must satisfy the requirements of *Nollan* and *Dolan* even when the government denies the permit and even when its demand is for money," the Court provided little guidance concerning a remedy. Just compensation under the Fifth Amendment is not relevant "[w]here the permit is denied and the condition is never imposed, [because] nothing has been taken." The Court directs that "[i]n cases where there is an excessive demand but no taking, whether money damages are available is not a question of federal constitutional law but of the cause of action—whether state or federal—on which the landowner relies." The implications of the case are not yet known, but Justice Kagan expressed in her dissenting opinion that her main concern was with how *Koontz* will constitutionalize the entire regulatory process. If *Nollan/Dolan* is applicable to all proposals and suggestions made during permit application negotiations, governments might desist altogether from communicating with applicants. Justice Kagan observes: "[The decision] deprives state and local governments of the flexibility they need to enhance their communities—to ensure environmentally sound and economically productive development. It places courts smack in the middle of the most everyday local government activity."

3.   COASTAL REGULATION AND NEW APPROACHES TO CONSTITUTIONAL TAKINGS: JUDICIAL TAKINGS AND FOURTH AMENDMENT "TAKINGS"

Because of the indeterminacy and unpredictability of regulatory takings cases, property owners often lack a clear test for making claims for compensation when coastal regulations have affected the value of their land. This situation has led property rights advocates to advance new theories that may affect the development of takings analysis and, consequently, coastal management law. In *Stop the Beach Renourishment v. Florida Department of Environmental Protection*, 130 S.Ct. 2592, 177 L. Ed. 184 (2010), the property owners claimed that the Florida Supreme Court had "taken" their right to accretions, a "vested property interest," by changing the law applicable to accretion in the context of beach restoration. Although the U.S. Supreme Court unanimously agreed that there had been no Fifth Amendment taking, the plurality, led by Justice Scalia, found that judicial opinions "effect a taking if they recharacterize as public property what was previously private property." Justice Scalia's test for a judicial taking focused on the effect on existing property rights: "If a legislature *or a court* declares that what was once an established right of private property no longer exists, it has taken that property. . . ." (Emphasis added). Justice Scalia explained judicial taking as follows: "Condemnation by eminent domain, for example, is always a taking, while a legislative, executive, *or judicial* restriction of property use may or may not be, depending on its nature and extent."

The four concurring justices did not adopt the concept of judicial taking, finding adoption of a novel constitutional concept unnecessary to disposition of the case. Justice Kennedy, joined by Justice Sotomayor, however, addressed the problems associated with applying the Fifth Amendment to judicial decisions and suggested that courts could be constrained appropriately from making arbitrary and irrational decisions that eliminate established property rights through the Due Process Clause. It is notable that none of the justices, however, categorically denied the existence of the concept of a judicial taking, and that six justices agreed that state supreme court decisions that eliminated existing property rights might be unconstitutional either as a judicial taking or as a due process violation.

The other novel theory is assertion of the Fourth Amendment to claim an unreasonable seizure of property (rather than a Fifth Amendment taking). In *Severance v. Patterson*, 566 F.3d 490 (5th Cir. 2009), the federal case that certified the question of "rolling" public beach access easements to the Texas Supreme Court, the federal Court of Appeals found that the Fourth Amendment claim was not subsumed in Severance's taking claim. In response to the Texas Supreme Court's ruling that the "rolling easement" is not part of Texas law, the Fifth Circuit remanded the case for further proceedings on the Fourth Amendment claim. The court stated that it was "unpersuaded" that the case has been rendered moot by the fact that Severance's property had in the interim been taken (and fully compensated for) through eminent domain proceedings. See *Severance v. Patterson*, 682 F.3d 360 (5th Cir. 2012).

It is too early to judge the effect of these decisions on regulation of property. It seems unlikely, however, that additional causes of action will provide property owners the "bright line" they seek to demarcate when a regulation "goes too far."

CHAPTER IV

OFFSHORE RESOURCE MANAGEMENT

A. THE TIDELANDS CONTROVERSY AND THE SUBMERGED LANDS ACT

Managers and planners today support theories of ecosystem management and comprehensive, integrated planning for ocean areas and resources. Unfortunately, our institutions, agencies, and laws have evolved in a manner that often frustrates attempts to approach management of coastal and ocean resources in a coherent and cooperative fashion. Rather than dealing directly with the issue of cooperative management of ocean and coastal resources that are of mutual importance, the state and federal governments have waged battles for sixty years over proprietary interests and preemption issues. Immeasurable funds and resources have been expended in endless controversies over ownership, jurisdiction, and boundaries.

Until the 1940s, little doubt seemed to exist that the coastal states, rather than the federal government, "owned" the lands under the territorial sea. These waters were presumed to be encompassed within the definitions of navigable waters or tidelands that belonged to the colonies upon becoming sovereign and to the subsequently admitted states under the equal footing doctrine. See Chapter I.A.

Most coastal states had legislation establishing offshore marine boundaries prior to 1940, and many state constitutions and federal acts admitting states to the Union described state boundaries as extending a marine league or more offshore. See, Gordon Ireland, *Marginal Seas Around the States,* 2 La. L. Rev. 252 (1940) (reviewing the offshore claims and law of each coastal state as of 1940). Numerous state courts had early concluded that the original colonies succeeded to the King's interest in the tidelands and adjacent seas and, therefore, title vested in the original colonies. Decisions of federal courts, including the United States Supreme Court, impliedly, if not expressly, supported the presumption of state ownership of the seabed and the territorial sea. See, e.g., *Manchester v. Massachusetts*, 139 U.S. 240, 11 S.Ct. 559, 35 L.Ed. 159 (1891); *The Abby Dodge v. United States*, 223 U.S. 166, 32 S.Ct. 310, 56 L.Ed. 390 (1912). Even Roosevelt's Secretary of the Interior, Harold L. Ickes, charged with administering United States public lands, stated that the federal government had no authority to lease the seabed for mineral exploration. In the now famous 1933 Proctor Letter, Ickes explained to a lease applicant that "[t]itle to the soil under the ocean within the 3-mile limit is in the State of California, and the land may not be appropriated except by authority of the State." Letter from Harold Ickes, Secretary of the Interior, to Olin S. Proctor (Dec. 22, 1933), reprinted in Ernest Barkley, The Tidelands Oil Controversy 129 (1953).

In the late 1930s, controversies emerged within California concerning oil recovered from submerged lands by slant drilling from shore and ownership of mineral rights in submerged lands granted by the state to coastal cities for harbor and recreational development. Apparently instigated by Secretary Ickes, and fired by the oil industry and by vocal individuals from California interested in settling the offshore ownership issue, Congress in 1938 began a series of hearings and attempted to pass resolutions addressing federal interests in the tidelands. These efforts culminated in 1946 in House Joint Resolution 225, which quitclaimed any rights of the federal government in lands beneath tidelands and navigable waters to the states. President Truman vetoed the resolution on August 2, 1946, citing the fact that the issue was currently before the Supreme Court.

On October 19, 1945, the United States Attorney General filed an original jurisdiction suit in the Supreme Court against the state of California. *United States v. California*, 332 U.S. 19, 67 S.Ct. 1658, 91 L.Ed. 1889 (1947). The suit sought to have the United States declared the owner of the seabed and minerals from the mean low water line to three nautical miles seaward. California argued that because the original colonies had acquired from the Crown of England all lands under navigable waters, including all marginal seas within their boundaries, these lands also vested in California upon admission into the Union by virtue of the equal footing doctrine as an element of sovereignty.

The Court quickly dismissed California's arguments, concluding that "acquisition . . . of the three-mile belt [had] been accomplished by the national Government," rather than the English Crown or the colonies. The Court depicted the federal government's role not as merely a property owner, but as the entity responsible for the security and defense of the marginal seas and for the conduct of foreign relations:

> The ocean, even its three-mile belt, is thus of vital consequence to the nation in its desire to engage in commerce and to live in peace with the world; it also becomes of crucial importance should it ever again become impossible to preserve that peace. And as peace and world commerce are the paramount responsibilities of the nation, rather than an individual state, so, if wars come, they must be fought by the nation. The state is not equipped in our constitutional system with the powers or the facilities for exercising the responsibilities which would be concomitant with the dominion which it seeks.

Id. (citations omitted). These vital interests apparently did not, however, necessitate ownership by the United States of the territorial sea. Instead, the Court held only "that California is not the owner of the three-mile marginal belt along its coast, and that the Federal Government rather than the state has *paramount rights* in and power over that belt, an incident to which is full dominion over the resources of the soil under that water area, including oil." (Emphasis added.)

On the heels of the *United States v. California* holding, the United States brought suit against both

Texas and Louisiana on the basis that the broad principles of the case also dictated federal ownership or control of the oil fields of the Gulf of Mexico. See *United States v. Texas*, 339 U.S. 707, 70 S.Ct. 918, 94 L.Ed. 1221 (1950) and *United States v. Louisiana*, 339 U.S. 699, 70 S.Ct. 914, 94 L.Ed. 1216 (1950). The Louisiana case, with little to distinguish the state's history from California, was found to be controlled by *United States v. California*, 332 U.S. 19, 67 S.Ct. 1658, 91 L.Ed. 1889 (1947). The Texas case, however, presented a clearly unique circumstance because of the state's preadmission history as a sovereign republic with a boundary and dominion extending three marine leagues into the Gulf of Mexico. The Court disposed of the case through application of the equal footing doctrine, finding that relinquishment of any "claim that Texas may have had to the marginal sea" to be incidental to the transfer of Texas' external sovereignty to the United States.

The Supreme Court cases created great controversy in Congress about the ownership of the marginal seas and its resources. Following another vetoed attempt at quitclaim legislation, Congress passed the 1953 Submerged Lands Act (SLA), 43 U.S.C.A. §§ 1301–1315, which was signed by newly elected President Eisenhower. The SLA quitclaimed to the coastal states all federal proprietary rights in the three-mile territorial sea and confirmed federal government rights in the seabed and subsoil beyond that. The SLA accomplished three objectives: (1) it established state title to the territorial sea and its resources; (2) it decreed the limit of state ocean boundaries; and (3) it reserved federal rights both within and beyond state territorial limits.

Although one of the purposes of the SLA was to relieve both the state and federal governments of the "interminable litigation" provoked by *United States v. California,* the boundary provisions of the Act created additional legal problems. Section 1312 of the SLA confirmed title of the original coastal states to three geographic miles and recognized the authority of subsequently admitted states to extend boundaries to that distance. However, the section went on to provide the basis for states to continue to assert claims beyond three miles:

> Any claim heretofore or hereafter asserted either by constitutional provision, statute, or otherwise, indicating the intent of a State so to extend its boundaries is hereby approved and confirmed, without prejudice to its claim, if any it has, that its boundaries extend beyond that line. Nothing in this section is to be construed as questioning or in any manner prejudicing the existence of any State's seaward boundary beyond three geographical miles if it was so provided by its constitution or laws prior to or at the time such State became a member of the Union, or if it has been heretofore approved by Congress.

43 U.S.C.A. § 1312. Congress left it to the courts to determine whether a state could establish a historic claim beyond three miles. Because the SLA did not address the methodology for establishing the

seaward boundary lines, the courts also had to address the legal problems of boundary delimitation.

Only Texas and Florida have been able to establish claims beyond three miles. In 1960, the Supreme Court recognized the three marine league boundaries in the Gulf of Mexico of both Florida, based on Congressional approval of its 1868 constitution, and Texas, based on its historic claim. See *United States v. Florida*, 363 U.S. 1, 363 U.S. 121, 80 S.Ct. 961, 4 L.Ed.2d 1025, 4 L.Ed.2d 1096 (1960); *United States v. Louisiana*, 363 U.S. 1, 363 U.S. 121, 80 S.Ct. 961, 4 L.Ed.2d 1025, 4 L.Ed.2d 1096 (1960). In 1969, the United States brought an action against the states bordering the Atlantic Ocean in which the Supreme Court upheld the reasoning in *California* and precluded claims beyond three miles. *United States v. Maine*, 420 U.S. 515, 95 S.Ct. 1155, 43 L.Ed.2d 363 (1975).

The Supreme Court's dismissal of the claims to extended jurisdiction in the Atlantic settled finally the question of the extent of coastal state boundaries, but litigation has continued for decades over the exact position of the seaward boundaries of coastal states. See Aaron L. Shalowitz, *Boundary Problems Raised by the Submerged Lands Act,* 54 Colum. L. Rev. 1021 (1954). See also Aaron L. Shalowitz, 1–2 Shore and Sea Boundaries (United States Government Printing Office 1962, 1964); Michael W. Reed, 3 Shore and Sea Boundaries (United States Government Printing Office 2000). Because the SLA did not provide a legal or technical basis for delimiting boundaries, the Supreme Court adopted the provisions of the 1958 Convention on the Territorial Sea and Contiguous Zone to deal with boundary delimitation questions. *United States v. California*, 381 U.S. 139, 85 S.Ct. 1401, 14 L.Ed.2d 296 (1965).

The most fundamental issue in boundary extension is identification of the baselines or basepoints from which the territorial sea is measured. As a general proposition, the boundary is measured from the mean low water line. Waters within baselines or closing lines of bays and the mouths of rivers, and between some fringe islands and the coast are internal or inland waters and not part of the territorial sea. See, e.g., *United States v. Alaska*, 521 U.S. 1, 117 S.Ct. 1888, 138 L.Ed.2d 231 (1997). In the case of rivers and bays, the limit of the territorial sea must be measured from closing lines across the mouth of the water body, not from the low water line. A true bay, as opposed to a mere indentation in the coastline, is identified by applying the semicircle, twenty-four mile closing line test. In order to qualify as a closed bay, a body of water must have an area larger than a semicircle that uses the closing line of the bay as its diameter. In no event, however, can the closing line be more than twenty-four miles.

Historic bays are an exception to the semicircle, twenty-four mile closing line rule. For example, in the *Alabama and Mississippi Boundary Case,* the U.S. Supreme Court found that Mississippi Sound qualifies as a historic bay. See *United States v. Louisiana*, 470 U.S. 93, 105 S.Ct. 1074, 84 L.Ed.2d 73

(1985). The Court identified factors that are taken into account in determining whether a water body is a historic bay to include: (1) continuous exercise of authority over the area; (2) acquiescence by foreign nations; and (3) the vital interests of the country, including geographical configuration, economic interests, and national security. In the *Louisiana Boundary Case, United States v. Louisiana*, 394 U.S. 11, 89 S.Ct. 773, 22 L.Ed.2d 44 (1969), the Court rejected Louisiana's claim to a historic bay, but it did recognize that a state could conceivably establish such a historic claim to internal waters even in the absence of an international claim by the United States. See also *Alaska v. United States*, 545 U.S. 75, 125 S.Ct. 2137, 162 L.Ed.2d 57 (2005); *United States v. Alaska*, 422 U.S. 184, 95 S.Ct. 2240, 45 L.Ed.2d 109 (1975).

As a technical matter, it should be noted that ocean boundaries are not generally measured by lines running parallel to the coast, but are enclosed by an "envelope of arcs." The envelope is created by connecting the outer limits of arcs extended from basepoints along the coast at a radius based on the breadth of the jurisdictional claim. The envelope of arcs method assures that, for example, a state seaward boundary is always three miles from the *nearest* point on the coastline.

Until relatively recently, the United States continued to assert a three-mile territorial sea because of national security interests, despite the fact that most countries were clearly moving toward customary acceptance of twelve-mile territorial claims. On December 27, 1988, the United States radically changed its policy when President Reagan announced the extension of the United States territorial sea to twelve miles by Presidential Proclamation No. 5928. 3 C.F.R. 547 (1988). The proclamation explains that it applies only to the United States' position internationally and does nothing to alter domestic law. And Congress has amended very little domestic legislation to reflect this international claim. The extension of the United States territorial sea from three miles to twelve miles has reopened the issue of what should be the extent of state waters. For a complete discussion of the issues surrounding the twelve-mile territorial sea extension, see 1–2 Territorial Sea Journal (1990–92).

B.   OIL AND GAS DEVELOPMENT ON THE OUTER CONTINENTAL SHELF

In 1953, the year in which the Submerged Lands Act was enacted, Congress also passed the Outer Continental Shelf Lands Act (OCSLA), 43 U.S.C.A. §§ 1331–1356. The OCSLA codified the Truman Proclamation of 1945, an executive order that asserted U.S. sovereignty over the resources within and on the submerged land that constitute the "natural prolongation" of the country under the adjacent seas. The OCSLA reaffirmed the United States' sovereignty and exclusive jurisdiction over its continental shelf resources and created authority for the Department of the Interior (DOI) to encourage discovery and development of oil through a leasing program. The Act defines the outer continental shelf (OCS) as the submerged lands seaward of state boundaries and which "appertain to the United States and are subject to its jurisdiction and control." Id. § 1331(a).

The OCSLA, as enacted in 1953, authorized the DOI to lease OCS lands to the highest bidder for mineral production. The Secretary of the Interior could adopt rules for conservation of natural resources that would be incorporated into leases. Imposing new rules on leases after their issuance on conservation and environmental grounds, however, subjected DOI to suits claiming a taking of private property and impairment or breach of contract. See, e.g., *Union Oil Co. of Cal. v. Morton*, 512 F.2d 743 (9th Cir. 1975); *Sun Oil Co. v. United States Marathon Oil Co. v. United States*, 215 Ct.Cl. 716, 572 F.2d 786 (1978). But see *Marathon Oil Co. v. United States*, 158 F.3d 1253 (Fed.Cir. 1998) (holding that delays due to a state Coastal Zone Management Act consistency objection to exploration under an OCS lease were not compensable), *reversed on other grounds, Mobil Oil Exploration v. United States*, 530 U.S. 604, 120 S.Ct. 2423, 147 L.Ed.2d 528 (2000). The disastrous Santa Barbara blowout and oil spill led to widespread recognition that the limited provisions in the OCSLA for emergency suspensions and the authority for the DOI to impose conditions only at the leasing stage were totally inadequate for protection of the environment.

The 1978 OCSLA amendments represented the first "overhaul" of the Act in twenty-five years. The oil and gas leasing program was substantially changed by provisions that made leases subject to subsequently enacted OCSLA regulations. The amendments also established criteria for suspension and cancellation of leases, incorporated environmental safeguards, and created a role for coastal states in OCS planning and development.

During President Reagan's administration, Secretary of Interior James Watt introduced areawide leasing, fundamentally changing the leasing process. Areawide leasing opened up entire OCS planning areas, millions of acres of continental shelf, in lease sales. The approach was intended to accelerate lease sales, and affected competition among bidders and the amount of bids and revenue to the U.S. It also made assessment of impacts of a lease sale difficult, increasing controversy between the federal government and the states.

Starting in 1982, Congress began regularly introducing limitations on leasing in certain areas of the OCS by restricting funding in DOI's appropriations bills. These Congressional moratoria continued for 27 years. In addition, presidential leasing withdrawals under OCSLA section 12(a), 43 U.S.C.A. § 1341(a), limited new leasing to the central and western Gulf of Mexico and the OCS off Alaska. President Bush implemented a moratorium in 1990 on lease sales for a large portion of the continental U.S. from 1990–2000, which was extended to 2012 by President Clinton.

In 2006 Congress passed the Gulf of Mexico Energy Security Act (GOMESA) which required leasing in 8.3 million acres in the Gulf, including 5.8 million acres that were previously under Congressional moratoria. GOMESA also established a new moratorium on leasing activities in a redefined Eastern Gulf planning area within 125 miles of the Florida coast, as well as a portion of the Central Gulf planning area within 100 miles of coast line of Florida, until June 30, 2022. A moratorium also applies east of the Military Mission Line in the Gulf of Mexico in an area that has been traditionally used for military testing and training activities. The Act further provided for exchanges, allowing companies to exchange certain leases in moratorium areas for bonus and royalty credits to be used on other Gulf of Mexico leases.

In 2008, President George W. Bush issued an executive memorandum that rescinded the presidential moratorium on the OCS created by the 1990 order of President George H. W. Bush and renewed by President Clinton. The memorandum left only areas designated as marine sanctuaries subject to the leasing moratorium. On March 31, 2010, President Obama withdrew Bristol Bay, offshore Alaska, from leasing consideration through June 30, 2017. The result is that large areas of the U.S. continental shelf are potentially open for leasing. The Obama Administration has continued to support calls for more extensive OCS development, including parts of the Cook Inlet and the Chukchi and Beaufort Seas off Alaska—areas where native groups and environmentalists have challenged leases and drilling plans in court.

1. THE OCSLA LEASING AND DEVELOPMENT PROGRAM

The 1978 OCSLA amendments created a process for OCS development that now comprises five phases: (1) a five-year lease program; (2) the lease sale; (3) exploration; (4) development and production; and (5) decommissioning with removal of structures. The program is administered by the Bureau of Ocean Energy Management (BOEM), formerly the Marine Minerals Service (MMS), within the Department of the Interior (DOI).

a. The Five-Year Lease Program

The Secretary of the Interior is charged by the OCSLA with preparation of an oil and gas leasing program which consists of five-year schedules of proposed lease sales indicating, as precisely as possible, size, timing, and location of such activities. 43 U.S.C.A. § 1344(a). To facilitate preparation of the program, the OCS has been divided into planning areas.

The 1978 amendments enumerated the considerations that must be taken into account in development of the lease program. In summary, these include: (1) the existing information for assessment, predictive, and environmental purposes concerning the geographical, geological, and ecological characteristics of such regions; (2) distribution of development benefits and environmental risks among regions; (3) the interest of potential oil and gas producers; (4) the relative environmental sensitivity and marine productivity of different areas and the potential for conflict with other ocean, seabed, and resource uses; and (5) laws and policies of affected states. Id. § 1344(a)(2)(A)–(H). The lease plan is intended to reflect, "to the maximum extent practicable . . . a proper balance between the potential for environmental damage, the potential for the discovery of oil and gas, and the potential for adverse impact on the coastal zone." Id. § 1344(a)(3). See *Center for Biological Diversity v. U.S. Dep't of Interior*, 563 F.3d 466 (D.C. Cir. 2009) (vacating the leasing program and remanding the program to the Secretary of Interior to conduct adequate analysis of statutory factors and obtain the "proper balance" required).

Governors of affected states are given several opportunities to review and comment on the proposed leasing program both before and after publication of the proposed program in the Federal Register. An "affected state" includes: (1) a state connected to an artificial island or structure; (2) a state that will receive OCS oil for processing or transshipment; (3) a state designated by the Secretary of Interior because of the probability of significant impact or damage to the coastal, marine, or human environment from OCS development; or (4) a state that the Secretary finds is subject to considerable risk from oil spills, blowouts, or other releases because of such factors as prevailing winds or currents. 43 U.S.C.A. § 1331(f). The Secretary must reply to the governors in writing, explaining his decision to grant or deny the governors' requested program modifications. The submission of the lease program to Congress and the President must include copies of all correspondence between the Secretary and the governors of affected states. 43 U.S.C.A. § 1344(c).

Development and adoption of a Five-Year Lease Program also involves extensive review and consultation with other agencies, the oil and gas industry, the public, and local governments. The procedural requirements of both the OCSLA and the National Environmental Policy Act (NEPA), 42 U.S.C.A. §§ 4321 370, must be met. See *Natural Resources Defense Council, Inc. v. Hodel*, 865 F.2d 288, 275 U.S.App.D.C. 69 (D.C.Cir. 1988) (remanding the program to the Secretary for failure-to meet NEPA requirements, i.e., failure to consider the cumulative impact on migratory marine mammals); but see *Center for Biological Diversity v. U.S. Dep't of Interior,* 563 F. 3d 466 (D.C. Cir. 2009) (Although the petitioners have standing to bring climate change claims, the NEPA-based claims are not ripe due to the multiple stage nature of the Leasing Program). NEPA provides states and the public an additional opportunity to participate in the OCS lease process by commenting on the draft and final EIS and through judicial review of the final EIS.

After publication of a proposed Five-Year Lease Program, states and local governments have an additional ninety days to make comments and recommendations. At least sixty days before approving the program, the Secretary must submit the program to Congress along with any comments and the Secretary's justification for rejecting the recommendations of a state or local government. 43

U.S.C.A. § 1344(d). The Secretary must review the leasing program yearly and may revise and reapprove it. A new program must be developed, however, every five years. Id. § 1344(e).

For sixty days after its approval by the Secretary, a five-year leasing program is subject to judicial review exclusively in the District of Columbia Court of Appeals through a suit by adversely affected or aggrieved persons who participated in the administrative proceedings related to the program. 43 U.S.C.A. § 1349(c)(1). But the reviewing court will accord the Secretary substantial deference. In *California v. Watt*, 668 F.2d 1290, 215 U.S.App.D.C. 258 (D.C.Cir. 1981), the court set out the standard of review for a five-year leasing program. In summary, the record must establish that: (1) the Secretary's factual findings are based on substantial evidence; (2) policy judgments are based on rational consideration of identified relevant factors; and (3) the Secretary's interpretation of the statute is a permissible construction. See also *Natural Resources Defense Council v. Hodel*, 865 F.2d 288, 275 U.S.App.D.C. 69 (D.C.Cir. 1988).

In *California v. Watt,* the D.C. Circuit Court of Appeals concluded that the Five-Year Lease Program approved in 1980 was deficient in specificity of areas and timing and in consideration of the OCSLA-mandated factors, including failure to quantify environmental costs and properly balance potential for environmental damage and adverse coastal impacts with potential for oil discovery. The court remanded the leasing program for reconsideration.

Subsequently, the lease program for 1982–1987 opened virtually all the OCS, almost one billion acres, for leasing. Environmental groups challenged the program on the same grounds as the previous program and also on the grounds that it violated the court's 1981 decree. This time, however, the court rejected the arguments and upheld the entire lease plan. *California v. Watt*, 712 F.2d 584, 229 U.S.App.D.C. 270 (D.C.Cir. 1983).

Similarly, the five-year lease program for 2007–2012 was vacated for violations of the OCSLA and NEPA. In January 2007, President George W. Bush lifted the Presidential moratorium for Alaska's Bristol Bay and extensively expanded areas for leasing in the Beaufort, Bering and Chukchi Seas. The final program included a lease sale in Bristol Bay scheduled for 2011. See *Center for Biological Diversity v. U.S. Dep't of the Interior* (D.C.C. 2009). The U.S. Court of Appeals for the District of Columbia Circuit remanded the 2007–2012 Program, requiring the Secretary to consider the comparative environmental sensitivity and marine productivity of areas of the OCS and to reassess the timing and location of the leasing program to properly apply the balancing requirements of 43 U.S.C.A. § 1344(a)(2)(A)–(H). The court upheld, however, the program's limiting its analysis of the program's effects to "production activities on climate change generally, and the present and future impact of climate change on the local OCS areas," rejecting an argument that DOI should consider the broader climate change effects of consumption of the oil produced on the world. Id.

The revised 2007–2012 program, announced in March 2010, includes 16 lease sales—some of which have been cancelled—in six areas. BOEMRE, *Revised Program Outer Continental Shelf Oil and Gas Leasing Program 2007–2012* (Dec. 2010). In conjunction with the revised program, President Obama reinstated protection for Bristol Bay through June 2017 and cancelled the lease sale that had been scheduled for 2011.

b. The Lease Sale

Before DOI may initiate a lease sale, environmental studies of the lease area must be conducted in cooperation with affected states. 43 U.S.C.A. § 1346. Data is used to predict, assess, and manage the possible effects of OCS development on human, marine, and coastal environments. The Secretary is to consider relevant environmental information in developing regulations, in issuing operating orders, and in making decisions relating to exploration, drilling, and development and production plans. The OCSLA also directs the Secretary to carry out post-development environmental studies to monitor changes resulting from OCS activities. Courts have required an additional EIS for individual lease sales. See, e.g., *Conservation Law Found. v. Andrus*, 623 F.2d 712 (1st Cir. 1979); *Natural Resources Defense Council, Inc. v. Morton*, 458 F.2d 827, 148 U.S.App.D.C. 5 (D.C.Cir. 1972).

The Secretary must provide notice and copies of documents for proposed lease sales to the governors of affected states. Governors of affected states and executives of local governments may submit recommendations to the Secretary on the size, timing, and location of proposed lease sales. 43 U.S.C.A. § 1345. The Secretary must accept the timely recommendations of a governor on lease sales if he determines that the recommendations provide for "a reasonable balance between the national interest and the well-being of the citizens of the affected [s]tate." See *Massachusetts v. Clark*, 594 F.Supp. 1373 (D.Mass. 1984); *Conservation Law Found. v. Watt*, 560 F.Supp. 561 (D.Mass. 1983). The Secretary has, however, rejected the recommendations of governors of coastal states on several occasions. The deferential standard that courts have applied in reviewing the Secretary's rejection of such recommendations effectively eviscerates the section's obligatory language, i.e., "shall accept recommendations of the Governor." See *California v. Watt*, 520 F.Supp. 1359 (C.D.Cal. 1981) (finding that although the Secretary violated the spirit of the OCSLA by rejecting the governor's recommendations, giving due deference to the Secretary's judgment, the determination was not arbitrary and capricious); *Tribal Village of Akutan v. Hodel*, 869 F.2d 1185 (9th Cir. 1988) (holding that the Secretary's rejection of the governor's recommendations was not arbitrary and capricious). The Secretary must respond to a governor, in writing, concerning his reasons for accepting or rejecting the recommendations. 43 U.S.C.A. § 1345.

OCS leases are granted to the highest responsible, qualified bidder through a competitive bidding process. The bidding is done by sealed bids based upon a notice of sale published in the Federal Register. The lease term is for a five-to ten-year period depending on the depth of the water. Id. § 1337. Prior to the 1978 OCSLA amendments, courts had described the nature of an OCS lease as not conveying title, but conveying a property interest enforceable against the government. See, e.g., *Union Oil Co. of Cal. v. Morton*, 512 F.2d 743 (9th Cir. 1975). However, in *Secretary of the Interior v. California*, 464 U.S. 312, 104 S.Ct. 656, 78 L.Ed.2d 496 (1984), the U.S. Supreme Court noted that, since 1978, "the purchase of a lease entitles the purchaser only to priority over other interested parties in submitting for federal approval a plan for exploration, production, or development." This interpretation leaves unclear what, if any, property interest a lessee receives. More recently, the Supreme Court described the interest as a "renewable lease contract." In *Mobil Oil Exploration & Producing Southeast, Inc. v. United States*, 530 U.S. 604 (2000), the Court held that Mobil was entitled to restitution for breach of the "contract" by Congress' enactment of new legislation (the Outer Banks Protection Act) that prevented Mobil from proceeding to the exploration stage of the lease.

Note, however, that both "lease contracts" and the OCSLA now provide that an OCS lease is issued subject to the OCSLA and not only all OCSLA regulations in force at the time of the lease, but also all regulations issued pursuant to the statute in the future which provide for the prevention of waste and conservation of the natural resources of the OCS and the protection of correlative rights therein (and certain other statutes, such as the CZMA). See 43 U.S.C. § 1334. In *Century Exploration New Orleans, LLC v. U.S.*, 745 F.3d 1168, 44 ELR 20060, 78 ERC (BNA) 1482 (Fed. Cir. 2014), the Federal Circuit Court of Appeals held that stringent new operating regulations issued following the Deepwater Horizon oil spill did not breach the lease agreements. The court found that the regulations were issued under authority of the OCSLA (not the Oil Pollution Act) and that the "government has not breached its implied duty of good faith and fair dealing because the lease expressly authorized the government action at issue . . . , changes to OCSLA regulatory requirements." Id.

DOI has the express power to temporarily suspend or cancel leases if the lessee fails to comply with the terms of the lease, or "if there is a threat of serious, irreparable, or immediate harm or damage to life (including fish and other aquatic life) . . . or to the marine, coastal, or human environment." 43 U.S.C.A. § 1334(1). A lease may be canceled only after suspension for a continuous period of five years and a hearing in which the Secretary determines that continuation would cause serious harm to the marine, coastal, or human environment and that the threat of harm will not be abated in a reasonable period. If a lease is canceled, the lessee is entitled to compensation based on the fair value of the canceled rights or the expenses incurred by the lessee, whichever is less. Moreover, a lease may be forfeited and canceled for failure to comply with the OCSLA, its regulations, or the lease conditions. Id.

Leases may also be suspended at the request of a lessee. Lease suspensions are routinely granted (and extended) when "in the national interest, to facilitate proper development of a lease or to allow for the construction or negotiation for use of transportation facilities." 43 U.S.C. § 1334(a). But see *Aera Energy LLC v. Salazar*, 642 F.3d 212 (2011), *cert. denied*, 132 S. Ct. 252 (2011) (holding the agency may, on the merits, allow a lease to expire despite lessee's request for suspension).

In the 1990 amendments to the Coastal Zone Management Act (CZMA), Congress reacted to the U.S. Supreme Court's holding in *Secretary of the Interior v. California*, 464 U.S. 312, 104 S.Ct. 656, 78 L.Ed.2d 496 (1984), which found that lease sales are not subject to the federal consistency provisions of the Act. Although the amendments to the CZMA did not address lease sales specifically, it is clear that such sales are now among the category of federal activities that must be consistent with state coastal management programs to the maximum extent practicable if the activity affects the coastal zone. Lease suspensions also cannot be categorically excluded from consistency review. See *California v. Norton*, 311 F.3d 1162 (9th Cir. 2002). DOI delays in approving lessee exploration plans due to consistency review of suspended leases issued prior to the 1990 amendments, however, have been held to be a repudiation of the leases in *Amber Resources Co. v. United States*, 538 F.3d 1358 (Fed. Cir. 2008) (holding that the government had effectively "repudiated the lease agreements by putting into practice new [court-mandated] rules applicable to the availability of requested suspensions").

Judicial challenges to lease sales are generally based on NEPA, the Endangered Species Act, 16 U.S.C.A. §§ 1531–1544, or the environmental provisions of the OCSLA itself. Challenges based on NEPA usually focus on the adequacy of the EIS, either in the scope of the alternatives considered or in the analysis of the environmental impact. *Natural Resources Defense Council, Inc. v. Morton*, 458 F.2d 827, 148 U.S.App.D.C. 5 (D.C.Cir. 1972) is the leading case on the scope of alternatives the DOI must consider in the EIS. NRDC sought to enjoin a Gulf of Mexico lease sale because the EIS had failed to consider a number of conservation alternatives to the energy problem. The D.C. Circuit Court of Appeals rejected the DOI's argument that it was required to consider only alternatives within its jurisdiction. The court applied a "rule of reason" in holding that the degree of consideration of an alternative depends upon its likelihood of being implemented.

In analyzing the adequacy of the consideration of environmental impacts at the lease sale stage, courts have focused on the fact that the OCS leasing process confers no development rights. As a general principle, the amount and specificity of information on environmental impacts will vary at each stage of the OCS development process. Because the environmental impacts are largely speculative at the lease sale stage, courts have asserted that the Secretary does not need to consider in detail potential impacts that can be addressed with more certainty at the exploration or development stage. See *Tribal Village of Akutan v. Hodel*, 869 F.2d 1185 (9th Cir. 1988); *Village of False Pass v. Clark*, 733 F.2d 605 (9th Cir. 1984); *California v. Watt*, 683 F.2d 1253 (9th Cir. 1982); *North Slope Borough v. Andrus*, 642 F.2d 589, 206 U.S.App.D.C. 184 (D.C.Cir. 1980). An EIS that omits speculative information at the lease sale stage is not the equivalent of an EIS that is "incomplete due to the omission of ascertainable facts, or the inclusion of erroneous information, violat[ing] the disclosure requirements of [NEPA]." See *Tribal Village of Akutan v. Hodel*, 869 F.2d 1185 (9th Cir. 1988); see also, *Native Village of Point Hope v. Salazar*, 730 F.Supp.2d 1009 (D.Ct. Alaska 2010) (remanding an EIS that acknowledged significant information gaps as inadequate, because it "failed to determine whether missing information identified by the agency was relevant or essential" and "failed to determine whether the cost of obtaining the missing in-formation was exorbitant, or the means of doing so unknown"). Likewise, challenges to lease sales based on the failure of the Secretary to incorporate sufficient environmental protections to meet OCSLA requirements have also been found insufficient to stop a lease sale, because opportunities to impose additional conditions exist at later stages. *Village of False Pass v. Clark*, 733 F.2d 605 (9th Cir. 1984).

Two provisions of the Endangered Species Act (ESA) are particularly relevant to the OCS oil leasing process. Section 7(a)(2) of the ESA, 16 U.S.C.A. § 1536(a)(2), requires federal agencies to "insure that any action authorized, funded, or carried out by such agency . . . is not likely to jeopardize the continued existence of any endangered species or threatened species or result in the destruction or adverse modification of habitat . . . determined by the Secretary . . . to be critical." Section 7(d), 16 U.S.C.A. § 1536(d), prohibits any agency or applicant from making "any irreversible or irretrievable commitment of resources with respect to the agency action which has the effect of foreclosing the formulation or implementation of any reasonable and prudent alternative measures." A lease sale is not considered an "irreversible or irretrievable commitment of resources" because the Secretary has the authority to halt any future potentially harmful activities. See, e.g., *Conservation Foundation v. Andrus*, 623 F.2d. 712, 715 (1st Cir. 1979); *North Slope Borough v. Andrus*, 642 F.2d 589, 612 (D.C. Cir. 1980).

When DOI proposes a lease sale that may affect an endangered species, the agency must consult with the U.S. Fish and Wildlife Service or the National Marine Fisheries Service (NMFS). The relevant service will issue a biological opinion concerning whether the proposed sale will jeopardize the endangered species or adversely modify its habitat. If a finding of jeopardy or adverse modification of habitat is made, the service will suggest "reasonable and prudent alternatives" the agency can implement. However, the agency is not required to adopt the alternatives. But see *Village of False Pass v. Watt*, 565 F.Supp. 1123 (D.Alaska 1983) (noting that if the Secretary deviates from the alternatives, "he does so subject to the risk that he has not satisfied the standard of section (7)(a)(2)"). A court may set aside an agency's determination to reject the service's proposed alternatives only if the decision was "arbitrary, capricious, an abuse of discretion, or otherwise not in accordance with the law" under the Administrative Procedure Act.

In *Tribal Village of Akutan v. Hodel*, 869 F.2d 1185 (9th Cir. 1988), and in *Village of False Pass v. Clark*, 733 F.2d 605 (9th Cir.1984), DOI had failed to adopt completely the reasonable and prudent alternatives proposed by NMFS to reduce the risk of oil spills that might harm endangered gray whales. In both cases, the Circuit Court of Appeals rejected the argument that DOI had violated section (7)(a) by not implementing all the alternatives at the lease sale stage. Again relying on the multistage nature of the OCS development process, the court found "no irreversible or irretrievable commitment of resources" at the time of the lease sale. See also *North Slope Borough v. Andrus*, 642 F.2d 589, 206 U.S.App.D.C. 184 (D.C.Cir. 1980); *Conservation Law Found. v. Andrus*, 623 F.2d 712 (1st Cir. 1979); cf., *Conservation Law Found. v. Watt*, 560 F.Supp. 561 (D. Mass. 1983) (enjoining a Georges Bank lease sale for violations of the ESA). The court's deferential standard of review and the "wait and see what happens" approach to ESA compliance disregards the impacts of preliminary activities on endangered species as well as the additional costs and conflicts associated with putting off such decisions to the final development stages. When OCS activities are acknowledged to have potential effects on endangered species, the ESA provides various mechanisms that allow projects to proceed nonetheless. E.g., 16 U.S.C. §§ 1536(b)(4) and (o) (Secretary may issue biological opinions or incidental take permits setting out certain conditions that will minimize impacts to endangered species).

Because oil and gas development on the OCS can cause direct user conflicts with fishermen, as well as the potential for destruction of fisheries resources by pollution, lease sales have also been challenged for the potential effects on fisheries resources. As a general proposition, a majority of states have taken the policy position that renewable resource development, such as fisheries, should be favored over nonrenewable resource development. States and environmentalists have also argued that the express language of the OCSLA requires that oil and gas development may only be conducted if there is no harm to fisheries. The OCSLA provides that the Act be "construed in such a manner that the character of the waters above the Outer Continental Shelf as high seas and the right to navigation and fishing therein shall not be affected." 43 U.S.C.A. § 1332(2). In *Massachusetts v. Andrus*, 594 F.2d 872 (1st Cir. 1979), the federal court of appeals rejected an interpretation of this section that imposed an absolute priority for fisheries over oil and gas development. Construing the Act as a whole and in conjunction with the Magnuson-Stevens Fishery Conservation and Management Act (MSA) and NEPA, the court found that the legislation was concerned with "balanced use of all resources of the area." The court did find, however, that the Secretary has "a duty to see that gas and oil exploration and drilling is conducted without unreasonable risk to the fisheries. His duty includes the obligation not to go forward with a lease sale in a particular area if it would create unreasonable risks in spite of all feasible safeguards." Id.

Conflict with the aboriginal rights of Native Alaskans to occupy and use the OCS may also prove to be a basis for challenging lease sales off Alaska coasts. "Aboriginal title or right is a right of exclusive use and occupancy held by Natives in lands and waters used by them and their ancestors prior to the assertion of sovereignty over such areas by the United States." *Village of Gambell v. Clark*, 746 F.2d 572 (9th Cir. 1984) (*Gambell I*). In 1983, the DOI began leasing over two million acres of the OCS lands off the west coast of Alaska. The tribal Villages of Gambell and Stebbins sought to enjoin the lease sale, claiming that oil leasing would adversely affect their aboriginal rights to hunt and fish on the OCS and that the Secretary had failed to comply with section 810 of the Alaska National Interest Lands Conservation Act (ANILCA), 16 U.S.C.A. § 3120, which requires federal agencies to consider the effect of the "use, occupancy, or disposition [of public lands] on subsistence uses and needs" in Alaska. The district court granted summary judgment in favor of the Secretary and the oil company intervenors, denying the injunction and allowing the lease sale to go forward. While the appeal was pending, the Secretary approved exploration plans for the leased areas. On appeal, the Ninth Circuit Court of Appeals in *Gambell I* found: (1) that aboriginal claims by Native Alaskans had been extinguished by the

Alaska Native Claims Settlement Act (ANCSA), 43 U.S.C.A. § 1603(b); and (2) that the Secretary was required to comply with ANILCA. The Secretary made a post-sale evaluation of the impacts of the leases and found that neither exploratory activities nor oil production would significantly restrict subsistence uses.

In 1985, the Villages again sought to enjoin exploratory drilling and a further lease sale. The district court found that the Secretary did not comply with ANILCA, but did not issue an injunction. On appeal, the Ninth Circuit found that the Villages had established a strong likelihood of success on the merits and stated: "Irreparable damage is presumed when an agency fails to evaluate thoroughly the environmental impact of a proposed action." The court found that an injunction was the "appropriate remedy for a violation of an environmental statute absent rare or unusual circumstances." *Village of Gambell v. Hodel*, 774 F.2d 1414 (9th Cir. 1985) (*Gambell II*). The U.S. Supreme Court granted certiorari and held that ANILCA applies only to activities in Alaska and not to activities on the OCS and that the injunction had been improperly issued. *Amoco Prod. Co. v. Village of Gambell*, 480 U.S. 531, 107 S.Ct. 1396, 94 L.Ed.2d 542 (1987). On remand, the Ninth Circuit found that if ANILCA applied only in Alaska, ANCSA similarly only extinguished aboriginal rights in Alaska. The court also held that "aboriginal rights may exist concurrently with a paramount federal interest" in the OCS. The case was remanded to the district court for a determination of whether aboriginal rights on the

OCS exist, whether oil and gas leasing and development interferes with such rights, and whether the OCSLA extinguishes aboriginal rights. *Village of Gambell v. Hodel*, 869 F.2d 1273 (9th Cir. 1989) (*Gambell III*).

By the time the case was before the federal district court again, the oil companies had completed exploration activities and relinquished the leases, and no further lease sales were scheduled. Upon appeal from the district court's summary judgment for the government without deciding any of the questions, the Ninth Circuit found the issue moot and that no basis for federal jurisdiction remained. *Village of Gambell v. Babbitt*, 999 F.2d 403 (9th Cir. 1993) (*Gambell IV*).

Subsequently, in *Native Village of Eyak v. Trawler Diane Marie, Inc.*, 154 F.3d 1090 (9th Cir. 1998) (*Eyak I*), the 9th Circuit held that the paramount rights of the United States in the OCS (the "paramountcy doctrine") barred aboriginal claims to *exclusive* rights to hunt and fish in the offshore area. See also *U.S. v. California*, 332 U.S. 19, 67 S.Ct. 1658, 91 L.Ed. 1889 (1947) and Chapter IV.A. supra. In *Eyak II*, the 9th Circuit attempted to address the apparent conflict in *Gambrell III* and *Eyak I* concerning the relation of aboriginal rights and the paramount rights of the national government in the OCS. Applying a test that required the Village to show not only "continuous use and occupancy," but also "an exclusive and unchallenged claim to the disputed areas," the court held that the Village had not provided sufficient evidence to establish aboriginal rights on the OCS. The court, therefore, had no need reach the issue of whether recognition of aboriginal rights creates a conflict with the federal paramountcy doctrine. *Native Village of Eyak v. Blank*, 688 F.3d 619 (9th Cir. 2012) *(Eyak II)*. The relationship between aboriginal rights of use of the OCS and the paramount rights of the federal government consequently remains unresolved.

c. Exploration Plans

Before embarking on exploration, the lessee must submit an exploration plan to DOI for approval. The plan must include a schedule of exploration activities, description of the equipment to be used, location of the well, and other information. An oil spill contingency plan and an environmental report must accompany the plan. Id. § 1340(c); 30 C.F.R. §§ 250.30–250.33. Each phase of an OCS development project is not a separate federal "action" for purposes of the Endangered Species Act, so additional consultation with NMFS or FWS is not required. See *North Slope Borough v. Andrus*, 642 F.2d 589, 206 U.S.App.D.C. 184 (D.C.Cir. 1980).

DOI may conduct an environmental assessment (EA) at this stage to determine whether it can make a Finding of No Significant Impact (FONSI) or if an EIS must be prepared. EAs are generally done for frontier areas, but for "mature areas" of the OCS, such as the Central and Western Gulf of Mexico, DOI had determined that EAs are generally not required. The agency had also adopted numerous "categorical exclusions"—categories of actions that do not normally, in the absence of extraordinary circumstances, result in individually or cumulatively significant environmental effects. DOI also applies a tiering process to prevent unnecessary duplication of effort by reviewers and to avoid repetitive discussions of issues that had been covered in previous studies. Basically, oil and gas exploration in the Western and Central Gulf of Mexico had become so routine by the time of the Deepwater Horizon oil spill that the NEPA process was no longer serving its purposes.

The Council on Environmental Quality (CEQ) in its *Report Regarding the Minerals Management Service's National Environmental Policy Act Policies, Practices, and Procedures as They Relate to Outer Continental Shelf Oil and Gas Exploration and Development* (August 16, 2010) detailed the failures of the NEPA process in that case and proposed comprehensive recommendations, most of which have been implemented for the 2012–2017 Five-Year Lease Program. Since 2010, CEQ has also issued a number of guidance documents intended to "modernize and reinvigorate" NEPA. See CEQ, *Steps to Modernize and Reinvigorate NEPA*, available at http://www.whitehouse.gov/administration/eop/ceq/initatives/nepa.

CEQ also criticized the OCSLA provision requiring DOI to approve, approve with modifications, or disapprove an exploration plan within 30 days once it is complete. 43 U.S.C. § 1340(c)(1). Whether Congress underestimated the potential impacts of exploration or simply intended to expedite OCS oil exploration, CEQ judged the time too short for proper evaluation of exploration plans and recommended elimination of the time limit. Id.

DOI cannot, however, issue a permit for exploration until the state has concurred, or is presumed to concur, with the consistency certification that must be submitted with the plan. 16 U.S.C.A. § 1456(c)(3)(B). A consistency certification asserts that the exploration plan is consistent with the state coastal management program. This process may involve an additional three to six months. (Concurrence by the state with the oil company's consistency determination is "conclusively presumed" if the state does not object within 6 months. 16 U.S.C. § 1456(c)(3)(A)–(B)).

d.   Development/Production Plans

Once a discovery has been made, a development/production plan must be submitted to DOI for approval before production activities can begin. The plan must include: a description of the activity; drilling facilities to be used; location and depth of wells; geological and geophysical data; environmental and safety standards; and a timetable for development and production. This plan must also be accompanied by an oil spill contingency plan and an environmental report. 43 U.S.C.A. § 1351(a), (c); 30 C.F.R. § 250.34.

There is only one provision in OCSLA mandating the preparation of an EIS, and it is directed at development and production plans in frontier areas. 43 U.S.C. § 351(e)(1) provides that:

[a]t least once the Secretary shall declare the approval of a development and production plan in any area or region . . . of the outer Continental Shelf, other than the Gulf of Mexico, to be a major Federal action.

Development plans are reviewed for environmental impacts to determine whether another EIS must be prepared. In mature areas, DOI generally finds it unnecessary to prepare an EA or an EIS because of the experience in that area. As in the case of exploration plans, however, the NEPA process has been substantially revised since the Deepwater Horizon oil spill to assure adequate review.

DOI must disapprove or require modification of a development plan if it is determined that the lessee has failed to demonstrate compliance with applicable laws, that the activities threaten national security or defense, or that the activities pose serious harm to life (including aquatic life), property, or to the marine, coastal, or human environment. Id. § 1351(h)(1). The plan also cannot be approved if it is inconsistent with the coastal management program of an affected state. Id. § 1351(d). If a plan is disapproved for failure to comply with statutory requirements of the OCSLA, including the consistency requirements of the CZMA, the lessee is entitled to no compensation. If a plan is disapproved for one of the other reasons specified in the section and an approvable, modified plan is not submitted within five years, the Secretary must cancel the lease and compensate the lessee. Id. § 1351(h)(2).

As in the case of a lease sale, the Secretary must provide notice and copies of documents for proposed exploration and development/production plans to the governors of affected states, who may submit recommendations to the Secretary with respect to a proposed development/production plan. Id. § 1345(c). The Secretary must accept a governor's recommendations if he determines that they provide for "a reasonable balance between the national interest and the well-being of the citizens of the affected [s]tate." Id.

e. Decommissioning

OCSLA regulations define decommissioning as: "(1) Ending oil, gas, or sulphur operations; and (2) Returning the lease or pipeline right-of-way to a condition that meets the requirements of regulations of MMS and other agencies that have jurisdiction over decommissioning activities." 30 C.F.R. § 250.1700. This definition applies to all forms of decommissioning covered by the regulations: permanently plugging wells, temporarily abandoned wells, removing platforms and other facilities, site clearance, and pipeline decommissioning. Id. at § 250.1703.

DOI regulations require that lessees "[p]romptly and permanently plug" their temporarily-abandoned oil wells if the government so orders, 30 C.F.R. § 250.1723, and they must in any event "permanently plug all wells on a lease within 1 year after the lease terminates." Id. § 250.1710. Generally, a lease is terminated when the last structure on the lease ceases production. A post-removal report is due within 30 days after removing a platform or other facility. After the decommissioning is complete, the agency must assess whether it has been undertaken properly.

In *Noble Energy, Inc. v. Salazar*, 671 F.3d 1241 (D.C. Cir. 2012), Noble Energy argued that it was not obligated to follow a DOI order to permanently plug and abandon oils well off the coast of California that had been temporarily plugged since 1985. Noble argued that because the government had been found to have repudiated their lease agreement, see *Amber Res. Co. v. United States,* 538 F.3d 1358 (Fed.Cir.2008), Noble was released from further compliance with statutory and regulatory obligations by the common law doctrine of discharge. Although DOI argued that the government's breach does not discharge Noble from compliance with independent statutory and regulatory requirements, the court hinged its analysis on the fact that the decommissioning regulations had never been interpreted to address whether they applied when the government breached its contract. The court remanded and required the agency "to interpret its regulations in the first instance and to determine whether they apply here. If they do, the government must explain why." The final disposition of this case affects numerous lessees and substantial amounts of money—in Noble's case, as much as $20 million.

2.   OCS REVENUE SHARING

Revenues from OCS leasing include bonuses, royalties, and rentals. During the period from 2007 through 2012, the federal government revenues ranged from $5.25 billion to over $18 billion per year from OCS oil and gas activities. The revenues are deposited primarily in the general treasury, but some money goes to the Land and Water Conservation Fund and the National Historic Preservation Fund to be distributed to the states for relevant projects.

In spite of the substantial environmental risks to states from OCS development and the costs states bear for onshore impacts of OCS activities, there is relatively little direct revenue sharing of OCS-generated funds with the coastal states. Unlike the policy for leasing activities on federally-owned lands within the inland areas of states, coastal states do not share directly in royalties, cannot impose severance taxes, and do not receive payments in lieu of taxes to mitigate the impact of federal OCS leasing activities. Congress has begun to address the OCS revenue sharing issue in an incremental fashion.

Section 8(g) of the OCSLA, 43 U.S.C.A. § 1337(g), originally provided for states to claim a "fair and equitable share" of revenues if a federal lease within three miles of a state's seaward boundary may tap a resource pool that underlies both federal and state lands. Apparently, however, these funds are not intended to be a general sharing of OCS revenues, but are instead compensation to the adjacent state for recovery of oil resources from lands under state waters. A 1984 case, *Texas v. Secretary of the Interior*,

580 F.Supp. 1197 (E.D.Tex. 1984), held that determination of a fair and equitable share included issues such as onshore impacts in addition to the issue of how much oil was drained from state lands. The court awarded the state fifty percent of the revenues. Congress amended section 8(g) in 1986 to provide for states to receive a twenty-seven percent share of revenues from such future leases, unless the Secretary and the governor of a state enter into an agreement for unitization or revenue sharing. The Energy Policy Act of 2005 further provides sharing of twenty-seven percent of revenue from renewable energy leases generated in the § 8(g) zone. See *Alabama v. U.S. Dept. of Interior*, 84 F.3d 410 (11th Cir. 1996); Richard G. Hildreth, *Federal-State Revenue Sharing and Resource Management Under Outer Continental Shelf Lands Act Section 8(g)*, 17 Coastal Mgmt. 171 (1989).

The Energy Policy Act of 2005 also created the Coastal Impact Assistance Program (CIAP) which allocated a portion of $250 million allocated annually in 2007–2010 to Alabama, Alaska, California, Louisiana, Mississippi, and Texas: the OCS oil-producing states. To qualify, the states had to develop approved CIAP plans and could use the funds for coastal conservation, restoration, mitigation, and public infrastructure.

When Congress enacted the 2006 Gulf of Mexico Energy Security Act (GOMESA), lifting the Congressional-leasing moratorium on 8.3 million acres of OCS and mandating sales in two areas of the Central and Eastern Gulf of Mexico planning areas, it also offered a new incentive for coastal state cooperation in OCS development in the Gulf of Mexico. The Act gives the Gulf oil-producing states— Texas, Louisiana, Alabama, and Mississippi—37.5% of the revenues from that newly opened territory. Starting in 2017, that same percent applies to all new production in the Gulf.

Neither the CIAP nor the GOMESA funds come with "no strings attached." Both programs require the funds to be spent on specified programs. GOMESA funds, for example, may only be used for:

—Projects and activities for the purposes of coastal protection, including conservation, coastal restoration, hurricane protections, and infrastructure directly affected by coastal wetland losses;

—Mitigation of damage to fish, wildlife, or natural resources;

—Implementation of a federally approved marine, coastal, or comprehensive conservation management plan;

—Mitigation of impacts of OCS activities through funding of onshore infrastructure projects; and

—Planning assistance and the administrative costs that do not to exceed 3%.

Arguably, these restrictions make the revenue-sharing less valuable to the states concerned. On the other hand, it can be argued that the program provides a dedicated source of funding directed at projects closely related to adaption to climate change and sea level rise, areas of great importance to coastal states. Legislation continues to be introduced to expand revenue sharing programs, but have been opposed by the administration. See, e.g., Nick Snow, *Administration opposes bill to share OCS revenue with coastal states*, Oil & Gas Journal (07/24/2013).

3.   OFFSHORE RENEWABLE ENERGY

Offshore renewable energy (ORE) projects using energy produced by waves, currents or thermal differences are being explored, but tax incentives and technological advances have led to offshore wind turbines or windfarms now being the focus of most ORE proposals—and sometimes controversy. The more than 10-year saga of Cape Wind Associates, the first offshore wind project to receive a permit for project construction, demonstrated the inefficiencies created by the gaps and overlaps in authority to regulate offshore wind siting and development.

Prior to 2005, the OCSLA had no specific language authorizing DOI to permit offshore windfarms on the OCS. The Army Corps of Engineers (Corps) assumed jurisdiction under § 10 of the Rivers and Harbors Act (RHA), 3 U.S.C. § 403, which gives the Corps authority to permit obstructions to navigation in the "navigable waters of the United States" and on the OCS. The Corps' permitting involved no planning or siting process or authority to convey to wind companies the right to occupy and use an area the OCS exclusively. The Energy Policy Act of 2005, § 388 (EPAct; P.L. 109–58) amended the OCSLA to provide for federal review and permitting of offshore energy projects. The Secretary of the Interior, in consultation with other federal agencies, is authorized to grant leases, easements, or rights-of-way on the OCS for wind energy and other development not authorized by other applicable law. The Corps retained jurisdiction under the Rivers and Harbors Act in regard to obstructions to navigation. An April 2009 MOU between the DOI and the Federal Energy Regulatory Commission (FERC) recognized exclusive jurisdiction of DOI over "the production, transportation, or transmission of energy from non-hydrokinetic renewable energy projects on the OCS."

The EPAct requires the Secretary of DOI:

- to issue leases, easements, and rights-of-way on a competitive basis (with some limited exceptions);
- to provide for suspension and cancellation of any lease, easement, or right-of-way;
- to create a system of "royalties, fees, rentals, bonuses, or other payments" that will ensure a fair return to the United States:
- to ensure that activities under the EPAct amendments are carried out in a manner that adequately addresses environmental protection, safety, protection of U.S. national security, and protection of the rights of others to use the OCS and its resources and prevent interference with reasonable uses of the seas;

- to take into consideration other uses of the sea or seabed, including use for a fishery, a sea lane, a potential site of a deepwater port, or navigation;

- to "provide for the restoration of the lease, easement, or right-of-way," including financial assurances; and

- to impose "such other requirements as the Secretary considers necessary to protect the interests of the public and the United States."

43 U.S.C. § 1337(p).

In addition to requiring DOI to carry out these activities in consultation with other federal agencies, the EPAct provides for coordination and consultation with the governor of any state or the executive of any local government that may be affected by a lease, easement, or right-of-way. In addition, for projects that are located wholly or partially within 3 miles of state waters, states will receive 27% of the revenues generated. States within 15 miles of the geographical center of the project will receive an "equitable distribution" of the 27%, based on proximity to the project.

The renewable offshore energy program is administered by Bureau of Ocean Energy Management, Regulation, and Enforcement (BOEM), within DOI, through regulations adopted in 2009 by its predecessor agency, the Marine Minerals Service (MMS). In addition, in 2010, the DOI Secretary Salazar announced the "Smart from the Start" program to expedite Atlantic coast wind energy projects. In addition to identifying Wind Energy Areas for leasing and development, the Secretary sought to make the permitting process more efficient. In addition to the Cape Wind Project, BOEM has also issued a noncompetitive lease to Bluewater Wind Delaware and held lease sales off Rhode Island/Massachusetts and Virginia in 2013.

C.   MARINE MINERALS MINING

1.   OCS HARD MINERAL MINING

United States jurisdiction over hard mineral resources of the outer continental shelf was also claimed in the 1945 Truman Proclamation and codified in the OCSLA. The majority of offshore minerals mining has occurred near Alaska for sand and gravel. In addition to sand and gravel, however, DOI believes there is the economic potential to mine other OCS mineral reserves, including heavy mineral placers (gold, chromium, platinum, tin, and titanium), phosphorite crusts and nodules, and phosphate. Technology and discoveries during the last three decades have also instigated interest in the mining of manganese nodules and polymetallic sulfides.

Increased attention to minerals mining of the OCS during the 1980s brought an increased awareness of the lack of comprehensive legislation or policy in the area. The OCSLA includes comprehensive authority for leasing and development of OCS lands for oil, gas, and sulfur exploitation. But only one sentence in the entire Act, section 8(k), mentions the leasing of "any mineral other than oil, gas, and sulphur." 43 U.S.C.A. § 1337(k). The extensive statutory framework that is in place for OCS oil and gas development does not exist for hard minerals mining. The 1978 amendments to the OCSLA that provide for environmental protections, state participation in the leasing process, and state coastal plan consistency are specifically applicable only to oil and gas leases.

During the 1980s, the federal government began to encourage development of offshore minerals as part of the National Minerals and Materials Program Plan. The government's position was that the lack of comprehensive regulations for prospecting, leasing, and recovering of marine minerals had inhibited development of a domestic marine mining industry. In 1988, MMS published rules on prelease prospecting of minerals other than oil, gas, and sulphur, 30 C.F.R. §§ 280.0–280.17, and in 1989, MMS issued rules for general leasing, 30 C.F.R. §§ 281.0–281.47, and for mining operations on the OCS, 30 C.F.R. §§ 282.0–282.50.

Both commercial prospectors and certain scientific researchers are required to have a permit and an approved plan before conducting OCS prospecting activities. Lease sales may be initiated by the Secretary or by unsolicited requests for a lease sale. The rules generally provide for a competitive bidding system for leases. Section 8(k) was amended in 1994 and 1999 to eliminate the requirement of competitive lease sales when OCS sand and gravel resources are needed for public works projects such as beach and coastal wetlands restoration.

General environmental assessment and protection provisions are included at all three stages of the mineral development process. The regulations are most controversial in regard to coordination with affected or adjacent states. The regulations clearly intended that intergovernmental coordination and consultation would be carried out through six regional federal/state task forces, rather than through provisions comparable to the requirements for oil and gas development. See 30 C.F.R. § 281.13.

The governors of adjacent states will receive copies of permit applications and plans for prospecting upon submission, but states will not have the authority to comment upon the activities unless the MMS determines to prepare an environmental assessment. Id. § 280.11. At the lease sale and mining stages, governors will receive notice and documents and will have the opportunity to have their comments "considered." The federal consistency provisions of the CZMA are not addressed in the rules. This is likely because MMS was taking the position in its leasing regulations, issued prior to the 1990 CZMA amendments, that "coastal zone consistency concurrence is not required prior to a lease sale of OCS minerals"—a currently unsupportable position. 54 Fed. Reg. 2042, 2046 (1989).

The most fundamental objection to the OCS hard mineral mining regime is that the MMS, now BOEM, lacks authority to promulgate the regulations under the OCSLA. Commentators have pointed out that the

1953 OCSLA and its amendments have dealt virtually exclusively with oil and gas development, and that one sentence in an act is inadequate to provide a statutory basis for a comprehensive regulatory program. One proposal is that hard mineral development should be addressed in comprehensive legislation for the U.S. Exclusive Economic Zone.

BOEM's Marine Minerals Program now focuses primarily on sand and gravel as the major "non-energy minerals" managed under the OCSLA. BOEM's role is characterized as a "steward" of these resources with responsibility to assure that removal for coastal restoration projects, including beach and wetlands restoration, is carried out in an environmentally sound manner, minimizing impacts on the marine and coastal environments.

2. DEEP SEABED HARD MINERAL RESOURCES

The 1982 United Nations Convention on the Law of the Sea (UNCLOS) creates a comprehensive international regime for the exploitation of the mineral resources of the deep seabed beyond coastal state jurisdiction. See Chapter VI.F. Based on the concept that the resources of the seabed are the common heritage of mankind, the principles proposed for governing the area met with strong opposition from the United States and from other developed countries.

The Deep Seabed Hard Mineral Resources Act (DSHMRA), 30 U.S.C.A. §§ 1401–1473, was enacted by the United States in 1980, prior to the conclusion of the UNCLOS negotiations. The Act set up a licensing scheme for mining of the seabed of the high seas beyond United States' jurisdiction. The licensing program was intended both as a spur to the UNCLOS negotiations and to provide an interim regime for seabed activities pending the Convention's coming into force that would provide a stable environment for U.S. investors. Other developed countries enacted similar legislation and entered into international agreements to deal with recognition of other countries' claims and to create mechanisms for conflict resolution.

The DSHMRA's "reciprocating states" provision allows the Administrator of NOAA to designate other nations as reciprocating states so their license and permit programs can be coordinated to respect each other's claims and to avoid conflicts. By 1983, France, Italy, Japan, the United Kingdom, and West Germany had enacted domestic seabed mining legislation and were designated by NOAA as reciprocating states The U.S. has subsequently negotiated agreements with Belgium, China, France, Germany, Japan, Russia, and the United Kingdom. The problem is that all of these cooperative agreements were concluded before the LOS Convention came into force and were, generally, intended to be interim arrangements. It is not clear whether these arrangements are all now considered viable.

The DSHMRA requires U.S. citizens and vessels to obtain a license from the Administrator of the

National Oceanic and Atmospheric Administration (NOAA) to explore for nodules. Ten year exploration licenses are issued on a first-come, first-served basis for a specifically identified area. The license holder has a priority to receive a permit allowing commercial recovery. The permit gives the holder the exclusive right to explore or mine a specific area, but only as against other U.S. citizens. NOAA regulations recognize seabed mining as a freedom of the high seas, and issuance of licenses should "not unreasonably interfere with the exercise of the freedoms of the high seas by other nations, as recognized under general principles of international law." 15 C.F.R. § 970.503.

Prior to issuing an exploration license or recovery permit, the NOAA Administrator must make a number of specific findings concerning the exploration or recovery plan: (1) the activity will not interfere with the exercise of high seas freedoms by other nations or conflict with other international obligations of the United States; (2) the activity will not lead to a breach of international peace; (3) the activity will not adversely affect the environment; and (4) the activity will not endanger life at sea. Id. § 1415(a).

Several provisions of the act address environmental concerns. The DSHMRA extends Clean Water Act (CWA) jurisdiction to any discharge of a pollutant from vessels and other floating craft engaged in exploration or commercial recovery, extending jurisdiction to vessels even when on the high seas. NOAA must prepare programmatic environmental impact statements in certain circumstances and is required to prepare a site-specific EIS for each license or permit. If a license or permit may adversely affect a fishery resource, NOAA must consult with the relevant regional fisheries management council.

Because the Act requires any shore-based processing of minerals to take place in the U.S., deep seabed mining may have some effects on U.S. coastal areas. There is no provision, however, for approval by or consultation with coastal states prior to license or permit issuance. The commercial recovery regulations fill the gap by providing extensive state consultation provisions even though the act itself does not require them.

The act has been reauthorized several times without significant change. Commercial recovery, however, remains a distant prospect.

D.   HISTORIC PRESERVATION AND MARINE SALVAGE

1.   BACKGROUND

Both the federal government and the coastal states view ancient shipwrecks off the coasts of the United States as having significance beyond the monetary value of the recoverable cargo. The historic importance of such shipwrecks is illustrated by the designation of the site of the wreck of the *U.S.S. Monitor* as the country's first national marine sanctuary. Marine archaeologists portray private salvage of historic wrecks as the equivalent of "looting" an archaeological, historic, or culturally significant site. Private salvors do not perceive themselves as looters and point out that without their investment of resources and capital, historic wrecks would never be located.

New technologies and improved research techniques have led to the discovery of an increasing number of vessels in recent years, and conflicts concerning ownership and jurisdiction over these vessels have led to complex court cases. During the last several decades, numerous shipwreck cases have addressed the appropriateness of the application of the maritime law of salvage or finds as well as issues of jurisdiction, preemption, ownership, and eleventh amendment immunity of states from suit. The courts have not been entirely consistent in their conclusions, and although a few principles have emerged, a myriad of issues are still unresolved.

In order for the United States to assert ownership or control of shipwrecks, the federal government must make an express claim. After adjudication of the boundary between state and federal submerged lands in *United States v. Florida*, 420 U.S. 531, 95 S.Ct. 1162, 43 L.Ed.2d 375 (1975) established that the wreck of the *Atocha* was located on the federal continental shelf rather than on state lands, the United States asserted title to the wreck and the recovered artifacts. The Fifth Circuit Court of Appeals held that it may be within the power of the federal government to exercise its "sovereign prerogative" to claim abandoned property found at sea, but the United States had never enacted legislation to assert such a claim. See *Treasure Salvors, Inc. v. Unidentified Wrecked and Abandoned Sailing Vessel*, 569 F.2d 330 (5th Cir. 1978). Specifically, the court found that the United States cannot claim ownership of wrecks on the continental shelf based on the Abandoned Property Act, 40 U.S.C.A. § 310, or on the Antiquities Act, 16 U.S.C.A. §§ 431–433, because the wreck was located beyond the jurisdiction of the Acts. The United States also could not base a claim on the Truman Proclamation or the Outer Continental Shelf Lands Act, because they were not intended to extend "control over non-resource-related material in the shelf area," such as shipwrecks. The federal government does, however, under the Antiquities Act, 16 U.S.C.A. §§ 431–433, protect shipwreck sites on lands owned or controlled by the federal government, including national parks and national marine sanctuaries. See also *Klein v. Unidentified Wrecked and Abandoned Sailing Vessel*, 758 F.2d 1511 (11th Cir. 1985) (holding that the United States was in constructive possession of a shipwreck embedded in the soil in Biscayne Bay National Park).

Historically, the most fundamental conflict in cases of shipwrecks found within state boundaries concerns whether federal admiralty law preempts state salvage or archaeological recovery laws. Although a majority of states have enacted legislation asserting ownership or the authority to regulate and manage historic shipwrecks, courts have failed to settle the question of whether such statutes are enforceable. See *Zych v. Unidentified, Wrecked and Abandoned Vessel, Believed to be the*

Seabird, 941 F.2d 525 (7th Cir. 1991). A number of federal courts have held that cases involving shipwrecks are within the federal courts' exclusive admiralty jurisdiction. See *Martha's Vineyard Scuba Headquarters, Inc. v. Unidentified, Wrecked and Abandoned Steam Vessel,* 833 F.2d 1059 (1st Cir. 1987); *Platoro Ltd. v. Unidentified Remains of a Vessel,* 614 F.2d 1051 (5th Cir. 1980); *Treasure Salvors, Inc. v. Unidentified Wrecked and Abandoned Sailing Vessel,* 569 F.2d 330 (5th Cir. 1978). Other courts have specifically found that state regulation of such shipwrecks is inconsistent with federal maritime principles and is preempted by federal admiralty law. See, e.g., *Cobb Coin Co. v. Unidentified, Wrecked and Abandoned Sailing Vessel (Cobb Coin I),* 525 F.Supp. 186 (S.D.Fla. 1981). However, some federal courts, even within the same circuit as courts asserting exclusive admiralty jurisdiction, have upheld the exercise of state authority over wrecks. See *Jupiter Wreck, Inc. v. Unidentified, Wrecked and Abandoned Sailing Vessel,* 691 F.Supp. 1377 (S.D.Fla. 1988); *Subaqueous Exploration & Archaeology, Ltd. v. Unidentified, Wrecked and Abandoned Vessel,* 577 F.Supp. 597 (D.Md. 1983).

Even in the application of federal maritime and admiralty law, questions persist concerning whether the law of salvage or the law of finds applies to such shipwrecks. Under the law of salvage, the original owner retains title to goods saved from peril by a salvor. However, the salvor who meets certain requirements is entitled to a reward for rescuing the goods from marine peril. The admiralty court sits as a court of equity in determining the salvage award. The U.S. Supreme Court has identified six main factors to consider in determining a salvage award:

(1.) The labor expended by the salvors in rendering the salvage service. (2.) The promptitude, skill, and energy displayed in rendering the service and saving the property. (3.) The value of the property employed by the salvors in rendering the service, and the danger to which such property was exposed. (4.) The risk incurred by the salvors in securing the property from the impending peril. (5.) The value of the property saved. (6.) The degree of danger from which the property was rescued.

The Blackwall, 77 U.S. 1, 19 L.Ed. 870 (1869). The salvage award is intended not only to compensate the salvor, but also to reward "meritorious services" and serve as an inducement to others. When the property recovered is unique or has special intrinsic value, an award *in specie* is generally found to be more appropriate than a monetary salvage award. See generally *Columbus-America Discovery Group v. Atlantic Mut. Ins. Co.*, 974 F.2d 450 (4th Cir. 1992).

Common law principles do not specifically address the issue of preservation of historical and archaeological artifacts during salvage operations, but admiralty courts have begun to fashion rules. For example, the court in *Columbus-America Discovery Group v. Atlantic Mutual Insurance Co.*, 974 F.2d 450 (4th Cir. 1992) stated that the degree to which salvors worked to protect the historical and archaeological value of the wreck and items salved is relevant to the salvage award. In *MDM Salvage, Inc. v. Unidentified, Wrecked and Abandoned Sailing Vessel*, 631 F.Supp. 308 (S.D.Fla. 1986), the federal district court considered the work that the salvors had done to protect the historical and archaeological integrity of the wreck and the salvaged items inadequate to award the salvor exclusive salvage rights. When the exclusive salvage rights to the *Titanic* were challenged, the court held that the preservation of the archaeological integrity of the wreck site as well as the preservation of the retrieved artifacts was evidence that the operation had been undertaken with due diligence. *R.M.S. Titanic Inc. v. Joslyn,* 924 F.Supp. 714 (E.D.Va. 1996).

In *Chance v. Certain Artifacts Found & Salvaged from The Nashville*, 606 F.Supp. 801 (S.D.Ga. 1984), the federal district court refused any salvage award because the handling of the property by the salvors was increasing the likelihood of deterioration of the antiquities rather than "rescuing" them from marine peril. The federal court in *Cobb Coin Co. v. Unidentified, Wrecked and Abandoned Sailing Vessel (Cobb Coin II)*, 549 F.Supp. 540 (S.D.Fla. 1982) held "that in order to state a claim for a salvage award on an ancient vessel of historical and archaeological significance, it is an essential element that the salvor document to the Admiralty Court's satisfaction that it has preserved the archaeological provenance of a shipwreck." In other words, numerous courts have now found that evidence of preservation is not just a standard for determining the amount of or enhancing the salvage award, but a threshold requirement for determining the right to exclusive salvage rights or entitlement to any salvage award.

In the case of ancient shipwrecks, a number of courts have rejected the legal fiction of salvage law that the "owner intends to return" and the application of salvage law. See, e.g., *Treasure Salvors, Inc. v. Unidentified Wrecked and Abandoned Sailing Vessel*, 569 F.2d 330 (5th Cir. 1978) (holding that "[d]isposition of a wrecked vessel whose very location has been lost for centuries as though its owner were still in existence stretches a fiction to absurd lengths"). Under the law of finds, a finder who takes possession and exercises control over lost or abandoned property acquires title. Two exceptions to the law of finds are that the property is not considered legally lost if it is embedded in the soil or if the owner of the land has constructive possession of the property. See, e.g., *Klein v. Unidentified, Wrecked and Abandoned Sailing Vessel*, 758 F.2d 1511 (11th Cir. 1985) (holding that the United States had constructive possession of a ship embedded in the soil of Biscayne Bay National Park, and a "finder" was entitled to no salvage award); and *Chance v. Certain Artifacts Found & Salvaged from The Nashville*, 606 F.Supp. 801 (S.D.Ga. 1984) (holding the state of Georgia to be the owner of a Confederate raider embedded in the state-owned submerged lands of the Ogeechee River).

In *Columbus-America Discovery Group v. Atlantic Mutual Insurance Co.*, 974 F.2d 450 (4th Cir. 1992), the Fourth Circuit Court of Appeals determined that the law of salvage, rather than the law of finds, applied to the recovery of up to a billion dollars in gold from the 1857 wreck of the *S.S. Central America* on the high seas off the South Carolina coast. The Columbus-America Discovery Group, which located the vessel in 1988 and had been recovering the gold that the ship was transporting from California to New York, sought to be declared owner of the treasure. However, the insurance underwriters who had paid the claims for the disaster and who had been subrogated to the rights of the original owners of the gold also asserted ownership. The district court found Columbus-America to be the "finder" and owner of the gold. The appellate court reversed, summarizing the applicable law as follows:

> [W]hen sunken ships or their cargo are rescued . . . courts favor applying the law of salvage over the law of finds. Finds law should be applied . . . where the previous owners are found to have abandoned their property. Such abandonment must be proved by clear and convincing evidence. . . . Should the property encompass an ancient and longlost [sic] shipwreck, a court may infer an abandonment. Such an inference would be improper, though, should a previous owner appear and assert his ownership interest; in such a case the normal presumptions would apply and an abandonment would have to be proved by strong and convincing evidence.

Id. The failure of the insurers to continue recovery efforts did not constitute abandonment of "long lost property that was involuntarily taken from [their] control," and the law of salvage was found applicable. Id.

In *Columbus-America Discovery Group,* the court favored the law of salvage because it diminished the incentive for secretive behavior and encouraged open, cooperative conduct to protect property. Id. at 460–61. In the case of historic shipwrecks, applying salvage law also preserves the court's equitable jurisdiction to impose standards on salvors that will insure that ancient shipwreck sites are excavated using proper methods and that artifacts recovered in a manner that maintains their historic significance.

Exploration for shipwrecks and salvage operations can be destructive of more than just the historic value of the site and the artifacts that are discovered. Many shipwrecks have occurred on coral reefs and in productive, shallow water areas. A common exploration technique involves anchoring the boat and using the boat's prop-wash deflectors to direct the prop-wash into the ocean floor. The prop-wash creates craters in the seabed soil that expedite exploratory activities, but the technique also creates substantial turbidity in the water and destroys the habitat. Both state governments and the Army Corps of Engineers contend that this activity constitutes dredging and discharges that require permits. See, e.g., *Lathrop v. Unidentified, Wrecked and Abandoned Vessel*, 817 F.Supp. 953 (M.D.Fla. 1993) (holding that admiralty jurisdiction may be supplemented by necessary restrictions on salvage operations to ensure safety and to protect navigation and the environment). In the Florida Keys National

Marine Sanctuary, exploration and salvage operations have been strictly limited to protect the Sanctuary's primary resource, the coral reefs. *United States v. Fisher*, 22 F.3d 262 (11th Cir. 1994); *United States v. Fisher*, 977 F.Supp. 1193 (S.D.Fla. 1997).

2. THE ABANDONED SHIPWRECK ACT OF 1987

Congress attempted to alleviate some of the confusion concerning the ownership and authority to regulate certain shipwrecks through passage of the Abandoned Shipwreck Act (ASA) of 1987, 43 U.S.C.A. §§ 2101–2106. In order to protect shipwrecks of historic significance, the Act asserts the title of the federal government and then transfers to the state:

. . . any abandoned shipwreck that is:

(1) embedded in submerged lands of a State;

(2) embedded in coralline formations protected by a State on submerged lands of a State; or

(3) on submerged lands of a State and is included in or determined eligible for inclusion in the National Register.

Id. § 2105(a). It is estimated that this definition only encompasses about five percent of the 50,000 shipwrecks in United States waters. "Abandoned" is not defined in the legislation. The ASA also does not cover shipwrecks that were the subject of proceedings brought prior to the effective date of the Act. Id. § 2106(b)–(c).

Congress found that abandoned shipwrecks of historical significance are the type of resources that states should manage, because they are "irreplaceable State resources for tourism, biological sanctuaries, and historical research," and they offer unique recreational and educational opportunities. Id. § 2103(a)(1). The ASA attempts to address the multi-use aspects of the resources by directing states to develop "appropriate and consistent" policies to:

(A) protect natural resources and habitat areas;

(B) guarantee recreational exploration of shipwreck sites; and

(C) allow for appropriate public and private sector recovery of shipwrecks consistent with the protection of historical values and environmental integrity of the shipwrecks and the sites.

Id. § 2103(a)(2). The ASA encourages states to create underwater parks to provide additional protection and provides funds under the National Historic Preservation Act for the "study, interpretation, protection, and preservation of historic shipwrecks and properties." Id. § 2103(b). Federal guidelines have been published "to assist" states in developing legislation and management programs for shipwreck sites covered by the legislation. See id. § 2104. The federal government is not given authority to review state programs, however, and the transfer of ownership of shipwrecks is not dependent on federal approval of state management schemes.

Finally, because Congress found both the law of salvage and the law of finds unsuitable for preservation of historic shipwrecks, the ASA specifically provides that neither shall apply to abandoned shipwrecks that have been transferred into state ownership. Id. § 2106(a).

In applying the ASA to newly discovered shipwrecks, a number of questions arise: (1) Is the wreck abandoned?; (2) Is the wreck embedded?; (3) Does Congress' attempt to carve out a limited exception to admiralty jurisdiction violate constitutional principles?; (4) Does the Eleventh Amendment preclude federal courts from adjudicating claims to ships that states may claim under the ASA?; and (5) Does the ASA preempt state statutes that make claims to wrecks beyond the rights bestowed by the ASA?

In *California and State Lands Comm. v. Deep Sea Research, Inc. (The Brother Jonathan)*, 523 U.S. 491, 118 S.Ct. 1464, 140 L.Ed.2d 626 (1998), the U.S. Supreme Court addressed the ASA for the first time. The Court found that "abandoned" under the ASA has the same meaning as under admiralty law, i.e., a shipwreck is abandoned if the title has been affirmatively renounced or when an inference of abandonment can be made from the circumstances. Therefore, although admiralty law is inapplicable to ships transferred to states under the ASA, it is still relevant for determining which ships are actually subject to transfer to state ownership.

Fairport Int'l Exploration v. The Shipwrecked Vessel known as The Captain Lawrence, 177 F.3d 491

(6th Cir. 1999) comprehensively reviews the federal maritime law applicable to the term "abandonment." Abandonment can be express or by inference. Neither lapse of time alone nor the owner's failure to return to a shipwreck site necessarily establishes abandonment, but these aspects do contribute to circumstantial evidence from which abandonment may be inferred. The case specifically addressed the issue of the burden of proof borne by the party asserting abandonment under the ASA and found: "The uniform rule in admiralty is that a finding of abandonment requires proof by clear and convincing evidence."

Sovereign vessels are treated differently than private vessels in regard to abandonment. A State Department letter included in the House Report on the ASA states, "the U.S. only abandons its sovereignty over, and title to, sunken U.S. warships by affirmative act; mere passage of time or lack of positive assertions of right are insufficient to establish such abandonment." The letter goes on to say that the United States accords the same presumption of non-abandonment to sovereign vessels of other nations that have sunk in U.S. waters while on the noncommercial service of that state. H.R. Rep. No. 100–514(II), at 13 (1988). Congress later codified this position in the Sunken Military Craft Act, Pub. L. No. 108–375, §§ 1401–08 (2004).

In *Sea Hunt v. The Unidentified Shipwrecked Vessel*, 221 F.3d 634 (4th Cir. 2000), the state of Virginia claimed ownership under the ASA of the *La Galga* and the *Juno*, Spanish Navy frigates that sank in 1750 and 1802, respectively. The state issued permits to Sea Hunt, a maritime salvage company, to conduct salvage operations and recover artifacts from the wrecks. Spain asserted ownership over the shipwrecks. The court upheld the title of Spain to the vessels, finding that governments retain "ownership of foreign warships sunk in waters of the United States without being captured, and . . . that title to such sunken warships is not lost absent express abandonment by the sovereign." See also *Odyssey Marine Exploration, Inc. v. Unidentified Shipwrecked Vessel*, 657 F.3d 1159 (11th Cir. 2011) (holding that the Spanish vessel and cargo were immune from judicial arrest under the Foreign Sovereign Immunities Act (FSIA), 28 U.S.C.S. §§ 1602–1611; also holding that the cargo aboard the *Mercedes* was not severable from the shipwreck because other statutes, including the Sunken Military Craft Act, which would govern the salvage claims against the *Mercedes*, treated cargo as part of the shipwreck).

In *Zych v. Unidentified, Wrecked and Abandoned Vessel, Believed to be the Seabird*, 941 F.2d 525 (7th Cir. 1991), the Seventh Circuit Court of Appeals identified the issues of embeddedness and constitutionality as controlling in the case of an 1868 shipwreck discovered in Lake Michigan within Illinois state waters. The court remanded the case for a determination of whether the ship was "embedded" within the definition of the ASA. "Embedded" is defined as "firmly affixed in the submerged lands or in coralline formations such that the use of tools of excavation is required in order to move the bottom sediments to gain access to the shipwreck, its cargo, and any part thereof[.]" 43 U.S.C.A. § 2102(a). The term is to be interpreted consistently with the common law exception from the law of finds.

If on remand the ship were found to be "embedded" and, therefore, within the scope of the ASA, the court of appeals in *Zych* found that the constitutionality of the ASA would then have to be decided. In remanding the issue to the district court, the court of appeals identified two grounds for challenging statutes that alter admiralty jurisdiction: (1) exclusion of "a thing falling clearly within [admiralty jurisdiction];" or (2) alteration of jurisdiction so that admiralty jurisdiction is non-uniform. The uniformity challenge is directly dependent on the determination of the first challenge.

On remand to the district court, the parties and the court found Zych's admission of embeddedness sufficient to bring the shipwreck within the scope of the ASA, making the constitutionality of the ASA the controlling issue. *Zych v. Unidentified, Wrecked and Abandoned Vessel*, 811 F.Supp. 1300 (N.D.Ill. 1992). The court found that the ASA did not alter admiralty jurisdiction by precluding application of the law of salvage and finds to abandoned shipwrecks, because these cases were not clearly within admiralty jurisdiction. The court stated:

> [B]ecause a salvor essentially had no claim in federal court for a salvage award against the state prior to enactment of the ASA, either because salvage law does not apply to claims against abandoned vessels [i.e., because they are

> subject to the law of finds], or because the
> eleventh amendment bars an award of salvage
> against the state as owner of the vessel, the
> [ASA] . . . would have virtually no effect on
> federal admiralty jurisdiction.

Id. Similarly, elimination of the law of finds and the
vesting of title in the state had no effect on admiralty
jurisdiction, because it simply accomplished the same
result as applying the embeddedness exception of the
common law of finds. The district court also found
that the concept of embeddedness was sufficiently
related to the historic significance of a shipwreck to
withstand a constitutional due process challenge.

In *The Brother Jonathan,* the state of California
claimed that the Eleventh Amendment precluded the
federal court from adjudicating the state's interest in
the shipwreck. *California and State Lands Comm'n
v. Deep Sea Research, Inc.*, 523 U.S. 491, 118 S.Ct.
1464, 140 L.Ed.2d 626 (1998). The state relied on
Florida Department of State v. Treasure Salvors, Inc.,
458 U.S. 670, 102 S.Ct. 3304, 73 L.Ed.2d 1057 (1982),
where four members of the plurality and four
dissenters had agreed that Treasure Salvors could
not sue Florida in federal admiralty court without the
state's consent to recover property owned by the
state. In that case, however, the state official was
found to have acted beyond his authority and the
state did "not have even a colorable claim to the
artifacts." Subsequent cases found federal courts to
have no *in rem* admiralty jurisdiction where the state
presents a "colorable claim" to the wreck. See, e.g.,
Marx v. Government of Guam, 866 F.2d 294 (9th Cir.

1989); *Maritime Underwater Surveys, Inc. v. Unidentified, Wrecked and Abandoned Sailing Vessel*, 717 F.2d 6 (1st Cir. 1983). The Supreme Court distinguished *The Brother Jonathan* by the fact that the *res* in *Treasure Salvors* was in the possession of the state. Noting the constitutional underpinnings of admiralty jurisdiction, the Court held that "the Eleventh Amendment does not bar federal jurisdiction over the *Brother Jonathan* and, therefore, that the District Court may adjudicate . . . the State claims to the shipwreck." Four concurring justices in the case would have based the holding not on the lack of possession by the state, but on the premise that the Eleventh Amendment does not bar *in rem* admiralty actions. The concurring justices specifically noted that in admiralty cases, it is "evident that the issue [of Eleventh Amendment state immunity] is open to reconsideration."

Once the exercise of admiralty jurisdiction over the conflicting claims was validated, the Supreme Court remanded the issue of whether the vessel was "abandoned" within the definition of the ASA. The Court clarified that the "meaning of 'abandoned' under the ASA conforms with its meaning under admiralty law." Thus, in spite of the statutory language rejecting the application of admiralty law to ships transferred to the states by the ASA, a large body of admiralty law concerning abandonment still remains relevant to determining, as a threshold issue, whether a vessel falls within the ASA.

The Supreme Court in *The Brother Jonathan* did not resolve the issue of whether the ASA preempts state law claims to shipwrecks not covered by the ASA. The Ninth Circuit Court of Appeals had concluded that the California law was pre-empted because shipwrecks that do not meet the requirements of the ASA are exclusively within the admiralty jurisdiction of the federal government. *Deep Sea Research, Inc. v. Brother Jonathan*, 102 F.3d 379 (9th Cir. 1996). Because of the possibility that the issue would be moot after the application of the ASA on remand, the Supreme Court declined to address the preemption issue and that question remains unresolved.

E.   MANAGEMENT OF SPECIAL MARINE AREAS

1.   NATIONAL MARINE SANCTUARIES

The National Marine Sanctuaries Program was created in 1972 as part of the Marine Protection, Research and Sanctuaries Act. 16 U.S.C.A. §§ 1431–1445a. The purpose of the program is to identify marine areas of special national or international significance due to their resource or human-use values and to provide authority for comprehensive conservation and management of such areas where existing regulatory authority is inadequate to assure coordinated conservation and management. Among the considerations in determining the national or international significance of a site are:

(A) the area's natural resource and ecological qualities, including its contribution to biological productivity, maintenance of ecosystem structure, maintenance of ecologically or commercially important or threatened species or species assemblages, maintenance of critical habitat of endangered species, and the biogeographic representation of the site; [and]

(B) the area's historical, cultural, archaeological, or paleontological significance;

. . .

Id. § 1433(b)(1)(A)–(B). The Act particularly identifies the importance of maintaining and restoring "living resources by providing places for species that depend upon these marine areas to survive and propagate." Id. § 1431(b)(9). Designation of a marine area as a sanctuary, in itself, does not prohibit all development or use, but does require special use permits from the Department of Commerce (DOC) to authorize specific activities that are compatible with the purposes of the sanctuary. Id. § 1441. See *Craft v. National Park Service*, 34 F.3d 918 (9th Cir. 1994); *United States v. Fisher*, 22 F.3d 262 (11th Cir. 1994); *United States v. Fisher*, 977 F.Supp. 1193 (S.D.Fla. 1997) (injunctions and civil penalties imposed on divers and salvors for altering sanctuary seabeds without permits).

The national marine sanctuaries program got off to a slow start. The Secretary of Commerce did not designate the first sanctuary, the U.S.S. Monitor National Marine Sanctuary (NMS), until 1975. During this first phase of the NMS program, designation was a slow process; sanctuaries included relatively small areas of ocean space within their boundaries and were managed for narrowly defined purposes. Eight sanctuaries were designated during this period: the *U.S.S. Monitor,* Key Largo and Looe Key off Florida, Gray's Reef off Georgia, the Channel Islands, Gulf of Farallones, and Cordell Banks in California, and Fagatele Bay in the American Samoas. Criticism of the designation process and the effectiveness of the NMS program led to reassessment of the marine sanctuaries program.

In 1988 and 1992 the program was amended substantially. Federal agencies were required to consult with the Secretary of Commerce prior to taking actions within or outside an NMS that was likely to destroy or injure a sanctuary resource. Similar to the ESA consultation process, the Secretary may provide alternatives to the proposed agency action if the action is likely to affect sanctuary resources. Subsequent amendments provide that if an agency takes an action other than a recommended alternative that injures or destroys sanctuary resources, the agency must prevent or mitigate further damage, as well as restore or replace the sanctuary resources. 16 U.S.C.A. § 1434(d).

During this period, important provisions for enforcement and liability were added that give sanctuary designation and sanctuary management plans greater authority. The amendments provide that it is unlawful to:

(1)   destroy, cause the loss of, or injure any sanctuary resource managed under law or regulations for that sanctuary;

(2) possess, sell, offer for sale, purchase, import, export, deliver, carry, transport, or ship by any means any sanctuary resource taken in violation of this section. . . .

Id. § 1436. A "Sanctuary resource" is "any living or nonliving resource . . . that contributes to the . . . value of the sanctuary." Id. § 1432(8). The amendments create a rebuttable presumption that all sanctuary resources on board a vessel were taken in violation of the act or regulations. Id. § 1437(d)(4). Enforcement authorities are granted broad powers to board, search, and seize vessels, and impose civil penalties of up to $100,000 per violation per day. Id. § 1437(b)–(c). In addition, persons damaging or injuring any sanctuary resources are liable for response costs and damages. Id. § 1443. See *United States v. M/V Jacquelyn L.*, 100 F.3d 1520 (11th Cir. 1996); *United States v. Fisher*, 977 F.Supp. 1193 (S.D.Fla. 1997); *United States v. M/V Miss Beholden*, 856 F.Supp. 668 (S.D.Fla.1994); *United States v. Great Lakes Dredge & Dock Co.*, 259 F.3d 1300 (11th Cir. 2001).

The designation process for marine sanctuaries has been streamlined, but Congress has also accelerated the process by designating or ordering the designation of certain sanctuaries. During this second phase of sanctuary designation, the Florida Keys (which incorporated Key Largo and Looe Key), Monterey Bay, Stellwagen Bank, the Hawaiian Islands Humpback Whale, the Flower Garden Banks, the Olympic Coast, and Thunder Bay national marine sanctuaries have been created. The National

Marine Sanctuary System now comprises more than 170,000 square miles of marine and Great Lakes waters and includes thirteen sanctuaries as well as the Papahānaumokuākea (originally the Northwestern Hawaiian Islands) Marine National Monument, which is discussed in part 2 of this section, and the Pacific Remote Islands Marine National Monument.

The current generation of sanctuaries differs from those designated earlier in two ways: (1) their size, and (2) their management approach. The newest marine sanctuaries encompass extensive ocean areas of both federal and state jurisdiction. Designation of large ocean areas allows management of more of the activities that affect sanctuary resources and provides the opportunity to develop an ecosystem-based approach to resource management. Management plans can be developed that deal with direct and indirect, as well as primary and secondary, effects on sanctuary resources. Federal and state cooperative programs are encouraged, and advisory councils have become an integral part of both the plan development process and subsequent plan implementation. Because designation of such large areas affects numerous user groups, conflict management is an important part of plan development and implementation. See, e.g., *Personal Watercraft Industry Association v. Department of Commerce*, 48 F.3d 540, 310 U.S.App.D.C. 364 (D.C.Cir. 1995). This new kind of national marine sanctuary depends on a cooperative intergovernmental approach to management of large marine areas and has provided a model for development of other marine protected areas.

2.   THE PAPAHĀNAUMOKUĀKEA MARINE NATIONAL MONUMENT AND OTHER PACIFIC OCEAN MONUMENTS

The Antiquities Act of 1906, 16 U.S.C.A. § 431, gave the president discretion to set aside "historic landmarks, historic and prehistoric structures, and other objects of historic or scientific interest that are situated upon the lands owned or controlled by the Government of the United States to be National Monuments. . . ." The language of the statute, which provides that the monuments encompass the "smallest area compatible with proper care and management of the objects to be protected," suggests that Congress was conferring this power on the president to be used to protect small, discreet areas. The language has not, however, deterred presidents since Theodore Roosevelt from declaring millions of acres of public lands to be national monuments. On June 15, 2006, President George Bush proclaimed the largest national monument to date, the Northwestern Hawaiian Islands (NWHI) National Monument, now the Papahānaumokuākea National Monument (PNM), comprising nearly 140,000 square miles of federal waters surrounding 10 islands and atolls in the Pacific Ocean and stretching more than 1,200 miles from Nihoa to Kure Atoll. Presidential Proclamation 8031 (71 F.R. 36443, June 26, 2006). At the time of its designation, the monument was the world's largest protected marine area.

The PNM is a unique environment with over 7,000 species, one quarter of which are found only in the Hawaiian Archipelago. Among the most endangered of the resident species is the Hawaiian monk seal, and the islands are also the breeding area for 90 percent of the threatened Hawaiian Island green sea turtles. Over 14 million birds inhabit these remote islands, and the waters teem with fish species and sensitive coral ecosystems. The islands also hold great cultural significance for native Hawaiians.

In 2005, the state of Hawaii had declared the state waters surrounding the NWHI as a marine reserve, prohibiting all extractive uses, including commercial and recreational fishing. The federal waters in the area had been protected as a Coral Reef Ecosystem Reserve under two Executive Orders of President Bill Clinton, and the area was under consideration for designation as a national marine sanctuary. The proclamation of the national monument, however, confers a significantly higher level of protection on the PNM than the sanctuary status would have provided.

The protections provided to the monument are unprecedented. Vessels must have permission to access the monument and are required to use vessel-monitoring systems. Even vessels merely passing through monument waters are required to give notice at least 72 hours before transiting the waters. Among the prohibited activities are: exploring for, developing, or producing oil, gas, or minerals; using or attempting to use poisons, electrical charges, or explosives in the collection or harvest of a monument resource; introducing or otherwise releasing an introduced species from within or into the monument; and anchoring on any living or dead coral. Commercial lobster fishing was terminated immediately by the proclamation, and commercial fishing for bottomfish and associated pelagic species was phased out within five years. Sustenance fishing outside of special preservation areas may, however, be permitted. Other uses of the monument are to be strictly regulated to assure the activities are "compatible with the purposes for which the monument is designated and with protection of monument resources." Id. The monument was the first to be under the jurisdiction of the Department of Commerce and NOAA, and is currently cooperatively managed by the Secretary of Commerce (NOAA) the Secretary of the Interior (U.S. Fish and Wildlife Service) and the State of Hawaii.

In January 2009, President Bush established three more marine national monuments in the Pacific totaling 195,274 square miles at the Marianas Trench, remote coral atolls designated as the Marianas Trench, the Pacific Remote Islands and Rose Atoll, and Rose Atoll in American Samoa. President Obama, on September 25, 2014, further expanded the Pacific Remote Islands Marine National Monument in the central Pacific from around 87,000 square miles to approximately an additional 408,000 square miles. Incorporating the 200-mile U.S. exclusive economic zone (EEZ) adjacent to seven uninhabited islands and atolls, the monument is the largest marine protected area on earth.

3. OTHER MARINE PROTECTED AREAS

The National Marine Sanctuaries Program was created specifically to protect natural and cultural features of the marine environment, but federal and state governments protect and conserve marine areas and resources under numerous other authorities and for many purposes. For example, marine areas are protected as national parks, national monuments, national wildlife refuges, fishery management zones, national estuarine research reserves and many other categories. Within their waters, states have also established and managed marine areas to protect marine resources. In recent years, marine protected areas (MPAs), ranging from multiple-use areas to no-take reserves, have proliferated as a conservation and management tool.

In 2000, President Clinton issued Executive Order 13158 on Marine Protected Areas (MPAs) directing federal agencies to work with state, local, and nongovernmental partners to create a comprehensive, nationwide network of marine protected areas. The Executive Order recognizes the need to integrate efforts to protect marine areas through an ecosystem-based approach to management and maximize opportunities for coordination of research and public education. The Executive Order defines "marine protected area" as "any area of the marine environment that has been reserved by federal, state, territorial, tribal, or local laws or regulations to provide lasting protection for part or all of the natural and cultural resources therein." As an initial step, the Marine Protected Areas Inventory (formerly the Marine Managed Areas Inventory), a comprehensive geospatial database designed to catalog and classify over 1,600 marine protected areas within US waters, was developed to contribute to the development of a national system of Marine Protected Areas. The Inventory revealed that 41% of all U.S. waters are in some form of MPA.

The National Marine Protected Areas Center and a 30-member MPA Federal Advisory Committee were created to develop a framework for a national MPA system and to work with agencies and stakeholders to develop regional systems of MPAs that can achieve ecosystem-wide goals and objectives. In 2008, NOAA and the Department of Interior published *Framework for the National System of Marine Protected Areas of the United States of America* (2008), identifying goals and conservation objections and providing guidance for the development of a national system of MPAs. The *Framework* established eligibility criteria and created a nomination process for existing MPAs to be included in the national system. In addition, to creating a process for improving regional and ecosystem-based coordination of MPAs, the *Framework* developed science-based processes for identifying natural and cultural resource conservation gaps in the national system. Prior to President Obama's latest extension of the Pacific Remote Islands National Monument, the National System of MPAs included 437 MPAs and covered an area of 191,030 square miles—4% of U.S. marine waters including the 200-mile EEZ. The new designation increased protected area by more than 400,000 square miles.

F.   MANAGEMENT OF FISHERY RESOURCES

1.   HISTORICAL BACKGROUND OF STATE FISHERIES MANAGEMENT

Prior to 1977, states were the primary managers of the country's fisheries. By virtue of the police power, the states had regulated fisheries in inland waters and the three-mile territorial sea since colonial times. See *McCready v. Virginia*, 94 U.S. 391 (1876) (holding a state owns "the tide-waters . . . and the fish in them, so far as they are capable of ownership while running;" see also *Manchester v. Massachusetts*, 139 U.S. 240, 11 S.Ct. 559, 35 L.Ed. 159 (1891) and *Douglas v. Seacoast Prods., Inc.*, 431 U.S. 265, 97 S.Ct. 1740, 52 L.Ed.2d 304 (1977) (explaining that state "ownership" of living resources was a "legal fiction expressing 'the importance to its people that a State have the power to preserve and regulate the exploitation of an important resource.' "). This jurisdiction was confirmed by the Submerged Lands Act of 1953 which specifically granted the states "title to and ownership of . . . natural resources," including the "right and power to manage, administer, lease, develop and use" marine resources within their boundaries, generally three miles offshore. 43 U.S.C.A. § 1311(a). Historically, however, state fisheries jurisdiction has not been limited to waters within its boundaries.

The landmark case, *Skiriotes v. Florida*, 313 U.S. 69, 61 S.Ct. 924, 85 L.Ed. 1193 (1941), recognized the right of a state to regulate its citizens outside territorial waters. In holding that state regulations on the taking of sponges would apply to a Florida resident even if he were not in state waters, the Supreme Court explained the citizenship basis for exercise of authority as follows:

> If the United States may control the conduct of its citizens upon the high seas, we see no reason why the State of Florida may not likewise govern the conduct of its citizens upon the high seas with respect to matters in which the State has a legitimate interest and where there is no conflict with acts of Congress. Save for the powers committed by the Constitution to the Union, the State of Florida has retained the status of a sovereign.
>
> . . . When its action does not conflict with federal legislation, the sovereign authority of the State over the conduct of its citizens upon the high seas is analogous to the sovereign authority of the United States over its citizens in like circumstances.

Id. The Court also reaffirmed the principle that a vessel is a bit of floating territory of a state and subject to the jurisdiction of the state even beyond territorial boundaries.

With state authority to regulate its citizens both within and outside state waters beyond dispute, the primary controversies that arose concerned state management of noncitizens. Early cases often involved protectionist state regulations. The Supreme Court had a number of opportunities to establish the principle that state regulations could not unreasonably discriminate against noncitizens. See *Toomer v. Witsell*, 334 U.S. 385, 68 S.Ct. 1156, 92 L.Ed. 1460 (1948) (A South Carolina law that charged a $25 fee for a shrimping license for residents and a $2500 license fee for nonresidents violated the Privileges and Immunities Clause of the Constitution.); *Torao Takahashi v. Fish & Game Comm'n*, 334 U.S. 410, 68 S.Ct. 1138, 92 L.Ed. 1478 (1948) (A California law prohibiting "persons ineligible for citizenship" from obtaining commercial fishing licenses violated the Equal Protection Clause when applied to discriminate against resident aliens.); *Douglas v. Seacoast Prods., Inc.*, 431 U.S. 265, 97 S.Ct. 1740, 52 L.Ed.2d 304 (1977) (Discrimination against vessels not meeting a Virginia statute's citizenship requirements was preempted by federal licensing and enrollment statutes.).

State regulation of noncitizens beyond state waters takes two forms: indirect and direct. A primary means of enforcement of state fishery laws has been the use of landing laws or the prohibition of the possession of certain fish or gear. In addition to regulating state citizens and other fishermen within the territorial sea, these kinds of laws indirectly and incidentally affect fisheries and fishermen outside the state as well as interstate commerce. In spite of the extraterritorial effects, the Supreme Court, prior to 1977, upheld landing and possession laws when they were necessary for enforcement of fishery management legislation. The difficulty of preventing evasion of the statutes and "covert depletion" of local fisheries provided the legal justification for such regulations. *Bayside Fish Flour Company v. Gentry*, 297 U.S. 422, 56 S.Ct. 513, 80 L.Ed. 772 (1936) (upholding a landing law on sardines to prevent waste and conserve the fish within California waters even though the state law indirectly regulated beyond state waters and had some effect on interstate commerce).

The U.S. Supreme Court has not addressed the issue of whether legitimate state interests can justify direct state regulation of activities of noncitizens beyond state boundaries. In *State v. Bundrant*, 546 P.2d 530 (Alaska 1976), the Alaska Supreme Court considered the legitimacy of the state's high seas crab fishery regulations that applied to both citizens and noncitizens of Alaska. After establishing that the state had a legitimate interest in regulation of the offshore crab fishery, the court considered whether *Skiriotes* limited the application of the regulation to Alaska citizens. The Alaska Supreme Court found it inconsistent to recognize the importance of conservation of the fishery and the legitimacy of the state interest in regulation of the fishery, and then to provide the means to "frustrate the legitimate objectives of these laws" by exempting citizens of other states and allowing the opportunity for Alaskans to elude the regulation by transferring citizenship to another state. Because the regulation did not discriminate or exhibit other constitutional infirmities, the court held that the extraterritorial crab fishery regulation could continue to be enforced. An appeal of the case to the U.S. Supreme Court was dismissed when comprehensive federal legislation was enacted for the 200-mile offshore fisheries zone in 1976.

2.   FEDERAL FISHERIES MANAGEMENT

By 1976, it had become clear that neither the twelve-mile fishing zone created around the United States in 1964 by the Bartlett Act nor international agreements for fisheries management were slowing the depletion of fish stocks by an increasing number of foreign high seas fishing fleets. The notion of the high seas as a global commons was quickly leading to the decimation of fish populations as technologies developed to more intensely harvest fishing grounds. By the mid-1970s, a number of countries were extending fisheries jurisdiction beyond territorial waters, and negotiations at the Third UN Conference on the Law of the Sea (UNCLOS III) had reached substantial consensus, at least in principal, that coastal states should have exclusive fishery jurisdiction to 200 miles offshore. Congress' perception that the UNCLOS III negotiations were proceeding too slowly to protect offshore fisheries and the American fishing industry led to the passage in 1976 of the Fishery Conservation and Management Act, now named the Magnuson-Stevens Fishery Conservation and Management Act (Magnuson-Stevens Act or MSA), 16 U.S.C.A. §§ 1801–1882, which extended exclusive United States fisheries jurisdiction to 200 miles offshore. The offshore management area was originally designated the fishery conservation zone, but the MSA was later amended to reflect the 1983 United States' claim to a 200-mile exclusive economic zone (EEZ) that incorporated fishery management jurisdiction. Congressional reauthorization of the MSA was pending as this edition went to press.

For purposes of the MSA, the EEZ extends from state seaward boundaries (generally three miles offshore) out 200 miles from shore. In this 197-mile wide EEZ, the United States claims exclusive authority to manage and regulate all fisheries. Id. § 1811(a). Jurisdiction over anadromous species (e.g., salmon) is claimed throughout their migratory range beyond the EEZ. Id. § 1811(b). The Act originally excluded highly migratory species (e.g., tuna) from the EEZ management regime, but the 1990 amendments extended the jurisdiction to include tuna. The policies and purposes of the act are directed toward the conservation, development, and management of fishery resources, as well as the development of domestic commercial and recreational fishing. Id. § 1801.

The MSA established eight regional fishery management councils (RFMCs) to formulate management plans that are enforced through regulations of the U.S. Department of Commerce (DOC). Id. § 1852(a). The councils include the regional director of the National Marine Fisheries Service (NMFS) and state fishery management officers, as well as individuals from each state who are recommended by state governors and appointed by the Secretary of Commerce. The appointed council members, who constitute more than half of the membership, must be persons who are knowledgeable about fishery conservation and management, commercial or recreational fishing, or the fisheries resources of a region. Id. § 1852(b). In making appointments, the Secretary is also required to apportion council membership between recreational and commercial fishery representatives based on such factors as the type of fisheries managed, the quantity of fish harvested, fishing and processing methods used, and the number of participants in the fisheries. Id. §§ 1852(b)(2)(A)–(B). Appointed members may only serve three consecutive three-year terms. Id. at § 1852(b)(3). See also Donna R. Christie, *Living Marine Resources Management: A Proposal for Integration of United States: Management Regimes,* 34 Environmental Law 107, 113 (2005).

In the first decades of the MSA, most of the RFMCs were dominated by commercial fishermen, leading to some commentators to view the process as hopelessly biased. See T.A. Okey, *Membership of the Eight Regional Fishery Management Councils in the United States: Are Special Interests Over-Represented?,* 27 Marine Policy 193 (2003). The Councils are also exempt from the Federal Advisory Committee Act, 5 U.S.C. App. 2. Id. § 1852(I). See T. Cloutier, *Comment, Conflicts of Interest on Regional Fishery Management Councils: Corruption or Cooperative Management,* 2 Ocean & Coastal L.J. 101 (1996). The 1996 amendments to the MSA began addressing some of the criticisms by requiring disclosure of financial interests of nominees in fisheries. *Id.* § 1852(j).

Responding to criticisms concerning the RFMCs, Congress instituted several changes through the MSA Reauthorization Act of 2006 (Reauthorization Act), which passed in the waning hours of the 2006 "lame duck" Congress. New council members are required to take a training course designed to prepare the members to deal with the scientific, social, economic, environmental, legal, and conflict of interest requirements of the fishery management process. Id. at § 1852(k). The Reauthorization Act also strengthens and clarifies the MSA requirements concerning conflict of interest and recusal. Id. at § 1852(j). Finally, the Act limits the discretion of the councils very significantly in setting annual catch levels that exceed scientifically determined levels. See id. § 1852(h)(6). The Reauthorization Act did not respond comprehensively to the criticism that the councils are dominated by the fishing industry and do not adequately represent broader public interests. See, e.g., Pew Oceans Commission, *America's Living Oceans: Charting a Course for Sea Change* 44–45 (2003). The appointment process for the Gulf of Mexico Fisheries Management Council was changed significantly, however, by requiring the nomination by state governors of three individuals representing the commercial, recreational and charter fishing sectors, as well as another individual "knowledgeable regarding the conservation and management of fisheries resources in the jurisdiction." If the Secretary determines a governor's nominees do not meet these requirements, the Act provides a process for residents of a state to make nominations that the Secretary may add to the list of nominees submitted by a state governor. Id. § 1852(b)(2)(D).

The 2006 Reauthorization Act purports to improve the decision-making by RFMCs by providing more consistency and aligning the process with NEPA requirements and procedures. To provide more consistent application of the Act, the RFMCs are authorized to create a Council Coordination Committee consisting of the chairs, vice chairs, and executive directors of the councils (or other members or staff) to provide a forum for discussion of issues of relevance to all Councils in implementing the MSA. Id. § 1852(l). Next, the Secretary is directed to revise agency procedures for compliance with the National Environmental Policy Act (NEPA). Id. § 1854(i)(1). In consultation with the Council on Environmental Quality (CEQ) and the Councils, and with public participation, the Secretary is to develop a uniform environmental review procedure for fishery management plans (FMPs) that integrates NEPA review, analysis and public input and conforms with time-lines for review and approval of FMPs under the MSA. Id. Once these new procedures are adopted, they "shall be the sole environmental impact assessment procedure for fishery management plans, amendments, regulations, and other action taken or approved pursuant to the [MSA]." Id. § 1854(i)(2). See also *Notice of Availability of Draft Revised and Updated National Environmental Policy Act (NEPA) Procedures for Magnuson Stevens Act Fishery Management Actions*, 79 Fed. Reg. 36726 (June 30, 2014).

RFMCs have the primary responsibility for preparing FMPs for EEZ fisheries, establishing management policies not only for how, when, where, and how many fish are caught, but also allocating the catch among users. See *Flaherty v. Bryson*, 850 F. Supp. 2d 38, 50 (D.D.C. 2012) (discussing the determination of what is a "fishery" for purposes of a management plan). FMPs and plan amendments developed by the RFMCs must be submitted to the Secretary, who must approve a plan if it is consistent with applicable law. Id. § 1854(a)(3). The Secretary's approval is not reviewed de novo and will not be overturned unless it is inconsistent with the national standards or other applicable law, or is arbitrary and capricious or an abuse of the Secretary's discretion. See, e.g., *Associated Fisheries of Maine v. Daley*, 127 F.3d 104 (1st Cir. 1997); *C & W Fish Co. v. Fox*, 931 F.2d 1556, 289 U.S.App.D.C. 323 (D.C.Cir. 1991); *Fishermen's Dock Cooperative, Inc. v. Brown*, 75 F.3d 164 (4th Cir. 1996); *Pacific Marine Conservation Council v. Evans*, 200 F.Supp.2d 1194 (N.D.Cal. 2002).

The Secretary has independent authority to prepare FMPs for Atlantic highly migratory species, and in a limited number of other circumstances. Id. § 1854. The Secretary also has discretion to prepare (i.e., "may prepare") an FMP when a Council fails to develop and submit a plan for a fishery requiring management "after a reasonable period" and when a Council fails to resubmit a revised plan or amendment after the Secretary has disapproved or partially disapproved the plan or amendment. *Id*. § 1854(c). When a Council does not submit a plan for rebuilding an overfished fishery within two years of notification by the Secretary of the overfished status of the fishery, the Secretary is required to prepare a plan. Id. § 1854(e)(5).

FMPs are developed based on ten national standards set out in the MSA. Id. §§ 1851(a)(1)–(10). National standards (1) and (2) require FMPs to establish conservation and management measures based on the best scientific information available to prevent overfishing and assure optimum yield. See *Hadaja, Inc. v. Evans,* 263 F.Supp.2d 346 (D.R.I. 2003) ("While National Standard Two does not compel the use of specific analytic methods or require that an agency gather all possible scientific data before acting, the Standard does prohibit an agency from simply creating a rule based on mere political compromise.") Optimum yield is defined to be:

the amount of fish which:

(A) will provide the greatest overall benefit to the Nation, particularly with respect to food production and recreational opportunities; and taking into account the protection of marine ecosystems;

(B) is prescribed as such on the basis of the maximum sustainable yield from the fishery, as reduced by any relevant economic, social, or ecological factor; and

(C) in the case of an overfished fishery, provides for rebuilding to a level consistent with producing the maximum sustainable yield in such fishery.

Id. § 1802(28).

The most significant limitations on the setting of optimum yield are that it must prevent overfishing and not exceed maximum sustainable yield. Maximum sustainable yield is a scientific determination of the level of harvest that can be taken consistently on a long-term basis without diminishing the stocks and that will assure an inexhaustible and perpetually renewable resource. Fishing at a level that jeopardizes the sustainable capacity of a fishery to produce maximum sustainable yield is defined as overfishing. See 16 U.S.C.A. § 1802(29); see also *Northwest Envtl. Defense Ctr. v. Brennen*, 958 F.2d 930 (9th Cir. 1992) (finding a similar definition of overfishing reasonable for purposes of determining the allowable harvest of a salmon fishery). The MSA Reauthorization Act now requires that *all* FMPs set annual catch limits at a level that prevents overfishing. See 16 U.S.C. § 1852(h)(6); 16 U.S.C. § 1853(A)(15). Notably, the Reauthorization Act restricts RFMCs to setting the annual catch limits at a level that does not exceed the recommendations of the Councils' scientific and statistical committees or the new peer review process established by the Act to improve the scientific data available for management. See id. § 1852(h)(6); see also, id. § 1852(g).

The 1996 Sustainable Fisheries Act (SFA) amendments to the MSA required the Secretary of Commerce to report annually to Congress and councils on the status of fisheries and identify fisheries that are overfished or are approaching a condition of being overfished. 16 U.S.C. § 1854(e)(1). "A fishery shall be classified as approaching a condition of being overfished if, based on trends in fishing effort, fishery resource size, and other appropriate factors, the Secretary estimates that the fishery will become overfished within two years." Id. § 1854(e)(1). As amended by the 2006 Reauthorization Act, the MSA requires that within two years of notification that a fishery is overfished, the responsible RFMC must submit an FMP, plan amendment, or proposed regulations that will *immediately* end overfishing and rebuild affected stocks of fish within a specified time, which will normally not exceed 10 years. Id. § 1854(e)(3–4). See *Natural Resources Defense Council v. NMFS,* 421 F.3d 872 (9th Cir. 2005) (finding an FMP for a seriously overfished fishery with a 33-year rebuilding time that also called for an increased annual quota "patently unreasonable"). If the Council does not act within the required period, the Secretary must prepare an FMP or plan amendment and regulations within nine months to stop overfishing and rebuild affected stocks of fish. Id. § 1854(e)(5). See *Natural Resources Defense Council v. Daley,* 209 F.3d 747, 341 U.S.App.D.C. 119 (D.C.Cir. 2000) (holding that the level of take allowed under a rebuilding plan must have at least a 50% likelihood of achieving the goal of rebuilding the stock).

The SFA also required FMPs to minimize the bycatch of non-target species pursuant to new national standard (9). 16 U.S.C.A. § 1853(a)(1). "Bycatch" is "fish which are harvested in a fishery, but which are not sold or kept for personal use, and include economic discards and regulatory discards, [but] does not include fish released alive under a recreational catch and release fishery management program." 16 U.S.C. § 1802(2). Bycatch must be avoided or minimized only "to the extent practicable." Id. § 1851(a)(9). The Reauthorization Act also directs the Secretary to undertake efforts to reduce seabird interaction and mortality in fisheries. National Standard Guidelines explain the implications of bycatch on fisheries management as follows:

> Bycatch can, in two ways, impede efforts to protect marine ecosystems and achieve sustainable fisheries and the full benefits they can provide to the Nation. First, bycatch can increase substantially the uncertainty concerning total fishing-related mortality, which makes it more difficult to assess the status of stocks, to set the appropriate [optimum yield (OY) and define overfishing levels, and to ensure that OYs are attained and overfishing levels are not exceeded. Second, bycatch may also preclude other more productive uses of fishery resources.

50 C.F.R. § 600.350(d). See also *Pacific Marine Conservation Council v. Evans*, 200 F.Supp.2d 1194 (N.D. Cal. 2002) (remanding an FMP amendment for failure to adequately consider whether measures, such as fishing capacity reduction, marine reserves and observers, were impracticable means of bycatch reduction).

FMPs must identify essential fish habitat (EFH) for the managed fishery. Id. § 1853(a)(7). EFH is defined as "those waters and substrate necessary to fish for spawning, breeding, feeding or growth to maturity." 16 U.S.C. § 1802(10). FMPs must include measures to minimize the adverse impacts of fishing on EFH and identify actions encouraging the conservation of EFH. Id. Federal agencies are required to consult with the Secretary on their actions that may adversely affect EFH. Id. § 1855(b)(2). The Councils are required to make recommendations to the Secretary on federal and state actions affecting anadromous fish habitat, including EFH, and may make recommendations on actions affecting the habitat of other species. Id. § 1855(b)(3).

The MSA has provided authority for FMPs to protect designated areas by restricting or prohibiting fishing, types of fishing gear or types of vessels. Id. § 1853(3)(A). The establishment of marine reserves that prohibit all fishing, however, has become quite controversial. The 2006 Reauthorization Act requires that closure of an area to *all fishing* by an FMP must ensure that the closure:

(i)   is based on the best scientific information available;

(ii) includes criteria to assess the conservation benefit of the closed area;

(iii) establishes a timetable for review of the closed area's performance that is consistent with the purposes of the closed area; and

(iv) is based on an assessment of the benefits and impacts of the closure, including its size, in relation to other management measures (either alone or in combination with such measures), including the benefits and impacts of limiting access to: users of the area, overall fishing activity, fishery science, and fishery and marine conservation.

Id. § 1853(b)(2)(B).

National standards (3)–(7) provide that nondiscriminatory means should be used to manage fisheries throughout their range. Measures should be taken to avoid duplication and promote efficiency, but cannot have economic allocation as a sole purpose. The limitation on economic allocation as a purpose has not been interpreted to prevent development of FMPs using limited entry or individual fishing quota (IFQ) systems as a management mechanism. See, e.g., *Sea Watch Int'l v. Mosbacher*, 762 F.Supp. 370 (D.C.Cir. 1991) (holding that the establishment of an IFQ system for the ocean quahog fishery did not violate the national standards). In fact, the MSA includes such limited access systems among the discretionary measures a Council may include in an FMP. Any limited access system must, however, take into account:

(A)   present participation in the fishery;

(B) historical fishing practices in, and dependence on, the fishery;

(C)   the economics of the fishery;

(D) the capability of fishing vessels used in the fishery to engage in other fisheries;

(E) the cultural and social framework relevant to the fishery;

(F) the fair and equitable distribution of access privileges in the fishery; and

(G) any other relevant considerations. . . .

16 U.S.C.A. § 1853(b)(6). Numerous decisions have upheld FMP limited access systems including IFQ systems. See *Alliance Against IFQs v. Brown*, 84 F.3d 343 (9th Cir. 1996); *Norbird Fisheries, Inc. v. National Marine Fisheries Service*, 112 F.3d 414 (9th Cir. 1997); *Hadaja, Inc. v. Evans*, 263 F.Supp.2d 346 (D.R.I. 2003). Most managed fisheries are now under a limited license program. But the controversial nature of IFQ programs led Congress in 1996 to repeal all IFQ programs established after January 1995 and to impose a moratorium on new IFQ systems until October 1, 2000 (and later extend it until 2002) while the National Academy of Sciences (NAS) studied the impact of IFQs on Fishery Management. 16 U.S.C.A. § 1853(d)(1). Since the moratorium has expired, new IFQ programs have had to consider the recommendations of the NAS report. Id. § 1853(d)(5).

The 2006 Reauthorization Act creates new "limited access privilege programs" (LAPPs) and establishes national guidelines for the programs. Id. § 1853(a). Fisheries that are already subject to a limited access system may qualify for management under a LAPP system which expands the concept of IFQs to include allocation of harvesting privileges to fishing communities and regional fishing organizations. A fishing community is one that is "substantially dependent on or substantially engaged in the harvest or processing of fishery resources to meet social and economic needs. . . ." Id. § 1801(16). To participate in a LAPP as a fishing community, residents who conduct commercial or recreational fishing, processing or fishery-dependent support businesses must meet participation criteria developed by the relevant RFMC and develop a "sustainability plan." Id. The plan must "address the social and economic development needs of coastal communities, including those that have not historically had the resources to participate in the fishery." Id. § 1853a(c)(3).

Councils may also create LAPPs through their own initiative, by petition by the majority of the fishermen in a limited entry fishery, or in the case of the Gulf or New England regions, a 2/3 vote in a referendum among eligible permit holders. Id. § 1853a(c)(6). See *Coastal Conservation Ass'n v. Blank*, 2011 WL 4530544 (M.D. Fla. Sept. 29, 2011) (upholding the GOM Council's eligibility criteria to participate in a referendum to create a grouper and tilefish IFQ program); *Newton v. Locke*, 701 F.3d 5 (1st Cir. Mass. 2012) (upholding an amendment to the FMP for the Northeast Multispecies Groundfish Fishery which, among other things, altered and expanded the fishery's preexisting "sector allocation program" and distinguished the program from an ITQ or LAPP program).

A regional fishery association is a specific form of limited access privilege program in the MSA. A regional fishery association is:

> an association formed for the mutual benefit of members—

> (A) to meet social and economic needs in a region or subregion; and

> (B) comprised of persons engaging in the harvest or processing of fishery resources in that specific region or subregion or who otherwise own or operate businesses substantially dependent upon a fishery.

Id. § 1802(13A). These associations are not eligible for allocations, but may hold members' allocations. Regional fisheries organizations comprising participants who hold quota shares may qualify for participation in a LAPP by developing and submitting a plan meeting criteria developed by the relevant RFMP. Id. § 1853a(c)(4).

In 2010, NOAA released its Catch Share Policy to clarify and simplify design and implementation of catch share programs and reduce impediments to adoption in appropriate fisheries. "Catch share" is a general term for fishery management strategies that allocate a specific portion of the annual catch limit of a fishery to individuals, cooperatives, communities, or other entities. This includes LAPPs, IFQs and "other exclusive allocative measures such as Territorial Use Rights Fisheries (TURFs) that grant an exclusive privilege to fish in a geographically designated fishing ground." The Policy contains criteria for Councils to apply to assess whether a fishery will benefit from a catch share program and guiding principles to apply in developing a catch share program. *NOAA Catch Share Program,* available at http://www.nmfs.noaa.gov/sfa/manage ment/catch_shares/about/documents/noaa_cs_policy. pdf. Each recipient of a catch share is directly accountable to stop fishing when its exclusive allocation is reached. But with a secure allocation of the catch, there is no pressure or need to race for fish. More time and flexibility to fish allows fishermen to fish more sustainably by avoiding bycatch, unwanted species, and reducing the amount of discards and more efficiently by avoiding derby fishing and maintaining the economies of coastal communities.

Since the 1990 amendments to the MSA, the contents of an FMP have been required to include a "fishery impact statement" to "assess, specify, and describe the likely effects . . . [on] participants in the fisheries and fishing communities affected by the plan or amendment. . . ." Id. § 1853(a)(9). The protection of fishing communities was raised to a governing standard in 1996. National Standard Eight was added to the MSA by the SFA and provides that to the extent "consistent with the conservation requirements" of the Act, management measures must take into account the importance of the resources to fishing communities and, "to the extent practicable," minimize the adverse economic impact on these communities and to sustain participation by the communities in the fisheries. Id. § 1851(a)(8). See also, generally, Michael C. Laurence, *A Call to Action: Saving America's Commercial Fishermen,* 26

Wm. & Mary Envtl. Pol'y L. Rev. 825 (2002) (describing the implementation of National Standard Eight and supporting government reduction of fishing capacity as a final, viable option for saving fishermen and fishing communities). In *Natural Resources Defense Council v. Daley*, 209 F.3d 747, 341 U.S.App.D.C. 119 (D.C.Cir. 2000), in spite of arguments that the FMP would result of closure of the dogfish fishery for at least five years, the Court of Appeals upheld the FMP. The court noted that a collapsed fishery that would not be economically viable for decades would create worse economic consequences than implementing the FMP. The court emphasized that the duty to prevent overfishing under Standard One takes precedence over Standard Eight. Regulations provide that the effect of Standard Eight is that when two alternatives achieve similar conservation goals, the agency will choose the alternative that better achieves Standard Eight goals. See 50 C.F.R. § 666.345(b).

3.   FOREIGN FISHING IN THE U.S. EEZ

One of the primary goals of the 1976 Fishery Conservation and Management Act was to "Americanize" the waters off the U.S. coast. The Act allowed for foreign fishing in the U.S. EEZ, but only to the extent that fisheries allocations exceed domestic harvesting capacity and only when pursuant to a fishing treaty or Governing International Fishery Agreement (GIFA). A GIFA requires compliance with numerous conditions, including the foreign nation's agreeing to acknowledge exclusive U.S. management authority, to abide by all fishery regulations, to allow boarding and inspection for enforcement of U.S. laws, to reimburse U.S. citizens for damages to vessels or gear caused by a fishing vessel of the nation, and to permit and pay the costs associated with a required onboard observer. 16 U.S.C.A. § 1821(c). Each foreign fishing vessel must have an annual permit and is subject to permit fees and poundage fees for fish caught. Id. § 1824. A vessel's permit can be revoked for violation of conditions, *United States v. Kaiyo Maru No. 53*, 503 F.Supp. 1075 (D.Alaska 1980), and the release of a nation's fishery allocation can be affected. 16 U.S.C.A. § 1821(e)(1)(D).

The total allowable level of foreign fishing (TALFF) is determined by the appropriate fishery management council for each fishery. The TALFF is calculated by determining the surplus of optimum yield that remains after taking account of the harvest by U.S. vessels, the domestic annual harvest or DAH. This calculation can be generally conceptualized as: OY minus DAH equals TALFF. The TALFF for each fishery is allocated to foreign nations by the Secretary of State, in cooperation with the Secretary of Commerce, based on a number of factors, including the degree and extent of: (1) tariff barriers on the importation of or restricted market access for U.S. fish and fish products, particularly for the fish for which the allocation is requested; (2) cooperation to advance U.S. fishery exports; (3) cooperation in fisheries research and technology transfer, enforcement of fishery regulations, and minimization of gear conflict with U.S. fishermen; (4) traditional fishing by the foreign nation in a fishery and the nation's dependence on the fishery for domestic consumption; and (5) other matters the Secretary of State "deems appropriate." Id. § 1821(e)(1)(E). A TALFF allocation could also be affected by a nation's failure to allow reciprocal U.S. fishing or by a "certification" by the Secretary that the nation engaged in fishery or trade practices that undermine the International Convention for the Regulation of Whaling. See *Associated Vessels Servs., Inc. v. Verity*, 688 F.Supp. 13 (D.D.C. 1988) (holding that the court has no authority to invade the policy-making realm and order a reallocation of TALFF). See also Gary M. Shinaver, Comment, *Fishery Conservation: Is the Categorical Exclusion of Foreign Fleets the Next Step,* 12 Cal. W. Int'l L.J. 154 (1982).

Foreign countries enhanced their access to fish from the U.S. EEZ through so-called "joint ventures" in which U.S. fishermen deliver harvests directly to foreign fish processing vessels. These arrangements were perceived as a loophole in the law by onshore processors and as a new market opportunity by U.S. fishermen. In an attempt to balance the interests of both domestic fishermen and processors, Congress amended the MSA to require permits for such joint ventures that limited transfers to the portion of the fishery harvest beyond U.S. onshore processing capacity. 16 U.S.C.A. § 1824 (b)(6)(B). See also Donna R. Christie, *Regulation of International Joint Ventures in the Fishery Conservation Zone,* 10 Ga. J. Int'l & Comp. L. 85 (1980).

Since enactment of the MSA in 1976, the Congressional goal of Americanizing fishing in the

U.S. EEZ largely has been achieved. No TALFF for foreign fishing has been set for the U.S. EEZ since 1991, and no foreign vessels have harvested any fish or participated in a joint venture since 2003. With 2.25 million square miles of EEZ, some illegal fishing takes place in U.S. EEZs, however, particularly in the Pacific Ocean in the no-take areas set aside as marine national monuments. See Mark Richardson and the Marine Conservation Institute, *Protecting America's Pacific Marine Monuments: A Review of Threats and Law Enforcement Issues* (2012). These and other EEZ incursions into U.S. EEZs and the U.S. response are addressed in the *U.S. National Plan of Action to Prevent, Deter, and Eliminate Illegal, Unregulated, and Unreported Fishing* published by NOAA.

4. STATE MANAGEMENT AFTER ENACTMENT OF THE MSA

MSA section 306(a)(1), 16 U.S.C.A. § 1856(a)(1), generally preserves state fisheries management authority within its boundaries. An exception arises when state action or lack of action "substantially and adversely affect[s]" the implementation of an FMP for a fishery located predominately within the EEZ. The Act then allows the Secretary to directly regulate the affected fishery seaward of the state internal waters. 16 U.S.C.A. § 1856(b). Such preemption is infrequently used.

Section 1856(a)(3), as amended in 1996, preserves *a Skiriotes*-type jurisdiction for vessels registered in a state operating beyond state waters where: (1) the state laws are consistent with any applicable federal FMP, laws, or regulations, or there is no applicable federal FMP, laws, or regulations; or (2) a federal FMP delegates management to the state and the state laws are consistent with the FMP. Issues have arisen involving federal preemption and other constitutional challenges, the meanings of registration and consistent, and state enforcement mechanisms.

a.   Interpretation of "Registered"

State registration for purposes of extraterritorial jurisdiction is not defined in the MSA, but courts have interpreted the term liberally. These interpretations either implicitly or explicitly start with the premise that Congress intended registration to be defined by local or state law. The idea that Congress intended section 1856(a)(3) to refer to federal registration requirements instead of state requirements has been rejected by at least two courts. See *State v. F/V Baranof*, 677 P.2d 1245 (Alaska 1984); *People v. Weeren*, 163 Cal.Rptr. 255, 607 P.2d 1279 (1980). Federal registration requirements may, however, provide a helpful background for the registration issue. To comply with federal registration requirements, vessels weighing more than five net tons are required to be enrolled and licensed or registered by the federal government. Ships engaged in foreign trade are "registered" to establish nationality. Ships engaged in domestic trade or fishing are "enrolled" as evidence of the national character of the vessel and "licensed" to regulate its use. See *Douglas v. Seacoast Products*,

431 U.S. 265, 97 S.Ct. 1740, 52 L.Ed.2d 304 (1977). Vessels weighing less than five tons are not required to register with the federal government, but instead can have a registration number issued by an appropriate state.

The state in which the vessel is principally used is deemed to be an appropriate state for state registration purposes. *United States v. Seafoam II*, 528 F.Supp. 1133 (D.Alaska 1982). In *People v. Weeren*, 163 Cal.Rptr. 255, 607 P.2d 1279 (1980), the California Supreme Court determined that state licensing for commercial fishing purposes sufficed as state "registration" under the MSA. The vessel in *Weeren* was arrested beyond state waters for violation of a state law prohibiting the use of aircraft for spotting swordfish. The vessel did not possess a state identification number because it was enrolled with a United States document number. The court analyzed the different purposes of federal licensing, registration, or enrollment and of state registration. The court reasoned that preventing a state from enforcing its regulations against a vessel that was not required to obtain a state identification because the vessel possessed a federal number would render section 1856(a) "virtually meaningless, limiting [state] jurisdiction to pleasure boats and those few commercial fishing vessels lighter than five net tons." The court concluded that its interpretation prevented "the anomalous result which would follow [if the state could enforce its laws against] those boats in which the state had asserted only a limited identification and record-keeping interest, but was precluded as to vessels . . . which it has specifically licensed to engage in [a particular fishing activity]."

Some states have statutorily defined the term "registration" for purposes of extraterritorial jurisdiction over fisheries. For example, Maine's fishing license statute defines a registered vessel as one owned or operated by the possessor of a fishing license. In *State v. Hayes*, 603 A.2d 869 (Me. 1992), the Maine Supreme Court determined that possession of a Maine commercial fishing and lobster license meant that the defendant's vessel was registered within the meaning of section 1856(a). The vessel did not possess a state identification or registration number. Interpreting section 1856(a) to give effect to each state's definition of registration may subject a vessel to the simultaneous, and possibly conflicting, regulation of more than one state while fishing in the EEZ, leading to confusion for the vessel owner and enforcement authorities.

b.   Meaning of "Consistent"

The SFA allowed substantial confusion to continue by not entirely preempting state regulation when a federal plan and regulations were in place. States may still regulate state-registered vessels if no federal FMP is in place or if their laws and regulations are "consistent" with "the fishery management plan and applicable Federal fishing regulations." 16 U.S.C. § 1856(a)(3)(A). Further, the state can regulate other fishing vessels beyond state waters if the Secretary delegates management to a state with laws and regulations consistent with the applicable federal FMP. 16 U.S.C. § 1856(a)(3)(B). Significantly, the term, "consistent," was not defined in either case. It is clear that less restrictive regulation would not be consistent with the conservation regime of FMPs, but it is not entirely clear that more restrictive state regulations are consistent. Several courts have held that because the purposes of the MSA include development of the fishing industry, state regulations that restrict fishing in the EEZ beyond the level allowed in federal FMPs are not consistent. See, e.g., *Southeastern Fisheries Ass'n, Inc. v. Chiles*, 979 F.2d 1504 (11th Cir. 1992); *State v. Sterling*, 448 A.2d 785 (R.I. 1982); *Vietnamese Fishermen Assn. of America v. California Department of Fish and Game*, 816 F.Supp. 1468 (N.D.Cal. 1993); but see *Louisiana Seafood Mgmt. Council v. Foster*, 917 F. Supp. 439 (The "spirit and purpose of the Magnuson Act is to protect and conserve saltwater finfish" and does not preempt state regulation).

c.   Federal Preemption

MSA 306(a)(3)'s approval of state EEZ fisheries regulations which are consistent with federal FMPs, laws, or regulations presents issues similar to federal preemption questions. A court's analysis of whether a federal law preempts state regulation generally focuses on three issues: (1) Did Congress intend to occupy the field?; (2) Is there a conflict?; and (3) Does the state regulation present an obstacle to the goals and purposes of the federal law? *Douglas v. Seacoast Products*, 431 U.S. 265, 97 S.Ct. 1740, 52 L.Ed.2d 304 (1977).

In the fisheries management context, the first issue involves the question of whether the mere enactment of the MSA preempts state fishery regulation in the EEZ. If by enacting the MSA Congress evidenced intent, either express or implied, to occupy the entire field of fishery regulation, then any state fishery regulation is preempted by the Act. *State v. F/V Baranof*, 677 P.2d 1245 (Alaska 1984) (holding that Alaska laws had not been expressly preempted by the MSA and that no federal regulations had impliedly displaced state regulation of the crab fishery). Most courts have determined that mere enactment of the MSA does not preempt state fishery regulations. E.g., *State v. Dupier*, 118 P.3d 1039 (Alaska 2005); *Louisiana Seafood Management Council, Inc. v. Foster*, 917 F.Supp. 439 (E.D.La. 1996); *Anderson Seafoods, Inc. v. Graham*, 529 F.Supp. 512 (N.D.Fla. 1982); *State v. Painter*, 695 P.2d 241 (Alaska App. 1985); *State v. F/V Baranof*, 677 P.2d 1245 (Alaska 1984); *Livings v. Davis*, 465 So.2d 507 (Fla. 1985). Although the enactment of the MSA manifests a strong federal interest in fisheries regulation, section 1856(a)(3) now expressly precludes a finding that Congress intended for the MSA to preempt all state EEZ fishery regulations through complete occupation of the field.

Preemption can also occur when a state law conflicts with a federal FMP, laws, or regulations. Obviously, state regulations that are more lenient than a federal FMP, laws, or regulations present a conflict. The harder question has arisen in the context of more restrictive state regulation, and courts have come to inconsistent conclusions. Some courts find no conflict if it is possible to comply with both laws. See, e.g., *Skiriotes v. Florida,* 313 U.S. 69, 61 S.Ct. 924, 85 L.Ed. 1193 (1941) (a Florida statute regulating equipment used for sponge fishing did not conflict with a federal law regulating the size of sponges that could be taken); *Potter v. McCullers*, 505 So.2d 510 (Fla.Dist.Ct.App. 1987) (finding application of a Florida shrimping regulation constitutional when enforced beyond state waters but outside of a federally regulated shrimp sanctuary).

As a general proposition, federal environmental laws usually do not preempt more protective state legislation. However, some courts have found state regulations preempted by less restrictive federal rules for the same fishery. See, e.g., *Southeastern Fisheries Ass'n, Inc. v. Chiles*, 979 F.2d 1504 (11th Cir. 1992); *State v. Sterling*, 448 A.2d 785 (R.I. 1982). A slight deviation between a state and a federal regulation that are "substantially the same" will not lead to preemption. *State v. Painter*, 695 P.2d 241 (Alaska App. 1985) (finding no conflict between state and federal regulations when the only difference between the two regulations was that the state law provided criminal sanctions and the federal regulation provided civil sanctions).

Consistent with section 306(a)(3)(B), 16 U.S.C.A. § 1856(a)(3)(A), state regulation has been upheld because a federal FMP, law, or regulation expressly permits enforcement of the stricter state law. *State v. Hayes*, 603 A.2d 869 (Me. 1992) (finding no conflict when federal regulations contained language that retained local and state "fishing, catch and gear" requirements and permitted enforcement of more restrictive state lobster regulations); *Raffield v. State*, 565 So.2d 704 (Fla. 1990) (finding no conflict when the preamble to federal red drum fishery rules expressly stated that state landing laws were not superseded by the rules). However, in *Southeastern Fisheries Ass'n v. Mosbacher*, 773 F.Supp. 435 (D.D.C. 1991), the D.C. District Court struck down federal regulations for the Gulf of Mexico red drum fishery that provided for state landing and possession laws to continue to be enforced. The court found that failure to preempt state landing laws was arbitrary and capricious and an abuse of the Secretary's discretion. In effect, the FMP allowed fishermen to catch redfish within the EEZ, but not land them, since four of five Gulf States prohibited or restricted landing.

Finally, preemption may occur when a state fishery regulation presents an obstacle to the goals and purposes of the federal FMP, law, or regulation. When a state enforces regulations stricter than the federal FMP, without specific authorization in the FMP, state regulations may be viewed as presenting an obstacle to MSA goals of promoting domestic commercial fishing and preventing piecemeal extraterritorial state regulation. *Bateman v. Gardner*, 716 F.Supp. 595 (S.D.Fla. 1989); *Southeastern Fisheries Ass'n v. Martinez*, 772 F.Supp. 1263 (S.D.Fla. 1991).

d. Other Constitutional Challenges

Other constitutional challenges to state fishery regulations have been premised on the notion that it is not fair to subject state-registered vessels to more restrictive requirements than out-of-state vessels in extraterritorial waters. These statutes are usually challenged as violations of the Equal Protection, the Privileges and Immunities, or the Commerce Clauses.

Privileges and Immunities Clause challenges have been unsuccessful, because the clause appears to be clearly inappropriate in this context. The clause only protects out-of-state residents from discriminatory treatment by another state. *State v. Hayes*, 603 A.2d 869 (Me. 1992) (citing *Toomer v. Witsell*, 334 U.S. 385, 68 S.Ct. 1156, 92 L.Ed. 1460 (1948): "[The Clause] was designed to insure to a citizen of State A who ventures into State B the same privileges which the citizens of State B enjoy."); *Tangier Sound Waterman's Ass'n v. Pruitt*, 4 F.3d 264 (4th Cir. 1993). There is no need for the Privileges and Immunities Clause to protect in-state residents from their own laws because in-state residents have a voice in their state's political process.

Equal Protection challenges also are grounded in a concept of "fairness" to state citizens. Rejecting an equal protection claim, the Maine Supreme Court noted that the unequal treatment between in-state and out-of-state citizens is a result of "limitations on sovereignty rather than from the creation of suspect classifications." *State v. Hayes*, 603 A.2d 869 (Me. 1992). See also *State v. Thomas*, 2010 ME 116, 8 A.3d

638 (Me. 2010) (Maine's enforcement of its marine
resource laws against only Maine registered vessels
does not violate equal protection). In *State v. Raffield*,
515 So.2d 283 (Fla.App. 1987), a Florida court
determined that a state fishery regulation did not
violate equal protection because regulating the
taking of food fish by Florida citizens was a
legitimate state interest, i.e., conservation of a
fishery resource. See also *Daley v. Commissioner*, 698
A.2d 1053 (Me. 1997) (exemption of family members
fishing from same vessel from state per vessel lobster
trip limit upheld); *Lane v. Chiles*, 698 So.2d 260 (Fla.
1997) (state restriction on marine net fishing
upheld); *State v. Norton*, 335 A.2d 607 (Me. 1975)
(local ordinance banning nonresident shellfish
harvesting struck down).

Fishermen have, however, successfully brought
Equal Protection challenges to several state fishery
regulations. In *Bateman v. Gardner*, 716 F.Supp. 595
(S.D.Fla. 1989), and *Southeastern Fisheries Ass'n,
Inc. v. Martinez*, 772 F.Supp. 1263 (S.D.Fla. 1991),
the federal district court found that Florida statutes
placing shrimping and mackerel catch restrictions on
Florida-registered vessels in federal waters violated
equal protection because of the statute's
discriminatory impact. The court implied that a
state's *Skiriotes* jurisdiction is limited to those
circumstances in which a state fishery regulation
mirrors federal regulations for the same area. State
EEZ regulations meeting the requirements of section
306(a)(3) as amended in 1996 should be less
vulnerable to such challenges.

A third type of constitutional challenge is the assertion that a state fishery regulation places an undue burden on interstate commerce in violation of the Commerce Clause. *Davrod Corp. v. Coates*, 971 F.2d 778 (1st Cir. 1992), involved a state statute that regulated the length of fishing vessels in state waters. The court determined that the statute was not discriminatory to commerce on its face because it affected intrastate and interstate vessels equally. Had the statute been discriminatory on its face, the state would have had the burden of showing that the statute had a legitimate state purpose and that this purpose could not be served as well by non-discriminatory means. Next, the court examined whether the statute was discriminatory in its effect, which required a determination of whether the burden on interstate trade was clearly excessive in relation to the benefits. Concluding that the vessel length limitation was a "proper regulation of the means of catching fish," and that conservation of fish stock was a legitimate state regulatory concern, the court found no violation of the Commerce Clause. In spite of the fact that no in-state vessels were affected by the law, the court found that it has only "incidental" effects on interstate commerce.

The Florida Supreme Court applied the strict "legitimate local purpose" test in evaluating whether a Florida statute prohibiting the taking of fish with a purse seine was a burden on interstate commerce. *Raffield v. Florida*, 565 So.2d 704 (Fla. 1990). The court found that the statute did not violate the commerce clause because Florida has a legitimate interest in "protecting fisheries that are a vital source of food for its residents, even though the fisheries lie beyond the territorial limits of the state," and that limiting the use of purse seines was the only "available nondiscriminatory means" of achieving this purpose. Id. See also *Ampro Fisheries, Inc. v. Yaskin*, 127 N.J. 602, 606 A.2d 1099 (1992) (Commerce Clause challenge to state prohibitions of industrial menhaden fishing rejected); *New York State Trawlers Ass'n v. Jorling*, 16 F.3d 1303 (2d Cir. 1994) (Commerce Clause challenge to state ban on lobster trawling rejected).

In *State v. Hayes*, 603 A.2d 869 (Me. 1992), Maine's highest court noted that a state statute could not violate the Commerce Clause when Congress expressly authorizes the state action. Hayes found no Commerce Clause violation because federal lobster regulations required federal permit holders to comply with state fishing, catch, and gear requirements.

e.   Enforcement Issues

Enactment of the MSA has also created enforcement problems for the states, even for regulations that apply only within state waters. Landing or possession laws are the primary means for enforcing fisheries regulations. These laws can have the effect of regulating out-of-state citizens in the EEZ. Even enforcement of possession laws against a state's citizens fishing in the EEZ can be problematic if the prohibited gear is expressly permitted by a federal FMP, law, or regulation. *Vietnamese Fishermen Ass'n v. California Fish & Game Dept.*, 816 F.Supp. 1468 (N.D.Cal. 1993). In

Southeastern Fisheries Ass'n v. Department of Natural Resources, 453 So.2d 1351 (Fla. 1984), the Florida Supreme Court found that a Florida law prohibiting the use or possession of fish traps within state waters unconstitutionally limited the legal use of the traps in the EEZ. Although the state could continue to prosecute fishermen for unlawful possession of fishtraps, the state "must prove, as an element of possession, the intent to unlawfully use the fish traps" in Florida waters—a virtually impossible burden in the majority of field enforcement situations.

G.   MANAGEMENT OF PROTECTED AND ENDANGERED MARINE SPECIES

1.   WHALES

a.   Background

Whales are found in every ocean of the world, and the whaling industry began as early as the eleventh or twelfth century. By the twentieth century, the excesses and waste of an unregulated whaling industry had decimated whale populations. Although the market for whale oil and products decreased with the increased availability of petroleum products, whaling continued to increase. At the turn of the twentieth century, fewer than 5,000 whales per year were taken; in 1931, over 40,000 whales were harvested.

The first efforts to control whaling in the 1920s culminated in the 1931 Convention for the

Regulation of Whaling, opened for signature Sept. 24, 1931, 49 Stat. 3079, 155 L.N.T.S. 349. The Convention prohibited the taking of right whales and bowhead whales. The primary provisions of the treaty were directed at controlling waste by prohibiting the taking of calves, immature whales, and females with suckling calves and by requiring that parties make the "fullest possible use" of all whales that were harvested. Negotiations in 1937 and 1938 resulted in further agreements to prohibit the taking of gray whales and established minimum lengths for species, limits for geographic areas, and whaling seasons for humpback whales. Nearly fifty countries, including the United States, were parties to the 1931 Convention, but the major whaling nations—Argentina, Chile, Germany, Japan, and the Soviet Union—were not parties.

These early efforts did not improve the status of whale populations. The interruption of commercial whaling during World War II and the failure of the 1931 Convention provided the impetus for negotiation of a new treaty following the war. The current regime for regulation of whaling is based on the 1946 International Convention for the Regulation of Whaling (Whaling Convention), done Dec. 2, 1946, 62 Stat. 1716, 161 U.N.T.S. 72. Although the 1946 Convention originally had fewer parties than the earlier treaty, all the major whaling nations were among the signatories. The preamble of the 1946 Whaling Convention sets out the dual purposes of the agreement which include both "safeguarding for future generations the great natural resources represented by the whale stocks" and "the orderly development of the whaling industry." The original intent of the Convention was clearly not preservation, but conservation and recovery of whale stocks to an "optimum level" as a basis for long-term exploitation. See William Burke, *Legal Aspects of the IWC Decision on the Southern Ocean Sanctuary,* 28 Ocean Devel. & Int'l L. 3113 (1997).

b. The 1946 International Whaling Convention

Unlike most international fishing agreements which are generally limited to activities on the high seas, the Whaling Convention extends to "all waters in which whaling is prosecuted." Whaling Convention, art. I(2). This means that the Convention applies not only within 200-mile fishery and exclusive economic zones, but also within territorial seas and inland waters. The Convention does not define "whale," but the treaty's jurisdiction has been extended primarily to larger cetaceans. In fact, in the first two decades of treaty implementation, whales were not regulated by species, but in terms of "blue whale units," a methodology that treated all species of large baleen whales as fungible.

The Whaling Convention established the International Whaling Commission (IWC), which is composed of one voting representative of each party to the treaty. The IWC is authorized to recommend and carry out research, to collect statistics on stocks and whaling operations, and to disseminate information on means of maintaining and increasing whale stocks. Id. art. IV(1).

The IWC governs the exploitation and protection of whales through a detailed set of regulations called the Schedule. Article V of the Whaling Convention gives the IWC the power to amend the Schedule by a three-fourths majority of the members voting. Measures that may be taken include designation of: "(a) protected and unprotected species; (b) open and closed seasons; (c) open and closed waters, including the designation of sanctuary areas; (d) size limits for each species; (e) time, methods, and intensity of whaling . . .; (f) types and specifications of gear . . .; (g) methods of measurement; and (h) . . . records." Id. art. V(1).

The Whaling Convention puts a number of limitations on amendments to the Schedule that are not in the direct interest of preserving whales. Amendments to the Schedule must be based on scientific findings. Id. art. V(2). Because information on stocks and conservation methods is extremely deficient in spite of over fifty years of research, this requirement impliedly rejects the so-called "precautionary principle" which is currently favored by environmentalists. This requirement also rejects popular notions that whales are intelligent mammals with an entitlement to life. Restrictions on amendments to the Schedule are clearly intended to safeguard the interests of whaling countries. In addition to providing for conservation of whale stocks, amendments must provide for "development, and optimum utilization of the whale resources" and consider "the interests of the consumers of whale products and the whaling industry." Id. Amendments cannot restrict the number or nationality of vessels or allocate specific quotas to vessels. Id.

The provision of the Whaling Convention that guaranteed participation by whaling nations also provides the treaty's biggest loophole. An amendment to the Schedule is not effective with respect to a party that objects to the measure within ninety days. Id. art. V(3). Throughout the history of the Convention, its effectiveness has been jeopardized or even nullified when major whaling countries have registered objections to conservation provisions. See Simon Lyster, International Wildlife Law 27–8 (1985).

The most controversial amendment to the Schedule was the adoption in 1982 of a temporary moratorium—which is still in effect—on all commercial whaling that took effect in 1986. The Soviet Union, Japan, and Norway registered objections to the moratorium. Japan charged that the moratorium was a significant departure from the original objectives of the Convention, and that it was motivated by emotion and politics, rather than by science. See generally Kazuo Sumi, *The "Whale War" Between Japan and the United States: Problems and Prospects,* 17 Denv. J. Int'l L. & Pol'y 317 (1989). Norway resumed whaling operations in the spring of 1993 and continues whaling today. Iceland, which did not register an objection to the moratorium, withdrew from the Convention in 1992. Although Iceland rejoined in 2004, it included an objection to the moratorium as part of its reentry. In 2006, Iceland resumed commercial whaling.

The IWC has designated two sanctuaries that prohibit all commercial whaling. The Indian Ocean Sanctuary was created in 1979 and comprises all of the Indian Ocean south of 55 degrees south latitude. The Southern Ocean Sanctuary surrounding Antarctica was created in 1994. Other proposals for sanctuaries have repeatedly failed to achieve the three-fourths vote necessary.

The IWC is also authorized to "make recommendations . . . which relate to whales or whaling and to the objectives and purposes of th[e] Convention" by a majority vote. An example is the 1979 recommendation by the IWC directed at "pirate" whaling. The IWC recommended that parties suspend imports of whale meat and products and suspend exports of whaling vessels and technology to non-party countries. Such recommendations do not have the force of law but have been widely effective.

The only exemption provided for in the Whaling Convention is for special permits to be issued by nations for scientific research. Whaling Convention, art. VIII. To prevent waste, the Convention provides that whales taken for scientific purposes should be processed so far as practicable. Id. Critics have asserted that the sanctioning of commercial disposal of such whales has led to abuse of the exemption, particularly by Japan. Japan withdrew its original objection to the commercial moratorium, but continued taking whales, purportedly for scientific research. In 2014, the International Court of Justice

(ICJ) ordered Japan to revoke existing scientific permits and to refrain from issuing additional permits under its scientific program. The ICJ found that the design and implementation of Japan's scientific program are not reasonable in relation to achieving its stated objectives and, consequently, the special permits granted by Japan for the killing, taking and treating of whales were not "for purposes of scientific research" as required by the Convention. *Whaling in the Antarctic (Australia v. Japan: New Zealand intervening)*, Judgment of 31 March 2014.

There is no exemption in the Convention for whaling for subsistence and cultural needs, which arguably had not threatened the survival of whales before excessive commercial whaling operations depleted stocks. The IWC does not treat such whaling the same as commercial whaling, however, and the moratorium does not apply to subsistence whaling. Governments must provide the IWC with a "Needs Statement" that details the cultural and nutritional basis for the hunt. The IWC's Scientific Committee assesses the sustainability of the hunt and advises on catch limits. The Schedule provides catch limits for aboriginal subsistence whaling for certain natives of Alaska, Chukotka and Washington State, Greenland, and St. Vincent and the Grenadines.

Japan has unsuccessfully argued to the IWC that the reliance of many of its small coastal communities upon subsistence whaling is virtually identical to aboriginal subsistence whaling. Although the IWC has continually refused to authorize a catch limit for these "small-type" coastal whaling operations,

Japan's argument is gaining support and will be reconsidered at future IWC meetings.

It has been argued that the Whaling Convention was not intended to cover subsistence whaling. In *Hopson v. Kreps*, 622 F.2d 1375 (9th Cir. 1980), the Ninth Circuit held that justiciable questions had been presented as to whether the IWC had exceeded its jurisdiction in eliminating certain native subsistence whaling. The decision reversed the district court holding that interpretation of the treaty was a nonjusticiable political question. The question is still unresolved, because it was never addressed on remand, presumably because the IWC continued to authorize subsistence hunting of bowhead whales by Native Alaskans. See also *Adams v. Vance*, 187 U.S.App.D.C. 41 (D.C.Cir. 1978).

The Whaling Convention places responsibility on each government to "take appropriate measures" to enforce the treaty and to punish "infractions . . . by persons or by vessels under its jurisdiction." Whaling Convention, art. IX(1). Infractions and punitive and remedial measures taken must be reported to the IWC. Id. art. IX(4). The Convention gives a party broad discretion in implementing the provisions and in defining the scope of the nation's jurisdiction. Some countries, like the United States, have taken extensive measures to implement the Convention provisions and to promote further conservation of whales and other marine mammals.

c. United States Enforcement of the International Whaling Convention

The combination of the Whaling Convention's dual purposes, the objection procedure, and a weak enforcement mechanism has resulted in continued depletion of many species of whales and has frustrated attempts by the non-whaling majority of the IWC to incorporate reforms for further conservation of whales. United States' domestic policy on whaling, however, has had a significant influence on the implementation of IWC policies. United States policy on whaling is implemented through four statutes: (1) the Endangered Species Act, 16 U.S.C.A. §§ 1531–1544; (2) the Marine Mammal Protection Act (MMPA), 16 U.S.C.A. §§ 1361–1421h; (3) the Pelly Amendment to the Fisherman's Protective Act of 1967, 22 U.S.C.A. § 1978; and (4) the Packwood Amendment to the Magnuson-Stevens Fishery Conservation and Management Act (MSA), 16 U.S.C.A. § 1821(e)(2).

The MMPA, which is discussed further below, provides a comprehensive management program for a wide array of ocean mammals. The Act is broader both in scope and in protective measures than the Whaling Convention. In the MMPA, Congress specifically directs United States' agencies to initiate negotiations to amend existing international treaties, e.g., the Whaling Convention, to make the treaties "consistent with the purposes and policies" of the MMPA. 16 U.S.C.A. § 1378(a)(4). The Act also encourages negotiation of additional bilateral and multilateral agreements to protect and conserve all marine mammals. Id. § 1378(1)–(2).

The Pelly Amendment, passed in 1967 due to concern over the implementation of international salmon treaties, directs the Secretary of Commerce to certify to the President findings that foreign nationals, "directly or indirectly, are conducting fishing operations in a manner or under circumstances which diminish the effectiveness of an international fishery conservation program." 22 U.S.C.A. § 1978(a)(i). The term "international fishery conservation program" is defined broadly to apply to programs pertaining to any "living resources of the sea" and was intended to include the Whaling Convention. Id. § 1978(h)(3). Upon certification, the President may direct the Secretary of Treasury to prohibit importation of fish products from the certified country. Id. § 1978(a)(4). The President's imposition of the sanction is, however, discretionary. Following enactment of the Pelly Amendment, the President imposed no sanctions in five cases of nations certified by the Secretary of Commerce as engaging in fishing that diminished the effectiveness of whaling quotas established by the IWC. The threat of sanctions did, however, result in negotiations that substantially changed the whaling practices of the nations involved.

Congress' impatience with delays in certification and the President's failure to impose sanctions under the Pelly Amendment[1] was reflected in the 1979

---

[1] Japan, for example, was certified three times—in 1988, 1995, and 2000, but no president had issued trade sanctions

Packwood Amendment to the MSA. The Secretary of Commerce is directed to monitor activities of foreign nationals and "promptly" investigate and "promptly" make certification decisions. See id. § 1978(a)(3)(A)–(C). The Packwood Amendment also attempted to eliminate discretion in the imposition of sanctions. If the Secretary of Commerce certifies that foreign nationals, "directly or indirectly, are conducting fishing operations or engaging in trade or taking [of whales] which diminishes the effectiveness of the International Convention on the Regulation of Whaling," the Secretary of State must reduce, by at least fifty percent, the certified nation's fishery allocation within the United States EEZ. 16 U.S.C.A. § 1821(e)(2)(A)–(B). Certification under the Packwood Amendment is also deemed a certification for purposes of the Pelly Amendment.

In *Japan Whaling Ass'n v. American Cetacean Society*, 478 U.S. 221, 106 S.Ct. 2860, 92 L.Ed.2d 166 (1986), the U.S. Supreme Court addressed the issue of whether the Secretary of Commerce was required to certify that Japan's practices had "diminished the effectiveness" of the Whaling Convention by exceeding quotas established by the IWC. In 1981, the IWC set a zero quota for certain sperm whales and in 1982, the IWC adopted the commercial whaling moratorium to be effective in 1986. Japan had filed timely objections to both actions and was not bound to comply with these IWC regulations.

---

against Japan under the Pelly Amendment. In December 2000, President Clinton declared Japan ineligible to conduct fishing operations within the United States EEZ, but since Japan had no fisheries allocation, this was a purely ritualistic action.

Japan's actions could, however, be interpreted as diminishing the effectiveness of the Whaling Convention and be subject to sanctions under the Pelly and Packwood Amendments. Rather than "certifying" Japan, the Secretary of Commerce entered into negotiations that resulted in an agreement in 1984 that Japan would withdraw its objections to the sperm whale quota and the commercial whaling moratorium effective in 1988. In return, the United States would agree that Japan could harvest additional whales in the interim without triggering certification. Before formal adoption of the agreement, several environmental groups filed suit to compel the Secretary of Commerce to certify Japan. The district court granted summary judgment and ordered the Secretary to certify Japan immediately for violating the sperm whale quota. A divided court of appeals affirmed.

In the five-four opinion, the Supreme Court first rejected the government's argument that the case involved foreign relations and was unsuitable for judicial review. The Court cast the issue as merely involving interpretation of United States legislation, i.e., the Pelly and Packwood Amendments. The Court noted first that Japan had filed timely objections and was not in violation of any obligation under the Whaling Convention. The Court then considered whether Congress intended that the Secretary must automatically certify any nation that violates IWC quotas. Finding that Congress had not directly addressed the issue of whether quota violations per se "diminish effectiveness" of the treaty, the Court applied the test set out in *Chevron, U.S.A., Inc. v. Natural Resources Defense Council, Inc.,* 467 U.S. 837, 104 S.Ct. 2778, 81 L.Ed.2d 694 (1984). That is, reviewing courts should defer to the "executive department's construction of a statutory scheme it is entrusted to administer," unless the legislative history clearly reveals that the construction is contrary to the will of Congress.

The Supreme Court found that the legislative history supported the Secretary's view that the phrase "diminish the effectiveness" in the amendments was intended to provide a range of discretion. Because Congress' "goal was to protect and conserve whales," Congress intended the Secretary to have the flexibility to consider what course "would contribute more to the effectiveness of the IWC." The Court concluded, therefore:

> that the Secretary's decision to secure the certainty of Japan's future compliance with the IWC's program through the 1984 executive agreement, rather than rely on the possibility that certification and imposition of economic sanctions would produce the same or better result, is a reasonable construction of the Pelly and Packwood Amendments.

The dissenting justices read the legislative history as clearly demonstrating Congress' intent to impose a nondiscretionary duty on the Secretary to certify nations that violate IWC quotas. The Secretary's interpretation of the certification power, the dissenters stated, was merely a new "means for [the

Executive Branch to] evad[e] the constraints of the
Packwood Amendment."

Although the president rarely uses his discretion
to impose sanctions, Pelly/Packwood certification (or
the threat of certification) has not been an entirely
symbolic gesture. The availability of sanctions
considerably bolsters the U.S. negotiating position
and has led to significant changes in the actions of
whaling countries. See Peter J. Stoett, The
International Politics of Whaling 86–88 (1997).

In January 2014, the Secretary of Commerce
certified Iceland under Pelly/Packwood amendments
for the third time. Iceland was certified in 2004 for
its scientific whaling program; the certification was
extended in 2006 when it resumed commercial
whaling; and Iceland was again certified for
diminishing the effectiveness of the IWC in 2011.
Recently, Iceland has drastically increased its take of
finwhales for export to Japan. Its announced 2014–
2019 quota of 154 finwhales per year is more than
three times the number that the IWC deems
biologically sustainable. The Obama administration
has decided, however, to continue diplomatic
approaches to deal with Iceland's whaling. See White
House Statement, *Message to the Congress—Iceland
and the Fisherman's Protective Act* (April 01, 2014),
available at http://www.whitehouse.gov/the-press-
office/2014/04/01/message-congress-iceland-and-fish
erman-s-protective-act.

It should be noted that if a case similar to
American Cetacean Society arose today, the standing
of the environmental group to bring the suit would be

a major threshold issue. In *American Cetacean Society*, the Supreme Court summarily dismissed the Secretary's standing challenge in a footnote. The Court stated that "it appears that respondents are sufficiently 'aggrieved' by the agency's action: [T]hey undoubtedly have alleged a sufficient 'injury in fact' in that the whale watching and studying of their members will be adversely affected by continued whale harvesting." In a more recent case, *Lujan v. Defenders of Wildlife*, 504 U.S. 555, 112 S.Ct. 2130, 119 L.Ed.2d 351 (1992), the Supreme Court more narrowly interpreted "injury in fact."

In *Defenders of Wildlife*, the environmental group challenged a new regulation reinterpreting the Endangered Species Act to require consultations with expert agencies only for federal agency actions taken in the United States or on the high seas. The group's standing was based on the affidavits of members stating that they traveled to certain foreign countries to observe particular endangered species and their habitats. The Supreme Court identified the three elements to establish standing as follows:

> First, the plaintiff must have suffered an "injury in fact" in invasion of a legally protected interest which is (a) concrete and particularized; and (b) "actual or imminent, not 'conjectural' or 'hypothetical.' " Second, there must be a causal connection between the injury and the conduct complained of the injury has to be "fairly . . . trace[able] to the challenged action . . . and not . . . th[e] result [of] the independent action of some third party not before the court." Third, it

must be "likely," as opposed to merely "speculative" that the injury will be "redressed by a favorable decision."

(Citations omitted). While the Court acknowledged that the desire to observe an animal, even for purely aesthetic reasons, is a "cognizable interest for purposes of standing," the Court stated that "injury in fact" requires that a party be "directly" affected. Specifically citing *American Cetacean Society,* the Court criticized the finding of direct harm in that case as going "to the outermost limit of plausibility."

In *Defenders of Wildlife,* the Court also found that the plaintiffs failed to meet the causation and redressability prongs of the standing test. That is, the plaintiffs did not show that the harm they would suffer by not being able to observe endangered species in foreign countries was caused by the agency action or could be prevented by the remedy they sought. In *American Cetacean Society,* the harm that was alleged was caused by third parties, Japanese whalers, who were not before the court, and the remedy sought, certification under the Pelly and Packwood Amendments, would not necessarily lead to Japan's cessation of whaling operations. The Supreme Court's decision in *Defenders of Wildlife* clearly adds additional hurdles for environmental groups seeking to use United States courts to enforce international standards for the conservation of whales. But see *Didrickson v. United States Dep't of the Interior,* 982 F.2d 1332 (9th Cir. 1992) (Friends of the Sea Otter had standing to intervene as a defendant in a case challenging a federal regulation prohibiting the use of sea otters for Native Alaskan crafts).

d. Other United States Actions to Protect Whales

The United States has designated two national marine sanctuaries for the protection of whales. The Stellwagon Bank National Marine Sanctuary, an ocean area about 35 miles long and 25 miles wide, is located off the coast of Massachusetts between Cape Cod and Cape Ann. The submerged sand bank is a feeding area and the summer habitat of humpback and other whale species, as well as the critical habitat of right whales. Right whales are among the most endangered marine species. NOAA has taken measures to minimize vessel strikes and entanglement with fixed and other fishing gear.

The Hawaiian Islands Humpback Whale National Marine Sanctuary is intended to protect the whales and one of their primary breeding grounds. Regulations strictly prohibit approaching humpback whales (by any means) within 100 yards. The purposes of that sanctuary designation also include management of human activities consistent with protection of the whales and their habitat and creation of public education and interpretation programs.

2. MARINE MAMMAL PROTECTION

a. The Marine Mammal Protection Act

The International Whaling Convention applies only to a relatively small number of marine mammals and has not been particularly effective in stemming the depletion of the whale stocks to which it applies. By 1970, eight species of whales and numerous other marine mammals were threatened with extinction. Public sentiment had also been aroused by the intelligence and beauty of marine mammals and in reaction to the harvesting of baby harp seals and the killing of dolphins by tuna fishermen. A large constituency continued, however, to view marine mammals as a renewable resource that could be managed and used for commercial and food purposes. Others realized that preservationist strategies could have a major impact on outer continental shelf (OCS) development and commercial fisheries that killed or injured marine mammals as an incidental byproduct of the activities. The Marine Mammal Protection Act of 1972 (MMPA), 16 U.S.C.A. §§ 1361–1421h, represented a compromise among these conflicting interests. See generally Michael J. Bean & Melanie J. Rowland, The Evolution of National Wildlife Law 109–111 (3d ed. 1997). The complexity of this compromise is reflected in the statement of Congressional policy:

[M]arine mammals have proven . . . to be resources of great international significance, esthetic and recreational as well as economic, and . . . should be protected and encouraged to develop to the greatest extent feasible commensurate with sound policies of resource management and . . . the primary objective of their management should be to maintain the health and stability of the marine ecosystem. Whenever consistent with this primary objective, it should be the goal to obtain an optimum sustainable population keeping in mind the carrying capacity of the habitat.

16 U.S.C.A. § 1361(6).

Marine mammals protected by the MMPA include both mammals that are "morphologically adapted" to ocean environments, such as whales, dolphins, seals, walruses, and sea otters, and mammals that "primarily inhabit[ ] marine environment[s]," such as polar bears. Id. § 1362(6).

The Departments of Commerce and the Interior administer the MMPA. Through the National Marine Fisheries Service (NMFS), the Secretary of Commerce has responsibility for whales, porpoises, dolphins, seals, and sea lions. The Secretary of Interior, through the Fish and Wildlife Service (FWS), is responsible for other marine mammals, including walruses, polar bears, manatees, and sea otters. Id. § 1362(12)(A). Both Secretaries are required to consult with the Marine Mammal Commission, an independent scientific advisory body set up by the Act. The three-member Commission is appointed by the President, subject to Senate confirmation, and is charged with continuing review and assessment of marine mammal stocks, conservation methods, and research programs. The

Commission's recommendations are directed to the development of both domestic policies and international arrangements for conservation of marine mammals. Id. §§ 1401–1402.

The heart of the MMPA is a moratorium on the taking and importation of marine mammals and marine mammal products. Id. § 1371(a). "The term 'take' means to harass, hunt, capture, or kill. . . ." Id. § 1362(13). In *United States v. Mitchell*, 553 F.2d 996 (5th Cir. 1977), the Fifth Circuit Court of Appeals defined the geographic scope of the moratorium. The court held that the moratorium extends to actions of United States citizens on the high seas, but not to taking marine mammals in the territorial waters of other nations. The court found that neither the Act nor the legislative history demonstrated the "clear intent required . . . to overcome the presumption against extraterritorial extension" of U.S. law into the jurisdiction of other sovereign countries.

The moratorium is not absolute and contains a waiver provision, a number of exceptions, and an exemption for Alaskan natives. The waiver effectively changes the focus of the MMPA from preservation to management and regulated taking for the affected populations. To authorize a waiver of the moratorium, the Secretary generally must determine that a species or stock is at its optimum sustainable population (OSP) and that the waiver will not reduce the population below that level. The concept of OSP is unique and is presumably something different from the principle of maximum sustainable yield (MSY), which is often used in the management of commercially exploited wildlife. However, the definition of OSP is ambiguous, factoring in the carrying capacity of the environment and the health of the ecosystem, as well as the maximum productivity of the species. Id. § 1362(9). Taking marine mammals subject to a waiver of the moratorium requires a permit setting the number and kind of animals to be taken, the time period and place, and other conditions. Waivers on the importation of marine mammals or products require the Secretary to certify that the program for taking marine mammals in the country of origin is "consistent" with the MMPA. Id. § 1371(a)(3)(A).

The first statutory exception to the moratorium is the authorization for the Secretary to issue permits "for purposes of scientific research, public display, or enhancing the survival or recovery of a species or stock." 16 U.S.C.A. § 1371(a)(1). Applicants for scientific research permits must demonstrate the bona fide, nonduplicative research need for taking the animal. Permits for lethal research are issued only in limited circumstances when alternatives are not feasible. Captive maintenance of an animal requires a showing that the benefits of the program outweigh the benefits of alternatives that do not involve removal of the animals from the wild and also mandates the return of the animals to their habitat as quickly as feasible. Permits for scientific or public display purposes are subject to the environmental assessment procedures of the National Environmental Policy Act. See *Jones v. Gordon*, 792 F.2d 821 (9th Cir. 1986) (permit for capture of killer whales for scientific and public display purposes invalid for failure to prepare an environmental impact statement).

Movies like *Free Willy* and *Blackfish* have raised public awareness about the effects of public display on marine mammals. The MMPA does, however, authorize issuance of permits to take or import marine mammals for public display to applicants who offer "a [public] program for education or conservation purposes . . . based on professionally recognized standards of the public display community." Id. § 1374(c)(2)(A)(i). See also *Animal Protection Inst. of Am. v. Mosbacher*, 799 F.Supp. 173 (D.D.C. 1992) (Secretary had not abused his discretion in issuing import permits for public display of whales without determining OSP when evidence indicated that stocks of the species were abundant). A permit to take a marine mammal for public display may not be issued for a stock that has been designated by the Secretary as depleted. "Depleted" means that the population is below OSP or that the species is listed as endangered or threatened under the Endangered Species Act. Id. § 1362(1). If a species is listed as threatened or endangered under the Endangered Species Act (ESA), a scientific research or enhancement permit is necessary for the marine mammal to be held at a public display facility.

Prior to the 1994 amendments to the MMPA, NMFS shared authority over marine mammals while in captivity with the Department of Agriculture (DOA). The 1994 MMPA amendments delegated primary authority to DOA to manage the care of marine mammals in public display facilities under the Animal Welfare Act (AWA) and removed the requirement for an MMPA permit to hold an animal for public display, 7 U.S.C.A. §§ 2131–2159. DOA developed rules for such facilities through a negotiated rulemaking process. Scientists and animal welfare advocates have expressed concern that the regulations do not meet the needs of the animals, that existing rules need stronger enforcement, and that the regulated facilities should exert less influence in standard setting.

DOA currently allows numerous programs for dolphin/human interaction including feeding pools and swim-with-dolphin programs. Critics claim these programs put the dolphins and humans at risk. Allowing such programs sends mixed signals to the public who are prohibited from having similar interactions with dolphins in the wild. Congress amended the MMPA in 1992 to direct the Secretary to carry out studies to determine if the feeding of dolphins in the wild had adverse effects on their health or behavior, but it did not require that vessel operators who take tourists to offshore sites to feed dolphins get a waiver or permit to take dolphins. NMFS regulations requiring a permit were upheld in *Strong v. Secretary of Commerce,* 5 F.3d 905 (5th Cir.1993). Current regulations categorize feeding marine mammals in the wild as prohibited harassment and taking under the MMPA. See 50 C.F.R. pt. 216.

Stranded sick or injured marine mammals are often rehabilitated in private facilities. Through the

Marine Mammal Health and Stranding Response Program, 16 U.S.C. §§ 1421, 1421b.2, NMFS has created a network of private and governmental stranding organizations to rescue and rehabilitate marine mammals. These organizations are deemed custodians of stranded marine mammals and are authorized to "take" stranded animals, attempt to rehabilitate them, and reintroduce them into the wild. Animals in rehabilitation are required to be released within six months unless they are determined to be unreleasable because of injuries, medical conditions, and behavioral issues. Prior to releasing a rehabilitated animal into the wild, the custodian is required to provide a release plan to NMFS for approval. 50 C.F.R. § 216.27(a). NMFS has discretion concerning animals considered non-releasable, including allowing the custodian to keep the animal or transfer it to an approved facility, or requiring the custodian to euthanize it. 50 C.F.R. § 216.27(b). NMFS may require that rehabilitated marine mammals be used for public display and educational purposes in lieu of animals taken from the wild. 50 C.F.R. § 216.27(b)(4); § 216.27(c)(1). See NMFS Procedural Directive, *Process for Placing Non-Releasable Marine Mammals from the Stranding Program into Permanent Care Facilities* (2012), available at http://www.nmfs.noaa.gov/op/pds/docu ments/2/308/02–308–02.pdf. See also *Inst. of Marine Mammal Studies v. Nat'l Marine Fisheries Serv.*, ___ F.Supp.2d ___, 2014 WL 2154348 (S.D.Miss. 2014) (remanding denial of a take permit for a releasable, stranded sea lion because NMFS improperly delegated federal authority to a stranding organization).

The second exception to the moratorium is for permits for taking marine mammals incidental to commercial fishing operations. Id. § 1371(a)(2). Marine mammal-commercial fishery interactions are discussed further below.

The final exception authorizes the Secretary to permit, upon request, the unintentional taking of "small numbers of marine mammals" incidental to interactions with activities other than fishing, such as OCS oil and gas development. Id. § 1371(a)(5). Before the Secretary can issue a Letter of Authorization (LOA), he must make specific findings that the taking will have a "negligible impact" on the species or its habitat. Such "small number" permits are allowed even for depleted species. In 1994, the MMPA was amended expedite short-term authorization to incidentally take small numbers of marine mammals by "harassment", Incidental Harassment Authorizations (IHAs). 16 U.S.C. § 1371(a)(5)(D). Most LOAs and IHAs are issued for the incidental acoustic harassment of marine mammals and involve noise created by seismic airguns (for scientific research or for seabed oil and gas exploration), ship and aircraft noise, high energy sonar systems, and explosives.

The most controversial authorizations are for acoustic harassment (and possibly killing) of marine mammals by the U.S. Navy in its testing and deployment of high-intensity active sonar systems. NMFS originally issued rules in 2002 authorizing the

Navy's one-year use of the active sonar program for "training, testing, and routine military operations" in roughly 75% of the world's oceans. In *Natural Resources Defense Council, Inc. v. Evans* (*Evans I*), 232 F. Supp.2d 1003 (N.D. Cal. 2002) and in *Natural Resources Defense Council, Inc. v. Evans* (*Evans II*), 364 F. Supp.2d 1083 (N.D. Cal. 2003), environmental groups succeeded in limiting the area of testing (*Evans I*) and then in receiving a permanent injunction on grounds that the authorization decision violated NEPA, the ESA, and the MMPA. However, the victories were incomplete and short-lived. The injunction did not prohibit the Navy from testing and training with the sonar outside a 12-mile buffer and outside certain deep ocean areas with concentrations of marine mammals and endangered species so long as additional measures were taken to avoid harm to marine life. *Evans II*. In late 2003, Congress amended the MMPA to create separate "harassment" provisions for the military and federally-supported scientific research and removed the "small numbers" and limited geographic area provisions in regard to military operations. Department of Defense Authorization Act of 2004, Pub. L. No. 108–136, 319, 117 Stat. 1392 (2003). Harassment for "military readiness activities" is limited to (1) acts that actually injure or have a significant potential to injure, and (2) acts that actually disturb or are likely to disturb by disrupting natural behavioral patterns to the point where they are abandoned or significantly altered. Id. § 319(a) (amending 16 U.S.C. § 1362(18)). The Secretary of Commerce can impose restrictions to ensure the least practicable adverse impact on the marine mammals only after taking into account personnel safety, practicality, the impact on military readiness, and the views of the Department of Defense. In addition, the Secretary of Defense was given power to exempt *any action or category of actions* from the MMPA for up to two years if "necessary for the national defense." Id., § 319(b), 117 Stat. at 1434 (adding 16 U.S.C. § 1371(f)).

When the NRDC again challenged authorization of the Navy's use of "mid-frequency active" (MFA) sonar in training exercises off southern California (SOCAL), the U.S. Supreme Court further limited protections potentially available to environmental groups to protect marine mammals.[2] In *Winter v. NRDC*, 555 U.S. 7 (2008), the Supreme Court vacated a preliminary injunction limiting the SOCAL exercises. See *NRDC v. Winter*, 518 F.3d 658 (9th Cir. Cal. 2008). The Court first found that NRDC had not met the irreparable injury requirement necessary for issuance of an injunction. The Court then held that even if it were the case that NRDC had shown irreparable injury, the plaintiffs had not met the

---

[2]   In addition, the Council on Environmental Quality (CEQ) authorized the Navy to implement "alternative arrangements" to NEPA compliance in light of "emergency circumstances," see 40 C.F.R. § 1506.11, and the President, granted the Navy an exemption from the CZMA pursuant to 16 U.S.C. § 1456(c)(1)(B) that permits such exemptions when the activity is "in the paramount interest of the United States." The President determined that the exercises were "essential to national security" and that an injunction would "undermine the Navy's ability to conduct realistic training exercises that are necessary to ensure the combat effectiveness of . . . strike groups."

further requirements involved in balancing the
equities and consideration of the public interest.
Finding that the injunction jeopardized national
security, the Court held:

> . . . We do not discount the importance of
> plaintiffs' ecological, scientific, and recreational
> interests in marine mammals. Those interests,
> however, are plainly outweighed by the Navy's
> need to conduct realistic training exercises to
> ensure that it is able to neutralize the threat
> posed by enemy submarines.

Not to be deterred, NRDC has continued to contest
the Navy's sonar operations, most recently through a
challenge to NMFS' Final Rule providing a 5-year
authorization of the Navy's use of LFA sonar in the
world's oceans. See 77 Fed. Reg. 50,290 (Aug. 20,
2012). In *NRDC v. Pritzker*, 2014 U.S. Dist. LEXIS
35404 (N.D. Cal. Mar. 17, 2014), the court rejected
most of NRDC's attacks on the rule, but found that
NMFS had used outdated population information on
bottlenose dolphins in making its required
determination that the authorized taking will have a
"negligible impact" on marine mammal species or
stock. See 16 U.S.C. § 1371(a)(5)(A), (D). Because
analysis of "negligible impact" must be "based on the
best scientific evidence available," the court granted
summary judgment on that issue. One July 1, 2014,
the Department of Defense announced that it would
prepare a supplemental environmental impact
statement "for the limited purpose of addressing the
single deficiency identified by the court"—the failure
to use the most recent data on bottlenose dolphin in

its analysis of the impact of the LFA sonar. See 79 Fed. Reg. 372959 (July 1, 2014).

The MMPA contains an exemption from the moratorium for takings by Native Alaskans (Indian, Aleut, or Eskimo) unless the Secretary imposes regulations for a species determined to be depleted. The exemption only applies, however, if the taking:

   (1)   is for subsistence purposes; or

   (2)   is done for purposes of creating and selling authentic native articles of handicrafts and clothing . . .; and

   (3)   in each case, is not accomplished in a wasteful manner.

Id. § 1371(b). In *Didrickson v. United States Dep't of the Interior*, 982 F.2d 1332 (9th Cir. 1992), the Ninth Circuit Court of Appeals struck down a regulation that limited "authentic" articles to those "commonly produced" prior to enactment of the MMPA and excluded all articles made from sea otter products. The court held that the MMPA sufficiently identified authentic native articles of handicrafts and clothing as being "made at least in part from 'natural materials,' and . . . [produced] . . . in traditional native ways, such as weaving, carving, and stitching." The agency had no discretion to impose additional requirements as to the type of articles or to exclude sea otter products.

Subsistence whaling by the Makah Tribe in the Pacific Northwest has been much more controversial than the whaling by Native Alaskans that is

authorized both by the IWC quotas and the MMPA.
In 1995, the Makah notified the government of their
interest in resuming their right to cultural and
subsistence whaling under the 1855 Treaty of Neah
Bay. The Makah were allocated a quota by NOAA in
1998, and the tribe struck and landed one gray whale
in 1999. Since that time, litigation has precluded
further whaling. First, the Ninth Circuit Court of
Appeals found that NOAA's environmental
assessment (EA) and the issuance of a quota to the
Makah violated NEPA. *Metcalf v. Daley,* 214 F. 3d
1135 (9th Cir. 2000). Then in 2002, the Ninth Circuit
ruled further that an EIS (rather than an EA) should
have been prepared to comply with NEPA and that
the Makah must comply with MMPA processes to
pursue its treaty rights. *Anderson v. Evans,* 371 F.3d
475 (9th Cir. 2002).

The MMPA was amended in 1994 to clarify that it
was not intended to alter Indian treaty rights (16
U.S.C.A. § 1361 note), such as the Makah tribe's 1855
treaty right to continue whaling for gray whales. See
Alma Soongi Beck, *The Makah Decision to Reinstate
Whaling: When Conservationists Clash with Native
Americans Over an Ancient Hunting Tradition,* 11 J.
of Envtl. L. & Litigation 359 (1996). In February
2005, the Makah Tribe submitted a request for a
waiver of the MMPA's take moratorium, and NOAA
began the NEPA process of reviewing the effects of
Makah whaling in 2005. In 2006, the review was
expanded to review the effects of issuing quotas to
the Makah under the Whaling Convention Act
(WCA), 16 U.S.C. § 916 et seq., because the Makah
whaling cannot continue without receiving

authorization under both the MMPA and WCA. See Carol B. Koppelman, Anderson v. Evans: *The Ninth Circuit Harmonizes Treaty Rights and the Marine Mammal Protection Act*, 16 Hastings W.-Nw. J. Envtl. L. & Pol'y 353 (2010) (discussing the impact of *Anderson v. Evans* on the Makah's treaty rights). In 2007, five Makah tribe members conducted a rogue whale hunt, killing a gray whale with a high-powered rifle. The Makah tribe denounced the illegal hunt.

The EIS process is still on-going. NMFS terminated the 2008 draft EIS in 2012 after the agency determined it did not reflect substantial new scientific information on the gray whales targeted by the hunt. In 2012, the IWC also extended a gray whale catch limit for the Makah for 6 years. The future of the Makah whale hunt continues to be as unresolved as the clash of environmental and cultural ethics that it presents.

Section 1371(a)(4) of the MMPA allows the use of deterrents to discourage marine mammals from damaging fish catch, gear or other private property and to deter a marine mammal from endangering personal safety, so long as the deterrents do not result in death or serious injury of marine mammal. A commonly used deterrent is called an acoustical harassment device (AHD). Like other noise in the environment, little is known about the broader or long-term ecological effects of the use of such devices. The burden of proof is currently on the government to establish whether particular deterrents have "significant adverse effects" that would justify prohibiting their use. In light of the insufficiency of scientific information, many groups have suggested that the law take a more precautionary approach and require manufacturers to demonstrate that specific deterrents have negligible effects before NMFS can authorize their use.

The 1994 amendments to the MMPA deleted a provision that allowed fishermen to kill certain pinnipeds as a last resort when deterrents did not work. Seals and sea lions can be very aggressive, and deterrents (and even removal) have not always proved effective. There are concerns that increasing populations of California sea lions and West Coast harbor seals may not only interfere directly with fishing operations, but adversely affect other marine resource populations (e.g., salmon), the development of aquaculture, and coastal land uses. Some commentators advocate the reinstatement of a limited lethal take provision for "nuisance animals," culling "over-populated" areas, and allowing local officials to deal with site-specific conflicts involving the above species. These proposals are strongly opposed by scientists and environmentalists who advocate development of better, non-lethal deterrents. See *Humane Soc'y of the United States v. Locke*, 626 F.3d 1040 (9th Cir. Or. 2010) (holding that because NMFS failed to adequately explain its finding that sea lions were having a "significant negative impact" on the decline or recovery of listed salmonid populations, NMFS violated the MMPA when it authorized Idaho, Oregon, and Washington to kill up to 85 California sea lions annually at the Bonneville Dam to protect salmon in the Columbia River).

The MMPA specifically preempts state laws. The Act provides that "[n]o State may enforce . . . any State law or regulation relating to the taking of any species . . . of marine mammal within the State." 16 U.S.C.A. § 1379(a). But see *UFO Chuting of Hawaii v. Smith*, 508 F.3d 1189 (9th Cir. 2007) (Coast Guard license did not preempt a state statute banning thrillcraft and parasailing seasonally in the Maui Humpback Whale Protected Waters); see also K.L. Kaulukukui, *The Brief and Unexpected Preemption of Hawaii's Humpback Whale Laws: The Authority of the States to Protect Endangered Marine Mammals Under the ESA and the MMPA*, 36 ELR 10712 (2006).

Although the state preemption provision refers expressly only to the taking of marine mammals, one federal district court opinion holds that the MMPA also preempts state laws regarding importation of marine mammals. See *Fouke Co. v. Mandel*, 386 F.Supp. 1341 (D.Md. 1974). Authority to manage the taking of a species of marine mammal must be transferred to a state if the Secretary finds that a state conservation and management program meets the stringent standards and procedures of MMPA § 1379 to ensure that the state program is consistent with the MMPA and international obligations. This authority has yet to be transferred to any state.

Penalties for violation of the MMPA are substantial. The entire cargo of any vessel involved in the unlawful taking of a marine mammal is subject to seizure and forfeiture. The vessel will also be liable for a civil penalty up to $25,000. 16 U.S.C.A. § 1376(b). In addition, individuals are subject to fines of up to $10,000 for each violation of the Act or a permit, and fines of up to $20,000 per violation and one year of imprisonment can be imposed for knowingly violating the Act. Id. § 1375.

b. Marine Mammal—Fisheries Interactions

(1) The Tuna-Dolphin Controversy

In the area from southern California to Chile and westward to Hawaii, known as the eastern tropical Pacific Ocean, yellowfin tuna tend to associate with schools of dolphin. In the late 1950s and the 1960s, United States tuna fishermen began to take advantage of this phenomenon by setting their nets "on porpoise." Speedboats deploy the nets, called purse seines, around the dolphins, and the bottom of the net is then drawn closed, trapping the tuna and often the air-breathing dolphins as well. By the early 1970s, incidental dolphin deaths had reached over 300,000 per year. A major purpose of the enactment of the MMPA was to reduce the incidental mortality of dolphins and porpoises in the tuna fishery.

Apparently in anticipation of new technologies and fishing methods quickly replacing the technique of fishing "on porpoise," Congress provided a special two-year exemption for commercial fishing when the MMPA was enacted. Following the initial two-year period, continued incidental take was by permit and subject to the same type of regulations governing issuance of permits for a waiver. The "immediate goal" was that incidental kill of marine mammals be "reduced to insignificant levels approaching a zero mortality . . . rate." 16 U.S.C.A. § 1371(a)(2).

In *Committee for Humane Legislation, Inc. v. Richardson*, 540 F.2d 1141, 176 U.S.App.D.C. 362 (D.C.Cir. 1976), the D.C. Circuit Court of Appeals struck down the regulations promulgated by NMFS for taking porpoise incidental to commercial fishing and invalidated a general permit issued to the American Tunaboat Association. Neither the regulations nor the permits met the statutory requirements, particularly the necessity of determining the impact on the species OSP. The next few years involved numerous court cases, industry shutdowns, interim quotas, and attempts to set statutory quotas. New regulations in late 1977 and 1980 continued to lower the incidental take based on NMFS' determination of an incidental take that was technologically and economically achievable. In 1981, the MMPA was amended to provide that the goal of achieving "insignificant levels" of marine mammal mortality would be satisfied "in the course of purse seine fishing for yellowfin tuna by a continuation of the application of the best . . . safety techniques and equipment that are economically and technologically practicable." 16 U.S.C.A. § 1371(a)(2). See generally Michael J. Bean & Melanie J. Rowland, The Evolution of National Wildlife Law 122–131 (3d ed. 1997).

Regulation of tuna fishermen during the 1980s brought the incidental kill of porpoises to below 20,000 per year, but tensions between preservationists and the industry led Congress to place additional restrictions on fishing in the 1988 amendments to the MMPA. Setting nets within thirty minutes after sundown, a period when dolphins feed near the surface, and herding porpoises with explosives were prohibited. The Secretary was required to establish performance standards for vessel operators, including a system to identify fishermen with a consistently high incidental take rate for supplemental training and for possible suspension or revocation of their licenses. In addition, all U.S. vessels were required to carry an official observer on all fishing trips. 16 U.S.C.A. § 1374(h). See also *Balelo v. Baldrige*, 724 F.2d 753 (9th Cir. 1984) (Secretary's placement of warrantless observers aboard tuna vessels and that the use of the data they gathered for enforcement purposes falls within the "closely regulated industry" exception to the Fourth Amendment's protection against unreasonable searches). With observers on all U.S. tuna vessels, the incidental death rate for dolphins dropped to 5,083 in 1990, 1,002 in 1991, 439 in 1992, and 0 in 1995. See *American Tunaboat Ass'n v. Brown*, 67 F.3d 1404 (9th Cir. 1995).

The decline in dolphin mortality by U.S. vessels over the period is also attributable to other factors. The number of U.S. tuna vessels dropped during the life of the MMPA from a high of 155 in 1976 to 5 in 1995. Regulatory pressures led some tuna boats to abandon the eastern Pacific fishery or move to other fishing areas. Other vessels relocated to countries with less restrictive fishing practices. The decline in mortality by U.S. vessels was not reflected in the statistics for foreign vessels that have continued purse seine fishing with high dolphin mortality rates. Amendments in 1984 and 1988 to the MMPA required the Secretary to impose bans on importation of tuna from nations that did not regulate incidental take of marine mammals to produce a rate of taking comparable to U.S. vessels. These amendments served three purposes: (1) they provided a disincentive for U.S. vessels to relocate in other countries to avoid regulation; (2) they removed the economic advantage foreign fishermen would have by using more efficient means for catching tuna; and (3) they provided a means for further protecting marine mammal populations beyond traditional United States jurisdiction. These provisions led to international trade disputes that are discussed fully infra.

The International Dolphin Conservation Act of 1992, Pub. L. No. 102–523, amended the MMPA by imposing a five-year moratorium upon the harvesting of tuna with purse seine nets and lifting tuna embargos upon those nations making a commitment to implement the moratorium and take further steps to reduce dolphin mortality. The same year, the U.S. entered into the La Jolla Agreement, a non-binding international agreement to protect dolphins from harm in the Eastern Tropical Pacific (ETP) and to allow purse seine fishing with dolphin mortality caps. This agreement led to the United States and eleven other nations signing the Declaration of Panama to strengthen the protection of dolphins by (a) reducing dolphin mortality to levels approaching zero, with the goal of eliminating dolphin mortality in the ETP; (b) establishing annual dolphin mortality limits (DMLs); (c) avoiding bycatch of immature yellowfin tuna and other non-target species such as sea turtles; (d) strengthening national scientific advisory committees; (e) creating incentives for vessel captains; and (f) enhancing the compliance of participating nations to these commitments. The Panama Declaration of 1995 served as the basis for an agreement to establish the International Dolphin Conservation Program (IDCP), contingent upon the U.S. amending its laws to lift the MMPA embargoes imposed, to permit the sale of both dolphin-safe and non-dolphin safe tuna in the U.S., and to change the definition of dolphin-safe tuna from tuna harvested without dolphin purse seine encirclement to tuna harvested without dolphin mortality.

In 1997, Congress enacted the International Dolphin Conservation Program Act (IDCPA), Pub. L. No. 105–42, to implement the Panama Declaration. This amendment represented a major change in U.S. policy to pursue dolphin and ecosystem protection primarily through international cooperation. The IDCPA revised the criteria for banning imports to permit export of tuna to the U.S. if the exporter provides evidence of participation in certain international agreements to manage tuna and protect dolphins and that dolphin take does not exceed DMLs. The Secretary has made "affirmative findings" for the tuna fisheries of Ecuador, Mexico, Spain, Guatemala and E1 Salvador, allowing tuna from those countries to be imported into the U.S. See 50 CFR 216.24 (f) (requirements for an affirmative finding). The tuna embargo remains in place for

Belize, Bolivia, Colombia, Honduras, Nicaragua, Panama, Peru, Vanuatu, and Venezuela. See NOAA Fisheries, *Tuna/Dolphin Embargo Status Update*, available at http://www.nmfs.noaa.gov/pr/dolphin safe/embargo2.htm.

The IDCPA also changed standards concerning dolphin-safe labeling. The 1990 Dolphin Protection Consumer Information Act (DPCIA), 16 U.S.C. § 1385, prohibited any producer, importer, exporter, distributor, or seller of any tuna product sold in or exported from the United States to label that product as "dolphin safe" if the product contained tuna harvested on the high seas by a vessel engaging in driftnet fishing or in the ETP by a vessel using the purse seine method, unless the tuna was accompanied by various statements that no dolphin was intentionally encircled during the trip in which the tuna was caught. The Secretary of Commerce was directed to conduct a study of the effects of chase and encirclement on dolphins in purse seine fisheries for yellowfin tuna in the eastern tropical Pacific. The study was intended to determine whether chase and encirclement are having a "significant adverse impact on any depleted dolphin stock in the eastern tropical Pacific Ocean." 16 U.S.C. § 1385(d)(2). In December 2002 the Secretary made a final finding of "no significant effect" which authorized him under the IDCPA to broaden the definition of dolphin-safe tuna to include all tuna harvested in sets in which no dolphin mortality or serious injury was observed.

The finding was immediately attacked by environmental organizations. The U.S. Ninth

District Court of Appeal issued an injunction in 2003 and in 2004, held the final finding of the Secretary arbitrary and capricious and contrary to the applicable law under the Administrative Procedure Act, because the finding had been motivated by policy considerations, rather than based solely on the best scientific evidence. See *Earth Island Institute v. Evans*, 2004 WL 1774221 (N.D.Cal. 2004). Following the case, the definition for dolphin-safe labeling reverted to section 1385(h)(2) of the DPCIA, which provides that tuna is deemed dolphin-safe only if "no tuna were caught in the trip in which such tuna were harvested using a purse seine net intentionally deployed on or to encircle dolphins, and no dolphins were killed or seriously injured during the sets in which the tuna were caught."

When the case was affirmed in *Earth Island Institute v. Hogarth,* 494 F.3d 757 (9th Cir. 2007) and no further Congressional action on the issue seemed imminent, Mexico (with the EU and 11 other countries waiting in the wings) requested that the World Trade Organization (WTO) set up a dispute settlement panel. The dispute panel's decision was ultimately appealed to the WTO Appellate Body, which found that the U.S. dolphin-safe labeling scheme accords "less favorable treatment" to Mexican tuna products in violation of its obligations under GATT and the Agreement on Technical Barriers to Trade, because the U.S. measures did not set conditions for using the label in a way that reflects the risks faced by dolphins in different oceans. In 2013, NOAA issued new final rules that attempt to conform to the WTO holding, U.S.

legislation, and concerns of environmental organizations. See 78 Fed. Reg. 40997 (July 9, 2013). The discrimination against Mexico is addressed primarily by broadening the scope of the rule to cover oceans other than the Eastern Tropical Pacific (ETP) and requiring uniform verification from all tuna fishermen that dolphin-safe standards are met. Following the issuance of the rule, Mexico requested the WTO to establish a compliance panel—a mechanism for determining whether the losing party in a trade dispute has conformed to the rulings of the WTO. The compliance body was established in January 2014, and its report is due in December 2014.

(2) Incidental Taking in Other Commercial Fisheries

Marine mammals are also killed, injured, or harassed in other commercial fishery operations. They may be injured or killed by becoming entangled or caught in fishing gear, often in an attempt to take bait or fish caught on the lines or in nets. At or near the top of the food chain, marine mammals are often in direct competition with fishermen for the same resources. The animals can destroy or damage gear and are often harassed to deter them from taking catch or harming gear. See *United States v. Hayashi*, 22 F.3d 859 (9th Cir. 1993).

Taking of marine mammals incidental to fishing operations can potentially be authorized under three provisions of the MMPA: (1) The Secretary can issue permits under a waiver; (2) the Secretary can issue a permit for marine mammals taken incidental to commercial fishing operations under the MMPA, 16 U.S.C.A. § 1371; or (3) under a 1981 amendment to the MMPA, id. § 1371(a)(4), the Secretary can issue general permits through formal rulemaking to allow the taking of "small numbers" of nondepleted marine mammals incidental to commercial fishing by U.S. citizens if the total taking has "negligible impact" on the species or stock. Importantly, none of these sections provides authority for permitting a taking in fishing operations of depleted species, i.e., species that are not at or above optimum sustainable population (OSP) or that are threatened or endangered. See *Earth Island Institute v. Brown*, 865 F.Supp. 1364 (N.D.Cal. 1994).

In *Kokechik Fishermen's Ass'n v. Secretary of Commerce*, 839 F.2d 795, 268 U.S.App.D.C. 116 (D.C.Cir. 1988), fishermen and environmentalists challenged the issuance of a permit to the Japan Salmon Fisheries Cooperative Association to take Dall's porpoises in the course of their salmon fishing in the North Pacific. The permit did not include northern fur seals and other marine mammals that would also foreseeably be taken. The Secretary had concluded that it was not possible to make a finding as to whether certain northern fur seal populations were at or above OSP. The federal court of appeals held that issuance of the permit was contrary to the MMPA, because "it allowed incidental taking of various species of protected marine mammals without first ascertaining as to each such species whether or not the population of that species was at the OSP level." Id.

The court's decision conflicted with the agency's past practice and had a number of immediate ramifications for both domestic and foreign fishermen. With no authority in the MMPA for issuing permits for the incidental take of depleted species, the Secretary's ability to issue *any* incidental take permits was questionable. First, no permit could be issued if it was known that even small numbers of depleted species would be taken in a fishery. Second, in almost any fishery, the Secretary would be unlikely to be able to make the findings required by the court in order to issue a permit either because information was inadequate to determine which animals were likely to be taken incidentally or because data was insufficient to determine whether the population was at OSP and would not be disadvantaged.

Because so little information was available about marine mammal interactions with fishing, other than with tuna fishing, Congress responded in 1988 by enacting a five-year interim exemption to allow commercial fisheries to operate while information necessary for management of interactions was compiled. See 16 U.S.C.A. § 1383a. This was followed by 1994 amendments requiring NMFS to prepare stock assessments for all marine mammal species under U.S. jurisdiction whether healthy or in decline. 16 U.S.C.A. § 1386. The assessments must include a determination of the stock potential biological removal level and a recovery factor and are subject to review by regional scientific review groups. The amendments reaffirmed the Act's overall goal of reducing the incidental kill or serious injury rate from commercial fishing operations to insignificant levels approaching zero, and for the first time set a specific deadline of seven years after enactment for its achievement. 16 U.S.C.A. § 1387. These new provisions require the Secretary to issue a general authorization for the incidental lethal takes occurring during fishing to those vessels that register under an extension of the existing vessel registration system provided by the Act in section 1383a. Mandatory fishing vessel reporting program for vessels with frequent and occasional interactions with marine mammals, a mandatory observer program for those vessels to verify data on mortality and injury, a prohibition on intentional lethal takes, and emergency authority for the Secretary to intervene when particular stocks are declining were also included in the 1994 provisions.

The Secretary has also established take reduction teams, composed of industry, government, and non-resource user group representatives, to prepare take reduction plans for populations most affected by commercial fishing. 16 U.S.C. § 1387(f)(7)(B)(i). The plans' goals are to reduce incidental take levels to below the potential biological removal level for these stocks within six months and to insignificant levels approaching zero within five years, and must recommend regulatory or voluntary measures to meet these reductions. 16 U.S.C. § 1387(f)(2). The Secretary must then implement an approved plan and set, *inter alia,* fishery-specific limits on takes and time as well as area restrictions on fishing operations. If a plan fails to achieve these targets, the

Secretary must revise it and set regulations to meet the goals.

The most controversial take reduction plan is the one developed for the large whales of the Northwest Atlantic that are entangled by fixed fishing gear such as lobster traps and gillnets. The Atlantic Large Whale Take Reduction Plan (ALWTRP) is intended to protect three whale species (fin, humpback, and North Atlantic right whales) from entanglement in fishing gear. The plan covers a large number of fixed-gear fisheries, the largest of which is the New England and Mid-Atlantic lobster trap fishery.

3.   THE ENDANGERED SPECIES ACT

Legislation to preserve endangered wildlife was first enacted in 1966, but the Endangered Species Act of 1973 (ESA), 16 U.S.C.A. §§ 1531–1544, created the current regulatory regime for endangered species. With the contemporary emphasis in environmental law on preservation of biodiversity, the ESA is increasingly important for the protection of marine mammals and a wide variety of other marine species. The ESA provides an additional level of protection to more than twenty species of marine mammals such as the endangered right whale. To protect that whale, ESA provisions such as prohibition of take (*Strahan v. Coxe*, 127 F.3d 155 (1st Cir. 1997)), designation of critical habitat (62 Fed. Reg. 16108 (April 4, 1997)), development of recovery plans (16 U.S.C.A. § 1533(f)), and section 11(f) (16 U.S.C.A. § 1540) regulatory enforcement (61 Fed. Reg. 41116 (1996); 62 Fed. Reg. 59335 (Nov. 3, 1997) are being utilized in addition to the MMPA (*Bays' Legal Fund v. Browner*, 828 F.Supp. 102 (D.Mass. 1993)) and Stellwagen Bank National Marine Sanctuary. It is the primary means of protecting endangered marine species such as sea turtles (*State of Louisiana, ex rel. Guste v. Verity*, 853 F.2d 322 (5th Cir. 1988)), salmon (*United States v. Glenn-Colusa*, 788 F.Supp. 1126 (E.D.Cal. 1992)), seabirds (*Marbled Murrelet v. Babbitt*, 83 F.3d 1060 (9th Cir. 1996), and sea turtles discussed further below.

Many of the provisions of the 1973 ESA were enacted to implement the Convention on International Trade in Endangered Species of Wild Fauna and Flora (CITES), done Mar. 3, 1973, 27 U.S.T. 1087, 993 U.N.T.S. 243. The major substantive provision of CITES is the prohibition on trade in endangered (Appendix I) and threatened (Appendix II) species and species protected unilaterally within certain jurisdictions (Appendix III species) except a provided in the treaty. See generally Michael J. Bean & Melanie J. Rowland, The Evolution of National Wildlife Law 495–500 (3d ed. 1997). See also *United States v. Ivey*, 949 F.2d 759 (5th Cir. 1991); *Cayman Turtle Farm, Ltd. v. Andrus*, 478 F.Supp. 125 (D.D.C. 1979).

The ESA creates two groups of protected species: endangered and threatened. Like the MMPA, the ESA defines species to include distinct geographic populations. An endangered species is one that is "in danger of extinction throughout all or a significant portion of its range." 16 U.S.C.A. § 1532(6). See also *Center for Biological Diversity v. Lohn*, 296

F.Supp.2d 1223 (W.D.Wash. 2003). A threatened species is one that is likely to become endangered in the foreseeable future. Id. § 1532(20). All endangered or threatened species are also categorized as "depleted" under the MMPA, although depleted marine mammal species may also include species that are below their OSP and thus likely to become threatened. See *Cook Inlet Beluga Whale v. Daley*, 156 F.Supp.2d 16 (D.D.C. 2001) (finding that the decision not to list the Cook Inlet Beluga whale as endangered was not arbitrary and capricious, when designation as depleted and moratorium legislation served to protect the species) and *Alaska v. Lubchenco*, 825 F. Supp. 2d 209, (D.D.C. 2011) (upholding subsequent listing of the species in 2008 as endangered because MMPA protections had been inadequate to halt further depletion of the species).

The Act defines a threatened species as "any species which is likely to become an endangered species within the *foreseeable* future." 16 U.S.C. § 1532(20). See *Safari Club Int'l v. Salazar (In re Polar Bear Endangered Species Act Listing & Section 4(d) Rule Litig.)*, 709 F.3d 1 (D.C. Cir. 2013) ("[T]the agency's reliance on climate projections was sufficient to support their definition of foreseeability.") The ESA category of threatened species was created not only to provide protection before a species becomes endangered, but also to phase down the level of protection for endangered species whose numbers are restored to survival levels. The Eastern North Pacific stock of gray whales was declared by the National Marine Fisheries Service (NMFS) to be "fully recovered" and was removed from the endangered list and threatened status, but remains subject to the Whaling Convention and the MMPA. See also *Trout Unlimited v. Lohn*, 559 F.3d 946 (9th Cir. Wash. 2009) (ruling that NMFS may consider natural and hatchery-spawned salmon and steelhead together in one evolutionary significant unit when listing species under the ESA, and affirming the agency's decision to downlist the Upper Columbia River steelhead from endangered to threatened under the ESA).

Similar to the MMPA, ESA § 9 prohibits any person subject to U.S. jurisdiction from taking any endangered species within territorial waters or on the high seas and from importing or exporting such species. 16 U.S.C.A. § 1538(a)(1). The term "take" includes "to harass, harm, pursue, hunt, shoot, wound, kill, trap, capture, or collect." Id. § 1532(19). Prohibited takings include significant habitat modifications that actually injure listed species by altering their essential behavior patterns. See *Babbitt v. Sweet Home Chapter of Communities for a Great Oregon*, 515 U.S. 687, 115 S.Ct. 2407, 132 L.Ed.2d 597 (1995). See also *U.S. v. Town of Plymouth, Mass.*, 6 F.Supp.2d 81 (D.Mass. 1998) (issuing preliminary injunction prohibiting the Town of Plymouth from allowing off-road vehicles to drive on Plymouth Long Beach unless precautions are taken to protect threatened piping plovers).

The ESA does not preempt more restrictive provisions of the MMPA where they are applicable. Id. § 1543. Civil penalties for knowing violations of the ESA may be up to $25,000 per violation; other violations may receive up to a $500 penalty. Id. § 1540(a)(1). See *Block v. Josephson*, 156 F.3d 1235 (9th Cir. 1998). Criminal penalties of up to $50,000 and one year imprisonment may also be imposed. Id. § 1540(b). Perhaps the farthest-reaching penalty, however, is the provision that not only protected species involved in an unlawful act, but also guns, traps, boats, aircraft, and vehicles involved, are subject to forfeiture. Id. § 1540(e)(4)(B).

In drafting the ESA, Congress also recognized that protection of critical habitat may be as important as direct prohibitions on taking in ensuring the survival of a species or population. "Critical habitats" for endangered or threatened species are specific areas that are "essential to the conservation of the species," or areas that require "special management considerations or protection." Id. § 1532(5)(A). In general, critical habitat does not include the entire range of the species. Id. § 1532(5)(C). To the "maximum extent prudent and determinable," the Secretary must make critical habitat designations concurrently with the listing of a species. Id. § 1533(a)(3) See also *Center for Biological Diversity v. Evans*, 2005 WL 1514102 (N.D.Cal. 2005) (NMFS had a statutory duty to make the hard decision, i.e., to designate or not, unless it reasonably found the habitat was not determinable). More extensive habitat may be found to be essential to the survivability of a species over the long term, but critical habitat must at least include the minimum area necessary to avoid short-term jeopardy to the species. See *Alaska Oil & Gas Ass'n v. Salazar*, 916 F. Supp. 2d 974 (2013) (overturning the FWS designation of 187,157 square miles of coastal lands, barrier islands, and ice-dotted marine waters as critical habitat for the polar bear, concluding that the area was too big to be justified). Designation of critical habitat must be based on "the best scientific data." See, e.g., *Conner v. Burford,* 848 F.2d 1441, 1444 (9th Cir. 1988) (finding the agency was required to consider the scientific information available at the time, giving the species the benefit of the doubt). The Secretary must consider the economic impact of the designation and may exclude areas from critical habitat where the benefits of exclusion outweigh the benefits of including the areas as critical habitat unless the failure to designate the critical habitat will result in extinction of the species. 16 U.S.C.A. § 1533(b)(2).

Like the MMPA, the ESA contains a number of exceptions to section 9 takings prohibition. The ESA provides for permitting for scientific purposes, to enhance survival, and for establishment of experimental populations, id. § 1539(a), (j). A self-defense provision effectively acts as an exemption if a person acted on a good faith belief that he or she was acting to prevent bodily harm from an endangered or threatened species. Id. § 1540(b)(3).

The ESA also contains an exemption similar to (but more limited than) the MMPA for the taking of endangered or threatened species by Native Alaskans, who may also sell the non-edible byproducts of the wildlife when incorporated into "authentic native articles of handicrafts and clothing." Id. § 1539(e). In *United States v. Nuesca,*

945 F.2d 254 (9th Cir. 1991), two native Hawaiians, Nuesca and Kaneholani, appealed their convictions for taking two endangered green sea turtles and an endangered monk seal on the basis of aboriginal rights. The Ninth Circuit Court of Appeals found no evidence that the taking of green sea turtles or monk seals was a "traditional aspect of native Hawaiian life" or that a treaty protected such rights. Nuesca and Kaneholani also argued that the ESA could not constitutionally exempt one aboriginal group without exempting similarly situated groups. They contended that the Equal Protection Clause requires that all persons in similar circumstances be treated alike. The court found that the Hawaiian natives were not similarly situated because the exemption was not created merely for indigenous populations, but for a particular indigenous group with subsistence needs and dependence on endangered and threatened species. The court also refused to apply a "strict scrutiny" analysis because the ESA discriminated on the basis of culture and food supply, not race. The court held that Congress had a rational basis for excepting Native Alaskans from the ESA, while not establishing an exception for other aboriginal groups, and upheld the convictions.

Because possession of endangered species or parts of such species is generally prohibited by the Act, two ESA exceptions deal with possession and importation in limited circumstances of antique articles and "pre-Act parts," particularly scrimshaw, made from endangered species. Id. § 1539(f)–(h). A 1982 amendment to the ESA added an exception for the Secretary to permit taking of endangered species that is "incidental to, and not the purpose of, the carrying out of an otherwise lawful activity." Id. § 1539(a)(1)(B). This section allowed incidental takings that had previously been prohibited under the Act. Because the provisions had rarely been enforced and had not been taken seriously in such circumstances, it has been argued that the permitting provisions for incidental taking actually strengthened the Act significantly. See Michael J. Bean & Melanie J. Rowland, The Evolution of National Wildlife Law 234–235 (3d ed. 1997). Applicants for an incidental taking permit must submit a conservation plan which specifies: (1) the impact of the taking; (2) a mitigation scheme that specifies measures to be taken to minimize the impacts and that assures adequate funding is available; and (3) the alternative actions considered and why they were not adopted. 16 U.S.C. § 1539(a)(2)(A). After the opportunity for public comment, the Secretary must make specific findings that the taking is incidental to lawful activity and that the applicant has adequate funding to implement a plan that minimizes and mitigates impacts of the taking to the maximum extent practicable. Finally, the Secretary must determine that "the taking will not appreciably reduce the likelihood of the survival and recovery of the species in the wild." Id. § 1539(a)(2)(B). See, e.g., *Loggerhead Turtle v. County Council of Volusia County, Florida*, 148 F.3d 1231 (11th Cir. 1998); *Sierra Club v. Babbitt*, 15 F.Supp.2d 1274 (S.D.Ala. 1988). The ESA also contains an incidental taking exception for federal agency actions under similar circumstances,

16 U.S.C.A. § 1536(b)(4), and provisions for the Endangered Species Committee to exempt certain agency actions. Id. § 1536(e)–(o).

Section 7 of the ESA sets out the primary responsibilities of federal agencies under the Act:

> Each Federal agency shall, in consultation with and with the assistance of the Secretary, insure that any action authorized, funded, or carried out by such agency . . . is not likely to jeopardize the continued existence of any endangered species or threatened species or result in the destruction or adverse modification of habitat of such species which is determined by the Secretary . . . to be critical. . . .

Id. § 1536(a)(2); and

> After initiation of consultation . . . the Federal agency and the permit or license applicant shall not make any irreversible or irretrievable commitment of resources . . . which has the effect of foreclosing the formulation or implementation of any reasonable and prudent alternative measures. . . .

Id. § 1536(d). See *Hawksbill Sea Turtle v. Federal Emergency Management Agency*, 939 F.Supp. 1195 (D.V.I. 1996); *Pacific Rivers Council v. Thomas*, 30 F.3d 1050 (9th Cir. 1994). In summary, ESA section 7 requires an initial determination of whether endangered or threatened species may be present in the area of a proposed activity. If so, the agency must consult with the National Marine Fisheries Service (NMFS) or the Fish and Wildlife Service (FWS) to prepare a Biological Opinion before irreversibly committing resources. If NMFS or FWS makes a determination that the activity will jeopardize an endangered species or adversely modify its critical habitat, the relevant service will suggest "reasonable and prudent measures" the agency may take. See *Greenpeace Foundation v. Mineta*, 122 F.Supp.2d 1123 (D.Ha. 2000) ("NMFS cannot speculate that no jeopardy to monk seals or adverse modification of their critical habitat will occur because it lacks enough information regarding the impact of the fishery on seals. Such a determination is arbitrary and capricious."); see also *Rarnsey v. Kantor*, 96 F.3d 434 (9th Cir. 1996).

Section 1533(d) of the ESA gives the Secretary authority to issue "regulations as he deems necessary and advisable to provide for the conservation" of threatened species. 16 U.S.C.A. § 1533(d). As with marine mammals, the regulation of interactions between endangered or threatened marine species and the fishing industry has proved to be a most controversial area. Five species of sea turtles, all of which are either endangered or threatened, are found in the waters of the Atlantic Ocean and the Gulf of Mexico where shrimping operations occur. Studies have established that drowning of turtles in nets during shrimp trawls is a major cause of sea turtle mortality. In 1987, NMFS promulgated regulations requiring that turtle excluder devices (TEDs) be used by boats over 25 feet long in shrimp trawls during certain seasons in designated areas. Challenges to the implementation of the regulations pending further study of the relation between shrimping and sea turtle deaths were unsuccessful. See *Louisiana ex rel. Guste v. Verity*, 853 F.2d 322 (5th Cir. 1988) (record need only demonstrate that the regulations do in fact prevent prohibited takings, not that the regulations will enhance the species' chance of survival); *Louisiana ex rel. Guste v. Mosbacher*, 1989 WL 87616 (E.D.La.1989) (refusing to enjoin enforcement of TED regulations pending a National Academy of Science study required by ESA amendments in 1988). Following publication in 1990 of a study by the National Academy of Science recommending more extensive use of TEDs, NMFS issued regulations extending the use of TEDs to the entire year and to all shrimp trawlers. 50 C.F.R. Pts. 217 & 227.

Noncompliance with TED regulations is reported to be widespread and the government has sought civil penalties as well as stiff fines for violations. See *United States v. Menendez*, 48 F.3d 1401 (5th Cir. 1995). See also *Center for Marine Conservation v. Brown*, 917 F.Supp. 1128 (S.D.Tex. 1996). In *United States v. Tran*, 765 F.Supp. 356 (S.D.Tex. 1991), the federal district court affirmed the application of a federal sentencing guideline that allows a sentence to be increased four levels if "the offense involved a quantity of fish, wildlife, or plants that was substantial in relation either to the overall population of the species, or to a discrete subpopulation." In spite of the fact that only a single Kemp's Ridley sea turtle was taken, the court found that the species' highly endangered status, the low rate of survival of eggs, and the length of time to reach reproductive maturity justified the increased sentence for possession of an endangered species and failure to use a TED.

4.   PROTECTED MARINE SPECIES AND GATT

Although the original MMPA contained a general provision banning imports of fish unless U.S. standards are met, subsequent amendments to the MMPA effectively imposed the Act's stringent standards for protection of marine mammals on countries that export fish, particularly tuna, to the United States. The statute mandated the Secretary of Treasury to ban imports of fish and fish products from a nation unless the Secretary of Commerce certified that the nation's incidental take of marine mammals is comparable to that of the United States. In 1990 Earth Island Institute obtained an injunction halting importation of tuna from Mexico pending NMFS' issuance of comparability findings. See *Earth Island Inst. v. Mosbacher*, 929 F.2d 1449 (9th Cir. 1991). Mexico's response to the injunction was to request consultations with the United States as provided for in the General Agreement on Tariffs and Trade (GATT), opened for signature Oct. 30, 1947, 61 Stat. A3, 55 U.N.T.S. 14.

GATT is an international agreement that forms both the basis and the forum for world trade negotiations. Originally drafted in 1947, GATT (now the WTO) has 160 members. The purpose of the GATT is to expand free and fair trade by removing trade barriers and eliminating discriminatory and protectionist trade practices. The GATT also provides a forum for settlement of international trade disputes by consultations, and when consultations are unsuccessful, by resort to a formal panel. In 1994, the nations party to GATT created the World Trade Organization (WTO) to administer GATT and additional related agreements governing international trade. See Marrakesh Agreement Establishing the World Trade Organization, April 15 1994, 33 I.L.M. 1125.

When the consultations requested by Mexico failed to resolve the dispute, Mexico requested that a GATT panel be established to consider whether the United States' restrictions on Mexican tuna—both directly and through intermediary countries—violated obligations under GATT which:

1) prohibit quantitative restrictions or prohibitions under GATT Article XI;[3]

2) prohibit discriminatory quantitative restrictions for a geographic area under Article XIII; and

3) mandate national treatment requirements for imported goods under Article III.[4]

---

[3]   Article XI of GATT provides, in relevant part, that:

"No prohibitions or restrictions . . . whether made effective through quotas, import or export licenses or other measures, shall be instituted or maintained by any contracting party on the importation of any product of the territory of any other contracting party. . . ."

[4]   Article III of GATT provides, in relevant part:

"The products of the territory of any contracting party imported into the territory of any contracting party shall be accorded treatment no less favourable than that

See GATT, United States Restrictions on the Import of Tuna, Adopted Sept. 3, 1991, Panel Report No. DS21/R, reprinted in 30 I.L.M. 1594.

The GATT panel rejected the argument by the United States that the ban was an internal regulation applied at the point of importation and that the foreign tuna was treated no less favorably than tuna caught by domestic vessels. The panel stated that Article III did allow imposition of internal regulations that were nondiscriminatory, not disguised protectionism, and provided national treatment. However, the panel found Article III inapplicable to the tuna embargo because the regulations related not to the product itself, but to its method of production. Article III applies solely to laws . . . affecting the internal sale . . . of products." Having found Article III inapplicable, the panel determined that the embargo violated Article XI's quantitative prohibitions.

The United States also argued that the embargo was justified by exceptions under Article XX(b) and XX(g) which allow trade measures "necessary to protect human, animal or plant life or health" and "relating to the conservation of exhaustible natural resources if such measures are made effective in conjunction with restrictions on domestic production or consumption." The panel found that neither provision had been intended to apply

---

accorded to like products of national origin in respect of all laws, regulations and requirements affecting their internal sale, offering for sale, purchase, transportation, distribution, or use."

extraterritorially. Application of such measures beyond a nation's jurisdiction would undermine the free trade regime, allowing nations to unilaterally dictate environmental policies to other countries and derogate from GATT on the basis of nonuniform protection of persons, animals, or resources. Even if the provisions of Article XX(b) and XX(g) could apply to animals or resources beyond U.S. jurisdiction, the panel found that they were inapplicable to the tuna embargo. The United States did not demonstrate that the embargo was "necessary," because there was no showing that less restrictive means, such as international agreements, could not have accomplished the protection.

There was also insufficient showing under Article XX(g) that the measure was "primarily aimed at conservation." The fact that the application of the regulation was unpredictable and based on the incidental mortality rate of U.S. vessels made the regulation appear more related to protection of the U.S. fishing industry than to conservation of dolphins. See Joel P. Trachtman, *GATT Dispute Settlement Panel*, 86 Am. J. Int'l L. 142 (1992).

Mexico's challenge to the Dolphin Protection Consumer Information Act (16 U.S.C.A. § 1385) "dolphin safe" labeling requirements was not successful, however. The GATT panel found that the labeling did not discriminate against a geographic area because the requirements applied to tuna harvested by any vessel in the eastern tropical Pacific regardless of the vessel's origin. The labeling standards did not restrict trade because they were not mandatory, and tuna with and without the labels could be sold; any disadvantage arose from the free choice of the consumer. The panel's decision stressed that "[t]he labeling provisions therefore did not make the right to sell tuna or tuna products . . . conditional upon the use of tuna harvesting methods." But see the latest WTO challenge to dolphin-safe labeling at Chapter IV.G.2.b(1).

The GATT panel decision was advisory and could not become effective unless adopted unanimously by the Council of Representatives.[5] Rather than voting to block adoption of the decision by the Council, the United States entered into further negotiations with Mexico, with the countries agreeing that the decision should not be brought to the Council. In 1994 a panel also ruled against the secondary embargo provisions of the U.S. legislation banning tuna imports from nations whose industries pack and ship tuna products caught by fishing vessels from countries with high dolphin incidental mortality rates.

In 1998, a WTO dispute resolution panel applied a similar analysis to U.S. legislation prohibiting imports of shrimp from countries whose harvesting techniques may adversely affect sea turtles, unless the countries have a comparable regulatory program and rate of take comparable to U.S. vessels (see 16 U.S.C.A. § 1537 note). The U.S. appealed the panel's adverse decision to the new WTO Appellate Body. The Appellate Body held that the U.S. shrimp import

---

[5]   Under the current WTO/GATT regime, WTO Appellate Body recommendations are adopted unless affirmatively rejected by the Council.

prohibition was provisionally justified under Article XX(g) quoted above. Specifically, it held that: (1) along with non-living resources, living resources such as the five species of sea turtles protected by the U.S. import prohibition are exhaustible natural resources; (2) the U.S. prohibition is a measure relating to the conservation of such resources; and (3) the prohibition is a measure made effective in conjunction with restrictions on domestic production. WTO, United States Import Prohibition of Certain Shrimp and Shrimp Products, adopted Oct. 12, 1998, Appellate Body Report No. AB–1998–4.

The Appellate Body invalidated the U.S. prohibition, however, under the Article XX introductory clauses (the chapeau) which require that measures otherwise justifiable under Article XX(g) are not applied in a manner which would constitute a means of arbitrary or unjustifiable discrimination between countries where the same conditions prevail. The prohibited discrimination resulted from inflexible judicial and administrative interpretations of U.S. statutory requirements by U.S. courts and officials which forced WTO members desiring to export shrimp to the U.S. to adopt sea turtle protection rules and technologies not merely *comparable,* but rather *essentially the same,* as that applied to the United States shrimp trawl vessels without any inquiry into the appropriateness of the regulatory program for the conditions prevailing in those exporting countries. Furthermore, U.S. procedures for certifying WTO members for eligibility to export shrimp to the U.S. were defective for not providing a transparent, predictable certification process. The Appellate Body also criticized the U.S. for failing to engage in serious, across-the-board negotiations for bilateral and multilateral sea turtle protection agreements beyond the 1996 Inter-American Convention for the Protection and Conservation of Sea Turtles with Brazil, Costa Rica, Mexico, Nicaragua, and Venezuela, and for failing to ratify relevant environmental conventions such as the 1982 Law of the Sea Convention and 1992 Biodiversity Convention.

While it does find the U.S. shrimp import prohibition in violation of the GATT provisions, the WTO Appellate Body report is noteworthy for its explicit attempts to restore a balance between GATT free trade principles and environmental protection through the report's several endorsements of sustainable development, the precautionary approach and other principles of international environmental law found in the 1994 WTO agreement itself, the 1982 Law of the Sea Convention, and other conventions. Like the previous tuna cases, however, the Appellate Body continually stressed the importance of international cooperation over unilateral action.

The Appellate Body opinion is also noteworthy for what it did not say: It did not exclude the possibility of giving effect to extraterritorial environmental legislation, and it did not preclude regulations that went to the means of production, rather than to the product itself.

Finally, the Appellate Body ruled that WTO dispute panels can, but are not required to, accept unsolicited information from non-governmental sources such as the NGO amicus briefs submitted (but rejected) in the U.S. shrimp import prohibition dispute.

The Shrimp/Turtle case is a clear example of "losing the battle, but winning the war." The U.S. did not prevail in the case, but the WTO Appellate Body did interpret the GATT in a way that unambiguously allows nations to use economic and trade measures to protect marine species beyond their own borders. In a subsequent case in which Malaysia attacked the U.S. shrimp embargo, the Appellate Body found that by revising its procedures to comply with the recommendations and rulings of the earlier case, the U.S. import prohibition was justified under Article XX as a trade restriction "relating to the conservation of exhaustible natural resources." WTO, United States Import Prohibition of Certain Shrimp and Shrimp Products, adopted 15 June 2001, Appellate Body Report No. AB–2001–4.

The broader ramifications of the GATT provisions on international environmental law and marine species protection are still not clear. GATT and WTO panels as well as the WTO Appellate Body repeatedly have stressed that international agreements are the best method for protecting the environment. Clearly, contracting parties can agree to terms among themselves that may contradict GATT principles. But a number of major multilateral, international treaties also use trade restrictions against nonparty nations to enforce the treaty provisions. Treaties such as the Convention on International Trade in Endangered Species of Wild Fauna and Flora (CITES), done Mar. 3, 1973, 27 U.S.T. 1087, 993 U.N.T.S. 243, the Montreal Protocol on Substances that Deplete the Ozone Layer, done Sept. 16, 1987, S. Treaty Doc. No. 10, 100th Cong., 1st Sess. 1 (1987), 26 I.L.M. 1541, and the Basel Convention on the Control of Transboundary Movements of Hazardous Wastes and Their Disposal, opened for signature Mar. 22, 1989, S. Treaty Doc. No. 5, 102d Cong., 1st Sess. 1 (1991), 28 I.L.M. 657, use trade restrictions as a primary means of implementing and enforcing the treaties. The U.N. Fish Stocks Agreement also has provisions that could lead to conflict with the GATT, Article V, Freedom of Transit provisions. Agreement for the Implementation of the Provisions of the United Nations Convention on the Law of the Sea of 10 Dec. 1982 Relating to the Conservation and Management of Straddling Fish Stocks and Highly Migratory Fish Stocks, opened for signature Dec. 4, 1995, S. Treaty Doc. No. 104–24, 34 I.L.M. 1542 (1995) (entered into force Dec. 11, 2001). The U.N. Fish Stocks Agreement, art. 23(3), provides authority for states to adopt regulations to "prohibit landings and transshipments where it has been established that the catch has been taken in a manner which undermines the effectiveness of subregional, regional, or global conservation and management measures on the high seas;" and art. 33(2) less directly implicates trade conflicts by encouraging states to "take measures consistent with the Agreement and international law to deter the activities of vessels flying the flag of non-parties which undermine the effective implementation of this Agreement." See U.N. Fish Stocks Agreement. But the GATT mechanisms for factoring substantive concerns for the international environment into trade principles remain imperfect at best.

In spite of concerns for potential conflicts, the U.N. Food and Agricultural Organization (FAO) encourages nations to assure its trade practices do not undermine the effectiveness of fisheries conservation measures and to adopt trade-related measures, developed through international consultation and consistent with the WTO, that promote the sustainability of fisheries and address illegal, unreported, and unregulated fishing (IUU). Because developed countries account for around 80% of the value of fisheries imports (the U.S. imports 90% of its seafood), trade measures are a potent tool for addressing IUU fishing, protecting endangered marine species, and encouraging sustainable fisheries practices. See *FAO Technical Guidelines for Responsible Fisheries: Responsible Fish Trade*, No. 11 (FAO 2009). The FAO has developed a voluntary international plan of action (IPOA) to deter IUU fishing that is not controlled by flag or coastal state action. Nations are encouraged to develop national plans of action that use "all available jurisdiction in accordance with international law" and to adopt not only market-related measures, but also port state measures, coastal state measures, and measures to ensure that their nationals do not support or engage in IUU fishing. See *International Plan of Action to*

Prevent, Deter and Eliminate Illegal, Unreported and Unregulated Fishing (FAO 2001).

5.   UNITED STATES PROTECTION OF MARINE SPECIES INTERNATIONALLY

The U.S. first set out its response to the FAO's voluntary IPOA with a *National Plan of Action of the United States of America to Prevent, Deter, and Eliminate Illegal, Unregulated, and Unreported Fishing* (2004) (NPOA), an effort coordinated by the U.S. Department of State in conjunction with NOAA, NMFS, the U.S. Coast Guard, the Office of the U.S. Trade Representative, the U.S. Fish and Wildlife Service and the U.S. Customs Service. The NPOA also made recommendations for strengthening U.S. efforts to address IUU fishing. The 2006 Reauthorization of the MSA implemented many of these recommendations.

The U.S. has taken unilateral action to address international fisheries and marine species protection for several decades. In addition to the MMPA provisions to protect dolphins in international tuna fisheries and ESA provisions to protect sea turtles in shrimp fisheries, other early U.S. legislation to protect species internationally included the High Seas Driftnet Fisheries Enforcement Act (1992) (building on the earlier Driftnet Impact Monitoring, Assessment, and Control Act of 1987), which bans imports of fish and sport fishing equipment from nations whose nationals are not respecting the United Nations' moratorium on large-scale high seas driftnet fishing and denies port privileges to offending vessels. 16 U.S.C.A. § 1826a; UNGA Resolution 46/215 (1991) (calling for a worldwide driftnet moratorium beginning December 31, 1992). The legislation was strengthened by the High Seas Driftnet Fishing Moratorium Protection Act (Moratorium Act) in 1995.

In the 2006 Reauthorization of the MSA (amending the Moratorium Act), Congress passed its most far-reaching legislation on international fisheries. The Reauthorization set out directives for the United States to address illegal, unreported, and unregulated (IUU) fishing, and the related issues of strengthening international fisheries management organizations, and preventing bycatch of protected living marine resources (PLMR).[6] 16 U.S.C.A. §§ 1826i–1826k. The Moratorium Protection Act was further amended in 2011 by the Shark Conservation Act, (Pub. L. 111–348), to extend the Act to domestic and international conservation of sharks. See 77 Fed. Reg. 40554 (July 10, 2012); see also the Shark Finning Prohibition Act, 16 U.S.C.A. § 1822, and *United States v. Approximately 64,695 Pounds of Shark Fins*, 520 F.3d 976 (2008) (holding the Shark Finning Act inapplicable to vessels transshipping fins; case led to amendment of the act). The Moratorium Act sets out guidelines for defining IUU fishing that are implemented at 50 CFR 300.201 as follows:

---

[6]   NMFS has compiled a list of protected living marine resources for purposes of applying the Act, available at http://www.nmfs.noaa.gov/msa2007/docs/list_of_protected_lmr_act_022610.pdf.

(1) Fishing activities that violate conservation and management measures required under an international fishery management agreement to which the United States is a party, including but not limited to catch limits or quotas, capacity restrictions, and bycatch reduction requirements;

(2) Overfishing of fish stocks shared by the United States, for which there are no applicable international conservation or management measures or in areas with no applicable international fishery management organization or agreement, that has adverse impacts on such stocks; or,

(3) Fishing activity that has a significant adverse impact on seamounts, hydrothermal vents, cold water corals and other vulnerable marine ecosystems located beyond any national jurisdiction, for which there are no applicable conservation or management measures, including those in areas with no applicable international fishery management organization or agreement.

NMFS is required to report biennially to Congress on nations identified as having vessels:

(1) engaged in IUU fishing,

(2) bycatch of PLMRs, and/or

(3) high seas fisheries targeting or incidentally catching sharks that are not regulated by a program for the conservation of

sharks comparable to that of the United States, taking into account different conditions.

16 U.S.C.A. § 1826h. The U.S. will consult with identified nations to provide the opportunity for nations to comply with international fisheries management and conservation agreements and to adopt bycatch reduction methods in international fisheries that are comparable to methods used in U.S. fisheries. An identified nation that is not certified by the Secretary of Commerce as having taken appropriate measures to address IUU fishing or bycatch of PLMRs is subject to import prohibitions on certain fish products and port access limitations. In 2011, NMFS published a final rule creating procedures for the identification and certification of nations under the provisions of the act. See 76 Fed. Reg. 2100 (Jan. 14, 2011).

In 2014, the U.S. bolstered its authority to prohibit imports of fish caught by IUU fishing by ratifying the FAO's Port State Measures Agreement (PSMA). The Agreement will come into force when it has the requisite 25 parties. In addition, on June 17, 2014, the president announced the intent to create a Comprehensive Framework to Combat Illegal, Unreported and Unregulated Fishing and Seafood Fraud. A Presidential Task Force is directed to report to the President "recommendations for the implementation of a comprehensive framework of integrated programs to combat IUU fishing and seafood fraud that emphasizes areas of greatest need."

The 2006 MSA Reauthorization also called on the U.S. to "improve the effectiveness of international fishery management organizations in conserving and managing fish stocks under their jurisdiction." 16 U.S.C.A. § 1826i. The United States is a member of numerous international regional fishery management organizations (RFMOs) to manage high seas fisheries in world's oceans—7 in the Pacific Ocean; 4 in the Atlantic Ocean, 2 in the Southern Ocean, and 2 in the Indian Ocean. See NOAA Fisheries, Regional Agreements at http://www.nmfs. noaa.gov/ia/agreements/regional_agreements/intl agree.html. An RFMO may manage all fisheries in a region of the oceans or may be directed to the management of particular species in a region or throughout the range of the species. The United States is a party to the 1995 UN Fish Stocks Agreement that empowers RFMOs to adopt appropriate fisheries management programs and take effective measures against IUU fishing. Several of the RFMOs now use catch documentation and certification schemes to ensure compliance with and enforcement of their management programs. For example, the Commission for the Conservation of Antarctic Marine Living Resources (CCAMLR) and the Inter-American Tropical Tuna Commission (IATTC) have adopted catch certification programs, and the International Commission for the Conservation of Atlantic Tunas (ICCAT) has adopted statistical document programs for several species. The United States seeks to encourage RMFOs to increase their effectiveness through adoption and authorization of more market-based measures against IUU fishing, better identification and monitoring of IUU fishing vessels, and adoption of stronger port state controls. By working through these and other international organizations, the United States hopes to avoid unilateral action and take effective action against IUU fishing that is consistent with WTO obligations.

CHAPTER V

POLLUTION AND THE MARINE ENVIRONMENT

A. INTRODUCTION

Incidents like the oil spills from the *Torrey Canyon* in 1967, the *Amoco Cadiz* in 1978, the *Exxon Valdez* in 1989, and the *Deepwater Horizon* rig in 2010 focused worldwide attention on the devastation caused by accidental discharges of large quantities of oil. They have served as catalysts for the development of law relating to oil spill clean up and damage liability. Although these disasters highlight the environmental tragedy of marine pollution, such accidents are not the primary, most widespread, or even most devastating source of pollution of the seas. Intentional discharges of oil from vessels, ocean dumping of wastes, and discharge of sewage and wastes from land-based sources have contributed much more to the present level of marine pollution than these "disasters." Fortunately, both international and domestic regimes have been created to begin to deal more effectively with the prevention of marine pollution and to provide a scheme for allocating responsibility for occasional, devastating oil spills.

Part XII of the 1982 United Nations Convention on the Law of the Sea (UNCLOS), 21 I.L.M. 1261, addresses the marine environment. The basic obligation of every coastal nation is "to protect and preserve the marine environment." UNCLOS, art.

192. In addition to recognizing traditional rights of nations to control pollution and to protect the territorial sea environment, the treaty extends national jurisdiction for protection of the environment through the 200-mile EEZ. See id. art. 56(1)(b)(iii). The Convention adopts the basic principle of international law that activities should be conducted in a manner that does not cause damage by pollution to other countries and extends the principle to protect areas beyond national jurisdiction, i.e., the high seas and deep seabed. Id. art. 194(2).

UNCLOS directs parties to "deal with all sources of pollution of the marine environment . . . [through measures] designed to minimize [pollution] *to the fullest possible extent.*" Id. art. 194(3) (emphasis added). The sources of pollution subject to control include vessels, offshore installations, and land-based sources. The drafters of UNCLOS envisioned that the treaty would serve as an "umbrella" and that nations would continue to regulate dumping and pollution from ships through regional and international agreements, such as the London Convention, the Cartagena Convention, and MARPOL 73/78. See arts. 197, 210, 211. The UNCLOS provisions for pollution control enforcement by coastal states in the EEZ do, however, substantially enhance the effectiveness of these treaties. See arts. 216 21 and supra Chapter V.A. 1.

UNCLOS is unique with regard to land-based sources of marine pollution, because it is the only global treaty that addresses this issue. The treaty calls on nations to control as much as possible:

> the release of toxic, harmful or noxious substances, especially those which are persistent, from land-based sources, from or through the atmosphere or by dumping[.]

Id. art. 194(3)(a). The Convention includes no provisions for enforcement, however, beyond calling upon nations to adopt and enforce laws that implement internationally recognized standards. Id. art. 213. The Convention encourages participation in international and regional efforts to control land-based sources of pollution, such as, the Barcelona Convention for the Mediterranean and the Lima Convention for the Southeast Pacific.

UNCLOS is the only treaty dealing with pollution of the seas resulting from exploration and exploitation of the deep seabed. Anticipating eventual mining of the deep seabed beyond national jurisdiction for manganese nodules, the treaty establishes an international obligation to protect the marine environment beyond national jurisdiction and obligates the Seabed Authority, an organization created under the treaty to oversee deep seabed mining, to develop regulations to assure that exploitation of the seabed does not harm marine or coastal flora, fauna, or natural resources. Id. art. 145. UNCLOS also provides that all contractors and applicants for contracts must have sponsoring States. Sponsoring States have the responsibility to ensure that seabed mining activities are carried out in conformity with the Convention.

In 2010, the Republic of Nauru submitted a request to the Seabed Authority to provide an interpretation of States' responsibilities. The Council—the executive and policy-making arm of the Authority—requested an advisory opinion from the specialized Seabed Disputes Chamber of the International Tribunal for the Law of the Sea (ITLOS), the judicial body created by the LOS Convention. This opinion provides the first judicial interpretation of the obligations and potential liability of States in regard to pollution and environmental damage from seabed mining operations. See Seabed Disputes Chamber of the International Tribunal for the Law of the Sea, Responsibilities and Obligations of States Sponsoring Persons and Entities with Respect to Activities in the Area (Case No. 17 (2011)).

The Chamber interpreted UNCLOS to impose two kinds of duties on a sponsoring State. First, the "responsibility to ensure" imposes a duty of "due diligence" on a sponsoring State to secure compliance by the sponsored contractors with the treaty and contract obligations—a duty the Chamber "characterized as an obligation 'of conduct' and not 'of result'." The due diligence obligation includes the duty to ensure that the contractor meets the requirement for adequate environmental impact assessment—a requirement the Chamber found to arise under both UNCLOS and customary international law. Due diligence also requires the sponsoring State to ensure that the obligations of a sponsored contractor are made enforceable through domestic laws and regulations. Id.

Second, the sponsoring State has direct obligations which include:

- an obligation to assist the Authority;
- the obligation to apply the "best environmental practices" set out in Authority's regulations;
- the obligation to apply a precautionary approach, made binding by inclusion in the Authority's regulations;
- the obligation to adopt measures to ensure the provision of guarantees; and
- the obligation to provide a system for compensation for damages.

Id.

The liability of a sponsoring State arises from its failure to fulfill its obligations under the Convention and related instruments and the actual occurrence of damage. A sponsoring State's liability requires that a causal link be established between the failure to comply with its obligations and the damage. A sponsored contractor's failure to comply with its obligations does not in itself give rise to sponsoring State liability. Id.

The LOS Convention specifies neither what constitutes compensable damage nor who may be entitled to claim compensation. Although UNCLOS does not specifically entitle the Authority to make a claim, article 137(2) does provide that Authority acts "on behalf" of mankind. The Chamber also posited: "Each State Party may also be entitled to claim compensation in light of the *erga omnes* character of the obligations relating to preservation of the environment of the high seas and in the Area."

B.   OIL POLLUTION AND OIL SPILLS

1.   THE INTERNATIONAL REGIME

Recognizing that pollution of the seas by oil is a truly international issue, nations have negotiated a number of treaties to control intentional discharges and in an attempt to minimize accidental discharges. The effort began with the 1954 International Convention for the Prevention of Pollution of the Sea by Oil opened for signature May 12, 1954, 12 U.S.T. 2989, 327 U.N.T.S. 3, as amended in 1962, 1969, and 1971. This treaty, as amended in 1962, 17 U.S.T. 1523, 600 U.N.T.S. 332, prohibited the discharge of oil and oily mixtures into the sea in certain areas and required recordkeeping to document discharges of oil and the surrounding circumstances. Prohibited zones included all seas within fifty miles of a coast. The 1969 amendments, 28 U.S.T. 1205, 9 I.L.M. 1, added a rule that discharges, such as ballast discharges, must be *en route* and proscribed a rate of discharge in addition to the distance from land rule. Amendments in 1971, 11 I.L.M. 267, related to tank size and arrangement and created a fifty-mile prohibited zone around the Great Barrier Reef.

The *Torrey Canyon* oil spill provoked the negotiation of a number of new treaties in the years following the 1967 disaster. First, the 1969 International Convention Relating to Intervention on the High Seas in Cases of Oil Pollution Casualties, done Nov. 29, 1969, 9 I.L.M. 25, 26 U.S.T. 765, 970 U.N.T.S. 211, and the 1973 Protocol (Intervention Convention), gave parties emergency response power beyond territorial waters. This treaty gives contracting parties the authority to "take such measures on the high seas as may be necessary to prevent, mitigate or eliminate grave and imminent danger to their coastline or related interests from pollution or threat of pollution of the sea by oil, following upon a maritime casualty . . . which may reasonably be expected to result in major harmful consequences." The 1973 Protocol, 34 U.S.T. 3407, 13 I.L.M. 605, extended intervention authority to hazardous substances other than oil. The Intervention Convention creates extraordinary coastal nation authority over vessels of other countries on the high seas. This authority must generally be exercised in consultation with and in consideration of the views of the flag state of the vessel and affected parties. Priority must be given to saving human lives.

The 1969 International Convention on Civil Liability for Oil Pollution Damage (CLC), done Nov. 29, 1969, S. Exec. Doc. G, 91st Cong., 2d Sess. 19 (1970), 9 I.L.M. 45, 973 U.N.T.S. 3, provides a legal basis for claims for damages to the territorial sea or coast of a nation. Shipowners are strictly liable for damages from an oil spill subject to certain defenses, such as an act of war, an act of God, or the act or omission of a third party. If the shipowner establishes that the spill occurred without his fault or privity, the CLC creates a limitation on liability and requires that all ships carrying over 2000 tons of oil have financial security or insurance to the limit of liability under the Convention. Claims under the CLC provide an exclusive remedy. But see *In re Oil Spill by the "Amoco Cadiz" Off the Coast of France on March 16, 1978*, 471 F.Supp. 473 (J.P.M.L. 1979) (rejecting Amoco's argument that the case should be dismissed because the CLC is an exclusive remedy and allows recovery only in the courts of countries that suffered the pollution damage or took steps to prevent it). The flag state is responsible for certifying that a vessel meets the financial responsibility requirements. Because vessel owners may attempt to avoid these requirements by flying "flags of convenience," parties to the CLC are required to enact domestic legislation requiring all vessels using its ports or terminals to have certificates of financial responsibility on board.

The 1971 International Convention on the Establishment of an International Fund for Compensation for Oil Pollution Damage (1971 Fund Convention), done Dec. 18, 1971, S. Exec. Doc. K, 92d Cong., 2d Sess. 1 (1972), 1110 U.N.T.S. 57, was intended to supplement the inadequate liability compensation limits of the CLC and to provide compensation to individuals who suffer pollution damage not covered by the CLC. For example, damages from an oil spill in a country that is a party to the 1971 Fund Convention are recoverable even if the flag state of the offending vessel is not a party. The Fund is maintained by oil companies in each treaty nation rather than by the oil tanker owners and operators and increases the potential for recovery substantially.

Several protocols to the CLC and 1971 Fund Convention have been negotiated since 1984 to increase the liability and to broaden coverage of the conventions to include damage within the EEZ and reasonable environmental damages. The United States was criticized for acting unilaterally to impose additional levels and standards of liability after the *Exxon Valdez* oil spill and jeopardizing the viability and effectiveness of the international liability and compensation regime. See *U.S. Failure to Ratify Protocols Could Undermine Pollution Control, IMO Says,* 13 Int'l Envtl. Rep. (BNA) 240 (June 13, 1990). The 1992 Protocol to the CLC, however, incorporated many of the changes adopted by the U.S.

The primary international agreement for prevention and control of oil discharges is now the 1973 International Convention for the Prevention of Pollution from Ships, done Nov. 2, 1973, S. Exec. Doc. E, 95th Cong., 1st Sess. 1 (1979), 12 I.L.M. 1319, as modified by the 1978 Protocol, done Feb. 17, 1978, S. Exec. Doc. C, 96th Cong., 1st Sess. 1 (1979), 17 I.L.M. 546 (MARPOL 73/78). MARPOL 73/78 supersedes the 1954 convention on oil pollution prevention and extends the scope of the international pollution prevention effort to discharges of any harmful substance and to virtually all vessels and oil platforms. As of 2014 the Convention had 152 parties, including all major shipping countries and covering over 90% of the world's shipping tonnage. MARPOL 73/78 Annex II contains both operational and technological requirements. Operational discharges of oil are limited. For example, within "special areas" and fifty miles from land, only clean, segregated ballast may be discharged from tankers. More than fifty miles from land, discharges containing limited quantities of oil may be released while the vessel is *en route*. Tankers over 150 gross tons and other ships over 400 gross tons must have discharge monitoring equipment and be inspected and certified that they meet convention requirements. All discharges must be documented in an Oil Record Book. MARPOL 73/78 Annex II emphasizes improved technology, such as segregated ballasts and double hulls. Port reception facilities are required to eliminate the necessity of flushing tanks at sea. The United States implements MARPOL 73/78 Annex II with legislation entitled Prevention of Pollution from Ships, 33 U.S.C. §§ 1901–1913.

Although international efforts have had a significant effect in the area of liability and cleanup costs for pollution from oil and hazardous substances, many commentators believe that the conventions have actually provided very little relief from chronic discharges from vessels. Enforcement is the responsibility of the flag country, and unfortunately, there is very little economic incentive for a country to engage in vigorous enforcement of the treaty obligations against its ships in distant waters. See Paul S. Dempsey, *Compliance and Enforcement in International Law—Oil Pollution of the Marine Environment by Ocean Vessels,* 6 Nw. J. Int'l L. & Bus. 459, 557–61 (1984). The United States has found a unique way to supplement enforcement against foreign ships calling in U.S. ports, however, by enforcing the requirement under MARPOL and U.S. implementing legislation that requires that ships maintain an Oil Record Book noting all discharges. See Act to Prevent Pollution from Ships (APPS), 33 U.S.C.A. § 1908. Several U.S. courts have upheld U.S. civil and criminal jurisdiction over vessels for falsification of and failure to maintain an oil record book, even when the underlying act of illegal discharge from the vessel occurred outside U.S. territorial jurisdiction. Maintaining a false oil record book and misrepresentation of the oil record book while in a U.S. port provided a basis for U.S. jurisdiction independent of the discharge itself. See, e.g., *Giuseppe Bottiglieri Shipping Co. S.P.A. v. United States,* CIV.A. 12–0059–WS–B, 2012 WL 527619 (S.D. Ala. 2012); *U.S. v. Jho,* 534 F.3d 398, 2008 A.M.C. 1746 (5th Cir. 2008); *U.S. v. Petraia Maritime, Ltd.*, 483 F. Supp. 2d 34, 2007 A.M.C. 2783 (D. Me. 2007); *U.S. v. Ionia Management S.A.*, 498 F. Supp. 2d 477, 2007 A.M.C. 2794 (D. Conn. 2007).

Provisions of UNCLOS were drafted with the expectation of a separate international regime, such as MARPOL, applying to vessel design and construction standards and operational rules. But UNCLOS offers increased opportunities for coastal state enforcement of international requirements. Port states are authorized to investigate and institute legal proceedings for discharges in violation of international standards against vessels voluntarily in port. UNCLOS, art. 218(1), 220(1). A coastal state may physically inspect and institute proceedings against a vessel navigating its territorial seas when there are "clear grounds for believing" that the vessel has violated international standards or the pollution control laws of the coastal state. UNCLOS, art. 220(2). A coastal state may only detain and institute proceedings against a vessel in the EEZ if there is "clear objective evidence" that a violation of international oil pollution control standards actually resulted in a "discharge causing major damage or threat of major damage to the coastline . . . of the coastal State, or to any resources of its territorial sea or [EEZ]." UNCLOS, art. 220(6).

Regional port state control agreements have led to more coordinated and regular inspections to assure vessels meet standards under MARPOL and other technical conventions. Originally intended as a back-up for flag state control, regional agreements have proved to be an efficient and effective way to identify and share information on sub-standard ships. Regional agreements or MOUs, now covering virtually all of the world's major ports, include: Europe and the north Atlantic (Paris MOU); Asia and the Pacific (Tokyo MOU); Latin America (Acuerdo de Viña del Mar); Caribbean (Caribbean MOU); West and Central Africa (Abuja MOU); the Black Sea region (Black Sea MOU); the Mediterranean (Mediterranean MOU); the Indian Ocean (Indian Ocean MOU); and the Riyadh MOU. The U.S. Coast Guard maintains a port state control program to inspect, and sometimes detain, vessels for lack of seaworthiness and compliance with U.S. and international standards. In appropriate circumstances, sub-standard vessels may be banned from U.S. waters. See U.S. Coast Guard, Foreign &

Offshore Compliance Division, available at http://www.uscg.mil/hq/cgcvc/cvc2/safety.asp.

The United States and 23 other countries[1] are also parties to the Convention for the Protection and Development of the Marine Environment of the Wider Caribbean Region (Cartagena Convention), done Mar. 24, 1983, T.I.A.S. No. 11,085, 22 I.L.M. 227, and the Protocol concerning Co-operation in Combating Oil Spills in the Wider Caribbean Region, done Mar. 24, 1983, 22 I.L.M. 240. An additional sixteen countries are participating in a Caribbean Action Plan to implement the treaty. The Convention is intended to address a number of sources of marine pollution including vessels, dumping, seabed activities, airborne pollution, and land-based sources, and to provide a dispute resolution procedure.

It should be noted that the MARPOL 73/78 regime now goes far beyond oil pollution, the subject of mandatory Annexes I and II of the convention. Additional voluntary annexes are: Annex III— Prevention of Pollution by Harmful Substances Carried by Sea in Packaged Form; Annex IV— Prevention of Pollution by Sewage from Ships; Annex V—Prevention of Pollution by Garbage from Ships; and Annex VI—Prevention of Air Pollution from

---

[1]   Antigua and Barbuda, Bahamas, Barbados, Belize, Colombia, Costa Rica, Cuba, Dominica, the Dominican Republic, France, Grenada, Guatemala, Guyana, Jamaica, Mexico, the Netherlands, Panama, St. Kitts and Nevis, Saint Lucia, St. Vincent and the Grenadines, Trinidad and Tobago, United Kingdom, and Venezuela are the other Contracting Parties to the Convention and Oil Spill Protocol.

Ships. The U.S. has accepted Annexes I, II, III, V and VI. The U.S. has not ratified Annex IV, but has equivalent regulation for the treatment and discharge standards of shipboard sewage. See 33 U.S.C. 1251; 33 C.F.R. 159.

2.   DOMESTIC OIL POLLUTION REGULATION

Since 1972, section 311 of the Clean Water Act (CWA) has been the primary mechanism for enforcing oil pollution control standards and establishing responsibility and liability for oil spill and hazardous substance clean up and damages. 33 U.S.C. § 1321. The 1990 Oil Pollution Act (OPA), 33 U.S.C. §§ 2701–761, replaced most of the CWA scheme for responsibility for clean up costs and damages and for oil spill contingency planning. However, section 311 of the CWA still provides the framework for civil and criminal enforcement by the federal government for oil spills and, because many provisions of the OPA are similar to the prior law, cases interpreting the former statute are useful. The Comprehensive Environmental Response, Compensation and Liability Act (CERCLA), 42 U.S.C. §§ 9601–675, creates a parallel scheme to section 311 and OPA for hazardous substances to which it applies.

a.   Prohibitions and Enforcement Under CWA Section 311

Section 31(b)(1) of the CWA prohibits the "discharge[ ] of oil or hazardous substances into or upon the navigable waters of the United States." This policy is reinforced in section 311(b)(3) and (4) by a flat prohibition on oil or hazardous substance discharges in quantities which "may be harmful." Id. § 1321(b)(3)–(4). This prohibition forms the basis for civil and criminal penalties and for allocating responsibility and liability for discharges.

Section 311's prohibitions apply to the "navigable waters of the United States," adjoining shorelines, the contiguous zone, the 200-mile EEZ, and waters affected by outer continental shelf (OCS) activities, which may extend beyond 200 miles. The term "navigable waters" is limited only by the reach of the Commerce Clause and not by navigability in fact. Nonnavigable waters that are subject to the ebb and flow of the tide and wetlands that are adjacent to navigable waters are included within the scope of "navigable waters" for purposes of section 311. See, e.g., *United States v. Jones*, 267 F. Supp. 2d 1349, (M.D. Ga. 2003); *United States v. Texas Pipe Line Co.*, 611 F.2d 345 (10th Cir. Okla. 1979).

For purposes of CWA section 311, oil is broadly defined as "oil of any kind or in any form, including but not limited to petroleum, fuel oil, sludge, oil refuse, and oil mixed with wastes other than dredged spoil." 33 U.S.C. § 1321(a)(1). Hazardous substances are likewise construed broadly to include substances "which, when discharged in any quantity into or upon the navigable waters of the United States . . . or which may affect natural resources . . . present an imminent and substantial danger to the public health or welfare." Id. § 1321(b)(2)(A). However, until the Administrator of EPA designates a substance as hazardous, the provisions of section 311 do not apply. See *United States v. Ohio Barge Lines*, 410 F.Supp. 625 (W.D. La.1975). Hazardous substances subject to section 311 are designated at 40 C.F.R. § 117.1 17.23. Spills of hazardous substances, other than petroleum products, in navigable waters are also subject to regulation and liability under CERCLA.

The discharge prohibition is limited to quantities of oil and hazardous substances that "may be harmful to the public health and welfare or environment of the United States" as determined by regulation. 33 U.S.C. § 1321(b)(4). Regulations identify "harmful quantities" to be amounts of oil or hazardous substances that:

   (a) Violate applicable water quality standards, or

   (b) Cause a film or sheen upon or discoloration of the surface of the water or adjoining shorelines or cause a sludge or emulsion to be deposited beneath the surface of the water or upon adjoining shorelines.

40 C.F.R. § 110.3. A "sheen" is "an iridescent appearance on the surface of water." Id. § 110.1. Spillers have an obligation, subject to criminal penalties, to report spills in harmful quantities. Obviously, a "sheen'" may be created by seemingly insignificant discharges, and the imposition of duties, penalties, and criminal liability based on the sheen test has been controversial.

The question of what constitutes a spill of a reportable quantity has been the subject of a saga concerning Chevron that spanned 15 years. An earlier version of section 311(b)(3) was written in terms of "harmful quantities," and Chevron challenged the sheen test, arguing that the statute required actual injury for a spill to be reportable or subject to a penalty. In *United States v. Chevron Oil Co.*, 583 F.2d 1357 (5th Cir. 1978), the Fifth Circuit Court of Appeals held that the sheen test created only a rebuttable presumption of harm to the environment. To alleviate any burden on the government to show harm in every case, section 311 was amended to prohibit even quantities that "may be harmful." Chevron continued, however, to contest the imposition of civil penalties when a reportable spill nevertheless has little or no actual impact on the environment. In *Chevron, U.S.A., Inc. v. Yost*, 919 F.2d 27 (5th Cir. 1990), the court of appeals upheld the "sheen test" as the basis for imposing civil liability. "While it is apparent that such an approach sometimes overregulates, it is equally apparent that this imprecision is a trade-off for the administrative burden of case-by-case proceedings." Quoting *Orgulf Transport Co. v. United States*, 711 F.Supp. 344 (W.D.Ky. 1989), the court reasoned:

[T]hat Congress could have prohibited all discharges through a specific declaration and chose not to do so does not negate the effect of the amendment, a common sense reading of which illustrates that Congress chose to prohibit discharges which might not be harmful. Whether a spill resulted in actual harm to the environment is irrelevant to the determination of whether Section 311's prohibition of discharges of oil in quantities which may be harmful has been violated. The only pertinent inquiry is whether the spill was in a quantity that may be harmful as determined by the EPA. Because EPA has determined that a spill of oil which creates a sheen is a quantity which "may be harmful," such a spill is subject to the penalty provisions of 33 U.S.C. § 1321 and 40 C.F.R. Part 110.3.

Both civil and criminal enforcement and penalties are available for enforcement of section 311's prohibitions on discharges. Civil enforcement, through administrative orders and injunctive relief, is available to abate an actual or threatened discharge that "may be an *imminent and substantial threat* to the public health or welfare . . . and other living and nonliving natural resources." 33 U.S.C. § 1321(e)(1) (emphasis added). Although the Act does not define "imminent and substantial threat," the amendment to the provision that changed the word "is" to "may be" indicates that no actual harm need be shown. This is also consistent with interpretations of similar language in the Resource Conservation and Recovery Act (RCRA), 42 U.S.C. § 6973, and CERCLA, id. § 9606. See, e.g., *United States v. Conservation Chemical Co.*, 619 F.Supp. 162 (W.D.Mo. 1985) (holding that endangerment means risk of harm, considering the nature of the threat and its likelihood).

Civil penalties are imposed in federal court or administrative proceedings for discharging in violation of the Act and for failure to remove the discharge or to comply with an order or regulation. 33 U.S.C. § 1321(b)(7). OPA substantially raised the limits for civil penalties and revised the criteria for consideration in assessing civil penalties. For example, civil penalties for discharges generally are raised from $5000 for each offense to an amount of up to $25,000 per day of violation or up to $1000 per barrel discharged. 33 U.S.C.A § 1321(b)(7)(A). For spills resulting from "gross negligence or willful misconduct" OPA requires a penalty of not less than $100,000 and not more than $3000 per barrel discharged. Id. § 1321(b)(7)(D). (Note that this means a minimum penalty of $100,000 will be imposed for the reckless discharge of only one barrel of oil.) The following factors are now considered in determining the amount of a civil penalty: (1) the seriousness of the violation; (2) the economic benefit to the violator resulting from the violation; (3) the degree of culpability; (4) other penalties involved in the same incident; (5) any history of prior violations; (6) the nature, extent, and degree of success of efforts by the violator in mitigating or minimizing the effects of the spill; (7) the economic impact of the penalty on the violator; and (8) other matters as justice may require. Id. § 1321(b)(8).

Several other aspects of civil penalties should be noted. First, they are in addition to, not in lieu of, any other removal costs and damages incurred by the government. Second, civil penalties may be imposed regardless of fault and even where the violator has reported the spill and taken total responsibility for its removal at his or her own expense. These strict liability penalties have been held to be constitutional.

In *United States v. Atlantic Richfield Co.*, 429 F.Supp. 830 (E.D.Pa. 1977), for example, the federal district court found that imposition of penalties in such circumstances did not violate due process because there is a rational nexus between the behavior penalized and the purposes of the clean up fund into which penalties are deposited. As noted above, penalties may also be imposed where the discharge causes no harm to the environment. See *Orgulf Transport Co. v. United States*, 711 F.Supp. 344 (W.D.Ky. 1989); *United States v. Jones (In re Jones)*, 311 B.R. 647, 2005 AMC 264 (Bankr. M.D. Ga. 2004); *In re Oil Spill by the Oil Rig*, 841 F. Supp. 2d 988, 2012 AMC 982 (E.D. La. 2012).

Criminal prosecution under section 311 may relate to either the reporting requirements or to the spill itself. The decision of the federal government to pursue criminal prosecution is discretionary. A number of factors, including the prior history of the violator, the preventative measures that were taken, the need for deterrence, and the extent of cooperation, are considered by the government in deciding whether to bring criminal charges.

Section 311(b)(5) requires that a "person in charge" of a vessel or of an onshore or offshore facility must notify the National Response Center as soon as she or he knows of the oil or hazardous substance spill of a reportable quantity. 33 U.S.C. § 1321(b)(5). Failure to report a spill or knowingly submitting false information in an oil spill report results in criminal liability. Id. § 1321(b)(5), (c)(4). In *United States v. Boyd*, 491 F.2d 1163 (9th Cir. 1973), the sheen test was upheld as a reasonable indicator of when a person must report a spill. The court noted that the test had advantages of simplicity and certainty over a quantitative test and was not unconstitutionally vague.

A person who knowingly or negligently discharges oil in violation of section 311's prohibitions or who knowingly endangers another person by such a violation is subject to criminal prosecution. See 33 U.S.C. § 1319(c). The penalties for such violations depend on the level of culpability. For example, negligent acts may be subject to fines of $2500 to $25,000 per day or no more than one year imprisonment or both, while knowing violations may incur fines of $5000 to $50,000 per day or be subject to no more than three years imprisonment or both. 33 U.S.C. § 1319(c)(1)–(2).

Reporting a spill does not insulate a violator from criminal prosecution for the discharge. However, section 311(b)(5), prior to OPA, created use immunity for the report by providing that "[n]otification received pursuant to this paragraph or information obtained by the exploitation of such notification shall not be used against any such person in any criminal case, except a prosecution for perjury or for giving a false statement." The "use immunity" provision protects against infringement of a defendant's privilege against self-incrimination. In *Hazelwood v. State*, 836 P.2d 943 (Alaska App. 1992), Joseph Hazelwood, captain of the *Exxon Valdez,* appealed his conviction on criminal charges for the negligent discharge of oil. Captain Hazelwood asserted that section 311's "use immunity" required suppression of evidence of his intoxication "obtained by exploitation" of his report and reversal of his conviction. The Court of Appeals of Alaska rejected the application of the "inevitable discovery doctrine" as inconsistent with the grant of immunity. The court also held that there was "no evidentiary basis for finding the actual existence of an independent source for the state's evidence." In reversing Hazelwood's conviction, the court noted that its adherence to the law should not "be mistaken for enthusiasm." The court went on: "But while we may feel sorely tempted, as individuals, to recast the law in a mold better suited to our personal sense of justice, we are bound, as judges, to resist this temptation. . . ." Congress, on the other hand, can "recast the law" and has subsequently deleted the prohibition on the use for criminal prosecution of information gathered by further government investigation. As amended by the 1990 OPA, use immunity now applies only to the notification by the person in charge. See 33 U.S.C. § 1321(b)(5).

"Use immunity" applies only to criminal prosecutions, not to the use of reporting information for assessment of civil penalties. In *United States v. Ward*, 448 U.S. 242, 100 S.Ct. 2636, 65 L.Ed.2d 742 (1980), the U.S. Supreme Court held that the CWA's civil penalties are not "quasi-criminal" and that the Fifth Amendment's protection against self-incrimination does not apply to civil penalty proceedings.

C.   LIABILITY FOR CLEAN UP
COSTS AND DAMAGES

Liability for clean up costs and damages from spills of oil or hazardous substances has proved to be an unending source of confusion for students, lawyers and courts, because of the number of potential sources of liability and their relationships. Rather than provide a single, comprehensive statute for liability, Congress has specifically retained certain available remedies and has often left it to the courts to determine whether other remedies have been preempted or displaced. In order to conceptualize the entire complex scheme, the discussion will begin with the common law and admiralty law background of maritime torts.

1.   TRADITIONAL MARITIME TORT AND COMMON LAW REMEDIES

Traditional state common law torts of negligence, nuisance, and strict liability may be available sources of liability for spills of oil or hazardous substances in some circumstances. However, in the ocean and coastal context, if a cause of action is based on a maritime tort, maritime law must be applied as the substantive law.

The U.S. Supreme Court set out the test for admiralty jurisdiction in tort cases in *Grubart, Inc. v. Great Lakes Dredge & Dock Co.*:

> [A] party seeking to invoke federal admiralty jurisdiction pursuant to 28 U.S.C. § 1333(1) over a tort claim must satisfy conditions both of

location and of connection with maritime
activity. A court applying the location test must
determine whether the tort occurred on
navigable water. The connection test raises two
issues. A court, first, must assess the general
features of the type of incident involved to
determine whether the incident has a
potentially disruptive impact on maritime
commerce. Second, a court must determine
whether the general character of the activity
giving rise of the incident shows a substantial
relationship to traditional maritime activity.

513 U.S. 527, 534 (1995) (citations omitted). In *In re
the Exxon Valdez*, 767 F.Supp. 1509 (D.Alaska 1991),
the federal district court characterized the "oil spill
from the *Exxon Valdez* as a classic maritime tort."
The location test clearly was met, and because
maritime commerce is the primary focus of admiralty
law, the maritime nexus test was also met. Likewise,
the *Deepwater Horizon* oil spill undoubtedly met the
location test and had a disruptive impact on
maritime commerce, and the operations of the
Deepwater Horizon bore a substantial relationship to
traditional maritime activity. See *In re Oil Spill by
the Oil Rig "Deepwater Horizon"*, 808 F.Supp.2d 943
(Dist. Ct. E.D. La. 2011), citing *Theriot v. Bay
Drilling Corp.*, 783 F.2d 527, 538–39 (5th Cir.1986)
("oil and gas drilling on navigable waters aboard a
vessel is recognized to be maritime commerce"). On
the final question of whether the *Deepwater Horizon*
was a "vessel" subject to admiralty jurisdiction, the
court stated that it "was at all material times a vessel
in navigation. It was practically capable of maritime

transportation. See *Stewart v. Dutra Constr. Co.*, 543 U.S. 481, 497 (2005). See also *Herb's Welding v. Grey*, 470 U.S. 414, 417 n.2 (1985) ('Offshore oil rigs are of two general sorts: fixed and floating. Floating structures have been treated as vessels by the lower courts.').'' Id. See also *Offshore Co. v. Robison*, 266 F.2d 769, 779 (5th Cir.1959).

The admiralty jurisdiction of federal courts for maritime torts is not exclusive. Maritime tort actions may be brought in federal courts under diversity jurisdiction or in state courts, but regardless of the venue or how the tort is characterized, maritime law is still controlling unless displaced by a specific federal statute. State law has been held to be applicable in some limited situations where there are substantive gaps in maritime law. In addition, states may "create rights and liabilities with respect to conduct within their borders, when the state action does not run counter to federal laws or the essential features of an exclusive federal jurisdiction." *Romero v. Int'l Terminal Operating Co.*, 358 U.S. 354, 375 n. 42 (1959). But, in general, maritime law leaves few gaps in the regime for maritime torts that occur on the OCS and EEZ for state law to fill. The application of substantive maritime law has had significant ramifications in limiting both the amount and scope of a spiller's liability.

The Limitation of Vessel Owner's Liability Act (Limitation of Liability Act), which is referred to in OPA as the Act of March 3, 1851, is an early enactment that was intended to promote commerce and shipping by limiting a shipowner's potential liability. 46 U.S.C. §§ 181–192. In summary, if a shipowner establishes that a loss caused by its vessel was not due to negligence within the owner's privity or knowledge, the owner's liability for the loss is limited to the value of the owner's interest in the vessel and her pending freight. In the case of a catastrophic accident without fault, the liability of the owner of a sunken vessel may be virtually nothing. In spite of a specific savings clause (see 33 U.S.C. §§ 2702, 2704), OPA effectively repeals the 1851 act's liability limits with respect to "responsible parties" for oil spill clean up costs and for damages recoverable under OPA. See *Matter of MetLife Capital Corp.*, 132 F.3d 818 (1st Cir. 1997); *Seaboats, Inc. v. Alex C Corp. (In re Alex C Corp.)*, 56 ERC (BNA) 1498, 2003 AMC 256 (D. Mass. 2003). Nonresponsible parties may still be able to take advantage of the limits, however.

Judge-made, general maritime law also limits liability by narrowly defining the parties entitled to recovery for damages. In *Robins Dry Dock & Repair Co. v. Flint*, 275 U.S. 303, 48 S.Ct. 134, 72 L.Ed. 290 (1927), the U.S. Supreme Court enunciated the rule that where negligence does not result in any physical harm and only economic injury is suffered, a plaintiff may not recover in maritime tort for the loss of the benefits of a contract or prospective trade (economic damages). In the context of an oil spill like the *Exxon Valdez* spill in Prince William Sound, the *Robins Dry Dock* rule would preclude recovery in maritime tort for businesses, such as fish processors, boat charterers, and lodges and for use and enjoyment claims by recreational users, such as kayakers, photographers, and sport fishermen. Commercial fishermen fall within a controversial exception to the *Robins Dry Dock* rule. In *Union Oil Co. v. Oppen*, 501 F.2d 558 (9th Cir. 1974), the Ninth Circuit allowed the recovery of lost profits by commercial fishermen because they make direct use of a resource of the sea. Although it is not entirely clear that there exists a principled rationale to distinguish commercial fishermen from others who use the sea, this exception has been followed.

a. The Oil Pollution Act of 1990

The massive damage done by the *Exxon Valdez* oil spill led Congress to accelerate its ongoing deliberations on modernizing liability laws. OPA represented the rejection of a new international liability scheme in favor of a stricter, unilateral approach to protection of our waters and shores. OPA applies only to oil spills. "[O]il means oil of any kind or in any form, including, but not limited to, petroleum, fuel oil, sludge, oil refuse, and oil mixed with wastes other than dredged spoil, but does not include petroleum, including crude oil or any fraction thereof, which is specifically listed or designated as a hazardous substance under . . . [CERCLA] . . . and which is subject to the provisions of that Act[.]" 33 U.S.C. § 2701(23).

Under OPA, each "responsible party" is strictly liable for clean up costs and damages for discharges of oil. Responsible parties include owners, operators, and demise charterers of a vessel, terminal and pipeline owners and operators, and licensees of deepwater ports. 33 U.S.C. § 2701(32). Like its predecessor, CWA section 311, OPA contains limits on liability and requires vessels to have evidence of financial responsibility sufficient to meet the maximum liability under the Act. Id. § 2716. The limits on liability are greatly increased over the levels set by CWA section 311, however, and are much greater than limits proposed in international schemes at the time.

The limit on liability will be lifted in a number of circumstances. First, the limit will not apply if the incident was proximately caused by gross negligence, willful misconduct, or violation of a federal safety, construction, or operating regulation by the responsible party, his agent or employee, or a person acting pursuant to a contractual relationship with the responsible party. Id. § 2704(c)(1). In addition, the limit will not apply if the responsible party fails to report the incident, does not cooperate in removal activities, or refuses to comply with administrative or judicial orders issued pursuant to the Act's clean up authority. Id. § 2704(c)(2). In contrast to the Limitation of Liability Act, the burden of proof is on the government to establish that the responsible party is ineligible to have the limit on liability applied.

OPA provides a number of affirmative defenses that are a complete defense to liability for removal costs and damages. The responsible party must establish by a preponderance of the evidence that the discharge or substantial threat of a discharge of oil and the resulting damages or removal costs were caused solely by:

(1)   an act of God;

(2)   an act of war;

(3)   an act or omission of a third party, other than an employee or agent of the responsible party or a third party whose act or omission occurs in connection with any contractual relationship . . . if the responsible party establishes . . . that [she or he]

(A)   exercised due care with respect to the oil concerned, taking into consideration the characteristics of the oil and in light of all relevant facts and circumstances; and

(B)   took precautions against foreseeable acts or omissions of any such third party and the foreseeable consequences of those acts or omissions; or

(4)   any combination of paragraphs (1), (2), and (3).

Id. § 2703(a). The provisions continue the defenses available under section 311 except that OPA omits the defense of negligence by the United States. This exclusion may be significant since the government is responsible for maintaining navigation aids and publishing charts. The government may, however, be considered a third party for purposes of an affirmative defense. Much of OPA's additional language merely codifies the narrow judicial interpretations of section 311. See, e.g., *Travelers Ins.*

Co. v. United States, 2 Cl.Ct. 758 (1983) (holding that
the owner of a vandalized oil storage facility was
liable for clean up costs where the owner failed to
take reasonable security precautions). Because of the
requirement that the act of God, war, or a third party
must be the *sole cause* of the spill, the defenses are
difficult to assert successfully.

The government will reimburse a responsible
party for removal costs if the party establishes a
complete defense. OPA now allows a responsible
party entitled to this exception to liability to make a
claim to the Fund for all costs and damages incurred
that exceed the limit on liability. Id. § 2708. Cases
under CWA section 311's limitation of liability
provision had held that any initial costs incurred by
a spiller in clean up or containment operations could
not be offset against the moneys owed to the United
States. These costs were, therefore, in addition to the
limitation on liability for large spills. See *United
States v. Dixie Carriers, Inc.*, 736 F.2d 18 (5th Cir.
1984); *Steuart Transp. Co. v. Allied Towing Corp.*,
596 F.2d 609 (4th Cir. 1979). These cases
undermined federal policy to encourage immediate
and effective containment and removal.

OPA does not prohibit indemnification
agreements, i.e., agreements to insure or hold
harmless a party. However, these agreements are
only effective as between the parties and do not
transfer liability under OPA. 33 U.S.C. § 2710. For
example, a contract between an otherwise
responsible party and an oil transporter to shift
responsibility for any liability for a spill will act only

as an indemnification and subrogation agreement and will not achieve a transfer of statutory liability.

The primary responsibility for clean up lies with the responsible party. Formerly, the language of CWA section 311 gave the President discretionary authority to intervene when a clean up response was not conducted properly. As amended by the OPA, the provision now appears to create a mandatory duty: "The President shall . . . ensure effective and immediate removal of a discharge, and mitigation or prevention of a substantial threat of a discharge, of oil or a hazardous substance. . . ." Id. § 1321(c)(1). The president also is required to prepare the National Contingency Plan (NCP), which creates the framework "for efficient, coordinated, and effective action to minimize damage from oil . . . , including containment, dispersal, and removal . . . ," and establish a National Response System that is consistent with the NCP. Id. § 1321(d), (j).

The first category of liability then for a spiller is removal cost. Removal costs include all costs of removal and containment incurred by the United States, a state, or an Indian tribe and any removal costs incurred by any person for acts taken by the person that are consistent with the NCP. Id. § 2702(b).

Prior to OPA, a person who attempted to assist in the clean up or containment of an oil spill could be liable to the discharger if the efforts negligently contributed to further damage from the spill. OPA provides a "good Samaritan" exception to CWA section 311. A person will not be liable for removal costs and damages for assisting or rendering care consistent with National Contingency Plan (NCP) unless "the person is grossly negligent or engages in willful misconduct." The exclusion does not apply to personal injury or wrongful death actions, however. Id. § 1321(c)(4). The responsible party must pay any additional costs that arise because of the exception. The "good Samaritan" may also recover costs incurred in the assistance effort from the responsible party if the actions are consistent with the NCP.

Similarly, this immunity extends to manufacturers of dispersants that are used in an oil spill clean up in compliance with the NCP. The potentially toxic effects of dispersants have made their use controversial, but their use is contemplated by the CWA and incorporated in the NCP. In a case against Nalco, the manufacturer of the dispersant Corexit, the court found the exception from liability applies to the situation where the dispersant was listed on the NCP Product Schedule and pre-approved for use in a "spill of national significance." The court stated that the Act anticipated that there would have to be a balancing of the costs and benefits of the use of dispersants in a major spill, and the Act gives the government the responsibility to weigh the dangers of toxicity against the consequences of not using it. The court suggested that without immunity from liability, manufacturers not would be likely to provide or even produce a product necessary for effective oil spill response. The OPA provisions were found to preempt state as well as maritime law actions. *In re Oil Spill by the Oil Rig "Deepwater Horizon"*, 2012 WL 5960192 (Dist.Ct. E.D. La. 2012).

Because the CWA also immunizes the federal government "for any damages arising from its actions or omissions relating to any response plan required by [Section 311 of the CWA]," the U.S. also has no liability for damage caused by toxic dispersants. 33 U.S.C. § 1321(j)(8). See also Abby J. Queale, *Responding to the Response: Reforming the Legal Framework for Dispersant Use in Oil Spill Response Efforts in the Wake of Deepwater Horizon*, 18 Hastings W.-Nw. J. Envtl. L. & Pol'y 63, 65 (2012).

Obviously, all the oil from a catastrophic spill is unlikely to be removed. "Clean" can be an extremely subjective standard, depending on whether "how clean is clean" is determined by the government, environmentalists, scientists, the spiller, or the affected community. OPA gives the authority to determine when "removal . . . shall be considered completed" to the President, in consultation with governors of affected states and trustees that have been designated for purposes of natural resources restoration. Id. § 2711.

The second category of liability for an oil spill is for the damages specified in OPA. Several categories of damages are recoverable only by governments. These include: (1) "[d]amages for injury to, destruction of, loss of, or loss of use of, natural resources;" (2) "[d]amages equal to the net loss of taxes, royalties, rents, fees, or net profit shares due to the injury, destruction, or loss of real property, personal property, or natural resources;" and (3) "[d]amages for net costs of providing increased or additional public services during or after removal activities,

including protection from fire, safety, or health
hazards, caused by a discharge of oil." Id.
§ 2702(b)(2)(A), (D), (F).

Neither the CWA section 311 nor CERCLA
contains provisions for private claimants. Prior to the
OPA, only the Deepwater Port Act, 33 U.S.C. § 1501
et seq., OCSLA, 43 U.S.C. § 1801 et seq., and Trans-
Alaska Pipeline Authorization Act, 43 U.S.C.
§§ 1651–1656, created a mechanism for recovery of
damages by individuals. When these laws were not
applicable, claims had to be made under state law or
maritime tort. Private parties may claim three types
of damages under OPA. First, owners and lessees
may recover damages for "injury to, or economic
losses resulting from destruction of, real or personal
property." Id. § 2702(b)(2)(B). A second category of
private damages is entitled "subsistence use," but the
term is not defined in the OPA nor is it expressly
limited to aboriginal use of a resource. The provision
covers "[d]amages for loss of subsistence use of
natural resources, which shall be recoverable by any
claimant who so uses natural resources which have
been injured, destroyed, or lost, without regard to the
ownership or management of the resources." Id.
§ 2702(b)(2)(C). The class of "subsistence claimant"
identified for *Deepwater Horizon* oil spill settlement
procedures has been defined as

> a person who fishes or hunts to harvest, catch,
> barter, consume or trade Gulf of Mexico natural
> resources, in a traditional or customary manner,
> to sustain basic personal or family dietary,
> economic security, shelter, tool or clothing

needs, and who relied upon such subsistence resources that were diminished or restricted in the geographic region used by the claimant due to or resulting from the spill.

See *In re Oil Spill by Oil Rig Deepwater Horizon*, 910 F. Supp. 2d 891, 908 (E.D. La. 2012).

The final provision for private claims is for "[d]amages equal to the loss of profits or impairment of earning capacity due to the injury, destruction, or loss of real property, personal property, or natural resources." Id. § 2702(b)(2)(E). This section may have been intended to codify the exception in maritime tort law, created in *Union Oil Co. v. Oppen*, 501 F.2d 558 (9th Cir. 1974), that allows damages for purely economic losses for commercial fishermen. See H.R. Conf. Rep. No. 653, 101st Cong., 2d Sess. 103 (1990), reprinted in 1990 U.S.C.C.A.N. 779, 781 (stating only that a claimant need not be the owner of damaged property or resources to recover lost profits and cites the example of commercial fishermen). Some commentators, however, have indicated that OPA "deletes a limitation . . . under case law requiring that the claimant show physical damage to a proprietary interest before economic damage could be awarded." Cynthia M. Wilkinson et al., *Slick Work: An Analysis of the Oil Pollution Act of 1990,* 12 J. Energy Nat. Resources & Envtl. L. 181, 204 (1992) (The authors, who were counsels with the House Merchant Marine and Fisheries Committee when the provisions were enacted, assert that lost profits and earnings "may be had by anyone").

The first case to interpret this provision did not read it broadly. In *In re Cleveland Tankers, Inc.*, 791 F.Supp. 669 (E.D.Mich. 1992), the federal district court dismissed claims for economic damages from an oil spill. Claimants included a trucking company that lost profits, commercial marinas that lost business because of the closing of the channel, a boat charterer, a steamship company whose trade was interrupted, and marine terminal and dock operators. First determining that the claims were not cognizable as maritime torts because of the "bright line" *Robins Dry Dock* rule, the court then held that damages were also unavailable under OPA because the claimants had not alleged "injury, destruction, or loss to *their* property." (Emphasis added.) The court basically read OPA as reaffirming the *Robins Dry Dock* rule. By way of dictum, the court in *Ballard Shipping Co. v. Beach Shellfish*, 32 F.3d 623 (1st Cir. 1994), reached the opposite conclusion. See also Gregg L. McCurdy, *An Overview of OPA 1990 and Its Relationship to Other Laws*, 5 U.S.F. Mar. L.J. 423 (1993), and Francis J. Gonynor, *The* Robins *Dry Dock Rule: Is the "Bright Line" Fading?*, 4 U.S.F. Mar. L.J. 85 (1992).

In the litigation surrounding the *Deepwater Horizon* oil spill, the court has unequivocally interpreted OPA as removing the *Robins Dry Dock* limitation from OPA claims. Judge Barbier of the U.S. District Court stated that "one major remedial purpose of OPA was to allow a broader class of claimants to recover for economic losses than allowed under general maritime law," and held that "OPA claims for economic loss need not allege physical damage to a proprietary interest." *In re Oil Spill by the Oil Rig "Deepwater Horizon"*, 808 F.Supp.2d 943 (Dist. Ct. E.D. La. 2011). This greatly expands the kind of damage and class of plaintiffs entitled to compensation in the case of a major oil spill and does not provide the certainty provided by *Robins Dry Dock*'s "bright line rule." In regard to linking the oil spill to damage, Judge Barbier noted:

> . . . OPA does not expressly require "proximate cause," but rather only that the loss is "due to" or "resulting from" the oil spill. While the Court need not define the precise contours of OPA causation at this time, it is worth noting that during oral argument both counsel for BP and the PSC conceded that OPA causation may lie somewhere between traditional "proximate cause" and simple "but for" causation. Id.

OPA does not provide for punitive damages, raising the question of whether OPA preempts punitive damages that were previously available under general maritime law. In the *Deepwater Horizon* litigation, Judge Barbier relied on the U.S. Supreme Court's reasoning in *Exxon Shipping Co. v. Baker*, 554 U.S. 471 (2008), that held that the CWA did not preempt the general maritime remedy available for punitive damages. As in the case of the CWA provisions analyzed in *Baker,* Congress demonstrated no intent or language in OPA to preempt maritime law punitive damages, and the availability of such punitive damages does not undermine OPA's remedial scheme. The court held, therefore, that claims for punitive damages are available for general maritime law claimants against both responsible parties and others responsible only under maritime law. Id. Note that in *Baker* the U.S. Supreme Court limited punitive damages in maritime cases, however, stating that it "consider[s] that [a] 1:1 ratio [between compensatory damages and punitive damages], is a fair upper limit in such maritime cases." *Baker* at 513.

Recovery under CWA section 311 had been specifically limited to damages in United States waters. In *In re Oswego Barge Corp.*, 664 F.2d 327 (2d Cir. 1981), the court found that section 311 provided no remedies for pollution of foreign waters. OPA allows foreign claimants, including both governments and individuals, to recover removal costs and damages resulting from an oil spill from a vessel in United States' waters, from a tanker at a pipeline terminal or deepwater port, or from an OCS facility. 33 U.S.C. § 2707.

The natural resources damages provisions are perhaps the most revolutionary aspect of OPA. "Natural resources" are defined to include:

land, fish, wildlife, biota, air, water, ground water, drinking water, supplies, and other such resources belonging to, managed by, held in trust by, appertaining to, or otherwise controlled by the United States (including the resources of the exclusive economic zone), any State or local government or Indian tribe, or any foreign government.

Id. § 2701(20). "Damages for injury to, destruction of, loss of, or loss of use of, natural resources, including the reasonable costs of assessing the damage," are recoverable only by natural resources trustees designated for the United States, a state, an Indian tribe, or a foreign government. Id. § 2702(b)(2)(A). The primary duties of the trustees are: (1) to assess damages to the natural resources belonging to, managed by, or appertaining to their respective areas; and (2) to "develop and implement a plan for the restoration, rehabilitation, replacement, or acquisition of the equivalent, of the natural resources under their trusteeship." Id. § 2706(c). An assessment of damages by a trustee is entitled to a rebuttable presumption of appropriateness in any administrative or judicial challenge. Id. § 2706(e)(2). Problems clearly may arise involving duplicative or overlapping claims among trustees. OPA does not have a mechanism for resolving such conflicts. However, OPA does prohibit double recoveries from a responsible party for natural resource damages from the same incident. Id. § 2706(d)(3).

Determining appropriate values and methodologies for assessment of natural resources damages has been a ubiquitous problem. Working with very little guidance under CERCLA's natural resources damages provisions, the Department of the Interior's CERCLA regulations limited recoverable natural resource damages to "the lesser of" (a) the cost of restoring or replacing the equivalent of an injured resource, or (b) the lost use value of the resource. In *Ohio v. United States Department of the Interior*, 880 F.2d 432, 279 U.S.App.D.C. 109

(D.C.Cir. 1989), the D.C. Court of Appeals invalidated the regulations as directly contrary to the intent of Congress. Lost use value is a useful methodology for calculating damages such as commercial fishermen's lost profits. However, the court found that natural resources have values beyond, for example, the board feet of lumber in a forest or the value of a seal's or otter's pelt. Use value in such circumstances seriously undervalues the resource. The court endorsed the inclusion of passive values, such as existence values, in the calculation of damages. Existence values represent the value to individuals who make no active use of a beach, waterbody, or other natural resource, but still derive satisfaction from its existence.

The provisions of OPA provide a bit more guidance by identifying the following factors in calculating the measure of natural resource damages:

The measure of natural resource damages . . . is

(A) the cost of restoring, rehabilitating, replacing, or acquiring the equivalent of, the damaged natural resources;

(B) the diminution in value of those natural resources pending restoration; plus

(C) the reasonable cost of assessing those damages.

33 U.S.C. § 2706(d)(1). Congress expressed a preference for restoring resources when possible. Even this approach is controversial, however. Although restoration is often the most cost effective

approach, the restoration costs may still be disproportionate to the resource's value. On the other hand, many environmentalists would challenge man's ability to restore a natural resource to its previous pristine state. The Department of Commerce, as designated trustee for the federal government for most natural resources under OPA also incorporated lost use values in its regulations. See 15 C.F.R. pt. 990. The regulations largely were upheld in *General Electric Co. v. U.S. Dept. of Commerce*, 128 F.3d 767, 327 U.S.App.D.C. 33 (D.C.Cir. 1997).

A primary limitation on assessment of natural resources damages seems to be the statutory language that the recovery may only be had for damages that "result from such incident." 33 U.S.C. § 2702(a). The same language in CERCLA was interpreted in *United States v. Montrose Chemical Corp. of California* (C.D.Cal. 1991). The federal district court defined the causation standard as requiring plaintiffs to "show that defendant's release . . . was the sole or substantially contributing cause of each alleged injury to natural resources." The court required detailed, particularized allegations as to what, where, and when natural resources injuries were sustained.

Although all claims for clean up costs and damages must be presented to the responsible party first, the Oil Spill Liability Trust Fund (Fund) has been expanded under OPA to provide up to a billion dollars per incident, not only for federal costs and damages, but also for uncompensated private and state claims if "full and adequate compensation is not available." See 33 U.S.C. § 2713(d). The most obvious examples of when private claims would be paid by the Fund are when the spiller is not known, when the spiller has successfully asserted a complete defense, or when the spiller's liability exceeds the Act's limitations. The Fund is financed primarily by a five-cent per barrel tax on oil and penalties and fund transfers from other liability statutes.

b. Which Law?

Liability for damages from spills of oil or hazardous substances has proved to be an unending source of confusion. Rather than provide a single, comprehensive statute for liability, Congress has seemed to specifically retain certain remedies in OPA, leaving it to the courts to sort out which remedies have been saved, preempted or displaced. The choice of law determination is often critical to who can recover damages and what the limits of the polluter's liability may be. In addition to maritime law, state common law, and federal statutory law,[2] at least 24 states have passed oil spill legislation. Nearly all are strict liability statutes, and most impose unlimited liability. Further, in *Askew v. American Waterways Operators, Inc.*, 411 U.S. 325, 93 S.Ct. 1590, 36 L.Ed.2d 280 (1973), the U.S. Supreme Court held that CWA section 311 did not preempt a state statute imposing strict liability for

---

[2]   In *Middlesex County Sewerage Authority v. National Sea Clammers Ass'n*, 453 U.S. 1, 101 S.Ct. 2615, 69 L.Ed.2d 435 (1981), the U.S. Supreme Court held that "the federal common law of nuisance has been fully preempted in the area of ocean pollution."

state removal costs and for state and private damages for spills in the state's waters.

OPA contains a specific savings clause in regard to state law and federal maritime law. Section 1018(a) explains the relationship to state law, providing that nothing in OPA shall:

(1)   affect, or be construed or interpreted as preempting, the authority of any State or political subdivision thereof from imposing any additional liability or requirements with respect to—

(A) the discharge of oil or other pollution by oil within such State; or

(B) any removal activities in connection with such a discharge; or

(2)   affect, or be construed or interpreted to affect or modify in any way the obligations or liabilities of any person under . . . State law, including common law.

The *Deepwater Horizon* litigation created the necessity for Judge Barbier to determine the effect of this language on state law claims. The court found that this language only protected existing state authority involving discharges "within such State," and in the case of oil spills on the OCS, state law had been preempted by federal maritime law. *In re Oil Spill by the Oil Rig "Deepwater Horizon"*, 808 F.Supp.2d 943 (Dist. Ct. E.D. La. 2011). In addition, the court found that the Supreme Court reasoning in *International Paper Co. v. Ouellette*, 479 U.S. 481

(1987), precluded application of state law. In that case, the CWA's savings provision did not allow application of state law to water pollution originating outside of the state because it would undermine the efficiency and predictability goals of the CWA. *Askew* was distinguished as applying only to spills that occurred in state waters, not to out-of-state polluters, and involved legislation that did not overlap with federal statutes. State law claims were, therefore, dismissed. See also, *In re Deepwater Horizon*, 745 F.3d 157, 2014 WL 700065 (5th Cir. La. 2014) (affirming preemption of state law because the spill occurred on the OCS).

The *Deepwater Horizon* litigation also addressed the relation of general maritime law to OPA. It should be noted that general maritime law covers a much broader realm of liability than OPA; for example, OPA does not apply to products liability, personal injury or death claims, or punitive damages. But to the extent that claims against "responsible parties" are addressed by OPA, general maritime claims are preempted, and all claims against responsible parties are subject to OPA's presentment requirement.[3] See also *Gabarick v. Laurin Maritime (America) Inc.*, 623 F.Supp.2d 741, 747 (E.D.La.2009) (holding that OPA preempts general maritime law claims that are recoverable under OPA). Claims against non-responsible parties under maritime law, however, are not preempted by OPA. Maritime law

---

[3] The statute provides that all claims for removal costs or damages shall be presented first to the responsible party, who is given 90 days to settle the claims. 33 U.S.C. § 2713. Presentment is a mandatory condition precedent to filing suit.

continues to be subject to judge-made limitations, such as the *Robins Dry Dock* rule, and to the Limitation on Liability Act.

c. Pollution Prevention and Spill Response

OPA incorporates provisions for manning and operation that reflect the experience gained from the *Exxon Valdez* oil spill.[4] OPA addresses problems related to drug and alcohol abuse by broadening authority for drug and alcohol testing of vessel personnel and for examination of criminal and traffic records in licensing merchant seamen. Procedures are established for relieving a captain of command when he is operating the ship under the influence of alcohol or drugs. The perception that vessels are poorly manned is addressed through new training, manning, and watch-keeping requirements. See 46 U.S.C. §§ 7101–114, 7701–705, 8101–104.

OPA also requires studies of tanker vessel safety standards and adds new requirements for the minimum plating thickness of commercial vessels and for communication equipment. Undoubtedly the most controversial equipment standard of OPA was the requirement for double hulls. All new tankers over 5000 gross tons were required to have double hulls. OPA sets up a schedule for conversion of existing single hull tankers to double hulls. Single hull tankers were prohibited from operating in United States navigable waters or in the EEZ after 2010. By 2015, the prohibition will extend to double

---

[4] No additional legislation was passed in the wake of the *Deepwater Horizon* oil spill.

bottomed and double sided vessels. 46 U.S.C. §§ 1274(a), 3703a, 3715(a). See *Maritrans v. United States*, 342 F.3d 1344 (Fed.Cir. 2003).

In *Ray* v. *Atlantic Richfield Co.,* 435 U. S. 151 (1978) and *United States v. Locke*, 529 U.S. 89 (2000), the Supreme Court affirmed that in areas like design, construction, alteration, repair, maintenance, operation, equipping, personnel qualification, and manning of tanker vessels. Congress has left no room for state regulation. OPA's savings clause, 33 U.S.C. § 2718, did not create new authority for the states to regulate in this field which had been preempted under other federal law. States retain "authority to regulate the peculiarities of local waters if there [is] no conflict with federal regulatory determinations." Id.

OPA also addresses oil spill preparedness by expanding and strengthening the National Contingency Plan under the CWA. 33 U.S.C. § 1321(d). The President is ordered to prepare a plan "for efficient, coordinated, and effective action to minimize damage from oil and hazardous stance discharges." Id. § 1321(d)(2). The Plan must address the removal of a "worst case discharge of oil" and include: (1) creation of Coast Guard strike force teams; (2) establishment of a national center for coordination and direction of Plan implementation; (3) a system for surveillance and notice; (4) procurement and storage of removal and containment equipment; (5) procedures for identifying, containing, dispersing, and removing spills; (6) procedures to assure coordination of clean up efforts; and (7) development of a fish and wildlife response plan. See id. Consistent with the Plan, the President must set up a National Response System (NRS), including a National Response Unit, District Response Groups, and Area Committees. Id. § 1321(j). Tank vessels and facilities must also submit response plans for worst case discharges and ensure the availability of personnel and equipment to carry out the response. Id. § 1321(j)(5). The effectiveness of the NCP, the NRS, and other aspects of the response to the *Deepwater Horizon* oil spill are subjected to review and critical analysis in the U.S. Coast Guard's *BP Deepwater Horizon Spill Incident Specific Preparedness Review*, available at https://www.uscg.mil/foia/docs/DWH/BPDWH.pdf.

D.   OCEAN DUMPING

The intentional discharge of dredged spoil, sewage sludge, and industrial wastes into the ocean probably constitutes about ten percent of the pollutants in the ocean. Eighty to ninety percent of the deliberately dumped material is dredged spoil from navigation, waterway, and harbor projects. As much as ten percent of dredged materials are contaminated with oil, heavy metals, and organochlorine compounds. Industrial wastes may be obvious sources of hazardous or toxic contaminants, but sewage sludge may also contain heavy metals and organic chemicals. Ocean disposal has not only contributed to the general degradation of the marine environment, but also has direct effects on habitats and organisms at dumpsites. See Maritime Affairs: A World Handbook 240–41 (Edgar Gold ed., 2d ed. 1991).

The Convention on the Prevention of Marine Pollution by Dumping of Wastes and Other Matter (London Convention), done Dec. 29, 1972, 26 U.S.T. 2406, 1046 U.N.T.S. 120, is the primary international agreement dealing with marine disposal of wastes. Ocean "dumping" is defined in the Convention as:

> (i) any deliberate disposal at sea of wastes or other matter from vessels, aircraft, platforms or other man-made structures at sea;

> (ii) any deliberate disposal at sea of vessels, aircraft, platforms or other man-made structures at sea.

Id. art. 111(1).

The nations that are party to the London Convention originally agreed to prohibit the dumping of materials listed in Annex I of the Convention, unless they are "rapidly rendered harmless by physical, chemical, or biological processes in the sea. . . ." (Annex I, No. 8, 26 U.S.T. at 2465). Dumping of material specifically listed in Annex II and other material was allowed only on the issuance of a prior permit. The Convention set forth a number of factors in Annex III to be considered in granting permits, including the characteristics of the waste and site, method of disposal, effect on marine organisms, other uses of the sea, and the availability of alternative methods of dumping. The Convention's 1996 Protocol greatly restricted permissible dumping by prohibiting the ocean dumping of all wastes except those listed in a revised Annex I, the so-called "reverse list." Revised Annex I only allows the dumping of dredged material, sewage sludge, fish wastes, inert geological materials, natural organic materials, abandoned vessels and platforms, and other bulky items made of iron, steel, concrete, and similar nonharmful materials. Revised Annexes II and III to the 1996 Protocol deal with waste assessment and arbitral procedures. The 1996 Protocol provided that it would come into force upon its ratification by 26 nations, including at least 15 of the 76 nations who are parties to the London Convention. The 1996 Protocol entered into force in 2006. Currently, the Protocol has 45 parties. The United States is one of the current 87 parties to the London Convention, but has not ratified the 1996 Protocol.

The fact that the oceans are natural "carbon sinks" has led to proposals to enhance that capability by "ocean fertilization" and to use the oceans and seabed for sequestration of carbon. Ocean fertilization does not technically involve "disposal" in the ocean, but the parties to the London Convention have agreed that a precautionary approach is called for in dealing with such projects and that "ocean fertilization activities other than legitimate scientific research should not be allowed." See Resolution LC–LP.1 (2008) on the Regulation of Ocean Fertilization and Statement of concern regarding the iron fertilization project in ocean waters west of Canada (adopted 2 November 2012, reaffirming the position of the London Convention adopted in 2008). Carbon sequestration is more clearly within the scope of the London Convention. In 2006, Annex I was amended to allow CO_2 streams from CO_2 capture to be disposed of in sub-seabed geological formations. The interpretation of the London Convention as prohibiting the export of CO_2 to other countries for injection into sub-seabed geological formations led to an amendment in 2009 to allow for cross-border transportation of CO_2 for sub-seabed storage. The requirement that the amendment be ratified by two thirds of Convention's parties to enter into force has slowed implementation.

In 1972, Congress enacted the Marine Protection, Research and Sanctuaries Act of 1972 (MPRSA), 33 U.S.C. §§ 1401–445, to implement the London Convention. The first two titles of MPRSA are commonly known as the Ocean Dumping Act (ODA). The ODA was enacted "to regulate the dumping of all types of materials into ocean waters," and grants the Environmental Protection Agency and the Secretary of the Army, through the U.S. Army Corps of Engineers (the Corps), the authority to regulate ocean dumping.

The ODA defines ocean "dumping" broadly as "a disposition of material." Id. § 1402(f). Material may include solid wastes, industrial waste, radioactive waste, sewage sludge, incinerator residue, and dredged materials. However, dumping does not include effluent from ocean sewage outfalls, construction of offshore structures or artificial islands, or the deposit of oyster shells or other materials for the purpose of developing fisheries resources. Id. In general, anything placed on the ocean floor for purposes other than disposal is excluded.

As with the Clean Water Act, the Administrator of the EPA is charged with the duty of enforcing the provisions of the ODA. Under the ODA, the Administrator may grant permits for ocean dumping of nondredged materials except "radiological, chemical, and biological warfare agents, high-level radioactive waste, and medical waste," for which no permits may be issued. Id. § 1412(a). In general, the EPA may only allow disposal that "will not unreasonably degrade or endanger human health; welfare, or amenities, or the marine environment, ecological systems, or economic potentialities." Id. More specifically, EPA permit criteria include consideration of: (1) the effect of dumping on human health and welfare, including economic, esthetic, and recreational values; (2) the effect of dumping on fisheries resources, plankton, fish, shellfish, wildlife, shorelines, and beaches; (3) the effect of dumping on marine ecosystems, particularly the concentration and dispersion of such material; potential changes in marine ecosystem diversity, productivity, and stability; and species and community population dynamics; (4) the persistence and permanence of the effects of the dumping; (5) the effect of dumping particular volumes and concentrations; (6) the appropriate locations and methods of disposal or recycling, including land-based alternatives and the probable impact of alternatives upon the public interest; (7) the effect on alternate uses of the oceans, such as scientific study, fishing, and other living and non-living resource exploitation; and (8) the need for the proposed dumping. See 40 C.F.R. Pts. 227–228.

The EPA Administrator also designates sites and times for ocean dumping "that will mitigate adverse impact on the environment to the greatest extent practicable." 33 U.S.C. § 1412(c)(1). Because most long-term dumping sites are for dredged materials, the EPA must develop management plans for those sites that include monitoring and protections for the environment. Id. § 1412(c)(3).

The ODA authorizes the Corps, with the concurrence of the EPA, to issue permits for the dumping of dredged material. Id. § 1413. Under section 404 of the CWA, the Corps also has authority to permit the discharge of dredged materials into navigable waters. Id. § 1344(a). Because ODA jurisdiction includes all ocean waters seaward of the territorial sea baseline and because "navigable waters" under the CWA includes waters three nautical miles seaward of that baseline, the Corps' programs for disposal of dredged material overlap in the ocean to three miles offshore. The Corps has published regulations addressing the issue of the overlapping jurisdiction of the CWA and the ODA in the territorial sea. All disposal in the ocean or territorial sea of material that has been excavated or dredged from navigable waters will be evaluated under the ODA. Only materials determined to be deposited primarily for the purpose of fill will be evaluated under section 404 of the CWA. See 33 C.F.R. § 336.0; see also 53 Fed. Reg. 14,902, 14,905 (1988).

Whether a permit for dredged spoil disposal is evaluated under the CWA or the ODA can be significant. First, although the criteria for evaluation are virtually the same, the ODA requires that the Corps "make an independent determination as to the need for the dumping[,] . . . other possible methods of disposal[,] and . . . appropriate locations for the dumping." 33 U.S.C. § 1413(b). The CWA does not have a comparable requirement.

In permitting discharges under the CWA, both the CWA's requirement for state certification that a project does not violate state water quality standards and the federal consistency requirements of the Coastal Zone Management Act (CZMA) are applicable to activities with effects within three miles of the coast. In its ODA regulations, the Corps rejected comments by states that federal consistency requirements should apply to dumping beyond coastal waters and asserted that the ODA may preempt both the CWA certification provisions and the CZMA. For dumping material from federal projects in state ocean waters, the ODA does limit the authority of states to adopt or enforce any rule or regulation more stringent than the requirements of the ODA. Id. § 1416(d)(2). Otherwise, state authority over dumping in the state ocean waters is preserved. Id. § 1416(d)(1). But the Corps regulations state that it will continue to seek state water quality certification and consistency determinations for dredged spoil disposal within three miles of shore only as a matter of comity and specifically reserved its legal rights on the issue. 33 C.F.R. § 336.2(c). When one considers that the Corps itself generates almost ninety percent of the dredged spoil dumped in the sea, it is clear that the "checks and balances" of the CWA and CZMA may be appropriate to help reconcile the Corps' roles as both generator and regulator.

The EPA does have oversight authority over the Corps in issuing ocean-dumping permits for dredged spoils and over the Corps' use of disposal sites not designated by the EPA 33 U.S.C. § 1413(c). The EPA must concur with the Corps' determination that a permit or alternative disposal site complies with the ODA's criteria and restrictions. If the EPA declines to concur, the Corps may not issue the permit. Id. If the Corps determines that there is no economically feasible method or other available site that will not violate ODA criteria, the EPA must grant a waiver unless it finds that the "dumping . . . will result in an unacceptably adverse impact on municipal water supplies, shellfish beds, wildlife, fisheries . . . , or recreational areas." Id. § 1413(d). The Corps does not administratively issue itself permits for dumping dredged spoils, but the same standards and criteria apply for federal dredged spoil disposal projects. Id. § 1413(e).

In 1977, Congress amended MPRSA to forbid the issuance of permits for dumping of sewage sludge into ocean waters after December 31, 1981. The amendment went on, however, to define sewage sludge as municipal waste "the ocean dumping of which *may unreasonably degrade or endanger* human health, welfare, amenities, or the marine environment, ecological systems, or economic potentialities" (emphasis added). In *City of New York v. United States Environmental Protection Agency,*

543 F.Supp. 1084 (S.D.N.Y. 1981), the federal district court rejected the argument that the amendment required an absolute end to dumping. The court held that EPA could not deny the continuance of New York's sludge dumping permit without considering the effects of alternatives to ocean dumping, such as land based disposal, in its determination of whether ocean dumping caused unacceptable harm. In the Ocean Dumping Ban Act of 1988, Congress amended MPRSA to reverse *City of New York.* All ocean dumping of both sewage sludge and industrial wastes was banned after December 31, 1991, and no permits were issued to "new entrants" during the interim period. 33 U.S.C. § 1414b(a).

The prohibition on ocean dumping of industrial wastes had an interesting impact on a form of waste disposal that many thought was a promising concept for disposing of a number of highly toxic and hazardous substances. EPA had for a long time considered ocean incineration to be "dumping" both in the sense that smokestack emissions are deposited in ocean waters and in the sense that incinerator residue is also disposed of at sea. When EPA suspended development of ocean incineration regulations and barred consideration of new permit applications because of the ban on new entrants and the complete prohibition on dumping industrial wastes after 1991, Seaburn, a commercial waste disposal company, challenged EPA's characterization of ocean incineration as dumping. *Seaburn, Inc. v. United States EPA,* 712 F.Supp. 218 (D.D.C. 1989). Seaburn argued that smokestack emissions could not rationally be equated with dumping and that incinerator residue did not fit the definition of industrial waste. The D.C. federal district court found that this time Congress had unequivocally intended a moratorium on dumping of industrial wastes. Finding that "EPA's interpretation of the Ocean Dumping Ban Act [was] sufficiently rational to be entitled to the traditional deference accorded an agency interpretation of a statute," the court granted the EPA's motion for summary judgment and closed the door on research and development of ocean incineration technology.

The 1993 amendments to the London Convention and the 1996 Protocol have now also banned the ocean incineration and dumping of industrial wastes.

E.   PERSISTENT MARINE DEBRIS—PLASTICS

Humans contribute large amounts of materials that can be categorized as persistent marine debris to ocean waters and beaches—oil tarballs, glass, metal—but over the last two decades, it has become clear that nondegradable plastics contribute the most significant threat to the marine environment. Vessels and offshore facilities generate much of this plastic debris, which includes monofilament line, driftnets and other fishing nets, ropes, plastic sheeting, containers, and food packaging. People incur direct economic costs from marine debris on beaches and from debris that damages vessels. Perhaps more tragic, however, is the impact on marine wildlife. Inestimable numbers of fish, marine mammals, birds, and sea turtles die annually from entanglement with or ingestion of plastic debris. Relatively recently, it has been discovered that plastics accumulate in huge oceans gyres that concentrate the pollution and multiply the deleterious effects. See, e.g., *Tracking Ocean Debris,* 8 IPRC Climate 14, 2008; Jose G.B. Derraik, *The pollution of the marine environment by plastic debris: a review*, 44 Marine Pollution Bulletin 842 (2002);

Under the London Convention plastics cannot be dumped at sea. The Convention only applies, however, to materials that are transported for the purpose of disposal in the ocean. The scope of the London Convention does not reach "[t]he disposal at sea of wastes or other matter incidental to, or derived from the normal operations of vessels . . . and their equipment." London Convention, art. III(1). "Normal operations of vessels" has entailed the disposal of hundreds of thousands of tons per year of ship-generated plastic garbage and lost or abandoned fishing gear.

The international community addressed this gap in the regulation of vessel operational wastes in Annex V of MARPOL 73/78. Regulations for the Prevention of Pollution by Garbage from Ships (Annex V of MARPOL 73/78), Oct. 31, 1973, S. Treaty Doc. No. 3, 100th Cong., 1st Sess. 1 (1987), 12 I.L.M. 1434. Annex V prohibits "the disposal into the sea of all plastics, including but not limited to synthetic ropes, synthetic fishing nets and plastic garbage bags." Id. reg. 3. Floatable, nonplastic materials may not be disposed of within twenty-five miles of land, and food wastes and other garbage must be discharged at least twelve miles from shore. Id. The only exemptions from the discharge prohibitions are: (1) disposal necessary for the safety of the ship or crew, or to save life at sea; (2) discharges resulting from damage to a ship or its equipment; and (3) accidental loss of synthetic fishing nets. Id. reg. 6. The third exemption continues to account for significant plastics pollution.

The at-sea disposal prohibition necessitates other waste disposal options. Annex V requires nations that are parties to provide garbage reception facilities at ports and terminals. Id. reg. 7.

The United States ratified Annex V in 1987; the Annex went into force internationally in 1988. The United States implemented Annex V through the enactment of the Marine Plastic Pollution Research and Control Act (MPPRCA), which amended the Act on Prevention of Pollution from Ships, 33 U.S.C. §§ 1901–1912. MPPRCA extends Annex V's prohibitions on plastics and garbage disposal to all U.S. ships wherever they are located in the world. In addition, foreign ships operating in U.S. navigable waters or the EEZ, whether flying the flag of a party to MARPOL or not, are subject to Annex V requirements. Id. § 1902(a)(1), (3). Pursuant to Annex V, the MPPRCA also requires ports and offshore terminals to provide garbage reception facilities. Id. § 1905. Large ports and terminals that receive oil or cargo tankers or that receive more than 500,000 tons of fish annually must have certificates of adequacy from the U.S. Coast Guard in order to continue to receive ships. 33 C.F.R. § 158.135.

The MPPRCA contains a number of enforcement provisions. The Act mandates regulations for certain ships to maintain refuse record books to account for waste production and disposal. 33 U.S.C. § 1903(b). While in port or in U.S. navigable waters or in the EEZ, domestic and foreign ships subject to Annex V may be inspected for violations. Id. § 1907(c)–(d). U.S. ships may be inspected anywhere. Id. § 1907(e). Civil penalties are substantial and can be up to $25,000 for each violation. Knowing violations of the statute or Annex V constitute a class D felony. Id. § 1908. Ships are also subject to *in rem* actions for penalties and may be denied clearance to enter ports or permits to proceed from port. Id. § 1908(d). To supplement enforcement, the MPPRCA contains a "whistle-blower" provision that allows a court to award up to one-half of a fine to persons providing information of violations. Id. § 1908(a). With the incentive of this provision, crew members and "video camera-toting" tourists have been providing evidence of illegal dumping of plastics and garbage by cruise ships. In 1993, Princess Cruise Lines plead guilty and paid a record $500,000 fine for illegal dumping plastics and garbage that had been video taped and reported by passengers, who received one-half of the penalty. See *Vacationers Go Undercover at Sea to Film Dumping*, N.Y. Times (July 31, 1993). See also *United States v. Wallenius ShipManagement Pte.*, No. 2:06–CR–00213 (D.N.J. Aug. 10, 2006) (court awarded one-half of a $5 million fine to four crew members who faxed information alleging that they were being ordered to engage in deliberate acts of pollution); *United States v. OMI*, No. 2:04–CR–00060 (D. N.J. 2004) (court awarded one-half of a $4.2 million criminal fine to a Second Engineer who upon arrival asked for directions to local police department and reported illegal discharges and falsified records); and *United States v. Regency Cruises, Inc.*, No. 94–245–CR–T–21(C) (M.D. Fla. Mar. 8, 1995) (court split one half of the $250,000 fine among two witnesses who reported the pollution).

F.   POINT SOURCE DISCHARGES FROM LAND AND OFFSHORE FACILITIES

At the same time the Ocean Dumping Act was pending, Congress was in the middle of a struggle to pass sweeping Federal Water Pollution Control Act (FWPCA, now known as CWA) amendments. This water pollution legislation, which passed into law over President Nixon's veto in October 1972, had as its original goal the elimination of polluting discharges into navigable waters by 1985. While much of this legislation was designed to deal with the nation's fresh and estuarine waters, see, e.g., *California Public Interest Research Group v. Shell Oil Co.*, 840 F.Supp. 712 (N.D.Cal.1993), involving oil refinery selenium discharges into San Francisco Bay, and *Northwest Env. Advocates v. U.S. EPA,* 2005 WL 756614 (N.D.Cal. 2005) involving vessel ballast water discharges of invasive species, two sections deal specifically with ocean discharges: Section 403 (33 U.S.C. § 1343) regulates the offshore discharge of nondredged materials from onshore outfall pipes, and other point sources, except vessels. See, e.g., *United States v. Weitzenhoff*, 35 F.3d 1275 (9th Cir. 1993) (criminal prosecution for toxic sludge discharges into ocean waters off Honolulu). Section 404 (33 U.S.C. § 1344) regulates discharges of dredged materials into waters seaward to three nautical miles and authorizes the Corps of Engineers to issue permits for the discharge of dredged or fill materials at EPA-specified disposal sites in navigable waters.

CWA section 403 utilizes a precautionary approach where information is insufficient, calls for prevention of unreasonable degradation of the marine environment, and authorizes the use of effluent limitations established by the EPA. The section provides for a prohibition of discharges, if necessary, to achieve those requirements. Although section 403 of the CWA and section 102 of the ODA are similar, they are not identical. In essence, the ODA applies to dumping from vessels into ocean waters and does not apply to discharges from pipes and outfalls, which are subject to control under the CWA. All such discharges seaward of the inner boundary of U.S. territorial seas are subject to section 403 requirements.

Section 301 of the CWA makes unlawful the unpermitted discharge of any pollutant by any person except in compliance with the terms of that and other specifically enumerated sections. In short, section 301 prohibits the discharge of untreated sewage. Permit criteria developed pursuant to CWA section 403 supplement section 301 requirements and are applicable to permit proceedings authorized by section 402 as well as to municipal marine dischargers seeking a modification of the normally

applicable   secondary   sewage   treatment
requirements as provided by section 301(h).

The administrative framework of the CWA differs
fundamentally from that provided in the ODA. The
ODA is a federal program explicitly preempting state
regulatory activity. With certain exceptions, the
CWA envisions state pollution control programs that
are reviewed and approved by EPA, thus giving
states permit authority over point sources of
pollution seaward to three nautical miles. See *Pacific
Legal Foundation v. Costle*, 586 F.2d 650 (9th Cir.
1978). Beyond three nautical miles, EPA administers
the discharge permit processes for outer continental
shelf (OCS) oil and gas facilities (see, e.g., *BP
Exploration & Oil, Inc. v. Environmental Protection
Agency*, 66 F.3d 784 (6th Cir. 1995)), deepwater ports
(see 33 U.S.C. § 1502(10)), ocean thermal energy
conversion facilities (see 42 U.S.C. § 9117(f), and
other offshore facilities (see 33 U.S.C. § 1316)). See
also *Sierra Club, Lone Star Chapter v. Cedar Point
Oil Co.*, 73 F.3d 546 (5th Cir. 1996) (EPA regulation
of discharges from offshore oil and gas operations in
state waters).

G.   POLLUTION FROM OTHER
LAND-BASED ACTIVITIES

Worldwide, about seventy to eighty percent of
marine pollution comes from land-based sources
(LBS) and activities rather than vessels. These
activities include industrial and sewage point source
discharges like those in the previous section and
more dispersed runoff pollution into rivers, estuaries,

and the ocean from agriculture, forestry, mining, and urban development. The international and United States legal responses to LBS pollution, especially the runoff type, are much less developed than for vessels. Articles 207(1) and 213 of the 1982 UNCLOS very generally obligate nations party to the convention to adopt laws to prevent, reduce, and control pollution of the marine environment from land-based point sources and runoff. Paragraphs 17.24 through 17.29 of Agenda 21 produced by the 1992 United Nations Conference on Environment and Development (U.N. Doc. A/CONF. 151/26 (1992)) contain recommendations for national action as do the 1985 Montreal Guidelines for the Protection of the Marine Against Pollution from Land-Based Sources (UNEP/GC. 13/9/Add. 3, UNEP/ GC/DEC/13/1811, UNEP ELPG No. 7 (1985)) issued by the United Nations Environmental Program (UNEP). More detailed is the UNEP 1995 Global Programme of Action for the Protection of the Marine Environment from Land-Based Activities (UNEP (OCA)/LBA/IG.2/7). See J. Karau, D. VanderZwaag, & P. Wells, *The Global Programme of Action for the Protection of the Marine Environment from Land-Based Activities: A Cacophony of Sounds, Will the World Listen?* in Ocean Yearbook 13 (E. Borgese, A. Chircop, M. McConnell, & J. Morgan, eds., 1997).

Nine multilateral regional conventions for specific ocean areas address LBS pollution, including the Cartagena Convention for the Caribbean Region to which the United States is a party. The United States and 10 other Cartagena Convention members are parties to the Protocol Concerning Pollution from

Land-Based Sources and Activities (LBS Protocol) to the Cartagena Convention which entered into force in 2010. The LBS Protocol applies to the wider Caribbean region, including the Gulf of Mexico and Atlantic Ocean south of 30 degrees north latitude and out to 200 miles from shore.

The LBS Protocol comprises 5 annexes with the following provisions:

- **Annex I** lists land-based sources and activities and their associated contaminants of greatest concern;

- **Annex II** establishes procedure to develop regional standards and practices for the prevention, reduction and control of the Annex I sources and contaminants;

- **Annex III** sets specific regional limitations for domestic sewage; and

- **Annex IV** requires each party to take measures, including plans, programs and other actions, to prevent, reduce and control agricultural non-point sources.

LBS Protocol parties must address Annex III and IV by creating legally-binding effluent limitations for domestic sewage and by developing plans for the reduction and control of agricultural non-point sources. See EPA, *Cartagena Convention and Land-Based Sources Protocol*, available at http://www2. epa.gov/international-ooperation/cartagena-conven tion-and-land-based-sources-protocol; and the Caribbean Environmental Program, available at http://cep.unep.org.

In the United States, regulation of both the point source and the runoff components of LBS pollution occurs primarily under the CWA. CWA runoff regulatory programs include those for concentrated animal feeding operations (see *Waterkeeper Alliance, Inc. v. U.S. EPA*, 399 F.3d 486 (2d Cir. 2005)), combined sewer overflows (see *Northwest Environmental Advocates v. City of Portland*, 56 F.3d 979 (9th Cir. 1995)), and stormwater (see *Molokai Chamber of Commerce v. Kukui (Molokai) Inc.*, 891 F.Supp. 1389 (D.Hawaii 1995); see also *Decker v. Northwest Envtl. Def. Ctr.*, 133 S. Ct. 1326 (2013) (holding that NPDES permits are not required for stormwater runoff from logging roads)). Other runoff pollution sources are addressed as nonpoint sources (NPS) through the state-implemented land use planning and pollution prevention process of CWA section 319 (33 U.S.C. § 1329) and the coastal NPS control provisions of the federal Coastal Zone Management Act (CZMA) (16 U.S.C. § 1455b). The latter requires state design and implementation of enforceable NPS pollution management measures against a broad range of NPS sources and includes federal consistency requirements paralleling those of CZMA section 307 (16 U.S.C. § 1456). When the cumulative impact of point and nonpoint source pollution in a particular water body results in a violation of its state-established CWA ambient water quality standards, the CWA's complex total maximum daily load (TMDL) process (see 33 U.S.C. § 1313(d)) can be invoked to force reductions in both types of pollution. See *Dioxin/Organoehlorine Center v. Clarke*, 57 F.3d 1517 (9th Cir.1995) (EPA-imposed

TMDL for dioxin in Columbia River upheld); *Pronsolino v. Nastri*, 291 F.3d 1123 (9th Cir. 2002) (TMDL requirements apply to water bodies impaired solely by NPS pollution).

H. AIR POLLUTION FROM VESSELS

Rather than addressing pollution of the ocean, MARPOL 73/78, Annex VI, primarily addresses the impact of air pollution from ships on the health and environment of affected land areas and populations. Annex VI was first adopted in 1997 and limits sulphur oxides (SO_x) and nitrous oxides (NO_x)—the main air pollutants contained in ships exhaust gas—and prohibits deliberate emissions of ozone-depleting substances. MARPOL Annex VI was revised in 2008 to continue reductions in emissions of SO_x, NO_x and particulate matter (PM) and to provide for designation of emission control areas (ECAs) requiring additional reductions of SO_x pollutants. The IMO approved a North American Emission Control Area (ECA) area including the U.S. continental EEZ and Hawaii's (and Canada's) EEZ that went into effect in 2012 and a United States Caribbean Sea ECA that went into effect in 2014. Within the ECAs, the United States can enforce strict SO_x emission limits from fuel, and beginning in 2016, ships must also achieve an 80% percent reduction in NO_x. See R. Hildreth & A. Torbitt, *International Treaties and U.S. Laws as Tools to Regulate the Greenhouse Gas Emissions from Ships and Ports*, 25 Int'l. J. of Marine & Coastal L. 347, 364–366 (2010). See also *Pac. Merch. Shipping Ass'n v. Goldstene*, 639 F.3d 1154 (9th Cir. Cal. 2011) (upholding California regulations that require ships engaged in international and interstate commerce to use specific low-sulfur fuels whenever they are going to or from California ports or travelling within twenty-four miles of the California coastline. The Supreme Court denied certiorari based on a brief requested from the Solicitor General recommending denial in spite of the apparent conflict with the U.S. "paramount authority to regulate maritime commerce," because the California regulations are "largely consistent" with federal requirements and would "be overtaken" by federal requirements to implement the ECA.)

CHAPTER VI

DOMESTIC OCEAN POLICY AND THE LAW OF THE SEA

A. THE CURRENT CONTEXT OF THE LAW OF THE SEA

There is broad consensus that the modern era of the law of the sea began in 1945 with the Truman Proclamation declaring U.S. sovereign rights over the continental shelf. Prior to that time, nations had made only limited jurisdictional claims to ocean space or resources. Most countries' offshore claims were limited to three-mile territorial seas. The U.S. continental shelf claim initiated a flood of offshore claims that has been called the "ocean enclosure movement." The 1945 Truman Proclamation on the Continental Shelf, 10 Fed. Reg. 12, 303 (1945), stated:

> Having concern for the urgency of conserving and prudently utilizing its natural resources, the Government of the United States regards the natural resources of the subsoil and sea bed of the continental shelf beneath the high seas but contiguous to the coasts of the United States as appertaining to the United States, subject to its jurisdiction and control. . . . The character as high seas of the waters above the continental shelf and the right to their free and unimpeded navigation are in no way thus affected.

Although the U.S. claim to the continental shelf had no basis in international law, there was little international objection to the claim, and the Proclamation became the starting point of the international law of the continental shelf. See *North Sea Continental Shelf Cases* (F.R.G./Den; F.R.G./Neth.), 1969 WL 1 (1969); see also Ann L. Hollick, *U.S. Oceans Policy: The Truman Proclamations,* 17 Va. J. Int'l L. 23 (1976).

International offshore claims proliferated during the 1950s. These claims ranged from extensions of 12-mile territorial seas to assertions by some Central and South American countries of sovereignty over the seas to 200 miles offshore. To harmonize international jurisdictional claims and lessen potential for conflict, codification of the law of sea became a goal of nations. The First United Nations Conference on the Law of the Sea in 1958 produced treaties on the territorial sea and contiguous zone, the continental shelf, the high seas, and high seas fisheries. Although these treaties were widely accepted as codifying international law, major issues, such as the allowable breadth of territorial sea and continental shelf claims, were not adequately addressed. The treaties were also inadequate to deal with the growing stresses on fishery stocks and the environment. A second conference in 1960 failed to resolve these critical issues.

During the 1960s, marine fishery resources began to decline dramatically. Although part of the decline was probably due to degradation of the marine environment, the decline was primarily attributable to the intense fishing efforts of large, distant water fishing fleets. To attempt to deal with both the environmental impact on marine ecosystems and the economic impact on coastal fishermen, nations began to regulate high seas fisheries first through largely ineffective multilateral negotiations and then through controversial extensions of exclusive fishery zones.

Also during the 1960s, a number of private consortia were formed to develop technology to mine manganese nodules from the deep seabed. Manganese nodules are potato-sized masses of high-grade metal ores that are found on the deep ocean floor virtually all over the world. The nodules are composed primarily of manganese, but also contain iron, nickel, cobalt, and copper. The density of occurrence and exact composition of the nodules varies from place to place. Their existence has been known since the 1870s voyage of HMS *The Challenger,* considered the first marine research expedition. Exploitation at depths of over 3000 meters, however, had not been considered feasible until recently. Changing markets for metals, particularly copper and cobalt, and new technologies made mining of the manganese nodules commercially attractive for the first time.

Developing countries viewed the exploitation of the deep seabed as another example of hegemony and neocolonialism by developed countries. If developed countries were free to mine the seabed, developing countries would lose twice, because they lacked the technology to exploit the seabed and because developing countries are the major land-based producers of the ores with which seabed minerals would compete. Arvid Pardo, the ambassador from Malta, brought the issue to the United Nations in 1967. He proposed that the seabed should be declared the "common heritage of mankind" and be governed by an international regime. In a 108 to zero vote (including an affirmative U.S. vote), the General Assembly adopted these principles in the Declaration of Principles Governing the Seabed and the Ocean Floor, and the Subsoil Thereof, beyond the Limits of National Jurisdiction. G.A. Res. 2749 (XXV), U.N. GAOR Supp. No. 28, at 28, U.N. Doc. A/8028 (1970). The U.N. General Assembly had earlier adopted a moratorium on seabed mineral exploitation by a less convincing majority—a vote of 62 in favor, 28 against (including the United States), and 28 abstentions. G.A. Res. 2574–D (XXIV), U.N. GAOR Supp. No. 30, at 11, U.N. Doc. A/7630 (1969).

The developments of the 1960s and the gaps in the 1958 treaty regimes set the stage for negotiation of a treaty that would deal with all aspects of the law of the sea. The Third United Nations Conference on the Law of the Sea (UNCLOS III) was convened in 1973, although preparations for negotiation of a single, comprehensive treaty had been in progress since 1970.

The procedures for negotiation and decision making were unique and contribute to the argument that the treaty is a "package" and that individual principles of the treaty cannot be accepted or rejected piecemeal. The Rules of Procedure for UNCLOS III, U.N. Doc. A/CONF.62/30/Rev. 3, included an appended agreement that established the following principles for negotiations: (1) The problems of the seabed are interrelated and need to be considered as a whole; (2) to be effective, the treaty must secure broad acceptance; (3) every effort should be made to reach agreement on substantive matters through consensus; and (4) there will be no voting until all consensus efforts are exhausted. The approach created an opportunity for trade-offs and political compromise across a broad spectrum of widely divergent issues, so that the final disposition of many seemingly unrelated matters were actually quite closely tied.

The work of the conference was divided among three main committees: The First Committee dealt with the international regime for exploitation of the deep seabed; the Second Committee was concerned with jurisdictional zones, maritime boundaries, and the rights and duties of nations; and the Third Committee dealt with marine scientific research and the marine environment. After a decade of draft texts, negotiations, and consensus building, the 1982 United Nations Convention on the Law of the Sea (UNCLOS) was adopted by a vote of 130 to 4, with 17 abstentions. UNCLOS, *opened for signature* Dee. 19, 1982, United Nations, Official Text of the United Nations Convention on the Law of the Sea with Annexes and Index, U.N. Doc. A/CONF.62/122, U.N. Sales No. E.83.V.5 (1983), *reprinted in* 21 I.L.M. 1261 One hundred and nineteen countries signed the Convention at Montego Bay, Jamaica, on December 10, 1982. The United States voted against the treaty because of disagreement with the provisions for governing the deep seabed beyond coastal nation jurisdiction. Most of the other major developed nations either voted against the Convention or abstained.

In late 1993, the treaty received the requisite 60 ratifications to come into force in November of 1994. Virtually all of the ratifications were, however, by developing countries. In anticipation of the treaty coming into force without support from developed countries, the Secretary-General of the United Nations had begun negotiations in 1990 to address the "defects and shortcomings" of the seabed provisions and to establish the "universality" of the treaty. Intense negotiations through the summer of 1994, in which the U.S. was a leading participant, resulted in the Agreement Relating to the Implementation of Part XI of UNCLOS, commonly called the Boat Paper, which effectively amends the deep seabed provisions of UNCLOS. See U.N. Doc. A/Res/48/263 (1994), *reprinted in* 33 I.L.M. 1309 (1994). The Agreement, which was cosponsored by the United States, addressed many of the concerns of developed countries and received no negative votes. With these issues addressed, most countries quickly acceded to the treaty, bringing the number of parties today to 166. The U.S. became a signatory of both the Boat Paper's implementing agreement and UNCLOS at that time, but not a party.

A key feature of signing the Agreement was accepting its provisional application when UNCLOS came into force on November 16, 1994. Provisional application gave signatories of the Agreement, like the United States, the opportunity to participate in the development of the deep seabed mining regime pending their ratification of the Convention and Agreement. Because all provisional application of the Agreement terminated on November 16, 1998, the United States and the United Arab Emirates, signatories who have not ratified the Convention, are no longer entitled to provisional membership in the International Seabed Authority (ISA or the Authority). Since November 1998, the United States has, however, had observer status at the ISA.

In late 1994, President Clinton transmitted the Convention to the Senate Foreign Relations Committee and, as required by the U.S. Constitution, requested the Senate's consent to ratification. It was not until February 2004 that the Senate Foreign Relations Committee recommended, by unanimous vote, that the Senate give its advice and consent and transmitted the treaty to the Senate on October 7, 2004. Although President Bush expressed support for the treaty in December 2004, at that point significant opposition again arose, and the Senate failed to act on the Convention. When the Senate Committee on Foreign Relations favorably reported out the Convention again in 2012, the Senate again failed to bring the treaty to a vote. The United States remains outside the treaty regime.

Even prior to UNCLOS coming into force as a multilateral treaty, many of the concepts developed by the treaty negotiators, including a number of jurisdictional concepts, passed into the realm of customary international law through tacit or express acceptance by the international community.

Customary law is international law that is evidenced by the actual practice of nations. While rejecting the deep seabed provisions of UNCLOS, even President Reagan early announced the U.S. position that:

> . . . the United States is prepared to accept and act in accordance with the balance of interests relating to traditional uses of the oceans—such as navigation and overflight. In this respect, the United States will recognize the rights of other states in the waters off their coasts, as reflected in the Convention, so long as the rights and freedoms of the United States and others under international law are recognized by such coastal states.

Statement by the President, 19 Weekly Comp. Pres. Doc. 383 (Mar. 10, 1983); U.S. Oceans Policy, 83 Dep't St. Bull., June 1983, at 70 (1983); 22 LL.M. 464. In addition, as a signatory to the Convention and the Agreement on Part XI, the United States has an obligation not to take actions which may "defeat the object and purpose" of the deep seabed provisions of UNCLOS. See Vienna Convention on the Law of Treaties, May 23, 1969, U.N. Doc. A/CONF. 39/27, art. 18. Through these actions the United States has recognized the legitimacy of the LOS regime, but still may be compromised in asserting rights under the regime without becoming a party.

B. THE TERRITORIAL SEA AND CONTIGUOUS ZONE

Cornelius van Bynkershoek, an 18th century Dutch jurist, is often attributed with originating the "cannon-shot rule" for determining the extent of coastal nation control and jurisdiction over adjacent ocean waters. Under international law, territorial claims can only be made to areas that can be occupied and controlled by a country. Areas within the range of shore armaments arguably could be effectively controlled by the coastal nation. The Italian publicist, Galiani, later equated "cannon-shot range" with a distance of three miles or a marine league.

In 1793, Secretary of State Thomas Jefferson, in diplomatic notes to the French and British ministers, provided the first records of the United States' claim to a three-mile territorial sea. The notes included the following explanation:

The greatest distance to which any respectable assent among nations has been at any time given, has been the extent of the human sight, estimated at upwards of 20 miles, and the smallest distance, I believe, claimed by any nation whatever, is the utmost range of a cannon bail, usually stated at one sea league.... The character of our coast . . . would entitle us, in reason, to as broad a margin of protected navigation as any nation whatever. Reserving, however, the ultimate extent of this for future deliberation, the President gives instructions to the officers acting under his authority to consider those heretofore given them as restrained for the present to the distance of one sea league or three geographical miles from the seashores. . . .

I John B. Moore, A Digest of International Law 702 (1906).

During the 19th and 20th centuries, Great Britain and the United States became known as the "champions of the three-mile limit." As maritime powers, these countries sought to preserve the freedoms of the high seas and limit expansive coastal nation claims which would encroach on the high seas and free navigation. Following World War II, preservation of a three-mile limit became a major national security issue for the United States. Submarine-based missiles were a major element of the United States' system of deterrence. The effectiveness of this system would be compromised if restrictions on territorial sea transit, especially passage through international straits, required permission of the coastal nation or surfacing of submarines. Extension of jurisdiction of all nations' territorial waters from three miles to 12 miles would bring over a hundred international straits within the territorial waters of coastal nations.

Negotiations leading to the 1958 Convention on the Territorial Sea and the Contiguous Zone (Territorial Sea Convention), *done* at Geneva, April 29, 1958, 15 U.S.T. 1606, 516 U.N.T.S. 205, provided no international consensus on the limit of territorial sea claims. By 1965, only 32 of 107 coastal nations continued to limit territorial sea claims to three miles. By the time the Third United Nations Conference on the Law of the Sea (UNCLOS III) convened in 1973 to develop a comprehensive oceans treaty, it was absurd for the U.S. and other maritime powers to assert that customary international law restricted territorial sea claims to three miles. Only 25 countries continued to assert three-mile claims; of the 86 coastal countries claiming more than three miles, 56 claimed a 12-mile territorial sea. At the conclusion of UNCLOS III negotiations in 1982, 77 of 135 nations claimed 12-mile territorial jurisdiction, and only 24 maintained a three-mile claim.

The 1982 Convention on the Law of the Sea (UNCLOS) recognizes the right of coastal countries to claim a 12-mile territorial sea. The provisions of UNCLOS attempted to mitigate the impact of 12-mile territorial seas on navigation through international straits by creating a right of "transit passage," distinct from the historic right of innocent passage through territorial seas. UNCLOS, arts. 34–45. Although the United States had not ratified the Convention, on December 27, 1988, President Reagan announced the extension of the United States territorial sea to 12 miles by Presidential Proclamation No. 5928 "[i]n accordance with international law, as reflected in the . . . 1982 United Nations Convention on the Law of the Sea," and recognized a right of transit passage for foreign vessels in U.S. waters. 3 C.F.R. § 547 (1989).

Beyond the territorial sea, a coastal nation may claim an additional zone to prevent infringement of sanitary, fiscal, customs, and immigration laws. The United States is a party to the 1958 Convention on the Territorial Sea and Contiguous Zone, *done* at Geneva, Apr. 29, 1958, 15 U.S.T. 1606, 516 U.N.T.S. 205, which allows a country to claim a contiguous zone beyond territorial waters to 12 miles from the shore. The United States claimed a nine-mile contiguous zone prior to the 1988 extension of the territorial sea from three miles to 12 miles. Apparently because the 1958 Convention limited the contiguous zone to no more than 12 miles, the Presidential declaration extending the territorial sea did not make a further claim to a 24-mile contiguous zone, which is recognized by UNCLOS. See UNCLOS, art. 33(2). In 1999, however, President Clinton declared a contiguous zone extending 24 nautical miles from U.S. baselines by Presidential Proclamation. See Presidential Proclamation No. 7219. August 2, 1999, 64 Fed. Reg. 48701.

1. BASELINES

The simple principle of law that the normal baseline from which the territorial sea is measured is the low water line belies the complicated nature of demarcation of the baseline on all but the most regular coastlines. See Territorial Sea Convention, art. 3; UNCLOS, art. 5. Neither the Territorial Sea Convention nor UNCLOS defines the low water line. In *United States v. California*, 381 U.S. 139, 85 S.Ct. 1401, 14 L.Ed.2d 296 (1965), the U.S. Supreme Court found that the Submerged Lands Act, 43 U.S.C. §§ 1301–1315, should be interpreted consistently with the 1958 Territorial Sea Convention and held that the average of the lower low tides establishes the baseline from which the U.S. territorial sea is measured.

Baselines also divide the territorial sea from internal waters. Baselines are drawn across the mouths of rivers that flow into the sea and across the mouths of bays. In *United States v. California*, 381 U.S. 139, 85 S.Ct. 1401, 14 L.Ed.2d 296 (1965), the Supreme Court also adopted the Territorial Sea Convention's "twenty-four mile, semi-circle" rule for determining whether a coastal indentation is a bay for purposes of the Submerged Lands Act. To qualify as a bay, and consequently internal waters, the rule requires that the area of indentation be at least as large as the area of a semicircle whose diameter is equal the distance across the mouth of the indentation, except that the closing line can be no more than 24 miles. Territorial Sea Convention art. 7. UNCLOS article 10 also adopts this rule. In *United States v. California,* Monterey Bay was found to qualify as a true bay. Id. Subsequently, in *United States v. Maine*, 469 U.S. 504, 105 S.Ct. 992, 83 L.Ed.2d 998 (1985), the Supreme Court held Long Island and Block Island Sounds to be a juridical bay under the terms of the Territorial Sea Convention. The United States has taken the position that baselines for rivers that flow into estuaries should be demarcated according to principles that apply to closing lines for bays. See 4 Marjorie M. Whiteman, Digest of International Law 336–43 (1965).

Historic bays are an exception to the normal bay-closing rule. Waters that would not ordinarily meet the definition of a bay may be considered inland waters through historic title if a nation exercises authority over the area for a long period with the acquiescence of other nations. Chesapeake Bay and

Delaware Bay have long been recognized as historic bays. The United States has often objected, however, to recognition of other historic bays both within the United States and on the shores of other countries. Domestically, the establishment of historic waters would change federal-state boundaries for purposes of oil development and fisheries management. See, e.g., *United States v. Alaska*, 422 U.S. 184, 95 S.Ct. 2240, 45 L.Ed.2d 109 (1975). Internationally, the United States' objections are usually related to preserving the freedom of navigation. For example, the United States has objected to Libya's historically based claim to the Gulf of Sidra, the former Soviet Union's claim to the Peter the Great Bay, and Canada's claim to waters in Hudson Bay. See generally 4 Marjorie M. Whiteman, Digest of International Law 233–42 (1965).

In certain geographic circumstances, both UNCLOS, articles 7, 46–47, and the Territorial Sea Convention, article 4, recognize the right of a country to measure its territorial sea from straight baselines connecting low-tide elevations. These situations are: (1) where there is a fringe of islands or a delta along the coast in its immediate vicinity; (2) where the coastline is deeply indented and cut into, e.g., Norway; and (3) where an archipelagic nation draws baselines joining the outermost points of its islands.

The International Court of Justice recognized the concept of straight baselines in the *Fisheries Case (U.K. v. Norway)*, 1951 WL 12 (1951). However, the case and subsequent treaties have established conditions on the use of straight baselines:

(1) The straight baselines must follow the general direction of the coast. Id.

(2) The enclosed waters must be sufficiently linked to the "land domain" to be considered internal waters. Id.

(3) Straight baselines may not be drawn using low-tide elevations unless permanent installations, such as lighthouses, are permanently built on them above sea level. (Low-tide elevations are areas that are above sea level only at low tide). Territorial Sea Convention, art. 4(3); UNCLOS, art. 7(4).

(4) Straight baselines may not be drawn to cut off the territorial sea of another country from the high seas or EEZ. Territorial Sea Convention, art. 4(5); UNCLOS, art. 7(6).

(5) Where straight baselines create internal waters in areas that had not previously been considered such, innocent passage through the waters must be granted. UNCLOS, art. 8(2).

The regime of archipelagic states is a new development of UNCLOS. An "archipelagic state" is a nation whose territory is constituted wholly by one or more archipelagos and other islands. Id. art. 46(a). A country composed of both mainland and archipelagoes, e.g., Greece, Canada, or the United States, is not an archipelagic state for purposes of the law of the sea. An archipelagic state is entitled to draw straight "baselines joining the outermost points of the outermost islands" and to extend its territorial waters from that baseline. Archipelagic straight baselines are subject to the same conditions as other baselines and, in addition, generally may not exceed 100 miles per segment. See id. art. 47.

Again reflecting concerns for freedom of navigation, the United States has narrowly interpreted the rights of nations to use straight baselines, particularly archipelagic baselines. The United States policy statement accepting the principles of UNCLOS apparently means, however, that the United States will acknowledge the right of archipelagic countries to use such baselines when navigation rights are recognized. The United States has not drawn straight baselines for purposes of measuring territorial waters. In *United States v. California*, 381 U.S. 139, 85 S.Ct. 1401, 14 L.Ed.2d 296 (1965), the U.S. Supreme Court rejected California's argument that straight baselines should be used along certain portions of the coast. The Court stated that the decision to use straight baselines "is one that rests with the Federal Government, and not with the individual States." More recently, the Supreme Court rejected Alaska's right to draw straight baselines between fringe or barrier islands and claim the enclosed areas as internal waters. *United States v. Alaska*, 521 U.S. 1, 117 S.Ct. 1888, 138 L.Ed.2d 231 (1997).

2. RIGHTS AND DUTIES OF COASTAL NATIONS—NAVIGATION

In general, a coastal nation has the same sovereign rights over the territorial sea, its waters, seabed, and air space, as it has over its land territory and inland waters, subject to the right of innocent passage. Territorial Sea Convention, arts. 1–2; UNCLOS, art. 2. The right of innocent passage does not include overflight by aircraft. Nations have a positive duty not to hamper innocent passage by imposing requirements that effectively deny such passage or by discriminating against the vessels of any nation. Coastal countries must also assist navigation by giving appropriate notice of navigational dangers in the territorial sea. Territorial Sea Convention, art. 15; UNCLOS, art. 24.

The right of innocent passage for vessels in the territorial sea has two rather obvious aspects: passage and innocence. Passage is continuous, expeditious navigation through the territorial waters for the purpose of either traversing them or proceeding to or from internal waters or a port. Ships may stop and anchor when incidental to normal navigation, when rendered necessary by *force majeure* or distress, and when required to render assistance to persons, ships, or aircraft in danger or distress. Territorial Sea Convention, art. 14; UNCLOS, art. 18.

The concept of "innocence" is not as straightforward as "passage" and has evolved over the last century. The primary problem in defining innocence is establishing criteria based on objective international standards rather than dictated by the laws or subjective determinations of each coastal nation. Article 14(4) of the Territorial Sea Convention adopted the following definition:

> Passage is innocent so long as it is not prejudicial to the peace, good order or security of the coastal State. Such passage shall take place in conformity with these articles and with other rules of international law.

The article does not require a specific act or violation of coastal country's law for passage to lose its innocent character; however, it also does not provide that innocence is lost merely by the violation of a coastal country's law. The only circumstance in which the treaty provides that a breach of coastal country law *ipso facto* negates innocent passage is in the case of violation of laws to prevent vessels from fishing in the territorial sea. Territorial Sea Convention, art. 14(5).

UNCLOS adopted the definition of the Territorial Sea Convention, but also added a list of specific activities that will be considered "prejudicial" to peace, good order, and security. This list includes: fishing; scientific research or surveys; willful and serious pollution; interference with communications systems; acts of propaganda or spying; loading or unloading of goods, currency, or persons in violation of customs, fiscal, sanitary, or immigration laws; weapons exercises and the landing or launching of aircraft or military devices; and "any threat or use of force against the sovereignty, territorial integrity or political independence of the coastal [nation]." UNCLOS, art. 19(2). The list concludes with the broad category of action: "any other activity not having a direct bearing on passage." Id. The detailed list was intended to provide more objectivity and reduce coastal nations' discretion in interpreting the international standard for innocent passage.

The duty not to hamper innocent passage does not mean that foreign vessels are not subject to any regulation by coastal nations. In addition to regulations relating to fishing and living resources in territorial waters, a coastal nation may regulate foreign vessels with respect to: (1) navigation safety, maritime traffic, and protection of navigational aids; (2) protection of offshore facilities and installations, cables, and pipelines; (3) marine research; (4) environmental protection and pollution control; and (5) prevention of infringement of customs, fiscal, immigration, and sanitary laws. Id. art. 21(1). A coastal country may not impose regulations as to the design, construction, manning, or equipment of foreign ships engaged in innocent passage unless the laws are giving effect to "generally accepted international rules or standards," e.g., MARPOL 73/78 standards. Id. art. 21(2).

As a general proposition, coastal countries should not exert criminal jurisdiction on board foreign vessels exercising innocent passage in connection with crimes conducted onboard the vessel during its passage. However, the coastal country may investigate or make arrests on board the vessel:

(a) if the consequences of the crime extend to the coastal State;

(b) if the crime is of a kind to disturb the peace of the country or the good order of the territorial sea;

(c)   if the assistance of the local authorities has been requested . . .; or

(d)   if such measures are necessary for the suppression of illicit traffic in narcotic drugs or psychotropic substances.

UNCLOS, art. 27(1); see also Territorial Sea Convention, art. 19(1).

A right of hot pursuit exists when the coastal country has reason to believe a vessel has violated the law within the country's internal waters or territorial sea. Pursuit must begin while the vessel is within territorial waters after the vessel has been signaled; the pursuit must be hot and continuous. The right of hot pursuit ceases when a vessel enters the territorial sea of another country. UNCLOS, art. 111. The right of hot pursuit also exists for violations within other offshore jurisdictional zones. However, pursuit may be undertaken only for violations of rights related to the basis for which the zone was established, e.g., for fishing violations within a fishery zone or EEZ. Id.

The right of military vessels, i.e., "warships," to innocent passage has been one of the most controversial issues in the law of the sea. Views have been so widely divergent that neither the Territorial Sea Convention nor UNCLOS address the issue directly. In the early 1900s, it seemed broadly accepted that warships did not enjoy a right of innocent passage. See _North Atlantic Coast Fisheries Arbitration,_ II Proceedings 2007 (1910); Phillip C. Jessup, The Law of Territorial Waters and Maritime

Jurisdiction 120 (1927). After World War II, the United States and the United Kingdom led Western naval powers in asserting that warships as well as merchant vessels were entitled to innocent territorial sea passage. Countries, such as the U.S.S.R., China, and many developing countries, sought to require notification and even authorization for passage of warships. Commentators suggest that even though two parallel rules have emerged, confrontations are unusual and that countries have "contrived to avoid direct confrontation" through informal, low-level contacts. See R.R. Churchill & A.V. Lows, The Law of the Sea 74–76 (1988); see also Shao Jiu, *The Question of Innocent Passage of Warships After UNCLOS III,* 13 Marine Pol'y 56 (1989).

It is clear under customary international law, as well as under Territorial Sea Convention article 14(6) and UNCLOS article 20, that "[i]n the territorial sea, submarines and other underwater vehicles are required to navigate on the surface and to show their flag." It is also unquestionable that neither military nor commercial aircraft have a right of passage through the airspace above territorial waters. These facts form the primary basis for the United States' long refusal to recognize the right to extend territorial sea boundaries beyond three miles. The extension of 12-mile boundaries incorporates in territorial waters as many as 135 international straits, many considered of strategic military importance to the United States.

The regime of international straits in customary international law was discussed by the International

Court of Justice (ICJ) in *The Corfu Channel Case* in 1949. *The Corfu Channel Case* (U.K. v. Alb.), 1949 WL 1 (1949). The United Kingdom had sent warships through the channel to assert its right of passage without prior notification to Albania. The ICJ held that ships, including warships, of all nations have a right of innocent passage "through straits used for international navigation between two parts of the high seas without the previous authorization of a coastal [nation]." The court rejected Albania's arguments which were based on the facts that the channel was only an alternative, secondary route and not necessary for transit between areas of the high seas. Finding these factors irrelevant, the court held that the decisive criteria were the "geographical situation as connecting two parts of the high seas" and its usefulness for international navigation.

This formulation regarding passage through international straits was adopted as part of the innocent passage regime of the Territorial Sea Convention. The right of transit through international straits differs from other innocent passage through territorial waters in that the bordering nations may not suspend passage under any circumstances. See Territorial Sea Convention, art. 16(4). The higher level of protection of passage through international straits is based on the rationale that such passage is necessary for exercise of freedom of the high sea.

UNCLOS took an additional step to mitigate the impact of the extension of 12-mile territorial seas on submerged passage of submarines and overflight in international straits by creating a new right of "transit passage." Transit passage is the "exercise . . . of the freedom of navigation and overflight solely for the purpose of continuous and expeditious transit of [an international] strait" subject to a number of conditions. UNCLOS, art. 38(2). Ships must proceed in normal modes of transit without delay, without threat or use of force, and in compliance with generally accepted international standards for safety and pollution control. Id. art. 39(1)–(2). The reference to "normal modes" of transit comprehends submerged passage of submarines. In contrast to the ICJ's identification of international straits subject to a right of passage, the UNCLOS regime of "transit passage shall not apply if there exists seaward of [an island bordering a strait and the mainland] a route through the high seas or through an [EEZ] of similar convenience with respect to navigational and hydrographical characteristics." Id. art. 38(1). The United States proclamation extending a 12-mile territorial sea provides that "[i]n accordance with international law, as reflected in the . . . 1982 United Nations Convention on the Law of the Sea," the United States will recognize a right of transit passage by ships of all countries through international straits. 3 C.F.R. § 547 (1989).

The regime created by UNCLOS for passage through "archipelagic waters," waters enclosed in archipelagic straight baselines, is similar to transit passage through international straits. For purposes of innocent passage, archipelagic waters are treated like territorial waters. UNCLOS, art. 52(1). In addition, the archipelagic nation may designate archipelagic sea lanes within which "rights of navigation and overflight in the normal mode" may be exercised. Id. art. 53(1)–(3). The Convention directs that sea lanes and air routes traversing archipelagic waters "shall include all normal passage routes used as routes for international navigation or overflight." Id. art. 53(4). If an archipelagic nation does not designate sea lanes or air routes, "the right of archipelagic sea lanes passage may be exercised through the routes normally used for international navigation." Id. art. 53(12).

C.   THE CONTINENTAL SHELF

The continental shelf is the part of the seabed that gently slopes down from the low water line to a point, usually around a depth of around 200 meters, where it drops off more steeply in an area known as the continental slope. The breadth of the geologic feature of continental shelf varies from less than the breadth of the territorial sea to over 300 miles. The 1945 Truman Proclamation based the United States' claim to control of the resources of the continental shelf on the fact that this geologic feature was "an extension of the land-mass of the [United States] and thus naturally appurtenant" and subject to its jurisdiction and control.

The fact that rights exercised by the coastal nations arise from jurisdiction over its land territory made the development of the regime of the continental shelf unique. Unlike rights to territorial waters, contiguous zones, or exclusive economic zones, which must be exercised through positive acts or claims by the coastal nation, the exclusive right to the continental shelf arises through international law. In the *North Sea Continental Shelf Cases (F.R.G./Den.; F.R.G./Neth.)*, 1969 WL 1 (1969), the International Court of Justice stated that:

the rights of the coastal State in respect of the area of continental shelf that constitutes a natural prolongation of its land territory into and under the sea exist *ipso facto* and *ab initio,* by virtue of its sovereignty over the land, and as an extension of it in an exercise of sovereign rights for the purpose of exploring the seabed and exploiting its natural resources. In short there is here an inherent right.

Both the 1958 Convention on the Continental Shelf (Continental Shelf Convention), *done* at Geneva, April 29, 1958, 15 U.S.T. 471, 499 U.N.T.S. 311, and UNCLOS recognize the inherent and exclusive nature of a coastal nation's rights over the continental shelf:

1.   The coastal State exercises over the continental shelf sovereign rights for the purpose of exploring it and exploiting its natural resources.

2.   The rights are exclusive in the sense that if the coastal State does not explore the continental shelf or exploit its natural resources, no one may undertake these activities, or make a claim to the continental shelf, without the express consent of the coastal State.

3.   The rights of the coastal State . . . do not
depend on occupation, effective or notional, or on
any express proclamation.

Continental Shelf Convention, art. 2; see also
UNCLOS, art. 77.

Although the continental shelf regime emerged
primarily to control exploitation of mineral
resources, it also extends coastal nation jurisdiction
over living resources of the shelf. "[S]edentary species
. . . which, at the harvestable stage, either are
immobile on or under the seabed or are unable to
move except in constant physical contact with the
seabed or the subsoil" are considered continental
shelf resources. Continental Shelf Convention, art.
2(4); see also UNCLOS, art. 77(4). For example,
lobsters, crabs, and sponges are continental shelf
resources, but scallops and finfish are not. See, e.g.,
16 U.S.C. § 1802(4).

The Truman Proclamation did not specifically
define or describe the geographic scope of the United
States' claim, but a White House press release on
September 28, 1945, offered the following
commentary:

   The policy proclaimed by the President in
   regard to the jurisdiction over the continental
   shelf . . . is concerned solely with establishing
   the jurisdiction of the United States from an
   international standpoint. It will, however, make
   possible the orderly development of an
   underwater area 750,000 square miles in extent.
   Generally, submerged land which is contiguous

to the continent and which is covered by no more than 100 fathoms (600 feet) of water is considered as the continental shelf. 13 Dep't St. Bull. 484 (1945).

The term "continental shelf" was obviously intended to refer to a geologically or geographically identifiable area appurtenant to the coast, but has since become a term of art. By the time the 1958 Continental Shelf Convention was drafted, countries were skeptical about restricting claims to shelf resources. Rather than limit the continental shelf to a distance from shore or a depth, the 1958 Convention recognized a coastal nation's inherent exclusive rights out to the 200-meter isobath in depth *or to the limits of exploitability* of the seabed. Continental Shelf Convention, art. 1.

The 1982 UNCLOS contains a more certain, but extremely complicated, formula for calculating the extent of a continental shelf claim. A continental shelf may be claimed to 200 miles from shore, or to the extent of the continental margin (the actual submerged land prolongation including the continental shelf, slope, and rise), whichever is further. The legal fiction recognizing a 200-mile continental shelf, even in the absence of an offshore physical land prolongation, completes the evolution of the legal concept of the continental shelf. The maximum seaward extent of the continental shelf is 350 miles or within 100 miles of the 2500-meter isobath, whichever is further. See UNCLOS, art. 76(5). UNCLOS provides that the proceeds of exploitation of the shelf beyond 200 miles must be shared with the International Seabed Authority. Id. art. 82(1).

Because the delimitation of the extent of the continental shelf continues to be an indeterminate and complex process, UNCLOS provides for the establishment of a Commission on the Limits of the Continental Shelf to review continental shelf claims beyond 200 miles. Id. art. 76(8) and Annex II. The Commission provides technical assistance to countries and when a country adopts a continental shelf limit based on the recommendations of the Commission, the limit of the shelf is "final and binding" (presumably in regard to the boundary between a coastal state's continental shelf and the deep seabed administered under U.N. authority). Id. The United Nations will serve as a depository for charts and data "permanently describing" coastal states continental shelf claims beyond 200 miles. Id. art. 76(9).

The United States, a party to the 1958 Convention on the Continental Shelf, has placed no specific limit on its continental shelf claim by decree or statute. The Outer Continental Shelf Lands Act defines the continental shelf only as "all submerged lands lying seaward and outside of [lands granted to the states by the Submerged Lands Act] and of which the subsoil and seabed appertain to the United States and are subject to its jurisdiction and control." 43 U.S.C. § 1331(a). The United States has currently embarked on an "Extended Continental Shelf Project . . . to establish the full extent of the continental shelf of the United States, consistent with international law." See Extended Continental Shelf Project at http://continentalshelf.gov/. The project is described as the "largest and potentially most significant inter-agency marine survey ever undertaken by the U.S." The melting of the Arctic Ocean ice cover due to global warming is a primary impetus for this project. Arctic seabed resources, previously unrecoverable, may soon be exploitable due the diminished ice cover, and nations surrounding the Arctic Ocean have been submitting claims to extended continental shelves to the CLCS for several years. If the United States ever joins the treaty, it will have ten years to submit a claim.

D. FISHERY ZONES AND EXCLUSIVE ECONOMIC ZONES

Following the 1945 Truman Proclamation, other countries made claims of extended jurisdictions over adjacent waters or fisheries, but such claims of extended fishing zones or sovereign rights to as far as 200 miles offshore were not widely accepted and did not rise to the level of customary international law. Prior to the convening of UNCLOS III, international law generally limited exclusive coastal nation jurisdiction over fishery resources to a maximum of 12 miles by customary law. In most cases, this was coterminous with the territorial sea. In 1966, the United States passed the Bartlett Act, §§ 1–4, Pub. L. No. 89–658, 80 Star. 908 (1966) (repealed 1976), to establish an exclusive fishing zone extending to 12 miles offshore contiguous to the territorial sea.

But concern for the decimation of high seas
fisheries and the economic needs of coastal countries
was clearly leading to changes in international law
by the 1970s. In 1972, Iceland declared a 50-mile
exclusive fishery zone, that was challenged by the
United Kingdom and Germany, countries that had
traditionally fished in the area. In the resulting
Fisheries Jurisdiction Cases, *F.R.G. v. Ice.*, 1974 WL
2 (1974) and *U.K. v. Ice.*, 1974 WL 1 (1974), the
International Court of Justice recognized the need for
conservation as well as the emergence of preferential
rights of coastal nations to fisheries in adjacent seas
based on special dependence on the fisheries for
livelihood or economic development. The ICJ held
that the traditional fishing rights of other nations
also had to be accommodated through negotiations.

The UNCLOS III negotiations led to an early
consensus concerning coastal nation jurisdiction over
economic and resource exploitation to 200 miles
offshore. This 200-mile exclusive economic zone
(EEZ) represented a compromise that incorporated
the breadth of the most extensive offshore claims, the
protection of navigation, the right of developing
countries to control offshore economic development,
and the need for better conservation of marine living
resources. The extension of EEZs to 200 miles places
approximately ninety percent of the ocean's fishery
and oil resources within the jurisdiction of coastal
countries, with the United States gaining control of
the largest extent of EEZ.

Within the EEZ, the 1982 UNCLOS recognizes
sovereign rights of coastal nations "for the purpose of

exploring and exploiting, conserving and managing the natural resources, whether living or non-living, of the waters superjacent to the sea-bed and of the sea-bed and its subsoil, and with regard to other activities for the economic exploitation and exploration of the zone, such as the production of energy from the water, currents and winds[.]" UNCLOS, art. 56(1)(a). In addition, coastal countries have jurisdiction with regard to artificial islands and offshore installations, marine scientific research, and marine environmental protection and preservation. Id. art. 56(1)(b). Within an EEZ, other nations enjoy freedom of navigation and overflight and the right to lay cables and pipelines. Id. art. 58(1).

The slow pace of UNCLOS III negotiations and the perception that overexploitation of North Atlantic fisheries required immediate action led the United States to pass the 1976 Fishery Conservation and Management Act (now known as the Magnuson-Stevens Act or MSA), 16 U.S.C. §§ 1801–1882, creating an exclusive fishery conservation zone from three to 200 miles offshore. See supra Part IV.F.2. Before the conclusion of the UNCLOS III negotiations, ninety nations had established 200-mile offshore jurisdictional zones. On March 10, 1983, President Reagan proclaimed a 200-mile EEZ based on customary international law. Proclamation No. 5030, 3 C.F.R. § 22 (1984). The MSA was subsequently amended to replace the fishery zone claim with the EEZ designation.

The basis for fishery management under UNCLOS and the Magnuson-Stevens Act is very similar.

Fisheries should be managed and conserved using the best scientific information available to assure maintenance of populations at a level of maximum sustainable yield "as qualified by relevant environmental and economic factors." See UNCLOS, art. 61(2)–(3); see also, 16 U.S.C. §§ 1802(21), 1851. UNCLOS requires coastal nations to "promote the objective of optimum utilization" of EEZ fishery resources, but does not require full utilization. Because countries have total discretion in establishing allowable catch, limited only by the duty not to overexploit, the requirement that other countries have access to surplus stocks can be illusory. See UNCLOS, arts. 61, 62(2). Foreign fishing nations have no recourse under UNCLOS if a coastal nation sets the allowable catch at the same level as domestic harvesting capacity, leaving no surplus.

When a coastal country sets its allowable catch at a level that yields a surplus that is available to foreign fishermen, UNCLOS provides that all relevant factors should be taken into account in allocating the surplus, including the coastal nation's economic and other national interests, the rights and needs of geographically disadvantaged and land-locked countries, the requirements of developing countries in the region, and the "need to minimize economic dislocation in [countries] whose nationals have habitually fished in the zone or which made substantial efforts in research and identification of stocks." Id. art. 62(3).

E. THE HIGH SEAS

The waters beyond national jurisdiction that are open to all and in which no nation can assert sovereignty are the high seas. Both the 1958 Convention on the High Seas (High Seas Convention), *done* at Geneva, April 29, 1958, 13 U.S.T. 2312, 450 U.N.T.S. 82, and the 1982 UNCLOS contain nonexclusive lists of the freedoms of the high seas. Both conventions identify the freedoms of navigation, overflight, fishing, and laying submerged lines and cable. High Seas Convention, art. 2(1)–(4); UNCLOS, art. 87(1). UNCLOS also specifically includes freedom of marine scientific research and construction of artificial islands and installations. UNCLOS, art. 87(1). High seas freedoms "shall be exercised . . . with reasonable regard to the interests of other States." High Seas Convention, art. 2; see also UNCLOS, art. 87(2).

As a general rule, only the flag country has jurisdiction over a vessel on the high seas. High Seas Convention, art. 6; UNCLOS, art. 92. This exclusive jurisdiction is subject to a number of exceptions, including:

(1) vessels or aircraft involved in acts of piracy (High Seas Convention, art. 14, UNCLOS, arts. 100–107);

(2) vessels engaged in unauthorized broadcasting from the high seas (UNCLOS, art. 110);

(3) ships of uncertain nationality, no nationality, or sailing under two or more flags

(High Seas Convention, arts. 6(2), 22; UNCLOS arts. 92, 110);

(4) vessels involved in maritime casualties threatening or causing major pollution and damage to a coastal country or its resources (UNCLOS, art. 221); and

(5) vessels that are the objects of hot pursuit for violation of laws within internal, territorial, or EEZ waters (High Seas Convention, art. 23; UNCLOS, art. 111).

The law of the sea does not place slave trade or drug trafficking in the same category as piracy, i.e., crimes that may be enforced by any nation on the high seas. Prohibition of slave trade is considered a duty of the flag country. A vessel that is reasonably suspected of engaging in slave trade may be boarded on the high seas, but the only action a foreign nation may take is to report its findings to the flag country. High Seas Convention, art. 13; UNCLOS, arts. 99, 110.

In the case of illicit drug trafficking, neither UNCLOS nor customary international law provides a basis for enforcement of laws on the high seas except with regard to a country's flag vessels or if the vessel has no nationality (including when this is imputed by the vessel's flying more than one flag). UNCLOS calls on nations to cooperate in the suppression of drug trade. UNCLOS, art. 108. United States intervention on the high seas of foreign flag vessels believed to be involved in drug trade is often carried out by obtaining permission of the flag country on a case-by-case basis, usually through radio or telephone communication with the country's officials. See, e.g., *United States v. Gonzalez*, 776 F.2d 931 (11th Cir. 1985) (holding that a formal treaty "arrangement" with a country is not necessary and that telephone communication with the flag country giving permission for the United States to act is sufficient). Modern communications have made this process workable for intercepting drug trade long before it enters the contiguous zone or territorial waters. United States drug trafficking legislation contains provisions for executive arrangements with other countries to designate the area around specific vessels as within U.S. "customs waters" for purposes of seizing the vessel and subjecting the persons on board to U.S. prosecution. The U.S. is also party to numerous interdiction agreements, mostly with nations in the wider Caribbean area, for cooperation in regard to maritime drug enforcement. See Department of State, United States Maritime Law Enforcement Agreements, available at http://www.state.gov/s/l/2005/87199.htm.

Article 88 of UNCLOS states that the "high seas shall be reserved for peaceful purposes." This does not mean that the naval forces cannot navigate the high seas and even conduct military exercises. The United States takes the position that military exercises are a traditional use of the high seas. The hampering of navigation by military exercises and weapons testing has not, however, been uncontroversial. For nuclear weapons testing in the Pacific Ocean after World War II, the United States established "warning areas" of as much as 400,000 square miles around detonation sites. The legality of such an interference with the freedoms of the high seas sparked great debate. See, e.g., Myres S. McDougal & Norbert A. Schlei, *The Hydrogen Bomb Tests in Perspective: Lawful Measures for Security,* 64 Yale L.J. 648 (1955); Emanuel Margolis, *The Hydrogen Bomb Experiments and International Law,* 64 Yale L.J. 629 (1955). The worldwide dangers of radioactive fallout soon overshadowed the legality debate, and in 1963, the United States became a party to the Limited Nuclear Test Ban Treaty, ending its atmospheric and high seas testing of nuclear weapons. France, which was not a party to the treaty, continued nuclear testing in the Pacific Ocean and even used force to prevent entry of vessels into test zones. The legality of this action was never finally resolved. Australia and New Zealand's appeal of the matter to the International Court of Justice (ICJ) was rendered moot when France announced it would stop atmospheric nuclear testing. See *Nuclear Tests Cases* (Austl. v. Fr., N.Z. v. Fr.), 1974 WL 4 (1974).

More than thirty years after the *Nuclear Test Cases,* nuclear weapons and testing are still controversial in the South Pacific region. The Treaty of Raratonga, a 1985 agreement by the members of the South Pacific Forum, created a South Pacific Nuclear Free Zone and bans placement and testing of nuclear devices in internal, territorial, or archipelagic waters. The treaty also recognizes the authority of nations to prohibit ships and aircraft carrying nuclear weapons from entering ports or transiting territorial waters or archipelagic waters except for purposes of innocent or sea lanes passage.

THE INTERNATIONAL

South Pacific Nuclear Free Zone Treaty, *done* Aug. 6, 1985, *reprinted in* 24 I.L.M. 1442.

When France announced in 1995 that it would resume underground nuclear testing at atolls in the Pacific, New Zealand unsuccessfully sought to reopen the 1974 *Nuclear Tests Case* in the ICJ to challenge the legality of these tests. *Request for Examination* (N.Z. v. Fr.), 1995 WL 805134 (1995). In spite of strong protests by the members of the South Pacific Forum, France briefly resumed its underground testing in October 1995, maintaining that such testing was neither violative of international law nor a significant threat to the environment. See generally Barbara Kwiatkowsksa, *New Zealand v. France Nuclear Tests: The Dismissed Case of Lasting Significance,* 37 Va. J. Int'l Law 107 (1996). In 1996, France announced an end to its nuclear testing, however, and in 1998 ratified the Comprehensive Test Ban Treaty.

F.   THE INTERNATIONAL SEABED AREA

The seabed beyond the continental shelf is the international seabed area or deep seabed. Prior to the 1960s, the legal status of the deep seabed was not a major issue and was presumed to be generally subject to the freedom of the high seas. This view allowed no country to claim sovereign rights over the seabed but, like high seas fishery resources, seabed resources could be exploited so long as due regard was given to the rights of other countries. This had been the United States' continuing position on the legal status of the deep seabed and its resources. See 2 Restatement (Third) Foreign Relations Law of the United States § 523(1)(a)–(b), cmts. a–c, reporter's notes 1–2 (1986).

The 1982 UNCLOS declares the deep seabed to be the common heritage of mankind. UNCLOS, arts. 136–137. The development of this concept of deep seabed resources required a different theoretical basis. As the common heritage, resources are considered *res communes*—belonging to everyone—and are not subject to appropriation by individual nations or persons. A third view that had been argued was that the seabed is *res nullius,* territory belonging to no one, and is subject to occupation and exploitation by the first country to make a claim.

1. THE INTERNATIONAL SEABED REGIME OF UNCLOS

Part XI of UNCLOS implements the concept of the "common heritage of mankind" through creation of a regime to govern the exploitation of minerals of the deep seabed, called the Area. The regime purports to be exclusive, prohibiting any claim, acquisition, or rights over seabed mineral except in accordance with the Convention. UNCLOS, art. 137.

The International Seabed Authority is the organization established to govern resource uses of the Area on behalf of "mankind." All parties to UNCLOS are members of the Authority. The organs of the Authority are the Assembly, the Council, and a Secretariat. Id. arts. 137, 156–158. The Assembly is composed of one representative of each party of the

Authority and is the "supreme organ" of the Authority. The Assembly elects the Council and the Secretary General and is responsible for setting general policies of the Authority. Id. arts. 158–160.

The Council is the executive organ of the Authority and is responsible for directly implementing the treaty through specific policies and approval of work plans for mining projects. Id. art. 162. The Council has 36 members. The distribution of membership is intended to assure representation of nations involved in seabed mining and in terrestrial production of minerals, consumer nations, and developing countries. See id. art. 161.

In addition to these governing and administrative organs of the Authority, the Enterprise is a separate organ created to engage in mining and marketing of seabed minerals. Id. art. 170. Operation of the Enterprise is to be funded initially by the parties to the Convention and facilitated by an obligation of contractors to transfer mining technology to the Enterprise.

Part XI originally provided for a parallel system of development allowing mining by both the Enterprise and by national or private ventures that contract with the Authority. See id., Annex III. Applicants for mining contracts were required to identify two areas of equal potential and submit a work plan. The Authority would allocate one site to the applicant and reserve the other for exploitation by the Enterprise or a developing country. A contractor was required to pay a $500,000 fee for processing of the application, an annual $1,000,000 fee until production is started, and a production charge thereafter. Production would be subject to quotas to protect developing country producers of minerals.

For a complete discussion of the seabed mining regime as originally conceived, see 2 E.D. Brown, Sea-Bed Energy and Minerals: The International Legal Regime (1992).

2.   THE UNITED STATES OBJECTIONS AND THE IMPLEMENTING AGREEMENT

The United States had not voted for the United Nations moratorium on seabed mining, but had anticipated that such mining would eventually be conducted under a regime established by UNCLOS. The Deep Seabed Hard Mineral Resources Act, 30 U.S.C. §§ 1401–1473, was enacted as interim legislation, with licenses issued under the Act subject to termination if UNCLOS should come into force with United States participation.

In summary, the United States' objections to the original seabed mining provisions of UNCLOS were the following:

1.   Technology Transfer. The United States objected to transfer of technology provisions as forced sales and unfair to private contractors who lose their technological advantage.

2.   Production Controls. The investment in technology development and production costs for seabed mining is extraordinarily high. Production controls would have been imposed by a three-fourths vote of the Council and subject to

dispute settlement procedures. The United States labeled the decision making process, however, as discretionary and discriminatory.

3. Decision-making Procedures. The United States did not receive adequate assurances that nations with major economic interests involved would have an affirmative influence on decision-making and the ability to prevent decisions adverse to their interests. The treaty also provided for amendments that could enter into force without ratification by the United States.

4. Assured Access. Private consortia wanted guarantees that mining rights would be automatically granted under the provisions of the treaty. The United States objected to the degree of discretion in the contract approval process that did not protect the great initial investment by investors.

5. Competitive Balance. The United States took the position that the regime did not protect the economic viability of U.S. mining operations and may create a competitive advantage for the Enterprise or land-based producers.

See James B. Morell, The Law of the Sea 96–154 (1992) (analyzing the U.S. objections and finding them "overstated"); see also Statement by President Reagan on July 9, 1982, 18 Weekly Comp. Pres. Doc. 887 (1982).

The 1994 Agreement Relating to the Implementation of Part XI of UNCLOS effectively amended the Convention to address all these issues raised by the United States and other Western developed countries. See Part VI.A. First, the Agreement removes mandatory transfers of technology, substituting a duty of cooperation "consistent with the effective protection of property rights." Production ceilings and limitations were also eliminated. Policy making by the Authority must be based on recommendations of the Council. The United States is guaranteed a seat on the Council. The Council will have four-member chambers that are likely to be controlled by developed countries; the Council can take actions with a two-thirds vote, unless opposed by the majority of a chamber, allowing three members of the Council to block votes. The Authority will not be able to choose among applicants, but must approve on a first-come, first-served basis, applicants meeting qualification standards. Finally, payment rates must be comparable to land-based mining in order to avoid any artificial competitive advantage for land-based producers. See Bernard Oxman, *The 1994 Agreement and the Convention,* 88 A.J.I.L. 687 (1994).

3.   THE SEABED PROVISIONS AND THE FUTURE OF UNCLOS

With the adoption of the Agreement Implementing Part XI, UNCLOS has received the overwhelming acceptance of the international community. As of August 2014, 166 countries have become parties to UNCLOS. The hope of "universality" has largely been achieved. Of the Western developed countries, only the United States has not ratified the treaty. Even the United States, however, has demonstrated acceptance of the non-seabed principles of the treaty through its state practice and declarations. In addition, although the U.S. signing of the Agreement only entails an international obligation not to take actions that may "defeat the object and purpose" of the new deep seabed provisions of UNCLOS, by co-sponsoring the Agreement the United States has shown more than tacit support of the new seabed regime. It is now clear that Part XI no longer should hold the Convention "hostage."

G.   MARITIME BOUNDARY DELIMITATION

1.   BACKGROUND

When offshore jurisdiction was limited to a three-mile territorial sea, boundary disputes were infrequent. Equidistant lines or extensions of land boundaries usually afforded equitable results within this short distance. More extensive offshore claims created more opportunities for claims to overlap and for boundary disputes to arise. For longer distances, through the breadth of the continental shelf or the 200-mile EEZ, delimitation by equidistant lines caused disproportionate results when the line was affected by irregularities in the coastlines, and extensions of land boundaries usually had no rational relation to the delimitation of far offshore areas.

The 1945 Truman Proclamation on the continental shelf anticipated the problem of overlapping claims to the continental shelf and provided the following:

In cases where the continental shelf extends to the shores of another [country], or is shared

with an adjacent [country], the boundary shall
be determined by the United States and the
[country] concerned in accordance with
equitable principles.

10 Fed. Reg. 12,303 (1945).

Years of study and debate by the International
Law Commission during the 1950s resulted in
recommendations for territorial sea and continental
shelf delimitation that were substantially
incorporated into the 1958 conventions. The
Territorial Sea Convention, article 12, provides that
failing agreement to the contrary, a coastal nation is
not "entitled . . . to extend its territorial sea beyond
the median line . . . except where [variance is]
necessary by reason of historic title or other special
circumstances." Article 6 of the Continental Shelf
Convention also adopts an "equidistance-special
circumstances" rule, stating that "[i]n the absence of
agreement, and unless another boundary line is
justified by special circumstances, the boundary is
the median line [for opposite countries and] shall be
determined by application of the principle of
equidistance [in the ease of adjacent countries]."

In the *North Sea Continental Shelf Cases* (F.R.G./
Den.; F.R.G./Neth.), 1969 WL 1 (1969), the
International Court of Justice (ICJ) was required to
assess the status of the customary international law
of continental shelf delimitation. Because of a
concave coastline, Germany, which was not a party
to the 1958 Continental Shelf Convention, found its
continental shelf prolongation cut off by the
intersecting claims to equidistance boundaries of its

neighbors, Denmark and the Netherlands. The ICJ found that the equidistance method did not rise to the status of customary international law. Delimitation on the basis of equitable principles, taking into account all relevant circumstances and maintaining each country's natural prolongation to the extent possible, was found to be controlling. In the particular geographic circumstances, the ICJ identified the relevant factors to include the concave configuration of the coast, the physical and geologic structure of the shelf as evidence of natural prolongation of the land mass, the unity of natural resources of the shelf, and a reasonable degree of proportionality between the amount of coastline and the area of continental shelf. The ICJ noted, however, that "there is no legal limit to the considerations which [countries] may take account of" for the purpose of assuring that they apply equitable principles.

The UNCLOS III negotiators were confronted with the task of devising a rule for delimitation not only for the continental shelf, but for the exclusive economic zone as well. This turned out to be one of the most difficult provisions in UNCLOS to resolve with intractable arguments for "equitable principles" on one side and for the "equidistance method" on the other. The 1977 Court of Arbitration in the France-United Kingdom Continental Shelf Case apparently hoped to quell this debate by holding that treaty law and customary law were not necessarily different. In applying the Continental Shelf Convention to the case, the arbitral court stated that the language of the Convention requiring delimitation by the equidistance method, except where special circumstances justified another line, was merely a restatement of the proposition that boundaries must be delimited according to equitable principles. Moreover, the court stated that the Convention did not create a burden on a party to establish that special circumstances existed in a particular situation. *Arbitration on the Delimitation of the Continental Shelf* (U.K. v. Fr.) (1977), reprinted in 18 LL.M. 397.

For the primary part of the U.K.-France boundary in the English Channel, the arbitral court used an equidistance or median line, which is usually equitable when delimiting areas between opposite coastlines. A special enclave was created for Britain's Channel Islands, located near the coast of France. When the southern part of the boundary was extended into the Atlantic Ocean, islands off the coasts of the two countries, particularly the Scilly Islands off the southwest coast of England, had a significant effect on the equidistance line and were considered a special circumstance justifying a different boundary. To rectify what the court determined was a disproportionate effect, the Scilly Islands were given *"half-effect"* by bisecting the angle created by lines drawn giving the islands full effect and giving them no effect on an equidistance line. The resulting line has been called an "equitable equidistance" line. The court discounted the importance of natural prolongation, finding that geologic discontinuities in the continental shelf, such as the Hurd Deep Fault Zone, were not relevant to the delimitation. The concepts of giving "half-effect" to islands having a disproportionate effect or creating enclaves for islands that are not near the coast of their nation's mainland have been used in numerous subsequent delimitations. See, e.g., *Case Concerning the Continental Shelf* (Tunis./Libyan Arab Jamahiriya), 1982 WL 247 (ICJ 1982); *Territorial and Maritime Dispute between Nicaragua and Honduras in the Caribbean Sea* (Nicaragua v. Honduras) (2007); *Between Canada and France: Decision in Case Concerning Delimitation of Maritime Areas (St. Pierre and Miquelon)* (Court of Arbitration 1992); Treaty between Australia and the Independent State of Papua New Guinea concerning sovereignty and maritime boundaries in the area between the two countries, including the area known as Torres Strait, and related matters (18 December 1978).

With UNCLOS III negotiations in their final stages, the ICJ had another opportunity to clarify customary international law in the Tunisia-Libya continental shelf delimitation. *Case Concerning the Continental Shelf* (Tunis./Libyan Arab Jamahiriya), 1982 WL 247 (ICJ 1982). Both countries based their continental shelf boundary claims on the theory of natural prolongation—a country's right to the seabed naturally appurtenant to its coasts. The ICJ clarified the role of natural prolongation in delimitation by explaining that although natural prolongation is the legal basis for continental shelf claims, it does not necessarily provide any criteria for an equitable delimitation of the shelf. The physical structure of the shelf, which may or may not indicate the clear natural prolongation of each country, is only one relevant factor in delimitation according to equitable principles. Equitable principles, the ICJ explained, cannot be determined in the abstract, but only in terms of whether their application results in an equitable delimitation.

The ICJ also discussed the status of the equidistance method in delimitation according to equitable principles. Equidistance was found to have no privileged status among methods of delimitation, not even as a starting point that could be adjusted if the results are inequitable. Other important aspects of the Tunisia-Libya delimitation involved the ICJ's rejection of economic factors as a relevant circumstance in the delimitation, the half-effect given to offshore islands, and the emphasis on the proportionality test.

The Tunisia-Libya boundary line was determined to be a line perpendicular to the coast fallowing the dividing line of Tunisian and Libyan oil concessions. This line was adjusted to the east about 50 miles from the coast to reflect the change in direction of the Tunisian coast and to give offshore islands half-effect. The court then circumscribed the area affected by the delimitation to verify that the delimitation created a roughly proportionate division when comparing length of coastline to area of continental shelf.

With little additional guidance from the International Court of Justice, the final versions of the delimitation provisions of UNCLOS were a last minute compromise that has been called "a masterpiece of vagueness." UNCLOS article 74 on

EEZ delimitation and article 83 on continental shelf delimitation both provide as follows:

> The delimitation of the [exclusive economic zone and continental shelf] between States with opposite or adjacent coasts shall be effected by agreement on the basis of international law, as referred to in Article 38 of the Statute of the International Court of Justice,[1] in order to achieve an equitable solution.

With the proliferation of 200-mile EEZs, overlapping maritime boundary claims have become even more common. A major part of the docket of the ICJ comprises maritime boundary disputes. However, the fact that the world community now has more case law to draw upon has not made the principles or the implementation of maritime boundary delimitation necessarily more clear or predictable. A trend has been noted to more emphasis

---

[1]   Article 38 of the Statute of the International Court of Justice describes the source of international law on which the ICJ's decision shall be based. Article 38(1) provides:

The Court, whose function is to decide in accordance with international law such disputes as are submitted to it, shall apply:

(a)   international conventions, whether general or particular, establishing rules expressly recognized by the contesting states;

(b)   international custom, as evidence of a general practice accepted as law;

(c)   the general principles of law recognized by civilized nations;

(d)   . . . judicial decisions and the teachings of the most highly qualified publicists of the various nations, as subsidiary means for the determination of rules of law.

on coastal geography, but the uniqueness of each delimitation remains a dominant theme, and the cases provide little concrete guidance to promote simpler settlement of such disputes. See generally, Jonathan Charney, *Progress in International Maritime Boundary Delimitation;* 88 A.J.I.L. 227 (1994).

In the 2009 delimitation between the Ukraine and Romania, the ICJ did, however, set out a methodology for delimitation that the Court will follow:

> First, the Court will establish a provisional delimitation line, using methods that are geometrically objective and also appropriate for the geography of the area in which the delimitation is to take place. So far as delimitation between adjacent coasts is concerned, an equidistance line will be drawn unless there are compelling reasons that make this unfeasible in the particular case. So far as opposite coasts are concerned, the provisional delimitation line will consist of a median line between the two coasts. . . . [T]he Court will at the next, second stage consider whether there are factors calling for the adjustment or shifting of the provisional equidistance line in order to achieve an equitable result. The Court has also made clear that . . . "the so-called equitable principles/relevant circumstances method may usefully be applied . . . 'to achiev[e]' an equitable result." Finally, and at a third stage, the Court will verify that the line (a provisional

equidistance line which may or may not have been adjusted by taking into account the relevant circumstances) does not, as it stands, lead to an inequitable result by reason of any marked disproportion between the ratio of the respective coastal lengths and the ratio between the relevant maritime area of each State by reference to the delimitation line. A final check for an equitable outcome entails a confirmation that no great disproportionality of maritime areas is evident by comparison to the ratio of coastal lengths.

Maritime Delimitation in the Black Sea (Romania v. Ukraine) (ICJ 2009). (Citations omitted.)

These interpretations and applications of the law of international maritime boundaries in cases and conventions provide the legal framework within which United States maritime boundary litigation and negotiations have proceeded.

2.   UNITED STATES MARITIME BOUNDARIES

With the extension of continental shelf, fishery, and EEZ claims from the coasts of the United States, Puerto Rico, and U.S. territories and possessions, the United States asserted resource jurisdiction over approximately three million square miles of ocean space and created at least 25 situations of overlapping boundary claims. See Mark B. Feldman and David Colson, *The Maritime Boundaries of the United States,* 75 Am. J. Int'l L. 729, 733 (1981). While the majority of these boundaries are still unresolved, a number of the established boundaries are discussed below. For a list of maritime boundary agreements, see U.S. Dep't of State, Maritime Boundaries: Agreements and Treaties, available at http://www.state.gov/e/oes/ocns/opa/c28187.htm.

a. Cuba-United States Boundary

In 1977, the United States and Cuba negotiated an "all purpose" maritime boundary. Maritime Boundary Agreement between the United States of America and the Republic of Cuba, sighed Dec. 16, 1977, S. Exec. Doc. H, 96th Cong., 1st Seas. (1979), 17 I.L.M. 110. The treaty has never been ratified, but has been applied through exchange of notes every two years. The delimitation was between opposite coasts, Cuba and the Florida Keys, and a portion of the boundary was based on an equidistance line and another part was negotiated. A compromise established a portion of the boundary between a median line using Cuba's straight baselines and a median line using basepoints on Cuba's low water line. The 313-nautical mile line extends from the Gulf of Mexico through the southern part of the Straits of Florida to a tri-point with the Bahamas. See 1 International Maritime Boundaries 417–25 (Jonathan I. Charney & Lewis M. Alexander eds. 1993). Additional issues are likely to arise in the eastern Gulf of Mexico, because of Cuba's submission of a claim to OCS beyond 200 miles to the UN Commission on the Limits of the Continental Shelf. See Submission to the Commission on the Limits of the Continental Shelf to Demonstrate the Natural Extension of the Continental Shelf of Cuba Beyond 200 Nautical Miles in the Eastern Sector of the Gulf of Mexico (Exec. Summary) (May 2009), available at http://www.un.org/depts/los/clcs_new/submissions_files/cub51_09/cub_2009execsummary.pdf.

b. Mexico-United States Boundaries

The Pacific Ocean and Gulf of Mexico boundaries are based on three agreements. In 1970, the first agreement established boundaries through the 12-mile territorial sea and contiguous zone. When the two countries extended 200-mile fishery zones in 1976, provisional boundaries based on simplified equidistance lines were established through exchange of notes. The provisional boundary was the basis for a maritime boundary treaty in 1978 that was ratified in 1979 by Mexico and has been used for fishery management purposes. See id. at 427–45. Recently, interest in oil development on the continental shelf in the center of the Gulf of Mexico beyond and enclosed by the two countries' EEZs has led to negotiations to divide the continental shelf in two areas known as the "gaps." In 2000, the two countries adopted a treaty dividing the continental shelf beyond the EEZs with an equidistance line and reserving a buffer zone on each side of the boundary to deal with possible transboundary oil and gas deposits. The treaty anticipated that the countries would "seek to reach agreement for the efficient and equitable exploitation of such transboundary reservoirs." In 2012 the countries concluded the treaty to "establish a legal frame-work to achieve safe, efficient, equitable and environmentally responsible exploitation of transboundary hydrocarbon reservoirs." See Agreement between the

United States of America and the United Mexican States Concerning Transboundary Hydrocarbon Reservoirs in the Gulf of Mexico, available at http:// www.state.gov/p/wha/rls/2012/185259.htm. See also Curry L. Hagerty and James C. Uzel, *Proposed U.S.- Mexico Transboundary Hydrocarbons Agreement: Background and Issues for Congress* (CRS Report No.7–5700 2013).

c. Russia-United States Boundary

The boundary between the United States and Russia, extending over 1600 miles through the Bering Strait and Chukchi Sea to the Arctic Ocean, is the world's longest maritime boundary. The boundary is based on a technical interpretation of the 1867 convention between Russia and the United States in connection with the purchase of Alaska. The final agreement was concluded with the then Soviet Union in 1990 and ratified by the United States in 1991. Russia has not yet ratified the agreement, but the provisions have been applied pursuant to exchange of notes. The boundary basically divides equally the total area that was subject to conflicting 200-mile claims. See 1 International Maritime Boundaries 447–60 (Jonathan I. Charney & Lewis M. Alexander eds. 1993).

The EEZ jurisdictions of the two countries enclose an area of the Bering Sea that is referred to as the "donut hole." Because the area is high seas and not subject to Russian or United States fishing regulation, exploitation of the pollack fishery by foreign vessels was uncontrolled. The situation is a classic example of the problem of so-called "straddling stocks." In the 1980s, Japan, Korea, China, and Poland vessels severely overfished the area of the central Bering Sea creating severe conservation problems for pollock. Negotiations were initiated in 1991 to develop a multilateral regime for pollock exploitation in the central Bering Sea. During the three-year period of negotiations, all the parties voluntarily suspended fishing for pollack in the "donut hole" as well as in adjacent EEZs. The Convention on the Conservation and Management of Pollock Resources in the Central Bering Sea, with Annex, *done* June 16, 1994, establishes an international regime for the conservation and management of pollock resources in the "donut hole." An Annual Conference will establish the allowable harvest level (AHL) and individual national quotas (INQs), as well as other conservation and management measures for pollock and define the plan of work for the Scientific and Technical Committee. The Convention contains strong enforcement provisions requiring that vessels fishing for pollock in the Convention area carry scientific observers and use real-time satellite position-fixing transmitters, and allowing boarding and inspection of all fishing vessels of any Party to the Convention by authorized officials of any other Party for compliance with the Convention.

d. U.S. Possessions and Territories

The United States has concluded six boundary agreements on behalf of territories or possessions. A 1978 agreement established the Caribbean boundary between Puerto Rico and the U.S. Virgin Islands and Venezuela. The equidistance line gives full weight to all islands and coastal fronts. See 1 International Maritime Boundaries 691–703 (Jonathan I. Charney & Lewis M. Alexander eds. 1993). The American Samoa boundaries between the Cook Islands and New Zealand's Tokelau were negotiated in 1980 and entered into force in 1983. Both boundaries are based on the equidistance method giving full effect to all islands and fringing reefs. Id. at 985–93, 1125–34. In 1993, two treaties established the boundaries between Puerto Rico/U.S. Virgin Islands and the British Virgin Islands and Anguilla. The maritime boundary between Samoa and Niue was established in 1997, and in 2014, a treaty was concluded to establish the boundary between Guam and the Federated States of Micronesia.

e. United States-Canada Boundary in the Gulf of Maine

The United States and Canada have four maritime geographic frontiers that have been sites of overlapping boundary claims: the Gulf of Maine area in the Atlantic Ocean; seaward of the Strait of Juan de Fuca off Washington; extending from the Dixon Entrance in southeast Alaska; and in the Beaufort Sea in the Arctic. The only delimitation that is finally resolved is the Gulf of Maine boundary.

Canada made the first overt assertion of jurisdiction over the Gulf of Maine area and Georges Bank in 1964 by issuing geologic exploration permits north of a line equidistant from Nova Scotia and New

England. Although Canada did not become a party to the Continental Shelf Convention until 1970, the claim was based on the Convention's provisions. The United States did not formally object to the claim until 1969, following the ICJ opinion in the North Sea Continental Shelf Cases, which rejected the equidistance method as a rule of law and emphasized natural prolongation. Although negotiations began in 1970 to delimit the continental shelf, very little had been accomplished by 1976, when the dispute was exacerbated by the imminent extension of 200-mile fishery zones by both countries.

In November 1976, Canada published the claim to its fishery zone in the Gulf of Maine and across Georges Bank based on an equidistance line. The United States responded by publishing a delimitation line that ran through the Northeast Channel, a "discontinuity" in the shelf about three-fourths of the distance from Cape Cod to Nova Scotia, which the United States asserted separated the natural prolongation of the U.S. land mass, i.e., Georges Bank, from the Canadian shelf. Following the U.K-France delimitation, Canada revised its limits in 1978 to claim an "equitable equidistance" line that disregarded Cape Cod and Nantucket because of their disproportionate effect on the boundary. The United States later made an additional claim based on a "modified perpendicular" line. Based on theories from the Tunisia-Libya delimitation, the line was a perpendicular to the coast modified to preserve the natural prolongation of Canada's shelf in certain areas.

Negotiations on both a boundary line and a comprehensive agreement on cooperative fishery management continued through 1978 and in March 1979, the United States and Canada signed two treaties, one an agreement on management and conservation of fishery resources and the other an agreement to submit the boundary dispute to binding third-party settlement. The treaties were specifically linked so that one could not come into force unless the other did also. The fishery agreement met immediate opposition from New England fishermen and senators. In March 1981, after two years delay on ratification, President Reagan withdrew the fishery treaty. The boundary treaty, which had been noncontroversial, received the advice and consent of the Senate within a month. In November 1981, Canada agreed to the separation of the treaties upon assurance that Canadian fishermen could continue to fish in disputed areas.

The dispute was submitted to a special, five-member chamber of the International Court of Justice. The Special Chamber was requested to determine "in accordance with the principles and rules of international law applicable in the matter . . . , the course of the *single maritime boundary* that divides the continental shelf and fisheries zones of [the parties]." Case Concerning Delimitation of the Maritime Boundary in the Gulf of Maine Area (Can. /U.S.) (1984) (emphasis added). The case was the first to include fishery zone issues and to delimit a boundary for purposes of both the water column and continental shelf.

On October 12, 1984, the ICJ Special Chamber announced a boundary line that to a large extent equally divided the disputed area, which was not surprising. On the other hand, the methodology and criteria applied by the Chamber were decidedly unexpected.

In describing the area to be delimited, the Special Chamber rejected the concept of natural boundaries in the seabed or waters in the Gulf of Maine-Georges Bank area. The parties conceded the basic unity of character and the absence of any features which "interrupt the geologic continuity of [the continental] shelf." The Chamber not only rejected the U.S. argument that the water column of the area was divided into three identifiable oceanographic and ecological regimes, but also questioned the "possibility of discerning any genuine, sure and stable 'natural boundaries' in so fluctuating an environment as the waters of the ocean, their flora and fauna."

In analyzing the law and criteria to be applied in the case, the Chamber rejected the application of the Continental Shelf Convention, although both countries were parties. The treaty would have been applicable to the determination of a continental shelf boundary only, but it could not be applied to a delimitation that also included the water column. The Chamber then stated what it referred to as a "reformulation of the 'fundamental norm' " of international law applicable to maritime boundary delimitation: "[D]elimitation is to be effected by the application of equitable criteria and by the use of practical methods capable of ensuring, with regard to geographic configuration of the area and other relevant circumstances, an equitable result."

The Chamber found each country's criteria and methods inappropriate. The United States gave too much weight to fisheries and ecological criteria, and Canada did not consider the special geographic circumstances of the area. In stating what criteria it would apply to the delimitation, the Chamber made its most disturbing pronouncement: Because the boundary was to be a single line for both the seabed and the water column, the Chamber excluded "application of any criterion found to be typically and exclusively bound up with the particular characteristics of one alone of the two natural realities that have to be delimited in conjunction." The Chamber may just as well have said that it would not consider anything that was particularly relevant, since allocation of resources was, after all, the reason for the delimitation. The approach made most of the evidence presented by the parties irrelevant. The Chamber settled upon criteria employing geometric methods based on coastal geography that it predicted would inevitably be adopted in complex delimitations in the future because of their "neutral character."

The boundary line was extended in three segments. Equal division of the "maritime projections" was found to be an equitable approach. The segments were not strictly median or equidistance lines, because the first segment was constructed to discount uninhabited islets, rocks, and low tide elevations; the second segment was adjusted from the median to reflect the relative lengths of coastlines and effect of islands; and the third segment, extending into the Atlantic Ocean, was a line perpendicular to a closing line drawn from Nantucket to Cape Sable, Nova Scotia.

In a final assessment of whether the delimitation was "intrinsically equitable," the Chamber refused to consider either Canada's assertion that existing fishing patterns must be maintained or the U.S. claim of antiquity and continuity of fishing activities on Georges Bank. The Chamber seemed to question the "clean hands" of parties seeking equitable consideration of historic fishing patterns and economic dependence on fisheries, when the parties had only recently ejected foreign fishing fleets from the area without apparent concern for the repercussions in those countries. Because the boundary would not have a catastrophic effect on the livelihood or well being of the populations of the two countries, the Chamber found no reason to adjust the line further.

The Chamber's analysis has been widely criticized. Some critics claim that the decision deviates from international law and have questioned whether the case will serve as authority for other single maritime boundary delimitations; others have viewed it as the beginning of a trend toward the use of more neutral geometric principles. The methodology adopted by the ICJ in the Ukraine-Romania boundary delimitation does resemble the Chamber's approach, but the proposition that a single maritime boundary should not consider factors that are particularly relevant to only the water or only the seabed regime does not seem to have become part of the jurisprudence concerning the identification of factors or circumstances relevant to the delimitation.

H. MARINE SCIENTIFIC RESEARCH

Conceptually, the free pursuit and publication of knowledge about the marine environment would seem to be beneficial to everyone. The scientific information would broaden the world's understanding of the oceans and be invaluable to a coastal country in understanding, managing, and conserving its marine resources. But the same information can be strategically important to other countries for military and resource exploitation purposes. In addition, countries have been known to use conduct of scientific research as a subterfuge for intelligence operations. Because most developing countries lack the expertise or wealth for distant water research, freedom of marine science research is often viewed as primarily benefitting developed countries. These observations set out the basic elements of the debate concerning coastal nation control over marine scientific research.

Traditionally, marine scientific research (MSR) was considered a freedom of the high seas, but could not be conducted in territorial waters without the coastal country's permission. Vessels could not engage in research while exercising the right of innocent passage through a territorial sea. The Continental Shelf Convention imposed the first restrictions on research outside territorial waters. Article 5(8) of the Convention provides:

> The consent of the coastal State shall be obtained in respect of any research concerning the continental shelf and undertaken there. Nevertheless, the coastal State shall not normally withhold its consent if the request is submitted by a qualified institution with a view to purely scientific research . . . subject to the proviso that the coastal State shall have the right, if it so desires, to participate or to be represented in the research, and that in any event the results shall be published.

The term "concerning the continental shelf" left unclear whether the consent requirement applied to research that was not physically conducted on the shelf. The term "purely scientific research" was also vague because the line between pure and applied research is not always easily discernible. Since the 1970s, the extension of fishery zones has also had the effect of limiting marine research. Because fishery research necessarily involves the taking of fish, such research within extended fishery zones and EEZs is generally subject to coastal country regulation.

UNCLOS III negotiations had to attempt to resolve the conflict created by developing countries demanding more control over MSR and by scientists seeking to bring down the barriers that had already seriously limited marine research. Scientists had found that the emerging consent regimes for continental shelf and fisheries research were vague and subject to multiple interpretations and that requests for clearance often got so bogged down in politics and developing country bureaucracies that research voyages had to be canceled.

UNCLOS specifically codified MSR among the freedoms of the high seas, UNCLOS, art. 87 and reaffirmed that research may be conducted in the territorial sea only with consent of the coastal country. Id. art. 245. The Convention creates a new regime for marine science research conducted in the EEZ or on the continental shelf. While recognizing the right of all nations to participate in marine research and encouraging international cooperation, the Convention gives coastal countries authority to regulate and to authorize MSR in their EEZs and on their continental shelves. Id. art. 246(1).

The UNCLOS consent regime for the EEZ and continental shelf distinguishes between applied and pure research. Applied research involves activities that are of "direct significance for the exploration and exploitation of natural resources," or that involve drilling, explosives, or construction of installations or artificial islands. Id. art. 246(5)(a)–(c). Pure research includes activities carried out "exclusively for peaceful purposes and in order to increase scientific knowledge of the marine environment for the benefit of all mankind." Id. art. 246(3). Consent for pure scientific research projects shall be granted "in normal circumstances." Id. The coastal country has total discretion as to whether to consent to applied research, to research that pollutes the marine environment, and to research by countries that have provided inaccurate information or that have outstanding obligations from a previous project. See id. 246(5).

To address the concerns of developing countries, UNCLOS subjects researching countries to certain obligations. First, the coastal country must receive specific, detailed information about the project at least six months in advance. UNCLOS, art. 248. Second, the Convention imposes a long list of detailed, and usually expensive, conditions on research projects which include:

(1) ensuring that scientists of the coastal country are able to be represented or to participate in the research on board the vessel at no cost to the coastal country;

(2) providing preliminary and final reports on the research project and access by the coastal country to data and samples;

(3) if requested, providing the coastal country with assessment and interpretation of data and samples;

(4) ensuring that research results are appropriately published as soon as practicable; and

(5) unless otherwise agreed, removing any installations and equipment.

Id. art. 249(1). If the researchers fail to meet these conditions, the coastal country may suspend research or shut down the project. Id. art. 253.

The treaty provisions attempt to address the concerns of marine scientists in a number of ways. First, to assure that consent is not unreasonably delayed or denied, countries must establish procedures and rules for processing clearance requests. Id. art. 246(3). Although the term "normal circumstances" for consent is not defined, the Convention does state that "normal circumstances may exist in spite of the absence of diplomatic relations between the coastal [country] and the researching [country]." Id. art. 246(4). Finally, the Convention provides for "implied consent" in certain circumstances. First, if research is to be carried out by or under the auspices of an international organization in which the coastal country participates, consent is implied if the country does not object within four months of notification. Id. art. 247. (The Intergovernmental Oceanographic Commission is the most prominent international marine science organization.) In other cases, if a researching nation has provided the coastal country with all necessary information concerning the research project, the project may proceed after six months unless within four months of notification, the coastal country gives notice that:

(a) it has withheld its consent . . .; or

(b) the information given . . . regarding the nature or objectives of the project does not conform to the manifestly evident facts;

(c) it requires supplementary information . . .; or

    (d) outstanding obligations exist with respect to a previous marine scientific research project. . . .

Id. art. 252. In addition, consent cannot be withheld for applied or pure research on the continental shelf beyond 200 miles unless the area is currently the focus of exploitation and development activity by the coastal country. Id. art. 246(6).

As far as researching nations are concerned, the consent regime has a major shortcoming in that it is not subject to effective dispute resolution procedures. In general, parties to UNCLOS may submit disputes concerning interpretation or implementation to compulsory third party settlement. However, the withholding of a coastal country's consent to MSR projects is not subject to those procedures. Id. art. 297(2). The effect on conduct of marine research may not be great, however, because the time and funding constraints on most marine research projects are not flexible enough to allow the project to continue after delays for dispute resolution.

Limitations by coastal countries on publication of research are considered an unacceptable condition by most researchers. UNCLOS recognizes a coastal country's authority to require prior permission for publication only in the case of applied MSR that produces results "of direct significance for the exploration and exploitation of natural resources." Id. art. 249(2). As noted earlier, the line between applied and pure scientific research is not always readily discernible.

There is no doubt that a consent regime for the EEZ and the continental shelf has become part of customary international law although the details may be vague. In a policy statement accompanying the 1983 proclamation that extended the 200-mile EEZ, the President specifically refrained from extending U.S. jurisdiction over MSR. Statement by the President, 19 Weekly Comp. Pres. Dec. 383 (Mar. 10, 1983); U.S. Oceans Policy, 83 Dep't St. Bull., June 1983, at 70 (1983); 22 I.L.M. 464. This has not affected the practice of other countries, however. A 1992 study indicated that 116 countries have asserted jurisdiction over marine research; only nine of these countries limit claims to areas within 12 miles. Of countries claiming 200-mile offshore jurisdictional zones, only the United States and eight other countries do not claim jurisdiction over research in these areas. See Judith Fenwick, International Profiles on Marine Scientific Research 182, 184 (1992). More questionable is whether the implied consent provisions can be relied upon as customary international law. Some commentators suggest that the provisions lack the "fundamentally norm-creating character necessary for custom" and are therefore incapable of becoming customary international law even if evidence of state practice supported it. See R.R. Churchill and A.V. Lowe, The Law of the Sea 295 (1988). It seems unlikely, however, that research organizations would risk projects, funding, and even their oceanographic vessels in reliance upon the UNCLOS implied consent provisions.

Although the U.S. does generally require consent for MSR, it does require permission if any portion of the research in the EEZ:

- is conducted within a national marine sanctuary, a marine national monument, or other marine protected areas;

- involves the study of marine mammals or endangered species;

- requires taking commercial quantities of marine resources;

- involves contact with the U.S. continental shelf; or

- involves ocean dumping research.

See Dep't of State, Marine Scientific Research Authorizations, available at http://www.state.gov/e/oes/ocns/opa/rvc/. The U.S. also reserves the right to participate on foreign research conducted in the EEZ. Id.

The United States continues to be one of the primary sponsors of marine scientific research around the world. The Department of State (DOS) has statutory responsibility for coordination and oversight of international science and technology activities and reports that the DOS processes "approximately 400 applications for foreign coastal State consent and 70 applications for U.S. consent" annually. In addition, the DOS handles the transfer of data for research in the EEZ of other countries. And since the attempted pirate attack on the RV *Maurice Ewing* off the coast of Somalia in 2001, the DOS also attempts to provide researchers timely information of travel warnings and risks in foreign waters. See Perspectives on International Oceanographic Research 30–32 (U.S. Dept. of State, 2002).

I.   DISPUTE RESOLUTION IN UNCLOS

UNCLOS includes comprehensive dispute resolution procedures. Disputes concerning interpretation or application of the treaty that cannot be settled by other peaceful means are subject to binding dispute resolution. Article 287 of the Convention provides four alternative fora for dispute settlement:

   (1) the International Tribunal for the Law of the Sea constituted under Annex VI;

   (2) the International Court of Justice;

   (3) an arbitral tribunal constituted in accordance with Annex VII;

   (4) a special arbitral tribunal constituted in accordance with Annex VIII for specified purposes.

The International Tribunal for the Law of the Sea (ITLOS) has jurisdiction over all disputes submitted in accordance with the Convention and exclusive jurisdiction, through its Seabed Disputes Chamber, for disputes related to the international deep seabed area. The 21-member tribunal was first elected in August 1996. The Seabed Disputes Chamber, first elected in 2005, is composed of eleven tribunal members selected by a majority of the Tribunal. To date, only 22 cases have been submitted to the

Tribunal. The majority of the cases, like its first case *The M/V "SAIGA"* (1997), have invoked the Tribunal's special jurisdiction under article 292 to address the prompt release of vessels detained for violation of coastal country or international law, or similar situations involving the request provisional measures. Few cases have actually reached the merits of the case, but ITLOS has issued an important advisory opinion addressing the responsibilities and obligations of States sponsoring deep seabed miners. See discussion at Chapter V Introduction.

Annex VII of the Convention provides for general jurisdiction, five-member arbitral tribunals set up on an ad hoc basis. Annex VIII arbitral tribunals have jurisdiction for disputes that require special scientific expertise and fact finding, such as fisheries, protection and preservation of the marine environment, marine scientific research, and navigation, including pollution or dumping from ships.

Countries may choose one or more of the dispute settlement fora when they ratify or accede to the Convention or by a written declaration after that. If the parties to a dispute have not accepted the same procedure or if a party has not chosen a forum, the dispute may be submitted to arbitration in accordance with Annex VII, unless the parties otherwise agree. In submitting the Convention to the Senate for its advice and consent, the Senate Foreign Relations Committee recommended that the United

States make the following declaration concerning choice of dispute resolution fora:

(A) a special arbitral tribunal constituted in accordance with Annex VIII for the settlement of disputes concerning the interpretation or application of the articles of the Convention relating (1) fisheries, (2) protection and preservation of the marine environment, (3) marine scientific research, (4) navigation, including pollution from vessels and by dumping, and

(B) an arbitral tribunal constituted in accordance with Annex VII for the settlement of disputes not covered by the declaration in (A) above.

Certain disputes concerning consent to foreign marine scientific research in the EEZ as well as most disputes concerning EEZ living resources are exceptions to the mandatory dispute resolution procedures. UNCLOS, art. 297(2)–(3). Specifically, in the case of fisheries a country is not required to submit to dispute resolution "any dispute relating to its sovereign rights with respect to the living resources in the [EEZ], including its discretionary powers for determining the allowable catch, its harvesting capacity, the allocation of surpluses . . . and the terms and conditions established by its conservation and management laws and regulations." Id. art. 297(3).

Countries may also exercise certain optional exceptions to compulsory jurisdiction under article

298. Under these provisions a country may declare that it does not accept the dispute procedures with respect to disputes concerning maritime boundaries between neighboring States, disputes concerning military activities and certain law enforcement activities, and disputes where the United Nations Security Council is exercising the functions assigned to it by the Charter of the United Nations. The Senate Foreign Relations Committee recommended that the United States exercise all three exceptions available as optional exclusions from mandatory dispute settlement under UNCLOS article 298.

In many cases that are excepted from the general dispute settlement procedures, the Convention provides for compulsory conciliation under Annex V procedures. For example, in the area of fisheries, disputes subject to compulsory conciliation include circumstances in which:

(i)   a coastal State has manifestly failed to comply with its obligations to ensure through proper conservation and management measures that the maintenance of the living resources in the exclusive economic zone is not seriously endangered;

(ii) a coastal State has arbitrarily refused to determine, at the request of another State, the allowable catch and its capacity to harvest living resources . . .; or

(iii) a coastal State has arbitrarily refused to allocate to any State . . . the whole or part of the surplus it has declared to exist.

Id. art. 297(b). The report of a five-member conciliation commission must be deposited with the United Nations and detail any agreements reached by the parties, the commission's findings of fact and law and, failing agreement by the parties, its recommendations for an "amicable settlement." The report of the commission is not, however, binding on the parties. See Annex V.

J. MARINE FISHERIES

Intense fishing effort after World War II led to increases in global marine catch from less than twenty million tons in 1950 to about 60 million tons in 1970. The extension of coastal state jurisdiction over EEZ fisheries in the mid-1970s did not, however, abate the intensity of marine fishing. Worldwide marine catch increased until it peaked in 1996 at a catch of around 87 million tons and has shown a trend of decline since then. Analysis by the FAO of the most important fisheries indicated that "in 2011, 28.8 percent of fish stocks were estimated as fished at a biologically unsustainable level and therefore overfished," and "fully fished stocks accounted for 61.3 percent and underfished stocks 9.9 percent" of the fish stocks. There are some indications that overfishing is declining slightly since it peaked in 2008. The FAO has noted a consistent downward trend in the proportion of fisheries with potential for expansion, concluding that indicators suggest that the global potential for marine capture fisheries has been reached. Fishing effort, in the form of fishing capacity and more efficient technologies, has increased in the past two decades much more quickly

than catch, but some nations are reducing over-
capacity in response to the FAO's *International Plan
of Action for the Management of Fishing Capacity.*
See The State of World Fisheries and Aquaculture
(FAO 2014).

As countries have limited access to EEZs by foreign
fishermen and new fishing technologies have
developed, fishing on the high seas has also
expanded. These high seas fisheries, particularly for
highly migratory species and "straddling stocks" in
areas adjacent to or surrounded by EEZs, are being
blamed by coastal states for contributing to their
inability to manage fisheries sustainably. Intense
fish harvesting in areas of the high seas created the
greatest controversy in: (1) the Northwest Atlantic
near Canadian waters where fishing by countries
who are not members of the Northwest Atlantic
Fisheries Organization is resulting in over-
harvesting and in demands in Canada for extension
of fishery jurisdiction to 300 miles; (2) the Bering Sea
"donut hole," an area of high seas surrounded by U.S.
and Russian EEZs; (3) the Sea of Okhotsk "peanut
hole," outside the Russian EEZ, in which Russia has
attempted to impose a moratorium because of
overfishing; (4) the Barents Sea "loophole," an area of
the high seas between Russia and Norway in which
cod is being overfished; and (5) the Southeast Pacific,
where large-scale exploitation of straddling stocks of
Chilean jack mackerel has led Chile to propose a
claim to a "presential sea" in a large area adjacent to
the EEZ. See Christopher C. Joyner & Peter N. De
Cola, *Chile's Presential Sea Proposal: Implications*

for Straddling Stocks and the International Law of Fisheries, 24 Ocean Dev. & Int'l L. 99 (1993).

Most international concern has focused on the effects on EEZ management of intense high seas fishing for straddling stocks and highly migratory species. However, coastal States cannot totally shift responsibility for the failure of fisheries management in the EEZ to distant water fishing fleets. Over 90 percent of the fish are harvested within 200 miles offshore, and high seas, distant water fishers account for only about five percent of the total marine landings. In spite of coastal state control over this large portion of the fisheries, commercial species located entirely within the EEZ or associated with the continental shelf continued to decline for decades after extension of EEZs.

Outside of the U.N. Law of the Sea context, fisheries management and conservation have received some attention within the context of the development of international environmental law. Although not specifically a marine conservation document, the Rio Declaration, adopted at the United Nations Conference on Environment and Development (UNCED) in 1992, officially introduced into international environmental law two dominant resource management themes for the 1990s—the goal of sustainable development and the application of the precautionary principle or precautionary approach. The theme of sustainable development is summarized in Principle 3: "The right of development must be fulfilled so as to equitably meet development and environmental needs of present and future generations." The precautionary approach as embodied in Principle 15 provides that "[w]here there are threats of serious irreversible damage, lack of full scientific certainty shall not be used as a reason for postponing cost-effective measures to prevent environmental degradation." See Rio Declaration on Environment and Development, *adopted* 13 June 1992, U.N. Doc. A/CONF.151/26, vol. I (1992), *reprinted in* 31 LL.M. 874 (1992). Agenda 21, the action plan adopted by the UNCED Plenary (and later endorsed by the General Assembly), sets out a strategy in Chapter 17 for protection and sustainable development of the marine and coastal environment and its resources which requires "new approaches . . . that are integrated in content and are precautionary and anticipatory in ambit." Agenda 21, Chapter 17.1. One of the most important recommendations of Agenda 21 was to convene a United Nations conference to effectively implement UNCLOS provisions on straddling and highly migratory fish stocks. The U.N. General Assembly subsequently adopted a resolution for such a conference, which, after three years of negotiations, resulted in the adoption of the Agreement for the Implementation of the Provisions of the United Nations Convention on the Law of the Sea of 10 December 1982 Relating to the Conservation and Management of Straddling Stocks and Highly Migratory Stocks (Fish Stocks Agreement), Aug. 4, 1995, U.N. Doc. A/CONF.164/37 (1995), *done* Sept. 8, 1995, *reprinted in* 34 I.L.M. 1542 (1995).

1. HIGH SEAS FISHERIES FOR MIGRATORY AND STRADDLING FISH STOCKS

Article 63 of UNCLOS contemplated that future agreements would be necessary to deal with issues related to migratory and straddling fish stocks. The U.N. Fish Stocks Agreement is viewed as a measure to implement article 63 and provide an impetus for cooperation and compatibility in fisheries management beyond and within EEZs. The obligation for cooperation under the Agreement can be implemented through existing treaties and international arrangements or by the creation of regional fisheries management organizations (RFMOs). Countries that fish for straddling or highly migratory species are obligated to cooperate through one of these arrangements. This obligation is somewhat controversial in that it purports to bind not only parties to the Agreement, but also non-parties. Article 8(3) and (4) provide that non-parties may not participate in managed high seas fisheries unless they are members of the regional fisheries organization or accept the organization's management measures. Moreover, article 17(2) directs non-complying and non-party states not to authorize fishing by their vessels in managed fisheries. Finally, the authority under articles 17(4) and 33(2) for parties to take "measures consistent with the Agreement and international law" to deter non-parties from undermining the effectiveness of regional management measures together with limited coastal state enforcement provisions under article 21, allow a limited degree of enforcement of the Agreement and regional fishery management standards over non-party vessels on the high seas. Although these provisions arguably encroach upon the basic international law principles that treaties cannot bind third parties and that, generally, vessels on the high seas are subject only to flag state jurisdiction, parties to the Agreement contend that it does no more than articulate obligations on all states made binding through art. 63 of UNCLOS.

The Fish Stocks Agreement expands upon outdated conservation and management concepts of UNCLOS, such as qualified maximum sustainable yield. The Agreement specifically incorporates more contemporary concepts recommended by UNCED and the FAO on sustainability, ecosystem management, and integrated management, including requirements to: (1) adopt measures to assure long-term sustainability of straddling and migratory fish stocks, art. 5(a); (2) adopt measures to protect species within the same ecosystem, art. 5(e); (3) take measures to prevent or eliminate overfishing and excess capacity to ensure fishing effort that will allow sustainable use of fishery resources, art. 5(h); (4) minimize pollution, waste, discards, and impact on associated or dependent species, art. 5(f); (5) protect biodiversity of the marine environment, art. 5(g); and (6) assess the impact of fishing, other human activities and environmental factors on target stocks, associate and dependent species, and other species in the ecosystem, art. 5(d). The Agreement also requires application of the precautionary approach. Agreement, articles 5(c), 6.

The Fish Stocks Agreement, which required only thirty ratifications to come into force in 2001, has 81 ratifications as of August 2014. (Interestingly, although the United States is not a party to UNCLOS, it was among the first countries to ratify this implementing agreement in August 1996.) During the decades since the negotiation of the Fish Stocks Agreement, regional fisheries organizations have become revitalized and proliferated, and the role of these organizations has evolved toward becoming true fisheries management bodies for regions of the high seas. In spite of problems related to cost, the inadequacy of information, and other implementation issues, these organizations are playing an increasingly important role in the management of high seas fisheries.

The U.S. has been acting proactively in participation in existing RFMOs and development of new regional fisheries arrangements that will facilitate the implementation of the Agreement. In particular, in November 1995 the United States joined the Northwest Atlantic Fisheries Organization (NAFO) and has been instrumental in the organization's adoption of the principles of the U.N. Fish Stocks Agreement as rules governing member compliance and non-member fishing. The United States has also participated in negotiation of the recently concluded Western and Central Pacific Fisheries Convention, which establishes conservation and management measures for all countries and vessels operating in the region. The area covered by this Convention encompasses the last major ocean region that had been not covered by a regional management regime. The United States participated in the creation of the new Western and Central Pacific Fisheries Commission under the Convention. A new regime has also been negotiated under the Convention on the Conservation and Management of Fishery Resources in the Southeast Atlantic Ocean. Like other new regional high seas organizations, the governing principles incorporate principles of the U.N. Fish Stocks Agreement. In addition, the U.S. has participated in the South Pacific Tuna Treaty since 1988 and has been a member of the International Commission for the Conservation of Atlantic Tunas (ICCAT) since 1976. ICCAT has also incorporated important principles of the U.N. Fish Stocks Agreement into rules for members and for nonmembers fishing within the region.

Finally, the United States has passed legislation to implement the Agreement to Promote Compliance with International Conservation and Management Measures by Fishing Vessels on the High Seas (the Compliance Agreement), which was adopted by the Conference of the FAO in 1993. The High Seas Fishing Compliance Act of 1995, 16 U.S.C. §§ 5501–5509, establishes a system of permitting, reporting and regulation for United States vessels on the high seas.

2.   EEZ FISHERIES MANAGEMENT

The grant of exclusive fishery management authority to coastal nations by Part V of UNCLOS was based on a number of premises, none of which turned out to be entirely valid. The first was the notion that coastal state jurisdiction could provide a more functional fisheries management regime, because most fisheries are located within 200 miles of a coast. Current problems with highly migratory and straddling stocks seem to belie that premise. The second premise was that by placing these areas under exclusive jurisdiction, entry into fisheries would be controlled, thereby reducing both the potential for overfishing and for overcapitalization of fishing fleets. Rather than control entry, however, coastal states have subsidized domestic fishing fleets and directly contributed to the overcapitalization of the fishing industry and overexploitation of many stocks. Finally, prevailing theories of fisheries management were presumed to be adequate to protect and maintain fisheries if jurisdictional control and effective enforcement authority were established. In fact, scientific information has been inadequate to manage fisheries effectively and the basic concept of maximum sustainable yield has been ineffective for management of rapidly declining stocks.

Neither UNCLOS nor most coastal state domestic fishery management regimes adequately deal with the issues currently identified as undermining the effective conservation of marine fisheries. UNCLOS standards for coastal State conservation and utilization of EEZ fisheries are largely ambiguous, incredibly flexible, and virtually unenforceable. State self-interest and the degree of coastal state autonomy authorized by UNCLOS support continuation of the "tragedy of the commons" even within exclusively controlled EEZs.

This situation has not escaped the attention of the international community and a number of efforts have been directed at dealing with the inadequacy of the present EEZ management regime. The FAO Code of Conduct for Responsible Fisheries was also developed in response to Agenda 21. This voluntary agreement is comprehensive in covering all aspects of fishery conservation, management and development, including fishing activities and operations, aquaculture, trade, research, legal and administrative institutions, and integration of fisheries into coastal area management. The Code is to be "interpreted and applied in conformity with relevant rules of international law, as reflected in the United Nations Convention on the Law of the Sea." The provisions of the Code of Conduct provide a detailed elaboration of fishery management principles and practices. For example, the Code of Conduct recognizes sustainable use as "the overriding objective" of fisheries management and adopts the precautionary approach for dealing with lack of information and uncertainties concerning the state of stocks or impacts of fisheries activities. See FAO, *Code of Conduct for Responsible Fisheries* (FAO, Rome 1995). The FAO has also drafted an International Plan of Action for Management of Fishing Capacity (FAO, Rome 1999).

The Convention on Biological Diversity, *done* June 5, 1992, *reprinted in* 31 I.L.M. 818 (1992), is also relevant to management of marine fisheries. The

Biodiversity Convention is a framework treaty devoted to "conservation of biological diversity, the sustainable use of its components and the fair and equitable sharing of the benefits . . . of genetic resources." The Jakarta Mandate on Marine and Coastal Diversity implements that Biodiversity Convention through recommendations that incorporate the precautionary approach and principles of integrated coastal and marine management. Although these international developments are clearly important, they provide few mandatory obligations or enforceable principles that will contribute to early modification of EEZ fisheries management regimes.

Surprisingly, the Fish Stocks Agreement, which applies to high seas fisheries, seems to incorporate incentives necessary for the most immediate changes in EEZ management. In order to require the adoption of compatible measures for management of adjacent high seas fisheries, coastal nations must adopt EEZ management strategies for straddling stocks and migratory species that integrate the precautionary approach, protection of biodiversity, principles of sustainability, and ecosystem management. Not only is it unlikely that coastal States would adopt different management regimes for other fish stocks within the EEZ, it is virtually impossible to conceive how such an integrated management approach could not incorporate and positively affect management of all fisheries within the EEZ.

CHAPTER VII

THE FUTURE OF UNITED STATES OCEAN AND COASTAL POLICY

A. THE BEGINNINGS OF MODERN OCEAN AND COASTAL POLICY DEVELOPMENT

As earlier chapters of this book have discussed, the decades following World War II were a time of great change for the United States' oceans and coasts. The promise of offshore oil and gas not only led to the Truman Proclamation and the creation of a new international doctrine concerning the continental shelf, but also to domestic federal conflicts over the offshore's resources. Development of oil and gas has also generated controversy due to its potential environmental and economic impacts. Large foreign fishing fleets and new technologies led to an overcapitalized and efficient world fishing industry capable of depleting the seemingly endless bounty of the seas. Largely uncontrolled land-based pollution led to numerous "dead zones" in coastal waters. Population in coastal areas grew at unprecedented rates. By the mid-1960s, in the midst of an era of growing environmental awareness, the need for a better understanding of the United States oceans and coasts became the focus of national attention.

The Marine Resources and Engineering Development Act of 1966, Pub. L. 89–54; 80 Star. 205 (June 17, 1966), created the Commission on Marine Sciences, Engineering, and Resources, which became known as the Stratton Commission. Over a two-year period, the 15-person commission held hearings and developed a report that became the first comprehensive study of United States ocean policy. The report, *Our Nation and the Sea,* focused attention on the importance of the oceans to the country and the need for a national ocean plan of action to address immediate problems and future use of resources. Going beyond issues of marine science and technology, the report stated:

> Like the oceans themselves, the Nation's marine interests are vast, complex, composed of many critical elements, and not susceptible to simplicity of treatment. Realization and accommodation of the Nation's many diverse interests require a plan for national action and for orderly development of the uses of the sea. The plan must provide for determined attack on immediate problems concurrently with initiation of a long-range program to develop knowledge, technology, and a framework of laws and institutions that will lay the foundation for efficient and productive marine activities in the years ahead.

Commission on Marine Science, Engineering, and Resources, *Our Nation and the Sea: A Plan for National Action* (1969). The report contained 126 recommendations intended to initiate the national planning process for the oceans and coasts.

The recommendations of the report created a focus on ocean issues and led to the creation in 1970 of the National Oceanic and Atmospheric Administration

(NOAA) within the Department of Commerce to provide federal leadership and management for many oceans uses and resources. In 1972, Congress enacted the Coastal Zone Management Act, recognizing the coasts as a national, not merely a state or local, resource. That year also saw enactment of the Marine Mammal Protection Act, the Clean Water Act, and the Marine Protection, Research, and Sanctuaries Act—which included the Ocean Dumping Act—and the Marine Sanctuary Program. In the same decade, the Endangered Species Act and major amendments to the Outer Continental Shelf Lands Act in 1978 provided further authority to create a framework of authorities for ocean and coastal management. Ocean management remained sector-based, however, and lacked any comprehensive or ecosystem-based approach.

B.   OCEAN POLICY FOR THE 21ST CENTURY

Over the following decades, the ocean and coastal management framework expanded to include at least 140 statutes administered by twenty federal agencies, highlighting a new problem for ocean management: the fragmented and often uncoordinated legal framework for ocean management. As the pressures on ocean and coastal resources increased, new environmental challenges arose, and the movement toward sustainable use of resources focusing on ecosystem-based management made the inadequacies of the ad hoc, fragmented approach even clearer. A 2000 report of the Senate Committee on Commerce, Science, and

Transportation summarized the issue as follows: "Today, people who work and live on the water . . . face a patchwork of confusing and sometimes contradictory federal and state authorities and regulations. No mechanism exists for establishing a common vision or set of objectives." Senate Committee on Commerce, Science, and Transportation, 106th Cong., 2d sess. (May 23, 2000), S. Rept. 106–30. In recognition of the need to address the ocean and coastal issues of the new century, Congress enacted the Oceans Act of 2000, 4 Pub. L. 106–256, 114 Star. 644 (August 7, 2000), which established the United States Commission on Ocean Policy (USCOP) to make recommendations for a new "coordinated and comprehensive national ocean policy."

Even before President Bush could appoint the members of USCOP, the Pew Oceans Commission, a bi-partisan independent commission funded by the Pew Charitable Trusts, began a similar study "to chart a new course for the nation's ocean policy" and to raise public awareness of ocean issues. The Pew Commission's study, *America's Living Oceans: Charting a Course for Sea Change,* published in May 2003, was considered by some critics to be alarmist in finding that the nation's oceans are in crisis. But the USCOP report, *An Ocean Blueprint for the 21st Century: Final Report of the U.S. Commission on Ocean Policy* (2004), released the next year, reinforced the findings of the Pew Oceans Commission. In the Executive Summary, the United States Ocean Policy Commission found that "[o]ur failure to properly manage the human activities that affect the nation's oceans, coasts, and Great Lakes is compromising their ecological integrity, diminishing our ability to fully realize their potential, costing us jobs and revenue, threatening human health, and putting our future at risk." The USCOP report goes on to identify the extensive scope of the problems affecting our nation's oceans and the opportunities for the future, and makes more than 200 recommendations to improve ocean management.

Although the two commissions varied greatly in their proposed approaches to implementing new national ocean policy, they were in fundamental agreement about the nature and direction of such a policy. First, both commissions envisioned a national ocean policy based on principles of stewardship arising from the public trust in which the government holds ocean and coastal resources. Second, the commissions found that management of the oceans requires an ecosystem-based approach. To achieve this, improved national leadership is necessary to move toward a national ocean policy, implemented through coordinated, regional mechanisms. Third, ocean scientific research and cutting edge data must be available for managers and decision makers. Finally, lifelong, ocean-related education is needed to create "ocean literacy" and a citizenry with a strong ocean stewardship ethic.

The Oceans Act of 2000 required that USCOP's report be submitted to Congress and the President. Pub. L. No. 106–256, § 3(f)(1). Within 90 days after submission of the report, the President was directed by the Act to submit to Congress his response to the

USCOP recommendations for a coordinated, comprehensive and long-range national policy for the oceans. Id. at § 4(a). The President's response was in the form of the *U.S. Ocean Action Plan,* issued on September 4, 2004. The *Ocean Action Plan's* primary approach to providing greater visibility for ocean issues and coordinating ocean-related matters is through creation of a Cabinet-level Committee on Ocean Policy, which was established by Executive Order. Exec. Order No. 13,366, 69 Fed. Reg. 76,591 (Dec. 17, 2004).

Although the *Ocean Action Plan* and the Executive Order called for more coordination at the federal level, neither required specific action toward regional, ecosystem-based ocean management either on the federal level or at the state or regional level. This initial response provided only an incremental step toward the regional, ecosystem-based management of the oceans called for by USCOP.

Ocean policy legislation was introduced in both the Senate and the House of Representatives, but failed to muster broad-based support. Because of concern that little action would be taken on the recommendations of their commissions, the chairmen of Pew Oceans Commission and USCOP, Mr. Leon Panetta and Admiral James Watkins respectively, created the bi-partisan Joint Ocean Commission Initiative (JOCI), guided by a 10-member Task Force, with five from each commission. The goal of the Initiative has been to accelerate the pace of the response to the commissions' reports and catalyze meaningful ocean policy reform. Noting that the initial pace of progress did not reflect the urgency of the situation, the chairmen issued a "report card" giving the nation a D + for progress on ocean issues in 2005. By 2012, the report card showed little change in the overall grade, except for the A- grade for advances in programs by regional ocean organizations.

In June 2006, JOCI responded to a request from 10 senators to submit a report prioritizing the actions Congress should be taking to implement the recommendations of the USCOP and the Pew Oceans Commission. The report, entitled *From Sea to Shining Sea: Priorities for Ocean Policy Reform,* summarized the consensus of the commissions on the major problems of the oceans and coasts as follows:

- Fragmented laws, confusing and overlapping jurisdictions, and the absence of a coherent national ocean policy hinder our management efforts.

- A lack of federal support for emerging regional ocean and coastal governance initiatives hampers the ability of these initiatives to help solve important ocean and coastal problems.

- Overexploited fisheries bring economic hardship to fishing communities and businesses and jeopardize the living marine resources held in trust for the benefit of all U.S. citizens.

- A dearth of U.S. leadership in international ocean and coastal forums threatens our national economic and security interests.

- Dwindling U.S. investment in ocean and coastal research, science, and education compromises our ability to tackle such problems as global warming, resource depletion, harmful algal blooms, invasive species, and nonpoint source water pollution, to name just a few.

- Inadequate funding for federal agencies and for nonfederal partners at the regional, state, and local level is a severe impediment to addressing current problems and to anticipating and planning for future challenges.

Joint Ocean Commission Initiative, *From Sea to Shining Sea: Priorities for Ocean Policy Reform 5* (2006). The report reiterated the JOCI's position that these problems were too critical not to be addressed by timely responses. JOCI continues to attempt to keep ocean issues before Washington's leadership.

To carry out his campaign promise to give a priority to national ocean policy, on July 19th, 2010, President Obama issued Exec. Order 13547 establishing the first United States national ocean policy. The Order described the purposes of the national ocean policy as:

> ... to ensure the protection, maintenance, and restoration of the health of ocean, coastal, and Great Lakes ecosystems and resources, enhance the sustainability of ocean and coastal economies, preserve our maritime heritage,

support sustainable uses and access, provide for adaptive management to enhance our understanding of and capacity to respond to climate change and ocean acidification, and coordinate with our national security and foreign policy interests.

The Executive Order establishes a National Ocean Council (NOC)[1] at the Executive level and directs executive agencies, under the guidance of the Council, to implement recommendations developed by an Interagency Ocean Policy Task Force and adopted by the Order. The Final Recommendations of the Interagency Task Force, available at http:// www.whitehouse.gov/files/documents/OPTF_Final Recs.pdf, provide:

(1) our Nation's first ever National Policy for the Stewardship of the Ocean, Our Coasts, and the Great Lakes (National Policy);

(2) a strengthened governance structure to provide sustained, high-level, and coordinated attention to ocean, coastal, and Great Lakes issues;

(3) a targeted implementation strategy that identifies and prioritizes nine categories for action that the United States should pursue; and

---

[1]   The National Ocean Council (NOC), a body of twenty-seven federal agencies, departments and offices co-chaired by the chair of the Council on Environmental Quality and the Director of the Office of Science and Technology Policy, was established to advise the president and provide guidance to agencies on implementation of national ocean policy.

(4) a framework for effective coastal and marine spatial planning (CMSP) that establishes a comprehensive, integrated, ecosystem-based approach to address conservation, economic activity, user conflict, and sustainable use of ocean, coastal, and Great Lakes resources.

The Recommendations of the Task Force focused on five priority areas or "areas of special emphasis"— resiliency and adaptation to climate change and ocean acidification; regional ecosystem protection and restoration; water quality and sustainable practices on land; changing conditions in the Arctic; and ocean, coastal, and Great Lakes observations, mapping, and infrastructure—to provide for better informed decisions and improved understanding and coordination and support of Federal, State, tribal, local, and regional management of the oceans and coasts. See Recommendations at 28.

The national ocean policy divides United States marine waters into nine planning regions based on large marine ecosystems: Alaska/Arctic, Pacific Islands, Caribbean, West Coast, Gulf of Mexico, South Atlantic, Mid-Atlantic, Northeast and Great Lakes. The geographic scope of planning and coordination envisioned by the Task Force incorporates not only the federal EEZ and continental shelf, but also the territorial sea, including state waters landward to the mean high-water line, including inland bays and estuaries. Because implementation of a national ocean policy has no legislative mandate, ocean policy planning must be based on existing authorities at both the federal and state levels.

The Task Force Recommendations for stewardship of the oceans anticipated that the national ocean policy would be implemented through comprehensive, integrated, coordinated ocean management, utilizing the best science and coastal and marine spatial planning (CMSP) on an eco-regional basis. CMSP is described as follows:

CMSP is a comprehensive, adaptive, integrated, ecosystem-based, and transparent spatial planning process, based on sound science, for analyzing current and anticipated uses of ocean, coastal, and Great Lakes areas. CMSP identifies areas most suitable for various types or classes of activities in order to reduce conflicts among uses, reduce environmental impacts, facilitate compatible uses, and preserve critical ecosystem services to meet economic, environmental, security, and social objectives. In practical terms, CMSP provides a public policy process for society to better determine how the ocean, coasts, and Great Lakes are sustainably used and protected now and for future generations.

See Interagency Ocean Policy Task Force, *Interim Framework for Effective Coastal and Marine Spatial Planning* at 1 (2009). The Recommendations envisioned regional planning bodies composed of federal, state, and tribal authorities being responsible for development of regional plans. State participation on regional planning bodies and in implementation of regional plans is necessarily voluntary.

In April 2013, the National Ocean Council released its *National Ocean Policy Implementation Plan* to "translate the goals of the National Ocean Policy into on-the-ground change" and provide "clear direction" for federal agencies, partners and stakeholders. Nat'l Ocean Council, *National Ocean Policy: Implementation Plan* (2013), *available at* http://www. whitehouse.gov/sites/default/files/national_ocean_ policy_implementation_plan.pdf. During the two years that the NOC was developing the plan, however, significant opposition grew to the President's national ocean policy, in particular, to the coastal and marine spatial planning (CMSP) aspects. The *Implementation Plan* reflected this opposition by placing emphasis on ocean economies, security, and resilience of coastal communities and the oceans, with the terms "CMSP" and "spatial planning" conspicuously missing from the *Plan*. The *Implementation Plan* also states, somewhat ambiguously, that: "[s]hould all [s]tates within a region choose not to participate in a regional planning body within their region, *a regional planning body will not be established*." The state of Alaska has already opted out of region planning. Other regions, however, are making progress in the establishment of regional planning bodies (RPBs). The Northeast RPB, the Mid-Atlantic RPB, and the Pacific Islands RPB have already been created, and the West Coast is in the process of developing an RPB. The Northeast, Mid-Atlantic, South Atlantic, Gulf of Mexico and West Coast regions have established regional ocean partnerships that may evolve into RMBs. The future of CMSP as the primary planning tool, however, remains unclear.

The *Implementation Plan* is clear that even if an RPB is not established to generate a regional ocean plan, federal agencies are still bound under Executive Order 13547 to proceed with implementation of the national ocean policy and the Task Force recommendations. Federal agencies will continue to coordinate with states and other non-federal authorities and stakeholders under those circumstances, but it will not be within the framework designed to make states partners in the process.

The climate for environmental and resource protection is quite different in the United States today than it was when the Stratton Commission released its report and made its recommendations. Even so, the implementation of the recommendations of that commission was spread over the next decade (and many recommendations were never implemented). But the Stratton Commission report did not present a picture of the oceans and coasts in the state of crisis documented in the USCOP and Pew reports. Issues concerning the health of the oceans and the significance of ocean and coastal resources to the nation have much more difficulty maintaining the attention of the public and the government in today's political environment. Without concerted efforts, like that of the Joint Ocean Commission Initiative, to keep these issues and recommendations before Congress and the public, the USCOP and Pew

Commission reports might simply join other reports on the shelf. Without a legislative mandate and dedicated funding, national ocean policy is unlikely to achieve the comprehensive results necessary and may become a topic of primarily academic interest. Timely action is important not only to assure that issues do not fade from the public consciousness, but also because many of the problems of the oceans are being exacerbated by global warming and climate change. Action is needed now.

INDEX OF TOPICS

References are to Pages

BEACH RESTORATION
Avulsion and, 18–19
Right to accretions and, 19
Strategy to address erosion and sea level rise, 120–122

CLEAN WATER ACT (common name for the Federal Water
    Pollution Control Act)
Section 311 (see Oil Spills)
Section 404 (see Wetlands)
Wetlands regulation (see Wetlands)

COASTAL BARRIER RESOURCES ACT
See Barrier islands; Coastal Development Regulation

COASTAL BOUNDARIES
    See also Ambulatory Boundaries; Maritime Boundary
        Delimitation; Navigable Waters; Territorial Sea; Tides
    Generally, 8–19
Baselines, 160–161
Effect of armoring on coastal boundaries, 125–126
Federal law, applicability, 16–18
Fixing coastal boundaries, 15–19
Mean or ordinary high tide line
    Borax Consolidated, 9–11
    Defined, 9–10
    Effect of topography, 10–11
    State variations on definition, 10
States using the mean low water line boundary, 10
Submerged Lands Act, 156–158
Tidelands controversy, 153–157
Tides, 8–9

COASTAL DEVELOPMENT REGULATION
    Generally, 105–119
Building codes, 117–118
    National Flood Insurance Program and, 117–118
Coastal Barrier Resources Act, 108–109
    Coastal Barrier Resources System, 109
    National Flood Insurance Program and, 108, 109
Coastal setback lines, 112–115
    Florida, 113, 115